KNOWLEDGE REPRESENTATION, REASONING, AND THE DESIGN OF INTELLIGENT AGENTS

Knowledge representation and reasoning is the foundation of artificial intelligence, declarative programming, and the design of knowledge-intensive software systems capable of performing intelligent tasks. Using logical and probabilistic formalisms based on Answer Set Prolog (ASP) and action languages, this book shows how knowledge-intensive systems can be given knowledge about the world and how it can be used to solve non-trivial computational problems. The authors maintain a balance between mathematical analysis and practical design of intelligent agents. All the concepts, such as answering queries, planning, diagnostics, and probabilistic reasoning, are illustrated by programs of ASP and its extensions. The text can be used for AI-related undergraduate and graduate classes and by researchers who would like to learn more about ASP and knowledge representation.

Dr. Michael Gelfond is a Professor of Computer Science at Texas Tech University. He received his PhD from the Institute of Mathematics of the Academy of Sciences, St. Petersburg, Russia. He is an AAAI Fellow and serves as an Area Editor for the *International Journal of Theory and Practice of Logic Programming* and as an Executive Editor of the *Journal of Logic and Computation*. In 2004 and 2012 he was the recipient of the award for most influential paper in twenty years by the International Association of Logic Programming.

Yulia Kahl is a member of the Texas Action Group and the Knowledge Representation Lab at Texas Tech. She received her Master's in Computer Science, focusing on the use of Answer Set Prolog for planning. She has also worked as a programmer at IBM.

KNOWLEDGE REPRESENTATION, REASONING, AND THE DESIGN OF INTELLIGENT AGENTS

The Answer-Set Programming Approach

MICHAEL GELFOND

Texas Tech University

YULIA KAHL

CAMBRIDGE
UNIVERSITY PRESS

CAMBRIDGE
UNIVERSITY PRESS

University Printing House, Cambridge CB2 8BS, United Kingdom

One Liberty Plaza, 20th Floor, New York, NY 10006, USA

477 Williamstown Road, Port Melbourne, VIC 3207, Australia

314-321, 3rd Floor, Plot 3, Splendor Forum, Jasola District Centre, New Delhi - 110025, India

79 Anson Road, #06-04/06, Singapore 079906

Cambridge University Press is part of the University of Cambridge.

It furthers the University's mission by disseminating knowledge in the pursuit of education, learning and research at the highest international levels of excellence.

www.cambridge.org
Information on this title: www.cambridge.org/9781107029569

© Michael Gelfond and Yulia Kahl 2014

First published 2014

A catalogue record for this publication is available from the British Library

Library of Congress Cataloguing in Publication data
Gelfond, Michael.
Knowledge representation, reasoning, and the design of intelligent agents : the answer-set programming approach / Michael Gelfond, Texas Tech University, Yulia Kahl.
pages cm
Includes bibliographical references and index.
ISBN 978-1-107-02956-9 (hardback : alk. paper)
1. Intelligent agents (Computer software) I. Kahl, Yulia, 1970– II. Title.
QA76.76.I58G45 2014
006.3–dc23 2013029651

ISBN 978-1-107-02956-9 Hardback

To Lara and Patrick, with love

Contents

Preface

This is a book about knowledge representation and reasoning (KRR) – a comparatively new branch of science that serves as the foundation of artificial intelligence, declarative programming, and the design of intelligent agents – knowledge-intensive software systems capable of exhibiting intelligent behavior. Our main goal is to show how a software system can be given knowledge about the world and itself and how this knowledge can be used to solve nontrivial computational problems. There are several approaches to KRR that both compete with and complement each other. The approaches differ primarily by the languages used to represent knowledge and by corresponding computational methods. This book is based on a knowledge representation language called Answer Set Prolog (ASP) and the answer-set programming paradigm – a comparatively recent branch of KRR with a well-developed theory, efficient reasoning systems, methodology of use, and a growing number of applications.

The text can be used for classes in knowledge representation, declarative programming, and artificial intelligence for advanced undergraduate or graduate students in computer science and related disciplines, including software engineering, logic, and cognitive science. It will also be useful to serious researchers in these fields who would like to learn more about the answer-set programming paradigm and its use for KRR. Finally, we hope that it will be of interest to anyone with a sense of wonder about the amazing ability of humans to derive volumes of knowledge from a collection of basic facts. Knowledge representation and reasoning, located at the intersection of mathematics, science and humanities, provides us with mathematical and computational models of human thought and gives some clues to the understanding of this ability. The reader is not required to know logic or to have previous experience with computational systems. However, some understanding of the mathematical method of thinking will be of substantial help.

We have attempted to maintain a proper balance between mathematical analysis of the subject and practical design of software systems capable of using knowledge about their environment to perform intelligent tasks. Beginning with simple question-answering agents, we progress to more and more complex ones and explain how important problems of knowledge representation and reasoning such as commonsense (default) reasoning, planning, diagnostics, and probabilistic reasoning are solved with ASP and its extensions. The precise mathematical definitions of basic concepts are always accompanied by informal discussions and by examples of their use for modeling various computational tasks performed by humans. Readers are encouraged to run programs to test their agent's ability to perform these tasks using available, state-of-the-art ASP reasoning systems.

Of course the worth of a particular KRR theory is tested by the ability of software agents built on the basis of this theory to behave intelligently. If, given a certain amount of knowledge, the agent exhibits behavior that we believe reasonable for a human with exactly the same knowledge, we deem the theory to be a step in the right direction.

We hope that serious readers will learn to appreciate the interplay between mathematical modeling of a phenomenon and system design, and will better understand the view of programming as the *refinement of specifications*. Even though the book does not discuss large practical projects, we believe that the skills learned will be of substantial use in the marketplace.

We meant for this book to be a foundation for those interested in KRR. Our desire to limit the material to one semester forced us to skip many topics closely related to our approach, such as various constraint and abductive logic programming languages and algorithms, descriptions of important ASP reasoning methods, the methodology of transforming ASP programs to improve their efficiency, and a large body of useful mathematical knowledge. The book does not cover other important KRR topics such as descriptive logics and their use for the Semantic Web and other applications, natural-language processing, and the like. To help those interested in building on the foundation presented and learning more about these other topics, we have included a section on references and further reading in each chapter. (These lists of references, however, are not even close to complete – the goal is simply to start the readers on their learning adventure.)

The first two chapters introduce the reader to the logic-based approach to agent design and to the main tool we use to create the agent's knowledge base – Answer Set Prolog. The third chapter discusses the roots of ASP and briefly covers several other important knowledge representation formalisms. The next two chapters are concerned with the use of ASP for design and implementation of question-answering agents. Chapter 4 illustrates the use of (possibly recursive) ASP definitions of relations for building simple knowledge bases that allow incompleteness of information and a hierarchical organization of knowledge. Chapter 5 covers ASP representation of defaults and their exceptions – one of the distinctive features of ASP that makes it suitable for formalization of defeasible, commonsense arguments. In Chapter 6 our agents become more powerful as we show how various problems related to nontrivial search can be reduced to ASP reasoning. Chapter 7 discusses implementations of ASP solvers used to perform such reasoning. Chapters 8–10 deal with agents capable of performing actions and functioning intelligently in dynamic (changing) environments. The material includes discussion of action languages – tools for concisely describing such environments – and ASP-based reasoning algorithms that allow the agents to perform complex reasoning tasks including planning and diagnostics. Chapter 11 introduces a dialect of ASP capable of representing and reasoning with probabilistic knowledge. The emphasis here is on combining logical and probabilistic reasoning and the use of formal language to clarify and expand some classical probabilistic notions, including that of the behavior of probability under updates of the agent's knowledge base. Finally, in Chapter 12, we give a brief introduction to a traditional logic programming language called Prolog, which can be viewed as a special case of ASP. The appendices are meant to help the reader run ASP code using available ASP solvers. Sections marked with an asterisk are optional.

Preliminary versions of the book were used by the first author for teaching graduate and undergraduate classes in AI and intelligent systems at Texas Tech University. In some cases, the constraint of a single semester made it necessary to omit or only present highlights of Chapters 3 and 12.

We would like to conclude by acknowledging the people who knowingly or unknowingly contributed to this book. The first author was fortunate to learn about declarative programming and the logical approach to AI from work and occasional conversations with such founders of these fields as Bob Kowalski, John McCarthy, Jack Minker, and Ray Reiter. Without them this book would not have been possible. His life-long friendship and collaboration with Vladimir Lifschitz played a crucial role in his development as a scientist. The second author is grateful to her teachers, especially her advisor, Chitta Baral, who allowed her to pursue her interest in KRR and ASP. Also, she feels truly blessed to have been allowed to be a part of the Knowledge Representation Lab, first at the University of Texas at El Paso and now at Texas Tech University. The seminars conducted there and all the great people she met helped her maintain contact with the field that she has found exciting and rewarding.

We thank Vladimir Lifschitz and other colleagues, collaborators, friends, and students, including Evgenii Balai, Marcello Balduccini, Chitta Baral, Matt Barry, Justin Blount, Piero Bonatti, Marc Denecker, Thomas Eiter, Alfredo Gabaldon, Gregory Gelfond, Georg Gottlob, Daniela Inclezan, Patrick Kahl, Nicola Leone, Jorge Lobo, Viktor Marek, Veena Mellarkord, Ricardo Morales, Ilkka Niemella, Monica Nogueira, Mauricio Osorio, Ramon Otero, David Pearce, Alessandro Provetti, Halina and Teodor Przymusinski, Nelson Rushton, Torsten Schaub, Richard Scherl, Tran Cao Son, Yana Todorova, Bonnie Trailor, Miroslaw Truszczynski, Richard Watson, Yuanlin Zhang, and Weijun Zhu; they helped us develop a better understanding of the topics covered. Many of them also provided valuable comments on the book. The authors owe a special thanks to Pedro Cabalar, Vinay K. Chaudhri, Sandeep Chintabathina, Mauricio Osorio, Tran Cao Son, Richard Watson, and Yuanlin Zhang who used the earlier drafts of this book as primary or supplementary material for AI-related courses. Their feedback is greatly appreciated.

Thanks also to the developers of ASPIDE – Onofrio Febbraro, Kristian Reale, and Francesco Ricca – for including the query interface and its epistemic mode so that their program could be used to simulate the kind of dialogue we wanted to have with the computer. Thanks also to Nicola Leone and his team at DLVSystems who supported the development of these features. Everyone has been very helpful!

We also thank the great people at Cambridge University Press for their support. Ada Brunstein, Lauren Cowles, and Dana Bricken have been very helpful throughout the publishing process. We also truly appreciate the great feedback from the anonymous reviewers who gave valuable time to help us improve the book. The people at Springer-Verlag have been kind in letting us use the parts assembly problem from Clocksin and Mellish's wonderful *Programming in Prolog*, and we thank them kindly.

Michael wishes to thank his wife, Larisa, for constant encouragement and support that helped him go back to research after emigrating from the Soviet Union and to enjoy his work ever since. Without her this book would never have been written.

Yulia wishes to thank her husband, Patrick, who has always given her love, support, and the freedom to do what she loves. Without him, her part in the writing of this book would have been nothing but a dream. She also wishes to thank her wonderful parents, Michael and Larisa, without whom she would not have had the joy of working on this book.

1

Logic-Based Approach to Agent Design

The goal of artificial intelligence is to learn how to build software components of intelligent agents capable of reasoning and acting in a changing environment. To exhibit intelligent behavior, an agent should have a mathematical model of its environment and its own capabilities and goals, as well as algorithms for achieving these goals. Our aim is to discover such models and algorithms and to learn how to use them to build practical intelligent systems. Why is this effort important? There are philosophical, scientific, and practical reasons. Scientists are getting closer to understanding ancient enigmas such as the origins and the physical and chemical structure of the universe, and the basic laws of development of living organisms, but still know comparatively little about the enigma of thinking. Now, however, we have the computer – a new tool that gives us the ability to test our theories of thought by designing intelligent software agents. In the short time that this tool has been applied to the study of reasoning, it has yielded a greater understanding of cognitive processes and continues to produce new insights on a regular basis, giving us much hope for the future. On the software engineering front, mathematical models of intelligent agents and the corresponding reasoning algorithms help develop the paradigm of declarative programming, which may lead to a simpler and more reliable programming methodology. And, of course, knowledge-intensive software systems, including decision support systems, intelligent search engines, and robots, are of great practical value. In addition, attempts to solve the problems of AI illuminate connections between different areas of computer science (CS) and between CS and other areas of science, including mathematical logic, philosophy, and linguistics.

1.1 Modeling an Intelligent Agent

In this book when we talk about an **agent**, we mean an entity that observes and acts on an environment and directs its activity toward achieving goals.

Note that this definition allows us to view even the simplest programs as agents. A program usually gets information from the outside world, performs an appointed reasoning task, and acts on the outside world, say, by printing the output, making the next chess move, starting a car, or giving advice. If the reasoning tasks that an agent performs are complex and lead to nontrivial behavior, we call it intelligent. If the agent readily adapts its behavior to changes in its environment, it is called adaptive. If it performs tasks independent of human control, we call it autonomous. An agent can possess some or all of these qualities in varying degrees. For example, consider a program in charge of controlling a large system for paper production. Among its many complex tasks, it can make decisions based on temperature readings or thickness measurements and adjust the speed of a conveyer belt and alert the operator. Clearly this program is supposed to observe, think, and act on the environment to achieve certain goals. It is intelligent, as well as adaptive in response to its sensors. And it is certainly autonomous to a certain degree, although its decisions can be overridden by an operator. Of course, the scope of the program and hence its ability for intelligent behavior are very limited.

As in many AI and computer science texts, we ignore engineering tasks related to the agent's physical interaction with the world and concentrate on modeling the agent and designing software components responsible for its decision making.

A mathematical model of an intelligent agent normally consists of the following elements:

- a *language(s)* for representing the agent's knowledge
- *reasoning algorithms* that use this knowledge to perform intelligent tasks, including planning, diagnostics, and learning; most such algorithms are based on sophisticated search and are capable of solving problems of non-polynomial complexity
- an *agent architecture*, which is the structure combining different submodels of an agent (normally related to different reasoning tasks) in one coherent whole.

In this book we consider the following typical agent architecture. An agent's memory contains knowledge both about the world and that entity's capabilities and goals. The agent follows these four steps:

1. observes the world, checks that its observations are consistent with its expectations, and updates its knowledge base
2. selects an appropriate goal G

3. searches for a plan (a sequence of actions) to achieve G
4. executes some initial part of the plan, updates the knowledge base, and goes back to step 1.

Sometimes we refer to these four steps as the **agent loop**. In step 1, notice that the agent does not assume that it is the sole manipulator of its environment. This allows for incorporation of external events and for failure analysis; for example, the agent can compare its expected world model to the one it observes and attempt to *explain* the possible discrepancies between the two. In step 2, goal selection can be implemented in many different ways, including prioritization, real-time user input, or random selection. Step 3, planning, is an art in itself, requiring reasoning skills, efficient search, and, possibly, weights on actions. Finally, in step 4, performing an action can involve hardware robots or, in other domains, "softbots," capable, say, of cleaning up directories or searching the Web. There are a myriad of issues involved in this simple outline.

This architecture is simple. A more sophisticated architecture may involve a complex structuring of various intelligent tasks and communication between modules performing these tasks in parallel, powerful learning and vision components, the ability to communicate and cooperate or compete with other agents, and the like. In this book, however, we limit ourselves to a sequential architecture presented in the agent loop and show that even this simple approach can lead to important insights and systems.

To implement this architecture we need to meet a number of difficult challenges. For example, how can we create a knowledge base for our agent? How can we make it function in a changing environment and maintain focus on its current goal without losing the ability to change goals in response to important events in its environment? How can we make it capable of explaining some of these events and using the explanations to fill gaps in its knowledge base? How can we get it to use its knowledge to do intelligent planning?

To answer these and other related questions, we chose to use the **logic-based approach**. The main idea is as follows. To make machines smart, we need to teach them how to reason and how to learn. Since most teaching comes from instruction, and most learning comes from the same, we need an efficient means of communication. As with any problem in computer science, the choice of language has a large impact on the elegance and efficiency of the solution. Languages differ according to the type of information their designers want to communicate to computers. There are two basic types: algorithmic and declarative. **Algorithmic languages** describe sequences of actions for a computer to perform. **Declarative languages** describe properties of objects in a given domain and relations between them. The **logic-based** approach proposes to

- use a declarative language to describe the domain,
- express various tasks (which may include requests to find plans or explanations of unexpected observations) as queries to the resulting program, and
- use an inference engine (i.e., a collection of reasoning algorithms) to answer these queries.

1.2 Simple Family Knowledge Base – An Example

To illustrate the logic-based approach used in this book, we teach our computer basic facts about families. For simplicity we consider a small family consisting of three people – John, Alice, and their son Sam. The domain is structured in terms of binary relations *father*, *mother*, and *gender_of*. In these terms the family can be described by statements:

$$father(john, sam).$$
$$mother(alice, sam).$$
$$gender\_of(john, male).$$
$$gender\_of(sam, male).$$
$$gender\_of(alice, female).$$

read as "John is the father of Sam," etc. (We are keeping things simple here and assuming that first names are enough to uniquely identify a person. Of course, if Sam had a father also named Sam, we would need to give each his own unique identifier.)

These basic relations can be used to teach a computer new notions. For instance, the following two rules can be viewed as a definition of relation *parent*. We say that X is a parent of Y if X is a father of Y or X is a mother of Y.

$$parent(X, Y) \leftarrow father(X, Y).$$
$$parent(X, Y) \leftarrow mother(X, Y).$$

Note that identifiers starting with capital letters denote variables, whereas those starting with lowercase letters denote names of objects (e.g., sam, john) and relations (e.g., father, parent).

The next rule defines the meaning of relation "X is a child of Y."

$$child(X, Y) \leftarrow parent(Y, X).$$

This program is written in a variant of a declarative language called **Answer Set Prolog (ASP)**. Replacing symbol ← by : - turns these statements into an executable program. We discuss the full syntax and semantics of the language in Chapter 2.

To make sure that the program allows the computer to "understand" the material, we test it by asking a number of questions. For example, "Is Sam a child of John?" or "Who are Sam's parents?" If the answers are satisfactory, the program has learned. (Notice that this is exactly the method we use to check human understanding.) In what follows we refer to an agent answering our questions as STUDENT. We can view STUDENT as a *theoretical* question-answering system. Doing this allows us to avoid the discussion of details of actual systems that we later use to automate STUDENT's reasoning.

Since STUDENT is not capable of understanding even basic English sentences, we express the questions in its own language. To ask if Sam is a child of John, we type

$$? \; child(sam, john)$$

STUDENT will use the available knowledge and its reasoning mechanism to answer this question in the affirmative.

To ask "Who are Sam's parents?" we use variables. Statement

$$? \; parent(X, sam)$$

is read as "Find X such that X is a parent of Sam." This time the reasoning mechanism of STUDENT will look for X satisfying this query and return the names of Sam's parents: John and Alice.

Note that the real syntax for queries varies slightly with the implementation used. Here we simply put a question mark to distinguish the query from a fact.

The system still does not know that Sam is Alice's son. This is not surprising because it does not know the meaning of the word "son." For practice you can define relation $son(X, Y) - X$ is a son of Y.

The family example exhibits typical features of logic-based programming. The knowledge about the domain is stated in precise mathematical language, and various search problems are expressed as queries, which are answered by the reasoning mechanism of STUDENT. The program is **elaboration tolerant**, which means that small changes in specifications do not cause global program changes. For instance, in the process of developing the family knowledge base, we expanded the original collection of facts to accommodate new relationships between family members. In each case, the new definitions were natural and did not require changes to the rest of the program. It is equally easy to modify existing definitions. Suppose, for instance, that we would like to incorporate facts from a Spanish-language database that has statements $padre(a, b)$ instead of $father(a, b)$. These statements can be simply added to our knowledge base. The Spanish-English translation will be given by the rule

$$father(X, Y) \leftarrow padre(X, Y)$$

which modifies our previous definition of $father$. Other statements from the Spanish database can be incorporated in the same manner. Note that all relations based on $father$ remain unchanged.

The intelligence of this system can be significantly improved and its vocabulary expanded. It can be supplied with a natural-language interface allowing the user to state questions in English. It can be taught to plan with the information it has been given, as well as to find explanations for possible discrepancies between its knowledge and its observations of the real world. In this book we discuss some of these enhancements. We also address models of intelligent agents whose knowledge contains probabilistic information about the agent's domain. Usually such agents are studied within the probabilistic approach to AI, which is frequently viewed as an alternative to the logic-based approach. We do not share this view. Instead *we view probabilistic reasoning as commonsense reasoning about degrees of belief of a rational agent.* We illustrate this view and its ramifications toward the end of the book.

1.3　A Historical Comment

The roots of the logic-based approach to agent design are very deep. Interested readers are encouraged to look for a serious discussion of these roots in the history of logic. The goal of this section is to give a brief introduction to the development of the basic ideas that formed the foundations of this approach. More information on the history of the subject and on various approaches to combining logic and artificial intelligence is found in Chapter 3.

1.3.1　The Axiomatic Method

The need to structure existing mathematical knowledge and to improve its reliability and coherence led mathematicians of ancient Greece to the development of the axiomatic method. The classical exposition of this method is given in Euclid's *Elements* in which all geometric knowledge available to

Euclid is logically derived from a small collection of *axioms* – geometric propositions accepted without proof. For more than two thousand years that book served as a model of rigorous argument. It was used to teach geometry from the time of its publication to the late 19th and early 20th centuries and long remained the second most read book in Europe after the Bible. Increased interest in the enigma of thinking, the 18th-century shift of emphasis from geometry to calculus with its notion of continuum, inclusion of infinity and infinite sets as one of the main subjects of mathematics, and the centuries-long quest for the development of reliable reasoning methods for these newly created mathematical notions led to substantial progress in the development of logic and the axiomatic method. At the beginning of the 20th century, logicians developed the general idea of *formal language* and used it to axiomatize set theory. Basic mathematical notions such as natural and real number, function, and geometric figure, were defined in terms of sets and their membership relations. As a result (almost) all of the mathematical knowledge of the early 20th century could be viewed as logical consequences of a collection of axioms that could fit on a medium-sized blackboard. This exceptional scientific achievement demonstrated the high degree of maturity of logic and is similar to the development of Mendeleev's periodic table in chemistry or the understanding of the structure of DNA in biology. Another important achievement of logic was the creation of the mathematical notion of a correct mathematical argument – the notion of proof. All these notions not only deepened our understanding of mathematical reasoning but also had a strong influence on mathematics.

1.3.2 Logic and Design of Intelligent Agents

For a long time the influence of the axiomatic method has been much weaker outside of mathematics. Most likely, Gottfried Wilhelm Leibniz was the first to suggest that the method can have a much broader applicability, adding to our understanding of other areas of science and even substantially changing human behavior. In his *The Art of Discovery* written in 1685, Leibniz wrote,

The only way to rectify our reasonings is to make them as tangible as those of the Mathematicians, so that we can find our error at a glance, and when there are disputes among persons, we can simply say: Let us calculate [calculemus], without further ado, to see who is right.

He was hoping that

humanity would have a new kind of instrument increasing the power of reason far more than any optical instrument has ever aided the power of vision.

The idea, often referred to as the *Leibniz Dream*, greatly contributed to the development of computing science.

In the 20th century, Alfred Tarski and others, partly influenced by the Leibniz Dream, developed a research program whose goal was to investigate if the axiomatic method could be successfully applied outside of mathematics. In the 1950s John McCarthy came up with a program of applying this method to artificial intelligence, which gave birth to what is now called the **logic-based approach to AI**. The original idea was to supply computer programs with a substantial amount of knowledge about their problem domain represented in the language of mathematical logic and to use logical inference to decide what actions are appropriate to achieve their goals. This idea served as the foundation of declarative logical languages. For instance, the logic programming language Prolog, developed in the late 1970s by Robert Kowalski, Alain Colmerauer, Philippe Roussel, and others, allows a programmer to supply the program with knowledge about its domain represented by so-called definite clauses – a small subset of the language of classical mathematical logic. A computation problem is then reduced to proving that objects in the domain have a given property. This is achieved by an inference mechanism called SLD resolution. The language is Turing complete, which means that it can be viewed as a universal programming language. The simplicity of the class of definite clauses and the effectiveness of its inference mechanism allow for efficient implementations. Unfortunately, Prolog has some nondeclarative features. For instance, a simple modification of a program that preserves its logical equivalence may cause the program to go into an infinite loop. Some other substantial limitations prevent Prolog from being used as a full-scale knowledge representation language suitable for the design and implementation of intelligent agents, but we do not discuss them in this chapter.

Another interesting declarative language, Datalog, significantly expands the more traditional query-answering languages of relational databases. It can be viewed as a subset of Prolog, but it is limited to representing domains with a finite number of objects. The inference mechanisms of Datalog, however, are quite different from those of Prolog and are tailored toward query answering. In recent years there has been a substantial resurgence of Datalog, leading to more research and more practical applications of the language.

Summary

Inspired by the Leibnitz Dream of applying the axiomatic method to understanding methods of correct reasoning, researchers have been applying the logic-based approach to the design of intelligent agents. This approach consists of using a declarative language for representation, defining reasoning tasks as queries to a program, and computing the results using an inference engine. One such branch of research involves Answer Set Prolog, a simple yet powerful language useful for creating formal representations of various kinds of knowledge. When coupled with an inference engine, these representations can yield answers to various nontrivial queries; in fact, complex reasoning tasks such as planning and diagnostics, as well as other important parts of the agent architecture, can be reduced to querying knowledge bases. It is important to note that the separation of knowledge representation from the reasoning algorithm allows for a high degree of elaboration tolerance and clarity. We used a query-answering system, generically termed STUDENT, to illustrate the knowledge gained by the computer given a specific representation. Based on what the system knows is true, false, or unknown, we can evaluate the worth of such a representation, elicit unspoken assumptions, and learn about our own view of a domain.

References and Further Reading

The ideas of the logic-based approach to artificial intelligence and declarative programming were advocated by Cordell Green (1969), Robert Kowalski (1979), and John McCarthy (1990), among others. The importance of elaboration tolerance for knowledge representation was stressed by John McCarthy (1998). The simple agent architecture used in this book was introduced in Baral and Gelfond (2000) and Balduccini and Gelfond (2008). It is similar to earlier architectures (Kowalski 1995) and can be viewed as a special case of a more general belief-desire-intentions (BDI) architecture from Rao (1991). A popular account of this architecture that includes historical references can be found in Wooldridge (2000).

The first account of the axiomatic method is given in Euclid's *Elements* (Fitzpatrick 2007). A new, simplified approach to the axiomatization of geometry was suggested by David Hilbert (1899/1980). The discovery of paradoxes of set theory in the beginning of the 20th century led to further advances in axiomatic methods and attempts to axiomatize all of mathematics. (See, for instance, the famous formalization of a large part of mathematics by Alfred Whitehead and Bertrand Russell (1910, 1912, 1913). Later work (Godel 1932/1991) demonstrated that the full axiomatization of set theory, if at all possible, would require substantial new advances in our understanding of the axiomatic method. The possibility of applying the axiomatic method to realms outside of mathematics was suggested by Gottfried Wilhelm

Leibniz (1951) and later expanded by Alfred Tarski (1941/1995) and others.

Valuable information about the early history of Prolog and logic programming can be found in Kowalski (1988), Colmerauer and Roussel (1996), and Cohen (1988). For more information on Datalog see, for instance, Abiteboul, Hull, and Vianu (1995); Ullman (1988); and Zaniolo (1999).

Exercises

1. Compare and contrast the words *intelligent* and *rational*.

2. How can intelligent systems improve our ability to reason about a specific question?

3. Do some independent reading on Leibniz and explain why some people might consider him to be the first computer scientist.

4. In an address titled *Under the Spell of Leibniz's Dream*, Edsger Dijkstra (2001) said,

   I think it absolutely astounding that he [Leibniz] foresaw how "the symbols would direct the reasoning," for how strongly they would do so was one of the most delightful discoveries of my professional life.

   Describe one way in which, in computer science, symbols direct reasoning.

5. Read John McCarthy's 1959 paper titled "Programs with Common Sense."
   (a) How does he define a program with common sense?
   (b) Compare and contrast STUDENT and the advice taker.

2

Answer Set Prolog (ASP)

Answer Set Prolog is a declarative language; thus, an ASP program is a collection of statements describing objects of a domain and relations between them. Its semantics defines the notion of an **answer set** – a possible set of beliefs of an agent associated with the program.[1] The valid consequences of the program are the statements that are true in all such sets of beliefs. A variety of tasks can be reduced to finding answer sets or subsets of answer sets, or computing the consequences of an ASP program.

2.1 Syntax

Whenever we define a formal language, we start with its alphabet. In logic, this alphabet is usually called a signature. Formally, a **signature**[2] is a four-tuple $\Sigma = \langle \mathcal{O}, \mathcal{F}, \mathcal{P}, \mathcal{V} \rangle$ of (disjoint) sets. These sets contain the names of the objects, functions, predicates, and variables used in the program. (Predicate is just a term logicians use instead of the word "relation." We use both words interchangeably.) Each function and predicate name is associated with its **arity** – a non-negative integer indicating the number of parameters. For simplicity we assume that functions always have at least one parameter. Normally, the arity is determined from the context. Elements of $\mathcal{O}, \mathcal{F}$, and $\mathcal{P}$ are often referred to as *object, function*, and *predicate constants*, respectively. Often the word *constant* in this context is replaced by the word *symbol*. In the family relations program from Chapter 1, our signature Σ_f is

$$\mathcal{O} = \{john, sam, alice, male, female\}$$
$$\mathcal{F} = \emptyset$$
$$\mathcal{P} = \{father, mother, parent, child, gender\}$$
$$\mathcal{V} = \{X, Y\}$$

---

[1] Historically, belief sets – under the name of *stable models* – were defined on a special class of logic programs written in the syntax of the programming language Prolog. After the definition was extended to apply to the broader class of programs defined in this chapter, the term *answer set* was adopted.

[2] In some books the definition of a signature slightly differs from the one used here in that it does not contain $\mathcal{O}$; instead, object constants are identified with function constants of arity 0.

Whenever necessary we assume that our signatures contain standard names for non-negative integers, functions, and relations of arithmetic (e.g., $+, *, \leq$, etc.).

Sometimes it is convenient to expand the notion of signature by including in it another collection of symbols called **sorts**. Sorts are normally used to restrict the parameters of predicates, as well as the parameters and values of functions.[3] For this purpose every object constant and every parameter of a predicate constant is assigned a sort, just as for parameters and values of functions. The resulting five-tuple is called a **sorted signature**. For instance, signature Σ_f can be turned into a sorted signature Σ_s by viewing *gender* as a sort (instead of a predicate symbol), introducing a new sort, *person*, and assigning proper sorts to object constants of the signature and to parameters of its predicate symbols. Sometimes these assignments are written as $gender = \{male, female\}, person = \{john, sam, alice\}$, $father(person, person)$, etc.

Object and function constants are used to construct terms. Terms not containing variables usually name objects of the domain. For instance, object constant *sam* is a name of a person, term $max(2, 1)$ is a name for the number 2, etc. Here is the definition.

Terms (over signature Σ) are defined as follows:

1. Variables and object constants are terms.
2. If $t_1, \ldots, t_n$ are terms and f is a function symbol of arity n, then $f(t_1, \ldots, t_n)$ is a term.

For simplicity arithmetic terms are written in the standard mathematical notation; for example, we write $2 + 3$ instead of $+(2, 3)$. Terms containing no symbols for arithmetic functions and no variables are called **ground**. Here are some examples from our family program:

- *john*, *sam*, and *alice* are ground terms.
- X and Y are terms that are variables.
- $father(X, Y)$ is *not* a term.

If a program contains natural numbers and arithmetic functions, then both $2 + 3$ and 5 are terms; 5 is a ground term, whereas $2 + 3$ is not.

Let's extend our program signature to include the function symbol *car*. (Intuitively, we are assuming here that a person X has exactly one car, denoted by $car(X)$.) Now we can also make ground terms $car(john)$,

---

[3] This idea is familiar to users of procedural languages as parameters of procedures and functions are often associated with a type. Output types of parameters of functions are also common.

$car(sam)$, and $car(alice)$ and nonground terms $car(X)$ and $car(Y)$. So far our naming seems reasonable. There is, however, a complication – according to our definition $car(car(sam))$ is also a ground term, but it does not seem to denote any reasonable object of our domain. To avoid this difficulty consider the sorted signature Σ_s defined as follows:

- Object constants of Σ_s are divided into sorts: $gender = \{male,$ $female\}$, $person = \{john, sam, alice\}$, and $thing = \{car(X) :$ $person(X)\}$.[4]
- $\mathcal{F} = \{car\}$ where car is a function symbol that maps elements of sort $person$ into that of $thing$ (e.g., car maps $john$ into $car(john)$).
- In addition to predicate symbols with sorted parameters such as $father(person, person)$, $mother(person, person)$, and so on, of Σ_f, we also add a new predicate symbol with parameters of two different sorts denoted by $owns(person, thing)$.

The definition of a term for a sorted signature is only slightly more complex than the one for an unsorted signature. For $f(t_1, \ldots, t_n)$ to be a term, we simply require sorts of the values of terms $t_1, \ldots, t_n$ to be compatible with that of the corresponding parameter sorts of f. So the terms of a sorted signature Σ_s are $john, X, car(sam), car(alice), car(X)$, etc. Note, however, that, because $car(sam)$ is of sort $thing$ and function symbol car requires sort $person$ as a parameter, $car(car(sam))$ is not a term of Σ_s.

Term and predicate symbols of a signature are used to define statements of our language. An **atomic statement**, or simply an **atom**, is an expression of the form $p(t_1, \ldots, t_n)$ where p is a predicate symbol of arity n and $t_1, \ldots, t_n$ are terms. If the signature is sorted, these terms should correspond to the sorts assigned to the parameters of p. (If p has arity 0 then parentheses are omitted.) For example, $father(john, sam)$ and $father(john, X)$ are atoms of signature Σ_s, whereas $father(john, car(sam))$ is not. If the signature were to contain a zero-arity predicate symbol $light\_is\_on$, then $light\_is\_on$ would be an atom. If the ts do not contain variables, then $p(t_1, \ldots, t_n)$ says that objects denoted by $t_1, \ldots, t_n$ satisfy property p. Otherwise, $p(t_1, \ldots, t_n)$ denotes a condition on its variables. Other statements of the language can be built from atoms using various logical connectives.

A **literal** is an atom, $p(t_1, \ldots, t_n)$ or its negation, $\neg p(t_1, \ldots, t_n)$; the latter is often read as $p(t_1, \ldots, t_n)$ *is false* and is referred to as a **negative**

---

[4] Here $\{t(X) : p(X)\}$, where $t(X)$ is a term and $p(X)$ a condition, is the standard set-building notation read as *the set of all $t(X)$ such that X satisfies p*.

literal. An atom and its negation are called **complementary**. The literal complementary to l is denoted by $\bar{l}$. An atom $p(t_1, \ldots, t_n)$ is called **ground** if every term $t_1, \ldots, t_n$ is ground. Ground atoms and their negations are referred to as **ground literals**.

Now we have enough vocabulary to describe the syntax of an ASP program. Such programs serve as an agent's knowledge base, so we often use the words "program" and "knowledge base" synonymously. A **program** Π of ASP consists of a signature Σ and a collection of **rules** of the form:

$$l_0 \; or \; \ldots \; or \; l_i \leftarrow l_{i+1}, \ldots, l_m, \; not \; l_{m+1}, \ldots, \; not \; l_n \qquad (2.1)$$

where ls are literals of Σ. (To make ASP programs executable, we replace $\neg$ with $-$, $\leftarrow$ with $:-$, and or with $|$.)

For simplicity we assume that, unless otherwise stated, signatures of programs consist only of symbols used in their rules.

Symbol not is a new logical connective called **default negation**, (or **negation as failure**); $not \; l$ is often read as "*it is not believed that l is true.*" Note that this does not imply that l is believed to be false. It is conceivable, and in fact is quite normal, for a rational reasoner to believe neither statement p nor its negation, $\neg p$. Clearly default negation not is different from classical $\neg$. Whereas $\neg p$ states that p is false, $not \; p$ is a statement about belief.

The disjunction or is also a new connective, sometimes called **epistemic disjunction**. The statement $l_1 \; or \; l_2$ is often read as "l_1 *is believed to be true or l_2 is believed to be true.*" It is also different from the classical disjunction $\vee$. The statement $p \vee \neg p$ of propositional logic, called *the law of the exclusive middle*, is a tautology; however, the statement $p \; or \; \neg p$ is not. The former states that proposition p is either true or false, whereas the latter states that p is believed to be true or believed to be false. Since a rational reasoner can remain undecided about the truth or falsity of propositions, this is certainly not a tautology.

The left-hand side of an ASP rule is called the **head** and the right-hand side is called the **body**. Literals, possibly preceded by default negation not, are often called **extended literals**. The body of the rule can be viewed as a set of extended literals (sometimes referred to as the *premises* of the rule).

The head or the body can be empty. A rule with an empty head is often referred to as a **constraint** and written as

$$\leftarrow l_{i+1}, \ldots, l_m, \; not \; l_{m+1}, \ldots, \; not \; l_n.$$

A rule with an empty body is often referred to as a **fact** and written as

$$l_0 \ or \ \ldots \ or \ l_i.$$

Following the Prolog convention, non-numeric object, function and predicate constants of Σ are denoted by identifiers starting with lowercase letters; variables are identifiers starting with capital letters. Variables of Π range over ground terms of Σ. A rule r with variables is viewed as the set of its **ground instantiations** – rules obtained from r by replacing r's variables by ground terms of Σ and by evaluating arithmetic terms (e.g., replacing $2+3$ by 5). The set of ground instantiations of rules of Π is called the **grounding** of Π; program Π with variables can be viewed simply as a shorthand for its grounding. This means that it is enough to define the semantics of ground programs. For example, consider the program Π_1 with signature Σ where

$$\mathcal{O} = \{a, b\}$$
$$\mathcal{F} = \emptyset$$
$$\mathcal{P} = \{p, q\}$$
$$\mathcal{V} = \{X\}$$

and rule

$$p(X) \leftarrow q(X).$$

Its rule can be converted to the two ground rules,

$$p(a) \leftarrow q(a).$$
$$p(b) \leftarrow q(b).$$

which constitute the grounding of Π_1, denoted by $gr(\Pi_1)$.

To proceed we also need to define what it means for a set of ground literals to satisfy a rule. We first define the notion for the parts that make up the rule and then show how the parts combine to define the satisfiability of the rule.

Definition 2.1.1. *(Satisfiability) A set S of ground literals* **satisfies***:*

1. *l **if** $l \in S$;*
2. *$not\ l$ **if** $l \notin S$;*
3. *$l_1\ or\ \ldots\ or\ l_n$ **if** for some $1 \leq i \leq n$, $l_i \in S$;*
4. *a set of ground extended literals* **if** *S satisfies every element of this set;*
5. *rule r **if**, whenever S satisfies r's body, it satisfies r's head.*

For example, let r be the rule

$$p(a) \; or \; p(b) \leftarrow q(b), \neg t(c), \; not \; t(b).$$

and let S be the set

$$\{\neg p(a), q(b), \neg t(c)\}.$$

Let's check if S satisfies r. First we check if the body of the rule is satisfied by S. The body consists of three extended literals: $q(b)$, $\neg t(c)$, and $not \; t(b)$. The first two are satisfied by clause (1) of the definition, and the last is satisfied by clause (2). By clause (4), we have that the body is satisfied. Since the body is satisfied, to satisfy the rule, S must satisfy the head (clause (5)). It does not, because neither $p(a)$ nor $p(b)$ is in S (clause(3)). Therefore, S does *not* satisfy r. There are many sets that do satisfy r including $\emptyset$, $\{p(a)\}$, $\{p(b)\}$, $\{q(b), t(c)\}$, and $\{p(a), q(b), \neg t(c)\}$. For practice, check to see that this is so.

2.2 Semantics

First we introduce the semantics of ASP informally to give a feeling for the nature of the reasoning involved. We state the basic principles and give a number of examples. Then we formally define the semantics by stating what it means for a program to entail a ground literal.

2.2.1 Informal Semantics

Informally, program Π can be viewed as a specification for answer sets – sets of beliefs that could be held by a rational reasoner associated with Π. Answer sets are represented by collections of ground literals. In forming such sets the reasoner must be guided by the following informal principles:

1. Satisfy the rules of Π. In other words, believe in the head of a rule if you believe in its body.
2. Do not believe in contradictions.
3. Adhere to the "Rationality Principle" that says, "Believe nothing you are not forced to believe."

Let's look at some examples. Recall that in accordance with our assumption, the signatures of programs in these examples consist only of symbols used in their rules.

Example 2.2.1.

$$p(b) \leftarrow q(a). \quad \text{"Believe } p(b) \text{ if you believe } q(a).\text{"}$$
$$q(a). \qquad\qquad \text{"Believe } q(a).\text{"}$$

Note that the second rule is a fact. Its body is empty. Clearly any set of literals satisfies an empty collection, and hence, according to our first principle, we must believe $q(a)$. The same principle applied to the first rule forces us to believe $p(b)$. The resulting set $S_1 = \{q(a), p(b)\}$ is consistent and satisfies the rules of the program. Moreover, we had to believe in each of its elements. Therefore, it is an answer set of our program. Now consider set $S_2 = \{q(a), p(b), q(b)\}$. It is consistent, satisfies the rules of the program, but contains the literal $q(b)$, which we were not forced to believe in by our rules. Therefore, S_2 is not an answer set of the program. You might have noticed that, because we did not have any choices in the construction of S_1, it is the *only* answer set of the program.

Example 2.2.2. *(Classical Negation)*

$$\neg p(b) \leftarrow \neg q(a). \quad \text{"Believe that } p(b) \text{ is false if you believe that } q(a) \text{ is}$$
$$\text{false."}$$
$$\neg q(a). \qquad\qquad \text{"Believe that } q(a) \text{ is false."}$$

There is no difference in reasoning about negative literals. In this case, the only answer set of the program is $\{\neg p(b), \neg q(a)\}$.

Example 2.2.3. *(Epistemic Disjunction)*

$$p(a) \; or \; p(b). \; \text{"Believe } p(a) \text{ or believe } p(b).\text{"}$$

There are three sets satisfying this rule – $\{p(a)\}$, $\{p(b)\}$, and $\{p(a), p(b)\}$. It is easy to see, however, that only the first two are answer sets of the program. According to our rationality principle, it would be irrational to adopt the third set as a possible set of beliefs – if we do we would clearly believe more than necessary.

Consider now the program

$$p(a) \; or \; p(b).$$
$$q(a) \leftarrow p(a).$$
$$q(a) \leftarrow p(b).$$

Here the first rule gives us two choices – believe $p(a)$ or believe $p(b)$. The next two rules force us to believe $q(a)$ regardless of this choice. This is

a typical example of so-called *reasoning by cases*. The program has two
answer sets: $\{p(a), q(a)\}$ and $\{p(b), q(a)\}$.

Another important thing to notice about epistemic disjunction is that it
is different from exclusive *or*. (Recall that if the disjunction between A and
B is understood as exclusive, then A is true or B is true but not both. A
regular disjunction, which is satisfied if at least one of its disjuncts is true,
is sometimes called inclusive.)

Consider the following program:

$$p(a) \ or \ p(b).$$
$$p(a).$$
$$p(b).$$

The answer set of this program is $\{p(a), p(b)\}$. Note that if *or* were
exclusive, the program would be contradictory.[5]

Of course the exclusive or of $p(a)$ and $p(b)$ can also be easily expressed
in our language. This can be done by using two rules:

$$p(a) \ or \ p(b).$$
$$\neg p(a) \ or \ \neg p(b).$$

which naturally correspond to the definition of exclusive or. It is easy to
check that, as expected, the program has two answer sets: $\{p(a), \neg p(b)\}$
and $\{\neg p(a), p(b)\}$.

Example 2.2.4. *(Constraints)*

$$p(a) \ or \ p(b). \quad \text{"Believe } p(a) \text{ or believe } p(b)\text{."}$$
$$\leftarrow p(a). \quad\quad \text{"It is impossible to believe } p(a)\text{."}$$

The first rule forces us to believe $p(a)$ or to believe $p(b)$. The second rule is
a constraint that prohibits the reasoner's belief in $p(a)$. Therefore, the first
possibility is eliminated, which leaves $\{p(b)\}$ as the only answer set of the
program. In this example you can see that the constraint limits the sets of
beliefs an agent can have, but does not serve to derive any new information.
Later we show that this is always the case.

---

[5] One may ask why anyone would bother putting in the disjunction when $p(a)$ and $p(b)$ are known.
Remember, however, that the facts could have been added (or learned) later. Also, in reality, the
program may not be so straightforward. The facts may be derived from other rules and seemingly
unrelated new information.

Example 2.2.5. *(Default Negation)*
Sometimes agents can make conclusions based on the absence of information. For example, an agent might assume that with the absence of evidence to the contrary, a class has not been canceled. Or, it might wish to assume that if a person does not know whether she is going to class the next day, then that day is not a holiday. Such reasoning is captured by default negation. Here are two examples.

$p(a) \leftarrow not\ q(a)$. "If $q(a)$ does not belong to your set of beliefs, then $p(a)$ must."

No rule of the program has $q(a)$ in its head, and hence, nothing forces the reasoner, which uses the program as its knowledge base, to believe $q(a)$. So, by the rationality principle, he does not. To satisfy the only rule of the program, the reasoner must believe $p(a)$; thus, $\{p(a)\}$ is the only answer set of the program.

Now consider the following program:

$p(a) \leftarrow not\ q(a)$. "If $q(a)$ does not belong to your set of beliefs, then $p(a)$ must."

$p(b) \leftarrow not\ q(b)$. "If $q(b)$ does not belong to your set of beliefs, then $p(b)$ must."

$q(a)$. "Believe $q(a)$."

Clearly, $q(a)$ must be believed (i.e., must belong to every answer set of the program). This means that the body of the first rule is never satisfied; therefore, the first rule does not contribute to our construction. Since there is no rule in the program whose head contains $q(b)$, we cannot be forced to believe $q(b)$; the body of the second rule is satisfied, and hence, $p(b)$ must be believed. Thus, the only answer set of this program is $\{q(a), p(b)\}$.

Given a definition of an answer set of a program, one can easily define the notion of entailment:

Definition 2.2.1. *(ASP Entailment)*
A program Π **entails** *a literal l ($\Pi \models l$) if l belongs to all answer sets of Π.*

Π entails a set of literals if it entails every literal in this set. Often instead of saying that Π entails l we say that l is a **consequence** of Π.

This seemingly simple notion is really very novel and deserves careful study. To see its novelty, let us recall that the entailment relation of classical logic that forms the basis for mathematical reasoning has the important property called **monotonicity**: The addition of new axioms to a theory T of classical logic cannot decrease the set of consequences of T. More formally, entailment relation $\models$ is called monotonic if for every A, B, and C if $A \models B$ then $A, C \models B$. This property guarantees that a mathematical theorem, once proven, stays proven. This is not the case for ASP entailment. Addition of new information to program Π may invalidate the previous conclusion. In other words for a nonmonotonic entailment relation, $\models$, $A \models B$ does not guarantee that $A, C \models B$. Clearly, program Π_1 consisting of the rule

$$p(a) \leftarrow \; not \; q(a).$$

entails $p(a)$, whereas program

$$\Pi_2 = \Pi_1 \cup \{q(a)\}$$

does not. Addition of $q(a)$ to the agent's knowledge base invalidates the previous conclusion. It forces the agent to stop believing in $p(a)$.

This feature seems to be typical of our commonsense reasoning, where our conclusions are often tentative. This quality of commonsense reasoning made a number of AI researchers doubt that the logical approach to AI would succeed. The discovery of **nonmonotonic** logics in the 1980s dispelled these doubts. It is exactly this nonmonotonic quality given to ASP by its unique connectives and entailment relation that makes it such a powerful knowledge representation language. Much more is said later about nonmonotonicity in this book, but for now we return to our definitions.

We use the notion of entailment to answer queries to program Π. By a **query** we mean a conjunction or disjunction of literals. Queries not containing variables are called ground.

Definition 2.2.2. *(Answer to a Query)*

- *The answer to a ground conjunctive query, $l_1 \wedge \cdots \wedge l_n$, where $n \geq 1$, is*
  - yes *if* $\Pi \models \{l_1, \ldots, l_n\}$,
  - no *if there is i such that* $\Pi \models \bar{l}_i$,
  - unknown *otherwise.*
- *The answer to a ground disjunctive query, l_1 or $\ldots$ or l_n, where $n \geq 1$, is*
  - yes *if there is i such that* $\Pi \models l_i$,
  - no *if* $\Pi \models \{\bar{l}_1, \ldots, \bar{l}_n\}$,
  - unknown *otherwise.*

- *An answer to a query $q(X_1, \ldots, X_n)$, where $X_1, \ldots, X_n$ is the list of variables occurring in q, is a sequence of ground terms $t_1, \ldots, t_n$ such that $\Pi \models q(t_1, \ldots, t_n)$.*

(Note that the actual reasoning system we are going to use to answer queries refers to them as *epistemic queries*, uses a comma instead of $\wedge$ for conjunction, and does not directly support disjunctive queries.)

Example 2.2.6.
Consider again program Π_1 consisting of a rule

$$p(a) \leftarrow not\ q(a).$$

It has the answer set $\{p(a)\}$ and thus answers *yes* and *unknown* to queries $?p(a)$ and $?q(a)$, respectively. Query $?(p(a) \wedge q(a))$ is answered by *unknown*; $?(p(a)\ or\ q(a))$ is answered by *yes*. Query $?p(X)$ has exactly one answer: $X = a$. Let's add one more rule to this program:

$$\neg q(X) \leftarrow not\ q(X). \quad \text{``If } q(X) \text{ is not believed to be true,}$$
$$\text{believe that it is false.''}$$

This rule is known as the **Closed World Assumption (CWA)**. It guarantees that answer sets of a program are complete with respect to the given predicate (i.e., every answer set must contain either $q(t)$ or $\neg q(t)$ for every ground term t from the signature of the program). The new program's answer set is $\{p(a), \neg q(a)\}$. This time queries $?p(a)$ and $?(p(a)\ or\ q(a))$ are still answered by *yes*, whereas the answers to queries $?q(a)$ and $?(p(a) \wedge q(a))$ change to *no*.

2.2.2 Formal Semantics

We first refine the notion of consistency of a set of literals. Pairs of literals of the form $p(t_1, \ldots, t_n)$ and $\neg p(t_1, \ldots, t_n)$ are called *contrary*. A set S of ground literals is called *consistent* if it contains no contrary literals.

All that is left is to precisely define the notion of an answer set. The definition consists of two parts. The first part of the definition is for programs without default negation. The second part explains how to remove default negation so that the first part of the definition can be applied.

Definition 2.2.3. *(Answer Sets, Part I)*
Let Π be a program not containing default negation (i.e., consisting of rules of the form)

$$l_0\ or\ \ldots\ or\ l_i \leftarrow l_{i+1}, \ldots, l_m.$$

*An **answer set** of* Π *is a consistent set* S *of ground literals such that*

- S *satisfies the rules of* Π *and*
- S *is minimal (i.e., there is no proper subset of* S *that satisfies the rules of* Π*).*

Let's look at some examples, this time employing the formal definition and *observe that it captures our intuition.*

Example 2.2.7. *(Example 2.2.1, Revisited)*
Let us now go back to Example 2.2.1 and check that our informal argument is compatible with Definition 2.2.3, namely that $S_1 = \{q(a), p(b)\}$ is the answer set of program Π_1:

$$p(b) \leftarrow q(a).$$
$$q(a).$$

S_1 satisfies fact $q(a)$ by clause (1) of the definition of satisfiability (Definition 2.1.1). Clause (4) of this definition guarantees that the (empty) body of the second rule is vacuously satisfied by S_1, and hence, by clause (5), the second rule is satisfied by S_1. Since the head $p(b)$ of the first rule is in S_1, S_1 also satisfies the first rule. Clearly S_1 is consistent and no proper subset of S_1 satisfies the rules of Π_1; therefore, S_1 is Π_1's answer set. Suppose now that S is an answer set of Π_1. It must satisfy the rules of Π_1, and hence, S contains S_1. From minimality we can conclude that $S = S_1$ (i.e., S_1 is the unique answer set of Π_1). Later we show that any program with neither *or* nor *not* has at most one answer set.

Now that we have the answer set, we can see that, by the definition of entailment, this program entails $q(a)$ and $p(b)$. The following table shows the answers to some possible ground queries created from the program's signature:

? $q(a)$	*yes*
? $\neg q(a)$	*no*
? $p(b)$	*yes*
? $\neg p(b)$	*no*

We skip Example 2.2.2 (the reader is encouraged to work it out as an exercise) and consider another example.

Example 2.2.8.
Consider a program consisting of two rules:

$$p(a) \leftarrow p(b).$$
$$\neg p(a).$$

Let $S_1 = \{\neg p(a)\}$. Clearly, S_1 is consistent. Since $p(b) \notin S_1$, by clause (1) of the definition of satisfiability, the body of the first rule is not satisfied by S_1. Hence, by clause (5), S_1 satisfies the first rule. The body of the second rule is empty. Hence, by clause (4), it is vacuously satisfied by S_1. Thus, by clause (5), S_1 satisfies the second rule of the program. The only proper subset, $\emptyset$, of S_1 does not satisfy the second rule; therefore, S_1 is an answer set of our program. To show that S_1 is the only answer set, consider an arbitrary answer set S. Clearly, S must contain $\neg p(a)$. This means that by the minimality requirement $S = S_1$.

By the definition of entailment we can see that this program entails $\neg p(a)$. The following table contains the answers to some possible ground queries created from the program's signature:

? $p(a)$	*no*
? $\neg p(a)$	*yes*
? $p(b)$	*unknown*
? $\neg p(b)$	*unknown*

It may be worth noticing that this example clearly illustrates the difference between logic programming connective $\leftarrow$ and classical implication (denoted by $\supset$). Recall that $p(b) \supset p(a)$ is classically equivalent to its *contrapositive*, $\neg p(a) \supset \neg p(b)$. Hence, the classical theory consisting of $p(b) \supset p(a)$ and $\neg p(a)$ entails $\neg p(b)$. Our example shows that this is not the case if $\supset$ is replaced by $\leftarrow$. If we want the contrapositive of $p(a) \leftarrow p(b)$, we need to explicitly add it to the program.[6] We suggest that the reader check that, as expected, the resulting program would have the answer set $\{\neg p(a), \neg p(b)\}$.

Example 2.2.9.

$$p(b) \leftarrow \neg p(a).$$
$$\neg p(a).$$

---

[6] Later chapters show why we do not want a built-in contrapositive for our $\leftarrow$ connective.

Let $S_1 = \{\neg p(a), p(b)\}$. S_1 is a consistent set of ground literals that clearly satisfies the rules of the program. To show that S_1 is an answer set we need to show that no proper subset of S_1 satisfies the program rules. To see that, it is enough to notice that $\neg p(a)$ must belong to every answer set of the program by clause (1) of the definition of satisfiability, and $p(b)$ is required by clause (5). Therefore, S_1 is minimal.

This time, the answer to query $?p(b)$ is *yes* and to $?\neg p(b)$ is *no*.

Example 2.2.10. *(Empty Answer Set)*

$$p(b) \leftarrow \neg p(a).$$

There are no facts, so we are not forced to include anything in S_1. Let's check if $S_1 = \emptyset$ is an answer set. S_1 satisfies the rule because it does not satisfy its body. Since $\emptyset$ has no proper subsets, it is the only answer set of the program. Note that an empty answer set is by no means the same as the absence of one.

Since neither $p(a) \in \emptyset$ nor $\neg p(a) \in \emptyset$, the truth of $p(a)$ is *unknown*; the same applies for $p(b)$.

Now let's look at several programs containing epistemic disjunction.

Example 2.2.11. *(Epistemic Disjunction, Revisited)*
We start with the first two programs from Example 2.2.3 from the previous section. Program

$$p(a) \; or \; p(b).$$

has two answer sets, $\{p(a)\}$ and $\{p(b)\}$. Each contains a literal required by clause (3) of the definition of satisfiability. Note that $\{p(a), p(b)\}$ is not minimal, so it is not an answer set. Since entailment requires literals to be true in *all* answer sets of a program, this program does not entail $p(a)$ nor $p(b)$ (i.e., their truth values, along with the truth values of their negative counterparts, are *unknown*).

Now consider program

$$p(a) \; or \; p(b).$$
$$q(a) \leftarrow p(a).$$
$$q(a) \leftarrow p(b).$$

In this case our definition clearly gives two answer sets: $\{p(a), q(a)\}$ and $\{p(b), q(a)\}$. This program entails $q(a)$. It entails no other literals (but does entail, say, the disjunction $p(a) \; or \; p(b)$).

Now let's look at a new example emphasizing the difference between epistemic and classical readings of disjunction.

Example 2.2.12. *($p(a)$ or $\neg p(a)$ Is Not a Tautology)*
Consider

$$p(b) \leftarrow \neg p(a).$$
$$p(b) \leftarrow p(a).$$
$$p(a) \text{ or } \neg p(a).$$

The program has two answer sets: $S_1 = \{p(a), p(b)\}$ and $S_2 = \{\neg p(a), p(b)\}$. S_1 satisfies the first rule because it does not satisfy the rule's body, the second rule because it contains $p(a)$ and $p(b)$, and the third rule because it contains $p(a)$. S_2 satisfies the first rule because it contains both $\neg p(a)$ and $p(b)$, the second because it does not satisfy the body, and the third because it contains $\neg p(a)$. Because each literal is required to satisfy some rule, the sets are minimal.

But now let us look at the program

$$p(b) \leftarrow \neg p(a).$$
$$p(b) \leftarrow p(a).$$

It is not difficult to check that $\emptyset$ is the only answer set of this program. This result is not surprising since, as we mentioned in Section 2.1 when we discussed syntax, $p(a)$ or $\neg p(a)$ is not a tautology. Without the presence of explicit disjunction, $p(a)$ or $\neg p(a)$, the reasoner remains undecided about the truth value of $p(a)$, neither believing that $p(a)$ is true nor that it is false. Thus $p(b)$ is not included in the answer set.

It may be strange that we cannot conclude $p(b)$. Indeed one may be tempted to reason as follows: Either $p(a)$ is true or $p(a)$ is false, and hence, $p(b)$ must be included in any answer set. But, of course, this reasoning is based on the wrong reading of epistemic *or* – it slides back to a classical reading of the disjunction. Since the reasoner may have no opinion on the truth values of $p(a)$, the argument fails.

Example 2.2.13. *(Constraints, Revisited)*

$$p(a) \text{ or } p(b).$$
$$\leftarrow p(a).$$

The first rule is (minimally) satisfied by either $S_1 = \{p(a)\}$ or $S_2 = \{p(b)\}$. However, S_1 does not satisfy the second rule because it is not possible to satisfy an empty head if the body is satisfied. Therefore, S_2 is the only answer set of the program. Note that, although we cannot include $p(a)$ in any answer set, we do not have enough information to entail $\neg p(a)$. The answers to queries $p(a)$ and $p(b)$ are *unknown* and *yes*, respectively.

So far we have not had to address default negation. The second part of the definition of answer sets addresses this question.

Definition 2.2.4. *(Answer Sets, Part II)*
Let Π *be an arbitrary program and* S *be a set of ground literals. By* Π^S *we denote the program obtained from* Π *by*

1. *removing all rules containing* not l *such that* $l \in S$;
2. *removing all other premises containing* not.

S is an answer set of Π *if S is an answer set of* Π^S.

We refer to Π^S as the **reduct** of Π with respect to S.

Example 2.2.14. *(Default Negation, Revisited)*
Consider a program Π from Example 2.2.5 (see the following table). Let's confirm that $S = \{q(a), p(b)\}$ is the answer set of Π. Π has default negation; therefore, we use Part II of our definition of answer sets to compute Π^S.

	Π	Π^S
r_1	$p(a) \leftarrow$ not $q(a)$.	(*deleted*)
r_2	$p(b) \leftarrow$ not $q(b)$.	$p(b)$.
r_3	$q(a)$.	$q(a)$.

1. We remove r_1 from Π because it has *not* $q(a)$ in its premise, whereas $q(a) \in S$.
2. Then, we remove the premise of r_2.

In this way, we eliminate all occurrences of default negation from Π. Clearly, S is the answer set of Π^S and, hence, of Π.

Note that, as mentioned in the definition, a reduct is always computed with respect to a candidate set of ground literals S. The algorithm for computing answer sets is not presented until Chapter 7; thus, we must still come up with candidate sets based on our intuition given by the informal semantics. (Of course, theoretically, we could test all possible sets of ground literals from the signature, but in practice this approach works only on small programs.) Meanwhile, the following proposition will be of some help for reasoning about answer sets.

Proposition 2.2.1. *Let S be an answer set of a ground ASP program* Π.

(a) *S satisfies every rule* $r \in$ Π.
(b) *If literal* $l \in S$ *then there is a rule* r *from* Π *such that the body of* r *is satisfied by* S *and* l *is the only literal in the head of* r *satisfied by* S. *(It is often said that* **rule** r **supports literal** l.*)*

The first part of the proposition guarantees that answer sets of a program satisfy its rules; the second guarantees that every element of an answer set of a program is supported by at least one of its rules.

Here are some more examples of answer sets of programs with default negation:

Example 2.2.15.

$$p(a) \leftarrow not\ p(a).$$

This program has no answer set. This result can be established by simply considering two available candidates, $S_1 = \emptyset$ and $S_2 = \{p(a)\}$. S_1 does not satisfy the program's single rule, and hence, according to the first clause of Proposotion 2.2.1, cannot be the program's answer set. The second clause of the proposition allows us to see that S_2 cannot be an answer set because $p(a)$ is not supported by any rule of the program.

Note that the absence of answer sets is not surprising. The rule, which tells the agent to believe $p(a)$ if it does not believe it, should naturally be rejected by a rational agent.

This is our first example of an ASP program without answer sets. We refer to such programs as **inconsistent**. There are, of course, many other inconsistent programs, such as

$$p(a).$$
$$\neg p(a).$$

or

$$p(a).$$
$$\leftarrow p(a).$$

but inconsistency normally appears only when the program is erroneous (i.e., it does not adequately represents the agent's knowledge). Later, however, we show how various interesting reasoning tasks can be reduced to discovering the inconsistency of a program.

Example 2.2.16.

$$p(a) \leftarrow not\ p(a).$$
$$p(a).$$

There are two candidate answer sets: $S_1 = \{p(a)\}$ and $S_2 = \emptyset$. Since the reduct of the program with respect to S_1 is $p(a)$, S_1 is an answer set. Clearly, S_2 does not satisfy the rules of the program; thus, S_1 is the only answer set.

Example 2.2.17.

$$p(a) \leftarrow not\ p(b).$$
$$p(b) \leftarrow not\ p(a).$$

This program has two answer sets: $\{p(a)\}$ and $\{p(b)\}$. Note that $\emptyset$ is not an answer set for this program because it does not satisfy the program's rules. The set $\{p(a), p(b)\}$ is not an answer set of the program since its elements are not supported by the rules of the program.

Example 2.2.18.

$$p(a) \leftarrow not\ p(b).$$
$$p(b) \leftarrow not\ p(a).$$
$$\leftarrow p(b).$$

The constraint eliminates $\{p(b)\}$, making $\{p(a)\}$ the only answer set of the program.

Example 2.2.19.

$$p(a) \leftarrow not\ p(b).$$
$$p(b) \leftarrow not\ p(a).$$
$$\leftarrow p(b).$$
$$\neg p(a).$$

This program has no answer set. Indeed by Proposition 2.2.1 an answer set must contain $\neg p(a)$ and cannot contain $p(b)$. Hence, by the first rule of the program it should contain $p(a)$, which is impossible.

In the next example we consider a slightly more complex program.

Example 2.2.20. Let Π consist of the rules

$$s(b).$$
$$r(a).$$
$$p(a) \ or \ p(b).$$
$$q(X) \leftarrow p(X), r(X), \ not \ s(X).$$

After grounding the program will have the form

$$s(b).$$
$$r(a).$$
$$p(a) \ or \ p(b).$$
$$q(a) \leftarrow p(a), r(a), \ not \ s(a).$$
$$q(b) \leftarrow p(b), r(b), \ not \ s(b).$$

Even though the number of candidate answer sets for this program is large, the answer sets of the program can still be obtained in a relatively simple way. It is easy to see that by Proposition 2.2.1 an answer set S of the program must satisfy the first three rules. Thus, S contains $\{s(b), r(a), p(a)\}$ or $\{s(b), r(a), p(b)\}$. The program has no rule that can possibly support $s(a)$, and hence, every answer set of the program satisfies *not* $s(a)$. This means that every answer set containing $\{p(a), r(a)\}$ must also contain $q(a)$. There is no rule that can support $r(b)$; thus, the body of the last rule cannot be satisfied and $q(b)$ cannot belong to any answer set of the program. This implies that the program may only have two answer sets: $\{s(b), r(a), p(a), q(a)\}$ and $\{s(b), r(a), p(b)\}$. Both of the candidates are indeed answer sets, which can be easily checked using the definition.

So far our computation of answer sets has been done by hand. There are a large number of efficient software systems, called **ASP solvers**, that automate this process. Appendix A contains instructions for downloading and using several such solvers. At this point we advise the readers to download an answer set solver and use it to compute answer sets for programs from the previous examples. For many of the programs in this book queries can be answered manually by examining these answer sets and applying Definition 2.2.2. STUDENT from Chapter 1 is implemented by a query-answering system based on ASP solvers as described in Appendix B.

The version of ASP described in this book and used by most of the existing ASP solvers is unsorted. Readers who, as do the authors of this book, prefer to program in a sorted language should consult Appendix C describing a sorted version of ASP, its solver, and query-answering system that implement STUDENT.

2.3 A Note on Translation from Natural Language

So far we have discussed the semantics of logical connectives of ASP. The question of translating fragments of natural language into ASP theories was addressed only briefly.[7] It is important to realize that, as in any translation, the translation from even simple English sentences to statements in ASP may be a nontrivial task. Consider the simple English sentence, "All professors are adults." The direct (literal) translation of this sentence seems to be

$$(1)\ adult(X) \leftarrow prof(X).$$

Used in conjunction with a list of professors, it will allow us to make conclusions about their adulthood; e.g., the program consisting of that rule and the fact $prof(john)$ entails $adult(john)$. But what happens if we expand this program by $\neg adult(alice)$? Intuitively we should be able to conclude that $\neg prof(alice)$. The literal translation of the English statement does not allow us to do that. This happens because some information implicitly present in the English text is missing from our translation. One can argue, for instance, that the translation is missing something akin to classical logic's law of the exclusive middle with respect to professors and adults; thus a good translation to ASP should include statements

$$(2)\ adult(X)\ or\ \neg adult(X).$$

$$(3)\ prof(X)\ or\ \neg prof(X).$$

where X ranges over some sort *person*. For simplicity we assume that there are only two persons, $john$ and $alice$. Let us denote the program consisting of the rules (1)–(3) and the sort *person* by Π_1. One can easily check that Π_1 combined with the two facts above has one answer set:

$$\{prof(john), adult(john), \neg prof(alice), \neg adult(alice)\}.$$

(We are not showing the sort *person*.) As is typical in natural-language translation, this is not the only reasonable representation of our statement

---

[7] Here we, of course, are only talking about *manual* translation. We do not discuss methods for *automatically* translating from English to a formal language; however, this task, known as *natural-language processing*, is also a very important part of the general problem of artificial intelligence.

in ASP. One can simply translate our English statement into program Π_2 consisting of the above sort *person* and two rules:

$$adult(X) \leftarrow prof(X).$$
$$\neg prof(X) \leftarrow \neg adult(X).$$

The first rule is a direct translation and the second is its contrapositive. Again the program, used together with $prof(john)$ and $\neg adult(alice)$, produces the expected answers. Note, however, that programs Π_1 and Π_2 are not equivalent (i.e., they do not have the same answer sets). Indeed, if we do not include the sort, $\emptyset$ is the only answer set of Π_2, whereas Π_1 has answer sets including

$$\{prof(alice), adult(alice), prof(john), adult(john)\}$$
$$\{prof(alice), adult(alice), \neg prof(john), \neg adult(john)\}$$
$$\{\neg prof(alice), \neg adult(alice), prof(john), adult(john)\}$$
$$\{\neg prof(alice), \neg adult(alice), \neg prof(john), \neg adult(john)\}.$$

Which representation is better may depend on the context of the sentence, the purpose of our representation, and simply the taste of the translator. Any type of translation is an art, and translation from English into ASP is no exception. One of the goals of this book is to help you to become better translators and to better understand the consequences of your translation decisions.

2.4 Properties of ASP Programs

In this section we give several useful properties of ASP programs. (In the rest of this book, unless otherwise stated, we use the terms "ASP program" and "logic program" interchangeably.) We start with conditions that guarantee program consistency.

In what follows we consider programs consisting of rules of the form

$$p_0 \ or \ \dots \ or \ p_i \leftarrow p_{i+1}, \dots, p_m, \ not \ p_{m+1}, \dots, \ not \ p_n \qquad (2.2)$$

where ps are atoms and $i \geq 0$ (in other words, programs containing no classical negation $\neg$ and no constraints).

Definition 2.4.1. *(Level Mapping)*
Let program Π *consist of rules of form (2.2). A function* $\| \ \|$ *from ground atoms of* Π *to natural numbers*[8] *is called a* **level mapping** *of* Π*. Level*

---

[8] For simplicity we consider a special case of the more general original definition that allows arbitrary countable ordinals.

$||D||$, *where D is a disjunction of atoms, is defined as the* minimum level of D's members.

Definition 2.4.2. *(Local Stratification)*
A program Π consisting of rules of form (2.2) is called **locally stratified** *if there is a level mapping $||\ ||$ of Π such that for every rule $r \in \Pi$, the following is true:*

> 1. *for every p_k where $i < k \leq m$, $||p_k|| \leq ||head(r)||$; and*
> 2. *for every p_k where $m < k \leq n$, $||p_k|| < ||head(r)||$.*

It is easy to see that any program without classical and default negation is locally stratified. A function mapping all atoms of such a program into, say, 0 is a level mapping that satisfies the corresponding conditions. A function $||p(a)|| = ||r(a)|| = 1$ and $||q(a)|| = 0$ is a level mapping of a program consisting of rule

$$p(a) \leftarrow not\ q(a), r(a).$$

Clearly the mapping satisfies the conditions from the definition, and hence, the program is locally stratified.

Proposition 2.4.1. *(Properties of Locally Stratified Programs)*

- *A locally stratified program is consistent.*
- *A locally stratified program without disjunction has exactly one answer set.*
- *The above conditions hold for the union of a locally stratified program and any collection of closed world assumptions; i.e. rules of the form*

$$\neg p(X) \leftarrow not\ p(X).$$

Proposition 2.4.1 immediately implies the existence and uniqueness of answer sets of programs from Examples 2.2.5 and 2.2.6. It is, however, not applicable to the program from Example 2.2.15.

Let's consider two more examples of locally stratified programs.

Example 2.4.1.
Consider a program

$$p(0).$$
$$p(f(I)) \leftarrow p(I).$$

It is not difficult to see that the minimal set of ground literals satisfying rules of this program is an infinite set:

$$S = \{p(0), p(f(0)), p(f(f(0))), \dots\}$$

The program contains no negations and, hence, is locally stratified. Therefore, it has no answer sets except S.

The next example is only slightly more sophisticated.

Example 2.4.2.
Consider the program Π

$$p(0).$$
$$p(f(I)) \leftarrow not\ p(I).$$

and a set

$$S = \{p(0), p(f(f(I))), p(f(f(f(f(I))))), \dots\}.$$

Using the definition one can easily prove that S is an answer set of Π. Clearly, Π is locally stratified. (Consider a level mapping assigning to each atom $p(t)$ the number of fs occurring in t and check that it satisfies the corresponding conditions.) Therefore, S is the only answer set of the program.

Another approach to proving consistency and, sometimes, uniqueness of a logic program is based on the notion of the program's dependency graph. Let Π be a (not-necessarily) ground program consisting of rules of form (2.2). A **dependency graph** of Π is a collection of nodes labeled by predicate symbols from the signature of Π and a collection of arcs of the form $\langle p_1, p_2, s \rangle$ where s is $+$ (positive link) or $-$ (negative link). The graph contains $\langle p_1, p_2, + \rangle$ if there is a rule of Π containing an atom formed by p_1 in the head and an atom formed by p_2 in the body; it contains $\langle p_1, p_2, - \rangle$ if there is a rule of Π containing an atom formed by p_1 in the head and an extended literal of the form $not\ l$ where l is formed by p_2 in the body. Note that two nodes can be connected by both positive and negative links. A cycle in the graph is said to be negative if it contains at least one edge labeled by $-$. A program is called **stratified** if its dependency graph contains no negative cycles.

Proposition 2.4.2. *Let Π be a program consisting of rules of form (2.2).*

- *If the dependency graph of Π contains no cycles with an odd number of negative links then Π is consistent (i.e., has an answer set).*
- *A stratified program without disjunction has exactly one answer set.*

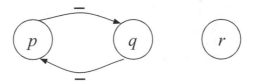

Figure 2.1. Dependency Graph.

The proposition can be used to prove consistency of programs

$$p(X) \leftarrow not\ q(X).$$
$$q(X) \leftarrow not\ p(X).$$
$$r(0).$$

and

$$p(X) \leftarrow not\ q(X).$$
$$r(0).$$

The first program has a dependency graph with an even number of negative cycles – see Figure 2.1. The second is stratified, thus having exactly one answer set. Despite substantial differences in their definitions, there is a close relationship between stratified and locally stratified programs. In fact, every stratified program is locally stratified.

The following proposition is useful for understanding the role of constraints.

Proposition 2.4.3. *Let* Π *be a logic program consisting of a collection* R *of rules with nonempty heads and a collection* C *of constraints. Then* S *is an answer set of* Π *iff* S *is an answer set of* R *that satisfies constraints from* C.

Last, we describe a procedure for removing negative literals and constraints from a program without changing its answer sets. For every predicate symbol p from the signature of Π,

1. Introduce a new predicate symbol p^+.
2. Replace every occurrence of a negative literal of the form $\neg p(\bar{t})$ in the program by a new, positive literal $p^+(\bar{t})$. We call this literal the *positive form* of $\neg p(\bar{t})$.
3. For every sequence of ground terms $\bar{t}$ that can serve as a parameter of p, expand Π by the axiom

$$\leftarrow p(\bar{t}), p^+(\bar{t})$$

4. Replace every constraint

$$\leftarrow body$$

of the program by rule

$$p \leftarrow body, \ not \ p$$

where p is a new atom.

It is not difficult to show that the new program Π^+, which contains neither classical negation nor constraints, has the following property:

Proposition 2.4.4. *Let S be a set of literals over signature Σ of Π. By S^+ we denote the set obtained by replacing negative literals of S by their positive forms. A consistent set S of literals from Σ is an answer set of Π iff S^+ is an answer set of Π^+.*

Summary

In this chapter we introduced our main knowledge representation tool – Answer Set Prolog. The logical connectives and the semantics of the language capture the intuition behind a particular notion of beliefs of rational agents as described by the rationality principle.

We hope that the reader agrees that the language satisfies the following important principles of good design: It has a simple syntax, its logical connectives have reasonably clear intuitive meaning, and the definition of its semantics is mathematically simple and transparent. The entailment relation of the language is nonmonotonic, which makes ASP dramatically different from the language of classical logic. In the following chapters we show the importance of this property for knowledge representation.

The chapter continued with a brief discussion of the subtleties of the translation of natural-language texts into Answer Set Prolog – a theme that permeates this book.

It concluded by describing several simple but important mathematical properties of the language. The first two give sufficient conditions guaranteeing the existence and uniqueness of answer sets of the programs. The last one illustrates the role of constraints as the means of limiting an agent's beliefs without generating new ones.

References and Further Reading

The syntax and semantics of Answer Set Prolog were introduced in Gelfond and Lifschitz (1991). The notion of stratification and its relation to dependency graphs was introduced in Apt, Blair, and Walker (1988). Local stratification first appeared in Przymusinski (1988). The properties of stratified and locally stratified programs were proven in these papers. There are many interesting extensions to these notions (see for instance Przymusinska and Przymusinski [1990]). Clause 1 of Proposition 2.4.2 is a simple special case of a more general result from Fages (1994). There are a substantial number of generalizations of Answer Set Prolog that allow rules whose heads and bodies contain more-complex formulas; see, for instance, Ferraris, Lee, and Lifschitz (2007) and Pearce (1997, 2006). Some of the other generalizations of the language are described in later chapters. The closed world assumption and its importance for knowledge representation and reasoning were first discussed in Reiter (1978). (Representation of CWA in Answer Set Prolog is from Gelfond and Lifschitz (1991)). The first efficient ASP system computing answer sets of nondisjunctive logic programs is described in Niemela, Simons, and Soininen (2002) and Niemela and Simons (1997). For a description of the corresponding system for programs with disjunction, see Leone, Rullo, and Scarcello (1997) and Calimeri et al. (2002). An interesting overview can be found in Minker and Seipal (2002). For information on natural-language processing see, for instance, Blackburn and Bos (2005).

Exercises

1. Given the following signature

$$\mathcal{O} = \{a\}$$
$$\mathcal{F} = \{f\}$$
$$\mathcal{P} = \{p\}$$
$$\mathcal{V} = \{X\}$$

specify which of the following are terms, atoms, literals, or none.

(a) a	(f) $\neg f(a)$	(k) $\neg p(a)$
(b) $\neg a$	(g) $f(p)$	(l) $p(f(a))$
(c) X	(h) $f(X)$	(m) $p(\neg f(a))$
(d) f	(i) p	(n) $\neg p(f(a))$
(e) $f(a)$	(j) $p(a)$	(o) $p(X)$

2. Given the following sorted signature

$$\mathcal{O} = \{pele, namath, jordan, soccer, football, basketball\}$$
$$Sorts = \{player, sport\}$$
$$player = \{pele, namath, jordan\}$$
$$sport = \{soccer, football, basketball\}$$
$$\mathcal{F} = \emptyset$$
$$\mathcal{P} = \{plays(player, sport)\}$$
$$\mathcal{V} = \{X, Y\}$$

   (a) Is $\neg plays(pele, soccer)$ a literal?
   (b) Is $plays(football, namath)$ a literal?
   (c) Is $basketball$ a term?

3. Given program Π,

$$p(a) \leftarrow not\ p(b).$$
$$p(b) \leftarrow not\ p(c).$$
$$p(c) \leftarrow not\ p(a).$$

   and set $S = \{p(c)\}$

   (a) Construct the program Π^S from the definition of an answer set.
   (b) Check if S is an answer set of Π. Justify your answer.

4. (a) Compute the answer sets of the following program:

$$p\ or\ q\ or\ r.$$
$$\neg p \leftarrow not\ s.$$

   (b) How does the above program answer queries $?p$ and $?q$?

5. Compute the answer sets of the following program:

$$p(a) \leftarrow not\ p(b), \neg p(c).$$
$$p(b) \leftarrow not\ p(a), \neg p(c).$$
$$\neg p(X) \leftarrow not\ p(X).$$

6. Compute the answer sets of the following program:

$$p \leftarrow not\ q.$$
$$q \leftarrow not\ p.$$
$$r \leftarrow not\ s.$$
$$s \leftarrow not\ r.$$
$$\neg s \leftarrow q.$$

7. (a) Compute the answer sets of the following program. *Assume that a and b are the object constants of this program's signature.*

$$\neg s(a).$$
$$p(X) \leftarrow not\ q(X), \neg s(X).$$
$$q(X) \leftarrow not\ p(X).$$
$$r(X) \leftarrow p(X).$$
$$r(X) \leftarrow q(X).$$

   (b) How does the program answer queries
       $?s(a),\ ?r(a),\ ?s(b),$ and $?q(b)$?

8. (a) Compute the answer sets of the following program:

$$p(a)\ or\ \neg p(b).$$
$$q(X) \leftarrow \neg p(X).$$
$$\neg q(X) \leftarrow not\ q(X).$$
$$r(X) \leftarrow not\ p(X).$$

   (b) How does the program answer queries
       $?q(a),\ ?r(a),\ ?q(b),$ and $?r(b)$?

9. (a) Compute the answer sets of the following program:

$$p(X)\ or\ q(X) \leftarrow not\ r(X).$$
$$\neg p(X) \leftarrow h(X),\ not\ r(X).$$
$$h(a).$$
$$h(b).$$
$$r(a).$$

   (b) How does the program answer queries
       $?p(b),\ ?q(b),$ and $?r(b)$?

10. (a) Compute the answer sets of the following program:

$$p(a) \leftarrow \ not \ p(b).$$
$$p(b) \leftarrow \ not \ p(a).$$
$$q(a).$$
$$\neg q(b) \leftarrow p(X), \ not \ r(X).$$

(b) How does the program answer queries
$?q(a), \ ?q(b), \ ?p(a)$, and $?r(b)$?

11. Translate the following story about dealing with high prices into ASP. Ignore the time factor. "Either the supply was increased or price controls were instituted. Instituting price controls leads to shortages. There are no shortages." Use zero-arity predicate symbols $increased\_supply$, $price\_controls$ and $shortages$. Compute the answer sets of this program. How does your program answer these queries:

$$? \ increased\_supply$$
$$? \ increased\_supply \wedge \neg price\_controls$$

Is that what you intended? (Note that the answer depends on your understanding of the disjunction in the first sentence of the story. Is it inclusive or exclusive?)

12. Consider the following story. "If Jim does not buy toys for his children, Jim's children will not receive toys for Christmas. If Jim's children do not write their Christmas letters, Jim will not buy them toys. Jim's children do receive toys for Christmas." Assume that the intended interpretation of this story implies that Jim's children wrote their Christmas letters.

(a) Translate the story into an ASP program and compute the answer set. Use disjunction to encode the law of the exclusive middle to allow the program to come to the proper conclusion.

(b) Translate the story into an ASP program and compute the answer set, this time making the contrapositive explicit for each statement.

3

Roots of Answer Set Prolog

Answer Set Prolog is a comparatively new knowledge representation (KR) language with roots in older nonmonotonic logics and the logic programming language Prolog. Early proponents of the logical approach to artificial intelligence believed that the classical logical formalism called *first-order logic* would serve as the basis for the application of the axiomatic method to the development of intelligent agents. In this chapter we briefly describe some important developments that forced them to question this belief and to work instead on the development of nonclassical knowledge representation languages including ASP. To make the chapter easier for people not familiar with mathematical logic, we give a very short introduction to one of its basic logical tools – first-order logic.

3.1 First-Order Logic (FOL)

First-order logic is a formal logical system that consists of a formal language, an entailment or consequence relation for this language, and a collection of inference rules that can be used to obtain these consequences. The language of FOL is parametrized with respect to a signature Σ. The notions of term and atom over Σ are the same as those defined in Section 2.1. The statements of FOL (called FOL formulas) are built from atoms using boolean logical connectives and quantifiers $\forall$ (for all) and $\exists$ (there exists). Atoms are formulas. If A and B are formulas and X is a variable, then $(A \land B)$, $(A \lor B)$, $(A \supset B)$, $\neg A$, $\forall X\, A$, $\exists X\, A$ are formulas. An occurrence of a variable X in a formula A is called *bound* if it belongs to a subformula of A that has the form $\forall X\, F$ or $\exists X\, F$; otherwise it is free. Formulas without free occurrences of variables are called *sentences*. $\forall X\, p(X)$ is a sentence; $p(X)$ is an FOL formula that is not a sentence. Sometimes, the latter are referred to as *conditions* on X. To simplify further presentation, we assume that, for every variable X, all occurrences of X in a formula are either free or bound, exclusively. This assumption eliminates formulas such as $(\forall X (p(X) \vee q(X)) \vee r(X))$ where the last occurrence of X is free and the first two are bound. A set of FOL sentences is often referred to as an FOL *theory*.

To illustrate, let's take our family example from Chapter 1. Its FOL signature, atoms, and terms are identical to the those given in Section 2.1. Here are some formulas made from the signature's symbols:

$$(father(john, sam) \wedge (mother(alice, sam) \vee mother(alice, john)))$$

$$\forall X, Y (parent(Y, X) \supset child(X, Y))$$

$$\neg \exists X \, gender\_of(X, male)$$

$$gender\_of(X, male)$$

The first three are sentences. The last one is a condition on X.

Note that so far we have only talked about the syntax of FOL. Nothing was said about the semantics (meaning) of these formulas and their truth or falsity. The meaning of a first-order formula depends on the interpretation of its nonlogical symbols. Such an interpretation is normally defined by specifying a nonempty set U called the *universe* and a mapping I that maps

- every object constant c of Σ into an element $I(c)$ of U,
- every function constant f of arity n into a function $I(f) : U^n \rightarrow U$,
- every predicate constant p of arity n into a subset $I(p)$ of U^n.

Using the first two clauses of this definition, function I can be naturally extended to arbitrary terms. Whenever convenient, we refer to an interpretation by its second element I.

To illustrate this notion let us consider the family example above, and define an interpretation, say I_1, of its symbols.

Suppose that our universe U_1 of I_1 consists of a group of four people and a group of two genders. Let us denote elements of U_1 by $d_1, \ldots, d_4, m, f$ where the ds stand for people and m and f for genders. (Note that these symbols do not belong to the signature of our FOL theory. Sometimes they are referred to as *meta-symbols*.) Mapping of object constants into elements of the universe can be viewed as naming these elements within the language. Making the value of $I_1(alice)$ to be d_1 simply means that, in our interpretation, the first person in the group has the name *alice*. The same goes for other constants. Let us assume that $I_1(john) = d_2$, $I_1(sam) = d_3$, $I_1(female) = f$, and $I_1(male) = m$. Let us also assume that our interpretation I_1 maps predicate *father* of arity 2 into the set $\{\langle d_2, d_3 \rangle\}$. Intuitively this means the only people in the group that satisfy the father-child relation are d_2 and d_3. The same goes for *mother* and *gender_of*.

I_1 is, of course, not the only possible interpretation. Interpretation I_2 may have the same universe and differ from I_1 only in its mapping of *father*: $I_2(father) = \{\langle d_4, d_3 \rangle\}$. Other interpretations may have completely different universes and mappings.[1]

Now we can define the truth value of an FOL sentence in interpretation I with universe U. First we expand the signature Σ by a collection of constant symbols, one for each element of the universe U; let's say that for each $d \in U$ the constant symbol c_d is added. The interpretation is extended so that each new constant symbol is assigned to its corresponding element of the domain.

Next we define the truth of sentences by induction on the definition of a sentence. A ground atom $p(t_1, \ldots, t_n)$ of the new signature is said to be true in I if $\langle I(t_1), \ldots, I(t_n) \rangle \in I(p)$. If A and B are FOL sentences then $\neg A$ is true in I if A is not true in I; $A \wedge B$ is true in I if both A and B are true in I; $\forall X\, A$ is true in I if for every $d \in U$, $A(c_d)$ is true in I. (Note that here by $A(c_d)$ we denote the result of replacing all occurrences of X in A by c_d.) An interpretation I satisfies a sentence F or is a *model* of F ($I \models F$) if F is true in I. An FOL theory T is *satisfiable* (or *consistent*) if it has a model. Finally, a sentence F is a *consequence* of theory T ($T \models F$) if F is true in all the models of T; $T \models F$ is often referred to as the *FOL entailment relation* and is read as T entails F. In what follows we often use a version of first-order logic whose syntax includes a special relation $=$. An interpretation I satisfies $t_1 = t_2$ iff I maps t_1 and t_2 to the same element of U.

By this definition, under interpretation I_1, $father(john, sam)$ is true, $father(sam, john)$ is false, $father(john, sam) \vee father(sam, john)$ is true, $\exists X\, father(X, sam)$ is true, $\forall X\, father(X, sam)$ is false, and so on. Under I_2, these formulas' truth values would become false, false, false, true, false, respectively.

Now suppose we have the following theory:

$$father(john, sam)$$
$$\neg father(sam, john)$$

---

[1] Note that this view of the universe is quite different from that which we intuitively use in logic programming where we normally have one (intended) universe. In our example the intended universe contains exactly three people and two genders (each uniquely named by the corresponding constant in the language). In some cases the ability to have arbitrary universes is very important. This is especially true for representing mathematical knowledge.

You can see that this theory is satisfiable because there exists an interpretation, for example I_1, in which all its sentences are true. Note that this theory entails $\neg(father(john, sam) \wedge father(sam, john))$, but does not entail $\neg(father(alice, sam))$ because there is an interpretation in which the parameters of predicate *father* are assigned this way.

In addition to the definition of formula and consequence relation, first-order logic normally includes a collection of inference rules – syntactic rules that usually consist of premises and a conclusion. The inference rules of first-order logic are *sound* (i.e., they preserve the truth of first-order sentences). Probably the most famous example of such a rule is *modus ponens*:

$$\frac{A, \ A \supset B}{B}$$

which says that if A is true and $A \supset B$ is true then B is also true. We say that a sentence F is derived from a theory T using a collection of inference rules R ($T \vdash_R F$) if there is a sequence of sentences $F_1, \ldots, F_n$ such that $F_n = F$ and every F_i is an axiom of T or is obtained from some previous elements of the sequence by an inference rule from R. We refer to such a sequence as a *derivation* of F from T in R. A collection R of first-order inference rules is called *complete* if for every theory T and formula F, $T \models F$ iff $T \vdash_R F$. There are a number of complete collections of inference rules of first-order logic. In Chapter 12 we discuss a logic programming version of an inference rule, called *resolution*, which is often used in automated reasoning systems.

This theoretical machinery allows us to refine our notion of the axiomatic method. We can view axioms as a theory T – a collection of FOL sentences. A sentence F is a consequence of T if $T \models F$. A mathematical proof of F can be viewed as shorthand for a derivation of F from T using some complete collection of inference rules. First-order logic provides a powerful tool for knowledge representation and reasoning. It has been shown to be sufficient for formalization of a very large part of contemporary mathematical knowledge and reasoning.

3.2 Nonmonotonic Logics

Surprisingly, further experience of applying the logic-based approach to the design of intelligent agents showed that first-order logic may not be a fully adequate tool for representing nonmathematical (especially commonsense) knowledge. The main problem is the difficulty of dealing with defeasible (or nonmonotonic) reasoning. Many researchers agree with the *Stanford Encyclopedia of Philosophy*, which states,

One of the most significant developments both in logic and artificial intelligence is the emergence of a number of non-monotonic formalisms, which were devised expressly for the purpose of capturing defeasible reasoning in a mathematically precise manner.

Among the pioneers of the field in the late 1970s were John McCarthy, Drew McDermott and Jon Doyle, and Raymond Reiter. An influential logical system developed by McCarthy is called **circumscription**. It is based on classical second-order logic and allows elegant model-theoretic characterization. McDermott and Doyle based their *nonmonotonic logics* on modal logics capturing the notion of belief. (A few years later Robert Moore introduced a particular logic of this type, called **autoepistemic logic**, which, among many other important things, served as a starting point for the development of the stable model semantics of the original Prolog. This semantics was the precursor of answer set semantics for more general logic programs we use in this book.) Reiter's formalism called **default logic** expands classical logic by allowing defeasible rules somewhat similar to those of ASP. The papers on circumscription, McDermott and Doyle's nonmonotonic logics, and default logic appeared in the same issue of the *Artificial Intelligence Journal* (vol. 13, 1980) dedicated to these new formalisms. Many people view this publication as the birth of nonmonotonic logic. In what follows we give a brief introduction to these formalisms.

3.2.1 Circumscription

Circumscription is a nonmonotonic logic based on the notion of *minimal entailment*. The basic idea is as follows. Let Σ be a first-order signature and $<$ be a partial order defined on interpretations of Σ. A model M is a $<$-*minimal model* of a first-order theory T if there is no other model M_0 of T such that $M_0 < M$. We say that T minimally entails formula F with respect to $<$ (or that $<$-circumscription of T entails F), and write $T \models_{min(<)} F$ or $circ(T, <) \models F$, if F is true in all $<$-*minimal* models of T.

Here is a simple example. Let Σ be a signature containing two object constants a and b and predicate constants p and q, and let T be a theory consisting of axioms

$$a \neq b$$
$$\forall X (X = a \lor X = b)$$
$$p(a)$$
$$q(a)$$

and $<_p$ be a partial order on interpretations of Σ defined as follows: $I_1 <_p I_2$ if I_1 and I_2 have the same universe and the same mapping of terms, and $I_1(p) \subset I_2(p)$. We show that

$$T \models_{<_p} \neg p(b)$$

$$T \not\models_{<_p} \neg q(b)$$

$$T \models_{<_p} \forall X\ X \neq b \supset q(X).$$

We start by finding $<_p$-minimal models of T. To satisfy the first two axioms of T, the universe of model M should consist of exactly two elements. To satisfy the third axiom, $M(p)$ should be equal to $\{M(a)\}$ or $\{M(a), M(b)\}$. However, the latter model is not minimal with respect to $<_p$ and should be discarded. $M(q)$ should be equal to $\{M(a)\}$ or $\{M(a), M(b)\}$. Since minimization of q is not required by relation $<_p$, both models are minimal. In more detailed notation a model of T has the universe consisting of two distinct elements, say, e_1 and e_2, with constants a and b mapped into these elements; e.g., $U = \{e_1, e_2\}$, $M(a) = e_1$ and $M(b) = e_2$. The corresponding $<_p$-minimal models M_1 and M_2 are obtained from M as follows:

$$M_1(p) = \{e_1\}$$

$$M_1(q) = \{e_1\}$$

and

$$M_2(p) = \{e_1\}$$

$$M_2(q) = \{e_1, e_2\}.$$

Note that strictly speaking we have an infinite collection of such models since $M(a)$ can be equal to e_2 and $M(b)$ to e_1, and moreover, elements of U can be arbitrary pairs. But it can be easily shown that such models are isomorphic to M_1 and M_2 and can be ignored.

This proves the above entailments. Of course, if we expand our theory by $p(b)$ the new theory entails $p(b)$. One can check that

$$T \cup \{p(b)\} \models_{<_p} p(b);$$

i.e., $p(b)$ is a consequence of the new theory. As expected, the new entailment relation is nonmonotonic.

It may be instructive to see what happens if we remove from T some of its equality axioms. Let T_1 be obtained from T by removing the first axiom. The new theory has a model M whose universe consists of one element, say e; the model maps both constants of the language into this element – $M(a) = M(b) = e$; both p and q are mapped into $\{e\}$; i.e., $M(p) = M(q) = \{e\}$. This implies that

$$T_1 \not\models_{<_p} \neg p(b).$$

Now let T_2 be obtained from the original theory T by removing the second axiom. T_2 has a $<_p$-minimal model M with the universe $U = \{a, b, c\}$, $M(a) = a$, $M(b) = b$, $M(p) = \{a\}$, and $M(q) = \{a, b\}$. This time we have

$$T_2 \not\models_{<_p} \forall X \, (X \neq b \supset q(X)).$$

Circumscription is a powerful nonmonotonic formalism that remains the language of choice for a number of researchers interested in knowledge representation and reasoning. Its minimality idea clearly influenced the development of ASP as well as other nonmonotonic formalisms. Recent work established a close mathematical connection between circumscription and some powerful generalizations of ASP, but full comprehension of the meaning of these results may require some additional nontrivial insights.

3.2.2 Autoepistemic Logic

Formulas of **autoepistemic logic** are built from propositional atoms using propositional connectives and the modal operator B. For instance, formula $Bp \supset p$ says that if p is believed then p is true, and so on. The semantics of autoepistemic logic is given via a notion of stable expansion.

Definition 3.2.1. *(Stable Expansion)*
For any sets T and E of autoepistemic formulas, E is said to be a **stable expansion** *of T iff*

$$E = Cn(T \cup \{B\phi : \phi \in E\} \cup \{\neg B\psi : \psi \notin E\})$$

where Cn is a propositional consequence operator.

Intuitively, T is a set of axioms and E is a possible collection of a reasoner's beliefs determined by T. A formula F is said to be *true* in T (or entailed by T) if F belongs to all stable expansions of T. If T does not contain the modal operator B, T has a unique stable expansion denoted by $Th(T)$. For instance, if $T = \{p, q \vee r\}$ then $Th(T)$ contains T together with an infinite collection of other formulas, including Bp, $\neg Bq$, $\neg Br$, $B(q \vee r)$, $B\neg Bq$, etc. There is a close connection between classes of autoepistemic theories and classes of theories of ASP. We describe one such connection that served as a starting point for the development of stable model semantics of logic programs.

Consider a class G of programs of Answer Set Prolog that consists of rules of the form:

$$
\begin{aligned}
(i) \quad & p_0 \leftarrow p_1, \ldots, p_m, \; not \; p_{m+1}, \ldots, \; not \; p_n \\
(ii) \quad & \neg p \leftarrow \; not \; p \quad \text{(for every atom } p\text{)}
\end{aligned}
\tag{3.1}
$$

where $0 \le m \le n$ and the ps are atoms. Let α be a mapping that maps rules (i) and (ii) into autoepistemic formulas:

$$
\begin{aligned}
\alpha(i) \quad & p_1 \wedge \cdots \wedge p_m \wedge \neg B\, p_{m+1} \wedge \cdots \wedge \neg B\, p_n \supset p_0 \\
\alpha(ii) \quad & \neg B\, p \supset \neg p
\end{aligned}
\tag{3.2}
$$

and let

$$
\alpha(\Pi) = \{\alpha(r) : r \in \Pi\}.
$$

Proposition 3.2.1. *For any program $\Pi \in G$, and any set A of literals in the language of Π, A is an answer set of Π iff $Th(A)$ is a stable expansion of $\alpha(\Pi)$. Moreover, every stable expansion of $\alpha(\Pi)$ can be represented in the above form.*

A similar proposition proven in 1987 for stratified logic programs showed that, at least in a simple case, default negation can be interpreted as an epistemic operator. This connection played an important role in the later development of stable model semantics. There are other interesting mappings of programs of Answer Set Prolog into autoepistemic logic and its variants, but none seem to provide a really good explanation of the meanings of the *or* and $\leftarrow$ connectives of Answer Set Prolog in terms of autoepistemic logic.

3.2.3 Reiter's Default Theories

A Reiter's *default* is an expression of the form

$$
\frac{p : M\, j_1, \ldots, M\, j_n}{f}
\tag{3.3}
$$

where p, f, and js are quantifier-free first-order formulas; f is called the *consequent* of the default, p is its *prerequisite*, and js are its *justifications*. A default may have no prerequisite or no justification. An expression $M\, j$ is interpreted as "it is consistent to believe j." A pair $\langle D, W \rangle$ where D is

a set of defaults and W is a set of first-order sentences is called Reiter's
default theory.

Definition 3.2.2. *(Extension of a Default Theory)*
Let $\langle D, W \rangle$ be a default theory and E be a set of first-order sentences.
Consider $E_0 = W$ and, for $i \geq 0$, let D_i be the set of defaults of form
(3.3) from D such that $p \in E_i$ and $\neg j_1 \notin E, \ldots, \neg j_n \notin E$. Finally, let
$E_{i+1} = Th(E_i) \cup \{conseq(\delta) : \delta \in D_i\}$ where $Th(E_i)$ is the set of all
classical consequences of E_i and $conseq(\delta)$ denotes δ's consequent. The
set E is called an **extension** *of $\langle D, W \rangle$ if*

$$E = \bigcup_0^\infty E_i.$$

Extensions of a default theory D play a role similar to that of stable
expansions of autoepistemic theories. The simple mapping α from programs
of ASP without disjunction to default theories identifies a rule r

$$l_0 \leftarrow l_1, \ldots, l_m, \ not \ l_{m+1}, \ldots, \ not \ l_n$$

with the default $\alpha(r)$

$$\frac{l_1 \wedge \cdots \wedge l_m : M \ \bar{l}_{m+1}, \ldots, M \ \bar{l}_n}{l_0} \tag{3.4}$$

(Recall that $\bar{l}$ stands for the literal complementary to l.)

Proposition 3.2.2. *For any nondisjunctive program Π of ASP*

   (i) *if S is an answer set of Π, then $Th(S)$ is an extension of $\alpha(\Pi)$;*
   (ii) *for every extension E of $\alpha(\Pi)$ there is exactly one answer set S of*
        Π such that $E = Th(S)$.

Thus, the class of nondisjunctive ASP programs can be identified with
the class of default theories with empty W and defaults of the form (3.4).
Perhaps somewhat surprisingly, the proposition is not easily generalized to
a program with disjunction. One of the problems in finding a natural translation from arbitrary ASP programs to default theories is related to these
theories' inability to use defaults with empty justifications in reasoning by
cases. The default theory with

$$D = \left\{ \frac{q :}{p}, \ \frac{r :}{p} \right\}$$

and

$$W = \{q \vee r\}$$

does not have an extension containing p and therefore does not entail p. The corresponding logic program

$$p \leftarrow q$$
$$p \leftarrow r$$
$$q \; or \; r.$$

has two answer sets, $\{p, q\}$ and $\{p, r\}$, and hence entails p.

3.3 ASP and Negation in Logic Programming

In the late 1970s and early 1980s different approaches to nonmonotonicity were investigated in the area of logic programming. The goal was to give a declarative semantics for the **negation as failure**[2] of the logic-based programming language Prolog. The new connective was initially defined in procedural terms referring to a particular inference mechanism of Prolog called SLDNF resolution (for more details, see Chapter 12). The statement *not a* is viewed as true if SLDNF resolution finitely fails to prove a. The attempts to find suitable declarative semantics of this nonmonotonic connective, together with the work on the general nonmonotonic reasoning formalisms discussed earlier, played a major role in the discovery of ASP and several other logic-programming-based KR formalisms. In this section we briefly outline some important developments in this area. In what follows we limit our attention to logic programs consisting of rules of the form

$$a_0 \leftarrow a_1, \ldots, a_m, \; not \; a_{m+1}, \ldots, \; not \; a_n \tag{3.5}$$

where the as are atoms. For historical reasons we refer to such programs as **normal logic programs** or *nlp*s.

3.3.1 Clark's Completion

The research on finding a declarative semantics for negation as failure in *nlp*s started with the pioneering work of Keith Clark. He suggested that, given an *nlp*, we could view the bodies of rules with a predicate p in their

---

[2] In other parts of this book, we refer to this as default negation. In this historical context, we have left the name as is.

heads as "sufficiency" conditions for inferring atoms formed by p from the program. Clark stated that the bodies of these rules could also be taken as "necessary" conditions, with the result that negative information about p could be assumed if none of these conditions are met. More precisely, let us consider the following two-step transformation of an *nlp* Π into a collection of first-order formulas:

Step 1: For every *nlp* rule (3.5) in Π, let $a_0 = p(t_1, \ldots, t_k)$ and $Y_1, \ldots, Y_s$ be the list of variables appearing in r. By $\alpha_1(r)$ we denote an FOL formula:

$$\exists\, Y_1 \ldots Y_s : X_1 = t_1 \wedge \cdots \wedge X_k = t_k \wedge$$
$$a_1 \wedge \cdots \wedge a_m \wedge \neg a_{m+1} \wedge \cdots \wedge \neg a_n \supset p(X_1, \ldots, X_k) \tag{3.6}$$

where, $X_1 \ldots X_k$ are variables not appearing in r.

$$\alpha_1(\Pi) = \{\alpha_1(r) : r \in \Pi\}$$

Step 2: For each predicate p rename its variables to make all the implications in $\alpha_1(\Pi)$ be of the form

$$E_1 \supset p(X_1, \ldots, X_k)$$
$$\vdots$$
$$E_j \supset p(X_1, \ldots, X_k).$$

Next, replace these formulas by

$$\forall\, X_1 \ldots X_k : p(X_1, \ldots, X_k) \equiv E_1 \vee \cdots \vee E_j$$

if $j \geq 1$ and by

$$\forall\, X_1 \ldots X_k : \neg p(X_1, \ldots, X_k)$$

if $j = 0$.

Definition 3.3.1. *(Clark's Completion)*
The resulting first-order theory combined with natural axioms for equality called free equality axioms[3] *is called* **Clark's completion** *of Π and is*

---

[3] In addition to the usual equality axioms, free equality axioms include

- $f(X_1, \ldots, X_n) \neq g(X_1, \ldots, X_n)$ for each distinct pair of function symbols f and g of arity n.
- $t(X) \neq X$ for each term $t(X)$ (other than X) in which X occurs.
- $f(X_1, \ldots, X_n) = f(Y_1, \ldots, Y_n) \supset X_1 = Y_1 \wedge \cdots \wedge X_n = Y_n$ for each n-ary function symbol f.

These axioms guarantee that ground terms are equal iff they are identical.

denoted by $Comp(\Pi)$. *A literal l is* entailed *by Π if l is the first-order consequence of $Comp(\Pi)$.*

To better understand the construction, let us consider the following example: Let Π be the program

$$p(a).$$
$$p(b).$$
$$q(Y) \leftarrow p(Y).$$
$$r \leftarrow not\ s.$$

Then $\alpha_1(\Pi)$ has the form, say,

$$X_1 = a \supset p(X_1)$$
$$X_2 = b \supset p(X_2)$$
$$\exists Y(X = Y \wedge p(X)) \supset q(X)$$
$$\neg s \supset r.$$

It is easy to check that the third axiom is equivalent to

$$p(X) \supset q(X).$$

To properly prepare for Step 2 in which we collect our formulas under the universal quantifier, we replace X_1 and X_2 in the first two axioms by, say, X. The result, $Comp(\Pi)$, is

$$\forall X : p(X) \equiv X = a \vee X = b$$
$$\forall X : q(X) \equiv \exists Y(X = Y \wedge p(X))$$
$$r \equiv \neg s$$
$$\neg s.$$

The second formula can be simplified to

$$q(X) \equiv p(X).$$

The following theorem establishes the relationship between models of Clark's completion of Π and the notion of a **supported model**. (A set S of atoms is supported by an *nlp* Π if, for every $a \in S$ there is a rule (3.5) such that $a = a_0, a_1, \ldots, a_m \in S$ and $a_{m+1}, \ldots, a_n \notin S$.)

Theorem 1. *A set S of atoms is a model of Clark's completion of Π iff S is supported and satisfies the rules of Π.*

Models of Clark's completion may obviously differ from answer sets of Π. Program $p \leftarrow p$ has two Clark's models, $\{\ \}$ and $\{p\}$, but only one answer set { }. This should not be surprising – the completion semantics intends to capture the notion of finite failure of a particular inference mechanism, SLDNF resolution, whereas answer set semantics formalizes the more general notion of default negation. It is also important to note that Theorem 1 immediately implies that every answer set of an *nlp* program Π is also a model of the completion of Π, and hence every literal entailed by Π with respect to Clark's semantics is also entailed by Π with respect to the answer set semantics.

The existence of Clark's declarative semantics facilitated the development of the theory of logic programs. It made possible the first proofs of correctness of the inference mechanism of Prolog based on SLDNF resolution, proofs of program equivalence, and some other properties of programs. It is still widely and successfully used for logic programming applications. Unfortunately in many situations Clark's semantics appears too weak. Consider, for instance, the following example:

Example 3.3.1. Suppose that we are given a graph, say,

$$edge(a, b). \ \ edge(c, d). \ \ edge(d, c).$$

and want to describe vertices of the graph reachable from a given vertex a. The natural solution seems to be to introduce these rules:

$$reachable(a).$$
$$reachable(X) \leftarrow edge(Y, X),$$
$$reachable(Y).$$

We clearly expect vertices c and d not to be reachable. However, Clark's completion of the predicate 'reachable' gives only

$$reachable(X) \equiv (X = a \lor \exists Y : reachable(Y) \land edge(Y, X))$$

from which such a conclusion cannot be derived.

This difficulty was recognized as serious and prompted the development of other logic programming semantics, including that of ASP. Even though now there are comparatively few knowledge representation languages that use Clark's completion as the basis for their semantics, the notion has not lost its importance for KR. As an illustration let us consider its use for computing answer sets of logic programs. We need the following terminology.

Definition 3.3.2. *A* nlp Π *is called* **tight** *if there is a mapping* $\| \ \|$ *of ground atoms of* Π *into the set of natural numbers such that for every* *rule (3.5) of* Π

$$||a_0|| > ||a_1||, \ldots, ||a_m|| \tag{3.7}$$

Theorem 2. *If* Π *is tight, then* S *is a model of* $Comp(\Pi)$ *iff* S *is an answer set of* Π.

Theorem 2 is due to François Fages. There are some recent results extending the notions of Clark's completion and of tightness, as well as discovering more general conditions for equivalence of the two semantics. Note that whenever the two semantics of Π are equivalent, Π's answer sets can be computed by satisfiability solvers (specialized inference engines for propositional theories). The connections between answer sets of a program and models of its Clark's completion have been recently used to substantially improve the efficiency of ASP solvers.

3.3.2 Well-Founded Semantics

In the late 1980s there were several attempts to deal with the problems of Clark's semantics of *nlp*. Two of them – stable model and well-founded semantics – are probably most relevant to the use of logic programs for knowledge representation. The stable model semantics has an epistemic character and can be viewed as a variant of ASP semantics in the context of *nlp*. The well-founded semantics of Allen Van Gelder, Kenneth A. Ross, and John S. Schlipf is based on a different idea. It defines the notion of a unique three-valued model of an *nlp* program Π, called Π's *well-founded* model.

For any *nlp* Π, the function Γ_Π from sets of atoms to sets of atoms is defined by equation

$$\Gamma_\Pi(X) = ans(\Pi^X) \tag{3.8}$$

where $ans(\Pi^X)$ is the answer set of the reduct Π^X from the definition of the answer set. It is clear that stable models of Π can be characterized as the fixpoints[4] of Γ_Π. It is not difficult to show that if $X \subset Y$ then $\Gamma_\Pi(Y) \subset \Gamma_\Pi(X)$. This implies that the function Γ_Π^2 is monotone and hence has, by the Knaster-Tarski Theorem, a least and a greatest fixpoint.

---

[4] An element x from the domain of a function f is called a *fixpoint* of f if $f(x) = x$. If f is defined on a collection of sets, then a fixpoint x is called a *least* fixpoint of f if no proper subset of x is a fixpoint of f; similarly, x is called a greatest fixpoint if no proper superset of x is a fixpoint of f.

(Γ_Π^2 is shorthand for $\Gamma_\Pi(\Gamma_\Pi(X))$.) Atoms belonging to the least fixpoint of Γ_Π^2 are called *well founded* relative to Π. Atoms belonging to the complement of the greatest fixpoint of Γ_Π^2 are called *unfounded* relative to Π.

Definition 3.3.3. *A three-valued function that assigns* 1 *(true) to atoms well founded relative to* Π, 0 *(false) to atoms unfounded relative to* Π, *and* $1/2$ *(undefined) to all the remaining atoms is called the* **well-founded model** *of* Π. *An atom is a* **well-founded consequence** *of* Π *if it is true in* Π's *well-founded model.*

From this definition one can easily see that every *nlp* has a unique well-founded model and that every well-founded consequence of Π is also Π's consequence with respect to the stable model semantics. To better understand the difference between the semantics, let us look at several examples.

Example 3.3.2. Consider the following program Π

$$a \leftarrow not\ b.$$
$$b \leftarrow not\ a.$$
$$c \leftarrow a.$$
$$c \leftarrow b.$$

To construct its well-founded model, we need to find the least fixpoint and the greatest fixpoint of Γ_Π^2. The empty set seems a good candidate for a least fixpoint, so we begin by letting $X = \emptyset$. The reduct $\Pi^\emptyset$ is

$$a.$$
$$b.$$
$$c \leftarrow a.$$
$$c \leftarrow b.$$

and because $\{a, b, c\}$ is the reduct's answer set, $\Gamma_\Pi(\emptyset) = \{a, b, c\}$. Applying Γ_Π to $\Gamma_\Pi(\emptyset)$ gives us the empty set, and thus, $\emptyset$ is a fixpoint of Γ_Π^2. Since the set is empty, there are no well-founded literals in the well-founded model of Π.

The set $\{a, b, c\}$ is the greatest candidate for a fixpoint we can test. The reduct of $\Pi^{\{a,b,c\}}$ is

$$c \leftarrow a.$$
$$c \leftarrow b.$$

and $\Gamma_\Pi(\{a, b, c\}) = \emptyset$. Applying Γ_Π again, we get $\Gamma_\Pi^2\{a, b, c\} = \{a, b, c\}$. Thus, $\{a, b, c\}$ is the greatest fixpoint of Π. Its complement is $\emptyset$, so there are no unfounded literals in the well-founded model of Π either. This means that, in the well-founded model, all of the program's literals are undefined.

This is not so for the stable model semantics under which there are two answer sets: $\{a, c\}$ and $\{b, c\}$. You can see that c is true in both models, and thus, under stable model semantics Π entails c, whereas under well-founded semantics it does not. This example demonstrates that well-founded semantics does not support reasoning by cases, whereas this ability is a built-in feature of stable model semantics.

Example 3.3.3. Consider a program Π consisting of the following rule:

$$p \leftarrow not\ p.$$

From the standpoint of stable model semantics, it is inconsistent. It has no stable model (and hence the set of stable consequences of Π contains all the *nlp* literals of the language of Π). In contrast, from the standpoint of the well-founded semantics, Π is consistent. It has empty sets of well-founded and unfounded atoms. Therefore, it has the well-founded model in which every *nlp* literal of Π is undefined (i.e., is assigned the value $1/2$). Hence the answer given by the program to query p is *undefined*.

Example 3.3.4. Consider the following program Π :

$$p \leftarrow not\ a.$$
$$p \leftarrow not\ b.$$
$$a \leftarrow not\ b.$$
$$b \leftarrow not\ a.$$

Π has two stable models: $\{p, a\}$ and $\{p, b\}$. As in the previous example, the well-founded model of Π has empty sets of well-founded and unfounded atoms. Hence the well-founded model of Π assigns *undefined* to every *nlp* literal of Π. This means that p is a consequence of Π in the stable model semantics, whereas the answer to p in the well-founded semantics is *undefined*.

Finally, let us look at the following example from Dix (1991).

Example 3.3.5. Consider Π consisting of rules:

$$a \leftarrow not\ b.$$
$$b \leftarrow c,\ not\ a.$$
$$c \leftarrow a.$$

This program has one answer set $\{a, c\}$, and thus has a and c as its consequences. The well-founded model of Π has no well-founded atoms. Its unfounded atoms are $\{a, b, c\}$, and hence, according to the well-founded semantics, atoms $a, b,$ and c are undefined.

There are large classes of programs for which both well-founded and stable model semantics coincide. For instance, this happens for programs without recursive definitions or, more generally, without recursive definitions through negation (i.e., stratified programs). A careful reader may notice that the programs in the earlier examples do have such definitions. Examples 3.3.2 and 3.3.4 both define a in terms of $not\ b$ and b in terms of $not\ a$. Example 3.3.3 defines p in terms of $not\ p$ and Example 3.3.5 defines a in terms of $not\ b$, and b is defined in terms of c and $not\ a$.

It is important to notice that the SLDNF resolution of Prolog is sound with respect to the well-founded semantics, but it is not complete. Several attempts were made to define variants of SLDNF resolution that compute answers to goals according to the well-founded entailment. One interesting approach, **SLS resolution**, was introduced by Teodor Przymusinski. SLS resolution is based on a type of oracle and, therefore, cannot be viewed as an algorithm. There are, however, several algorithms and systems that can be viewed as SLS-based approximations of the well-founded semantics. One of the most powerful of such systems, **XSB**, expands SLDNF with tabling and loop checking. (It can be found at `www.cs.sunysb.edu/~sbprolog/xsb-page.html`.) Its use allows the avoidance of many of the loop-related problems of Prolog. For instance, XSB's answer to query $reachable(c)$ for the program from Example 3.3.1 will be *no*, whereas Prolog interpreters will loop on this query.

It is not difficult to expand well-founded semantics of *nlp* to programs allowing classical negation. Of course in this case, not every program will be consistent even according to well-founded semantics. ($\{a., \neg a.\}$ is a simple example of a program that is inconsistent under both semantics). However, it proved to be more difficult to find an elegant extension of well-founded semantics to disjunctive programs. There are interesting knowledge representation languages based on the well-founded semantics of logic programs. The future may show if any of those languages will be competitive with ASP as a general KR language or will be preferable to ASP in some special cases. Well-founded semantics has already proven to be very useful for the development of efficient ASP solvers and question-answering systems that are sound with respect to ASP, such as XSB.

Summary

The chapter started with a brief introduction to classical first-order logic with its notions of objects, functions, and relations; the methodology of describing the world in these terms; clear separation of syntax and semantics; and ideas of interpretation, model, and entailment. This was followed by a review of early nonmonotonic formalisms that strongly influenced the development of ASP. We discussed *circumscription*, which uses the language of first-order logic but only considers models minimal with respect to some ordering, and *autoepistemic logic* and *default logic*, which are propositional theories whose semantics are aimed at capturing the notion of rational belief. Next, we gave a brief review of the negation as failure operator of Prolog and Clark's completion – the earliest attempt to give a declarative semantics of *nlp*. We concluded with a section on well-founded semantics that, for programs without disjunction, can be viewed as an alternative to the stable model semantics used in this book. The intent was to allow the reader to better understand the background in which ASP has been developed. Each of the formalisms outlined in this chapter is of independent interest and can be seriously studied using other sources.

References and Further Reading

Gottlob Frege (1879/2002) presented a logical formalism similar to first-order logic. In addition to boolean connectives (Boole 1854), the formalism contained quantified variables, which became a major tool in mathematics and mathematical logic. A good description of FOL and its relation to Knowledge Representation can be found in Lifschitz, Morgenstern, and Plaisted (2008). As a comprehensive introduction to logic for computer scientists, we recommend Nerode and Shore (1997). The original papers on circumscription, autoepistemic logic, and default logic appeared in the same issue of the *Journal of Artificial Intelligence*: McCarthy (1980), McDermott and Doyle (1980), and Reiter (1980). The original formalisms were quickly extended and generalized by multiple authors; see, for instance, Lifschitz (1985) and Moore (1983). The monograph by Marek and Truszczynski (1993) gives a mathematically rigorous but very readable introduction to the field. Procedural definition of the negation as failure operator of Prolog can be found in Lloyd (1987). Clark's completion was first presented in Clark (1978), well-founded semantics in Gelder, Ross, and Schlipf (1991); and stable model semantics in Gelfond and Lifschitz (1988). The last work was based on the

discovery of the relationship between negation as failure of Prolog and
the belief operator of autoepistemic logic (Gelfond 1987). The relationship between logic programs (without disjunction) and Reiter's default
logic was independently established in Gelfond and Lifschitz (1991) and
Bidoit and Froidevaux (1987, 1991). A good early (and still very useful)
survey of different declarative formalizations of negation as failure can
be found in Apt and Bol (1994). SLS resolution, published as a technical
report in 1987, appeared as a journal publication in Przymusinski (1995).
(See also related work in Ross (1989)). To learn more about the XSB system, one can consult Chen, Swift, and Warren (1995). Jack Minker (1982)
expanded the language of logic programs without default negation by disjunction. Theorem 1 first appeared in Marek and Subrahmanian (1989).
The notion of tightness (under a different name) together with Theorem 2
was introduced in Fages (1994) and generalized by a number of authors;
see, for instance, Erdem and Lifschitz (2003). The relationship between
generalized stable model semantics and circumscription is presented in
Ferraris, Lee, and Lifschitz (2011).

Exercises

1. Given universe $\{a, t, d, b, c\}$, FOL signature:

$$\mathcal{O} = \{ant,\ tarantula,\ dragonfly,\ butterfly,\ centipede\}$$
$$\mathcal{F} = \{\,\}$$
$$\mathcal{P} = \{insect,\ spider,\ bigger\}$$
$$\mathcal{V} = \{X, Y\}$$

and interpretation

$$I(ant) = \{a\},$$
$$I(tarantula) = \{t\},$$
$$I(dragonfly) = \{d\},$$
$$I(butterfly) = \{b\},$$
$$I(centipede) = \{c\},$$
$$I(insect) = \{a, d, b\}$$
$$I(spider) = \{t\}$$
$$I(bigger) = \{t, a\}$$

check if the following formulas are true under this interpretation:

(a) $bigger(butterfly, ant)$
(b) $\forall X\,(insect(X) \supset \neg spider(X))$

(c) $\neg \exists X \, (insect(X) \land spider(X))$

(d) $\forall X \, (insect(X) \lor spider(X))$

2. Consider an FOL theory consisting of all four sentences of Exercise 1. Is it satisfiable? Justify.

3. Given the signature from Exercise 1, show that the theory consisting of sentence

$$\forall X \, insect(X)$$

entails $insect(tarantula)$.

4. Given a signature consisting of object constants a and b, predicate constants p and q, and a partial order $<_p$ as defined in the chapter, use circumscription to find $<_p$-minimal models of theory:

$$a \neq b$$
$$\forall X (X = a \lor X = b)$$
$$p(a) \lor q(a)$$

Assume that the universe consists of two elements, e_1 and e_2, and $M(a) = e_1$ and $M(b) = e_2$.

5. Use the relationship between Answer Set Prolog and autoepistemic logic outlined in Proposition 3.2.1 to find a stable expansion of

$$\neg Bp \supset q$$
$$\neg Bq \supset \neg q$$

6. Use the relationship between Answer Set Prolog and default theory outlined in Proposition 3.2.2 to find an expansion of the default theory given by

$$\left\{ \frac{p(a) : Mp(b)}{p(c)}, \quad \frac{M \neg p(a)}{p(a)} \right\}$$

7. Find Clark's completion of predicate $edge$ given in Example 3.3.1.

8. Find Clark's completion of the following program:

$$tool(hammer).$$
$$person(fred).$$
$$animal(horse).$$
$$animate(X) \leftarrow person(X).$$
$$animate(X) \leftarrow animal(X).$$
$$inanimate(X) \leftarrow not\ animate(X).$$

9. Using the definitions in Section 3.3.2 and given the following program Π:

$$p.$$
$$q \leftarrow p.$$
$$r \leftarrow not\ q.$$

(a) Find the least fixpoint of Γ_Π^2.

(b) Find the greatest fixpoint of Γ_Π^2.

(c) Find the well-founded model of Π.

4

Creating a Knowledge Base

To reason about the world, an agent must have information about it. Because it is unreasonable to teach an agent everything there is to know, we decide on what kind of agent we are building and educate it accordingly. The collection of statements about the world we choose to give the agent is called a knowledge base. In this chapter we create several knowledge bases using the declarative approach. The emphasis is on the methodology of knowledge representation and the use of ASP. Using examples in several, very different domains, we emphasize the importance of the following:

- modeling the domain with relations that ensure a high degree of elaboration tolerance;
- the difference between knowledge representation of closed vs open domains; i.e., we need to know when we can assume that our information about a relation is complete and when we should instead reason with incomplete information, but realize that we are doing so (reasoning with incomplete information is covered much more thoroughly in Chapter 5);
- representing commonsense knowledge along with expert knowledge;
- recursive definitions and hierarchical organization of knowledge.

The first knowledge base contains various relationships within the family group, the second models electrical circuits, and the third deals with a basic taxonomic hierarchy that includes classes such as "submarine" and "vehicle." (For now we only make use of basic rules and recursion. More sophisticated knowledge bases are discussed in later chapters.)

> Examples in this chapter are given using notation necessary
> to run programs on real systems.
> To make ASP programs executable, we replace
> ¬ with -, ← with :-, and *or* with |.
> For information on these systems,
> please see Appendix A and B.

4.1 Reasoning about Family

In this section we consider several extensions of the simple family knowledge base (KB) from Chapter 1. The first extension familiarizes the program with such basic terms as *brother*, *sister*, and so on. The second defines a notion of orphan. The third deals with a recursive definition of the notion of ancestor. Each extension has its own assumptions about completeness of information for various relations of the domain.

4.1.1 Basic Family Relationships

To represent knowledge about family relationships we start with defining the sorts that exist in our domain. Let us use the same sorts we had in the old KB in Chapter 1 – *person* and *gender*. Their membership is represented by the following atoms:

```
1  person(john).
2  person(sam).
3  person(alice).
4
5  gender(male).
6  gender(female).
```

Next we define the relationships between the objects of our domain – binary relations *father*, *mother*, *parent*, and *child* with parameters of type *person* and relation *gender_of* with parameters *person* and *gender*.

```
7   father(john,sam).
8   mother(alice,sam).
9
10  gender_of(john,male).
11  gender_of(alice,female).
12  gender_of(sam,male).
13
14  parent(X,Y) :- father(X,Y).
15  parent(X,Y) :- mother(X,Y).
16
17  child(X,Y) :- parent(Y,X).
```

Lines of code numbered 1–17 give the complete program from Chapter 1.

> In this book, lines of code that are numbered sequentially can be executed as a single program; code that is not numbered usually represents a (possibly incorrect) alternative.

We proceed by showing how this initial knowledge can be expanded. Suppose, for instance, that our family from Chapter 1 has an exciting announcement – John and Alice had another baby boy, Bill. To record this joyous event, we add new statements to our knowledge base:

```
18  person(bill).
19  father(john,bill).
20  mother(alice,bill).
21  gender_of(bill,male).
```

This may be an appropriate moment for teaching our agent a new family relation – "X is a brother of Y." Let us denote this relation by $brother(X, Y)$ where X and Y are of sort *person*.

At first glance, the following simple rule should suffice to define the new notion:

```
brother(X,Y) :- gender_of(X,male),
                father(F,X),
                father(F,Y),
                mother(M,X),
                mother(M,Y).
```

This rule says that X is a brother of Y if X is male and X and Y have the same parents. To check if the rule is properly understood, we can create a program consisting of lines 1–21 together with the above rule for *brother* and use an implementation of STUDENT to answer queries $?brother(sam, bill)$ and $?brother(sam, X)$. Although the first query is answered correctly, the second gives a surprising answer – $brother(sam, sam)$.

The agent is not at fault – we are. Of course, every one of us knows that a boy cannot be his own brother, but STUDENT does not share this knowledge. It must be explicitly stated in the rule. To do that we will use the built-in operator != that stands for $\neq$. Here is the correct definition:

```
22  brother(X,Y) :- gender_of(X,male),
23                  father(F,X),
24                  father(F,Y),
25                  mother(M,X),
26                  mother(M,Y),
27                  X != Y.
```

We can test the new program and see that now the answers are correct. We succeeded in teaching the agent a new family relation!

The problem we experienced in defining the notion of brother is symptomatic of a serious difficulty confronted by a programmer in the process of knowledge representation. *A very large part of our knowledge is so deeply engrained in us that we do not normally think about it.* Bringing this knowledge out in the open requires discipline and a well-developed power of introspection. (In this sense declarative programming is not very different from procedural programming.)

Several fascinating subareas of AI deal with discovering and codifying such hidden "commonsense" knowledge and with finding ways of its efficient and elegant representation. In the following chapters we discuss some recent advances in this field.

Even though our agent can answer a large number of questions about relationships within the family, an experienced teacher will be able to discover serious gaps in its knowledge of the domain. Let's add the name Bob to our *person* sort and consider the questions:

$$? \; father(alice, bill)$$

$$? \; father(bill, sam)$$

$$? \; father(john, bob)$$

What are the expected answers to these queries? Well, the answer to the first two questions we expect from humans is obviously *no*. STUDENT, however, will return *unknown* to both of them. This result is again not surprising. To answer the first query correctly, the program should know that females cannot father children. This information can be easily incorporated into the program by the rule

```
28  -father(X,Y)  :-  gender_of(X,female).
```

The second answer is justified because we know that a person can have only one father. This is expressed by the rule

```
-father(X,Y)  :-  father(Z,Y),
                  X != Z.
```

It is at this point that we run into an unpleasant aspect of ASP as it is currently implemented. If you run the program that incorporates the last rule with one of the currently available solvers, you will get a mysterious message about safety. The "safety" requirement comes from serious concerns about the efficiency of the solver. The general definition of this notion of safety differs from system to system. For our purpose it is sufficient to say that *a rule is* **unsafe** *if it contains an unsafe variable (i.e., one that does not occur in a literal in the body that is neither built in nor preceded by default negation)*. (For a more detailed explanation of rule safety, please see your chosen ASP solver manual.)

One can easily see that the previous rule is unsafe because the only literal in the body containing variable X is formed by the built-in predicate !=. Hence, variable X is unsafe. We can make the rule safe by noting that, since X is a parameter of predicate *father*, it must be of the sort *person*, and then adding this information to the body of the rule:

```
29  -father(X,Y)  :-  person(X),
30                     father(Z,Y),
31                     X != Z.
```

This strategy is rather general. If you took care to define the sorts of parameters of predicates, a rule with an unsafe variable X can be turned into a safe rule by adding the sort of X to the body. The problem with the safety of rules disappears if one uses SPARC, an extension of ASP that requires an explicit definition of a program's sorts. Appendix C gives a brief introduction to this language and its corresponding software tools.

Let's return to our discussion of representing $\neg father$ and note that, strictly speaking, the given rule is not sufficient to represent the statement that a person cannot have more than one father. Our program also needs to know that Bill and John are two different people. We do not need to add anything, though, because ASP has a built-in **Unique-Name Assumption (UNA)**. This means that the objects in our program are considered distinct if their names are different unless we have specified otherwise. In other words, our agent considers "John" and "Dad" to be distinct people, even though in real life, he may answer to both. With the UNA, the first two questions are correctly answered by *no*.

Now try to use your common sense to answer the third question: "Is John the father of Bob?" Informal tests conducted with a fairly large number of students show that the responders are divided into two groups: a big one whose members respond with a definite *no*, and a smaller one with people that give a hesitant *maybe*. The difference can be explained by their varying understandings of the context of our family story. The larger group apparently makes the so-called Closed World Assumption (CWA) – they assume that the story contains *complete* information about John's family. This justifies the following simple argument: "The story does not mention that John is the father of Bob and, therefore, he is not." The members of the second group do not assume that the given information about John's family is complete (e.g., Bob can be John's son from a previous marriage); hence, the cautious answer.

It is easy to check that the reasoner associated with our program belongs to the second, more cautious and deliberate group. To see that, we simply need to expand the program by the fact

```
32  person(bob).
```

and ask our query. The answer will be *unknown*.

If we want to model the reasoning of the first group, we should be able to explicitly state that our information about John's fatherhood is complete. This can be done by using the default negation of ASP. The rule

```
33  -father(X,Y) :- person(X), person(Y),
34                  not father(X,Y).
```

says that if there is no reason to believe that X is the father of Y, then he is not. This is exactly the closed world assumption for fathers mentioned earlier. It is easy to see that our new program containing this rule will answer *no* to the third query.

Note that statements $person(X)$ and $person(Y)$ cannot be removed without violating the safety requirement. Note also that similar rules can be added for other relations of our program. We suggest that the reader test the additions to the program to see that they do indeed give the correct results. For more practice, experiment with closed world assumptions for *mother*, *parent*, and *brother*.

Notice that expanding our original knowledge base required only the addition of rules but no modification of them, indicating a reasonably high degree of elaboration tolerance.

4.1.2 Defining Orphans

Here is another example. Consider a collection of people represented by the sort *person*:

```
1  person(mary).
2  person(bob).
3  person(mike).
4  person(rich).
5  person(kathy).
6  person(patty).
```

Assume that we have a complete list of children represented by the relation *child*(*person*):

```
 7  child(mary).
 8  child(bob).
```

For each child our knowledge base includes the name of the child's mother (*mother*(*person, person*)), and the same for the child's father.

```
 9  father(mike,mary).
10  father(rich,bob).
11  mother(kathy,mary).
12  mother(patty,bob).
```

Let us also assume that the knowledge base contains a complete record of deaths, represented by *dead*(*person*):

```
13  dead(rich).
14  dead(patty).
```

Completeness of information about the above relations can be expressed by closed-world assumptions:

```
15  -child(X)  :- person(X),
16                 not child(X).
17  -father(F,C)  :- person(F),
18                    child(C),
19                    not father(F,C).
20  -mother(M,C)  :- person(M),
21                    child(C),
22                    not mother(M,C).
23  -dead(X)  :- person(X),
24               not dead(X).
```

Our knowledge base has the record of a child, Mary, whose parents are Mike and Kathy. Since their death is not recorded, they must be alive. Another child recorded in the knowledge base is named Bob. His parents, Rich and Patty, have died.

   Assume now that our goal is to teach an agent the notion of an orphan. Before we try to create a mathematical definition, we must first understand what it means for someone to be an orphan. One dictionary defines an orphan as a child whose father and mother are dead. Another notes that sometimes a child who has lost only one parent can be considered an orphan. The question of which definition to use must be resolved by the "users" prior to coding.

Let's stick with the first definition of orphan. The definition can be given by the following rules:

```
25  parents_dead(P)  :-  father(F,P),
26                        mother(M,P),
27                        dead(F),
28                        dead(M).
29
30  orphan(P)  :-  child(P),
31                 parents_dead(P).
32  -orphan(X)  :-  person(X),
33                  not orphan(X).
```

Here *parents_dead* is an auxiliary predicate added for readability. For simplicity we assume that users of the program are not even aware of its existence. This allows us to skip defining when *parents_dead*(*P*) is false. The next rules encode the definition of the orphan. The closed world assumption is justified by completeness of our death records and the information about the names of children's parents. Let's construct a program called `orphans.lp` from lines 1–33 and see what STUDENT knows. Extension `.lp` (for logic program) is arbitrary. If we ask whether Bob is an orphan, we get *yes*. Query *orphan*(*mary*) is answered by *no*. These are, of course, the expected answers. Note, however, that if we expand our program by the following,

```
person(perry).
child(perry).
mother(patty,perry).
```

and ask the new program whether Perry is an orphan, the answer is a definite *no*. Intuitively, however, this may not be a correct answer, since the unknown father of Perry could also be dead. The program is not responsible for the wrong answer, because we have violated the assumption requiring that the knowledge base contain names of both parents of each child. Nevertheless, it may be more prudent to modify our program to reject the new input (see Exercise 4).

4.1.3 Defining Ancestors

You are given Bill's family tree shown in Figure 4.1.

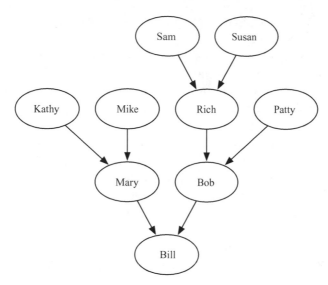

Figure 4.1. Ancestors.

We can encode it as follows:

```
1  person(bill).   person(mary).   person(bob).
2  person(kathy).  person(mike).   person(rich).
3  person(patty).  person(sam).    person(susan).
4
5  father(bob,bill).
6  father(rich,bob).
7  father(mike,mary).
8  father(sam,rich).
9  mother(mary,bill).
10 mother(patty,bob).
11 mother(kathy,mary).
12 mother(susan,rich).
```

We assume that the knowledge base contains complete information about the parents of each child in the domain, which can be expressed by the rules

```
13 -father(F,C) :- person(F), person(C),
14                  not father(F,C).
15 -mother(M,C) :- person(M), person(C),
16                  not mother(M,C).
```

(Note that by children we mean everyone except Sam, Susan, Mike, Kathy, and Patty whose parents are unknown. But because the domain contains no persons not mentioned in the family tree, this closed world assumption is justified even for them.)

Our goal is to teach the agent the notion of $ancestor(X, Y)$ – "X is an ancestor of Y" – where X and Y are of sort *person*. How would we define the notion of ancestor? Are your parents your ancestors? There are different definitions. Let us pick one and assume that they are, as are their parents' parents, and so on and so on. Unfortunately, the computer does not understand that last English expression, but with the proper language, it can be made to reason about it using **recursive definitions**.

The general structure of a recursive definition requires that the base case for a concept be defined. For example, our closest ancestors are our parents. Then we assume that we know how to define some ancestor n and concentrate on expressing what it means to be an $(n + 1)$-th ancestor.

ASP lends itself naturally to recursive definitions. This gives it a substantial advantage over knowledge representation languages that do not allow recursion (e.g., traditional relational databases). The end result is both more elegant and more economical. Here is an ASP definition of ancestor:

```
17  parent(X,Y) :- father(X,Y).
18  parent(X,Y) :- mother(X,Y).
19  -parent(X,Y) :- person(X), person(Y),
20                  not parent(X,Y).
21
22  ancestor(X,Y) :- parent(X,Y).
23  ancestor(X,Y) :- parent(Z,Y),
24                   ancestor(X,Z).
25  -ancestor(X,Y) :- person(X), person(Y),
26                    not ancestor(X,Y).
```

Note that the assumption of completeness of our information about children justifies the CWA rules for parents and ancestors. This program allows our agent to conclude that Bob is Bill's ancestor, as well as Mary, Rich, Patty, Mike, Kathy, Sam and Susan. We also conclude that Mary is not Bob's ancestor, and so on. In general the program gives a definite answer to a question $ancestor(a, b)$ for any two persons a and b.

The definition of ancestors concludes our discussion of family relationships. We hope that even these simple programs are sufficient to give some insight into the power of ASP. The process of programming in ASP is rather natural and does not require a lot of knowledge about the language. The resulting programs are clear, concise, and elaboration tolerant. Writing

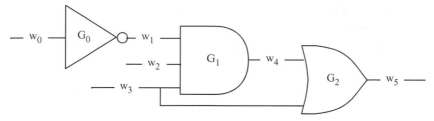

Figure 4.2. Electrical Circuit.

something comparable in traditional procedural or object-oriented programming languages such as *C* or *C++* would require good knowledge of data structures and substantially more effort. The result would be less readable and more difficult to modify. A really good programmer, however, might achieve better efficiency than that which can be achieved by existing ASP inference engines; however, this increased efficiency would hardly matter for this domain (even for a family with hundreds of thousands of members). Of course, implementations of ASP are constantly improving as well, so without extra effort by the knowledge base programmer, the efficiency of the implementation is increasing all the time, although it is unlikely to ever match a truly expert implementation in a lower level language. The choice of language for a particular task, as always, depends on the importance of program efficiency versus the price paid in developers' time.

4.2 Reasoning about Electrical Circuits

Suppose you were asked to describe a simple electrical circuit in ASP. What would be the first thing you would try to do? Desperately look for your old EE book to review what a circuit looks like? Describe gates? Wires? Connections? Just so we are all on the same footing, let's look at a picture of what we mean by a simple circuit (Fig. 4.2). G_0 is a NOT gate, G_1 is an AND gate, and G_2 is an OR gate. Let's keep it simple and limit ourselves to two-valued circuits.

So what next? When writing any logic program, a person should always ask oneself: "What are the objects and the relations that I am trying to represent?" The objects are wires and gates, and the connections are the relationships between them. Though it sounds obvious, this identification is not a trivial step. For example, it is tempting to think of a gate and its inputs and outputs as a single object. It turns out, however, that doing so would complicate the representations. Gates can have different numbers of inputs, forcing us to distinguish between gates that are otherwise similar.

Output wires of some gates can be input wires to others, but storing them with the gates does not specify their function. The identification of objects and relations in a domain greatly affects the representation and the ease and elegance of programming.

So, if we choose gates and wires as our objects, we can describe the circuit in Figure 4.2 as follows:

```
1  wire(w0).    wire(w1).    wire(w2).
2  wire(w3).    wire(w4).    wire(w5).
3
4  gate(g0).
5  type(g0,not_g).
6  input(g0,w0).
7  output(g0,w1).
8
9  gate(g1).
10 type(g1,and_g).
11 input(g1,w1).
12 input(g1,w2).
13 input(g1,w3).
14 output(g1,w4).
15
16 gate(g2).
17 type(g2,or_g).
18 input(g2,w4).
19 input(g2,w3).
20 output(g2,w5).
```

Now consider current that runs along the wire. We can represent its value by adding a new sort:

```
21 signal(0).
22 signal(1).
```

and predicate *val* that gives the value of the signal for a given wire. For example,

```
23 val(w0,1).
24 val(w2,0).
25 val(w3,1).
```

Given the values on input wires, the agent should be able to predict values on all other wires. To do this, it must know how NOT, AND, and OR

gates function. This is accomplished by the following recursive definition
of relation *val*:

```
26  % A NOT gate flips the value of the signal:
27
28  opposite(0,1).
29  opposite(1,0).
30
31  val(W1,V1) :- output(G,W1),
32                type(G,not_gate),
33                input(G,W0),
34                val(W0,V0),
35                opposite(V1,V0).
36
37  % The output of an AND gate is 0 if at least one input is 0:
38
39  val(W1,0) :- output(G,W1),
40                type(G,and_gate),
41                input(G,W0),
42                val(W0,0).
43
44  % It is 1 otherwise:
45
46  val(W1,1) :- output(G,W1),
47                type(G,and_gate),
48                -val(W1,0).
49
50  % The output of an OR gate is 1 if at least one input is 1:
51
52  val(W1,1) :- output(G,W1),
53                type(G,or_gate),
54                input(G,W0),
55                val(W0,1).
56
57  % It is 0 otherwise:
58
59  val(W1,0) :- output(G,W1),
60                type(G,or_gate),
61                -val(W1,1).
```

Finally, negation of the relation val is defined by the closed world assumption:

```
62  -val(W,V)  :-  wire(W),  signal(V),
63                  not val(W,V).
```

We may also add the rule

```
64  -val(W,V1)  :-  signal(V1),
65                  val(W,V2),
66                  V1 != V2.
```

to avoid erroneous input that assigns both 0 and 1 to an input wire. (Note that the statements describing sorts of variables in the bodies of the last two rules guarantee the rules' safety.) It is not difficult to show that, given the proper values of these wires, the program computes the unique value for every other wire of the circuit.

Query STUDENT with $val(W, V)$. Does it predict the output values correctly? For more practice, run the program on several other sets of inputs.

Notice that it is easy to build on to the circuit. Adding objects amounts to naming them. If they are gates, we must specify their type. Hooking them up to the configuration requires stating the gate's inputs and outputs. The existing definitions do not need to be changed in any way.

What we just encoded can be viewed as a kind of expert knowledge about circuits. It is not unreasonable to imagine that this simple example could be expanded into some sort of advice-giving system for humans dealing with complex circuitry. If humans were to safely rely on it for procedural instructions, this system must have some commonsense knowledge on top of its expert knowledge. Suppose this system was smart enough to determine that one of the gates was defective. First, it might need to be able to draw the conclusion that, if a component is defective, it must be replaced. Second, it may need to know that it is dangerous to replace a component in a system if there is current running through it. ASP gives us the power to add this knowledge without changing languages, systems, and the like. A possible implementation of this idea looks like this:

```
67  %% Assume we have a sensor that tells us the actual
68  %% value of the output wire of a gate by setting the
69  %% value of predicate sensor_val for that wire.
70  %% Then if the sensor value does not match the
71  %% predicted value, the gate must be defective.
```

```
72  %% To test the program, we artificially set sensor_val:
73  sensor_val(w1,1).
74
75  defective(G) :- output(G,Output_wire),
76                  sensor_val(Output_wire, SV),
77                  val(Output_wire,V),
78                  SV != V.
79
80  needs_replacing(G) :- defective(G).
81
82  %% We can also encode the knowledge that a gate is
83  %% dangerous to replace if any of its input wires
84  %% might have the value 1; i.e., if it is not known
85  %% whether the value of W is 0.
86
87  dangerous_to_replace(G) :- input(G,W),
88                             not val(W,0).
```

(Note that if we assume completeness of information about *val*, then not val(W,0) can be replaced by -val(W,0).) Based on this information, the system might perform some prearranged function such as notifying the operator or shutting off the current.

4.3 Hierarchical Information and Inheritance

Consider how one might represent the following information in ASP.

- The *Narwhal* is a submarine.
- A submarine is a vehicle.
- Submarines are black.[1]
- The *Narwhal* is a part of the U.S. Navy.

Here is one possible solution:

```
1  sub(narwhal).
2  vehicle(X) :- sub(X).
3  black(X) :- sub(X).
4  part_of(narwhal,us_navy).
```

---

[1] The reader has probably noticed that our specification makes a generalization about the color of submarines. It would have been better to say that *normally* submarines are black. In the next chapter, we revisit hierarchies and show how to express such statements, known as defaults.

This program is short and encodes exactly what was given. It allows an agent to conclude that the *Narwhal* is a submarine, is a vehicle and is black. However, when a human hears the story, there is much commonsense information that is assumed. For example, suppose we ask our agent whether the *Narwhal* is a car. A human could answer this question without further information, but STUDENT would rightfully answer *unknown*, because we did not teach it that cars are not submarines. Likewise, if we wanted to know if the submarine was red, we would have the same problem. This lack of negative information could be remedied by adding the following axioms to the program:

```
5  -car(X)  :- sub(X).
6  -sub(X)  :- car(X).
7  -red(X)  :- black(X).
8  -black(X) :- red(X).
```

Note that as soon as we decide we want to allow other types of vehicles and other colors in our program, we need to add two lines for each addition just so that the agent could correctly answer some simple commonsensical queries.

We can come up with a better representation if we exploit the hierarchical nature of the information from our story. Humans are good at organizing information about the world into tree-like structures of classes and subclasses. For example, when we are told that the *Narwhal* is a submarine, we understand that it belongs to a class of things that are called submarines and, thus, has certain properties that all submarines are assumed to have. With a submarine being a vehicle, objects that are submarines will inherit properties of vehicles as well. An **inheritance hierarchy** is a collection of classes organized into a tree formed by the subclass relation. Figure 4.3 shows the hierarchical structure of the classes in the story. Note that children of the class do not necessarily form its partition. In other words we do not exclude the existence of classes not mentioned in our representation. Thus, there is the possibility that our domain contains unknown or irrelevant classes that the designer decided not to include in the signature of our program. As a result the reasoner associated with the program will not be able to conclude that a vehicle x is either a submarine or a car – it could belong to some other class of vehicle left outside of our representation and not included in the hierarchy.

To represent this hierarchy we identify the implicit classes relevant to our story and make them objects of our domain. Once concepts become objects of the domain, we can define relations on them and explicitly reason about

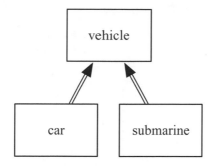

Figure 4.3. Subclasses in the Expanded Submarine Story.

whether they satisfy these relations. This process, often called **reification**, is frequently used to generalize and improve the quality of knowledge representation.

Syntactically reification of classes is accomplished by introducing a new sort *class*

```
1  class(sub).
2  class(car).
3  class(vehicle).
```

Relation $is\_subclass(C_1, C_2)$ corresponding to a subclass link of the hierarchy is defined as follows:

```
4  is_subclass(sub,vehicle).
5  is_subclass(car,vehicle).
```

The subclass relation is defined as the transitive closure[2] of $is\_subclass$:

```
6  subclass(C1,C2) :- is_subclass(C1,C2).
7
8  subclass(C1,C2) :- is_subclass(C1,C3),
9                     subclass(C3,C2).
```

As usual in recursive definitions we also add

```
10  -subclass(C1,C2) :- class(C1),
11                      class(C2),
12                      not subclass(C1,C2).
```

---

[2] A binary relation R^* is called the transitive closure of binary relation R if $R \subseteq R^*$ and for all X, Y, Z if $R(X, Z)$ and $R(Z, Y)$ then $R(X, Y)$ and no proper subset of R^* satisfies these properties.

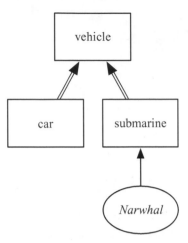

Figure 4.4. Adding an *is_a* Link.

To be able to talk about *objects of the classes* of the hierarchy, such as the *Narwhal*, we expand our picture by allowing a new type of link connecting objects to their corresponding classes (see Fig. 4.4).

To represent these new links we introduce a new sort, *object*:

```
13  object(narwhal).
```

and a new relation, $is\_a(X, C)$, where X is an object and C is a class:

```
14  is_a(narwhal,sub).
```

Now we define the main relation between objects and classes, called $member(X, C)$. The positive part of membership is defined as follows:

```
15  member(X,C)  :-  is_a(X,C).
16  member(X,C)  :-  is_a(X,C0),
17                   subclass(C0,C).
```

But, unlike the case of the *subclass* relation, we do not have complete information about membership. For example, Figure 4.5 shows a vehicle called the *Mystery*, but we do not know what kind of vehicle it is.

```
18  object(mystery).
19  is_a(mystery,vehicle).
```

We allow such members in our hierarchies and expect an agent to answer *unknown* to queries about whether the *Mystery* is a car or a sub. Therefore, we do not wish to use the CWA to represent negative information about membership.

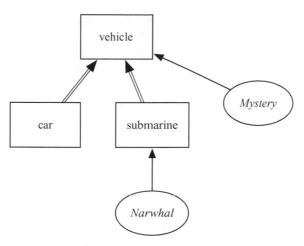

Figure 4.5. Incomplete Information about the Classification of the *Mystery*.

However, the designers of hierarchies often make a weaker assumption: *Normally, children of a class in a hierarchy are disjoint.* Thus in the absence of information to the contrary, it is reasonable to conclude that the *Narwhal* cannot be both a submarine and a car. Of course, it is possible to have exceptions to this rule – plenty of action heroes have vehicles that are difficult to categorize – but we do not discuss handling such cases until the next chapter. For now, we drop the word "normally" and assume that sibling subclasses are disjoint. This can be expressed by the following rules:

```
20  siblings(C1,C2)  :- is_subclass(C1,C),
21                      is_subclass(C2,C),
22                      C1 != C2.
23  -member(X,C2)  :- member(X,C1),
24                    siblings(C1,C2),
25                    C1 != C2.
```

These rules are sufficient to define the hierarchical structure.

In addition to classes of vehicles and their members, the story also talks about colors. Their representation is substantially facilitated by the same process of reification we used for classes. We make colors full-fledged citizens of our domain by introducing a sort *color*

```
26  color(black).
27  color(red).
```

The fact that the submarines are black is expressed as

```
28  has_color(X,black) :- member(X,sub).
```

Note that now we can ask what color something is, not just whether it is black. Recall that in our first implementation of the story, we wanted our program to realize that, if a submarine is black, then it is not red. In other words, we had an implicit assumption that objects can only have one color. With our new representation this assumption can be made explicit by the following axiom that, unlike the axioms we were forced to add to the first version, will work once and for all, no matter how many colors we choose to introduce:

```
29  -has_color(X,C2) :- has_color(X,C1),
30                      color(C2),
31                      C1 != C2.
```

(If we want to talk about multicolored objects, we simply introduce new colors, such as *black_red*.)

The last line of the original program

```
32  part_of(narwhal,us_navy).
```

remains unchanged.

The new program (lines 1–32) is clearly more powerful than the first one. Anything the old program can do, this program can do better. Not only can our agent answer all previous questions correctly, including that the *Narwhal* is not a car and is not red, but it also understands some deep, general notions about the nature of hierarchies and colors. With the first program, we can only ask if a particular submarine is a vehicle, not whether submarines in general are vehicles. It is easy to formulate these questions for the second program. It correctly answers both queries $member(narwhal, vehicle)$ and $subclass(sub, vehicle)$.

Reification has made our program not only more general but also more elaboration tolerant (i.e., more easily modifiable). For instance, to conclude that the *Narwhal* is not white, we simply familiarize our agent with that color by adding *white* to the definition of the sort *color*:

```
33  color(white).
```

If we wanted to say that vehicles are a type of machine, we could write

```
34  class(machine).
35  is_subclass(vehicle, machine).
```

Thanks to our subclass axioms, the whole tree structure would be adjusted automatically. Our agent would know that the *Narwhal* is a submarine, which is a type of vehicle, which is a type of machine. It would also know that it is not a car. Try asking $member(narwhal, X)$.

If we said that a vehicle is something that can be used for traveling, the second program could easily be expanded to allow the agent to deduce that this property would be true for all subclasses of vehicle. It would need no changes, just the following addition:

```
36  used_for_travel(X)  :- member(X,vehicle).
```

If we wanted to say that machines are not alive, we could just add

```
37  -alive(X)  :- member(X,machine).
```

We could then derive that machines, vehicles, cars, and submarines are not alive.

We have seen how the process of reification and the methodology of hierarchical organization can be very useful in creating elaboration-tolerant programs. The main differences between the two solutions of the original problem are their brevity, generality, and modifiability. Initially, the first program was shorter, but with minor subsequent changes, it lost this advantage. The second program is more general and more elaboration tolerant, which allows it to incorporate changes without substantial growth in size.

It is important to realize that the quest for elaboration-tolerant programming paradigms has been ongoing since the beginning of computer science and has included such developments as high-level languages, the notion of procedure and module, and object-oriented programming. However, having helpful tools does not necessarily lead to their appropriate use. When developing programs in any language, we must always strive to predict just how much a program will be expected to change and then balance compactness with elaboration tolerance.

Summary

In this chapter we have seen that the ASP-based declarative approach to knowledge representation is applicable to a wide variety of domains. We showed it to be capable of representing definitions (including recursive ones), open and closed world assumptions, and hierarchical knowledge. In practice this approach has been used successfully in circuit design, decision support systems for space shuttle controllers, team building that ensures fair scheduling of employees with necessary skills, automatic systems for software configuration management, data integration, semantic-web programming, and more, and applications are emerging in such varying fields as molecular biology, psychology, and linguistics.

We also discussed the basic methodology of representing knowledge in ASP, including the importance of the good selection of objects and relations of the domain, the power of reification, and the necessity of explicitly stating commonsense assumptions and thinking about possible extensions of the domain and the degree of elaboration tolerance of your program. In the next chapter we show how this methodology can be extended to represent another important concept of knowledge representation – defaults and their exceptions.

References and Further Reading

A good source for learning more about representing knowledge in Answer Set Prolog is *Knowledge Representation, Reasoning, and Declarative Problem Solving* by Chitta Baral (2003). The family example and various forms of inheritance hierarchies have been discussed in many books on logic programming and Prolog. These, however, assume the CWA for all relations of the domain; making this assumption for individual predicates requires explicit representation. In logic programming, such a representation became possible after the introduction of classical negation in Gelfond and Lifschitz (1991). Our representation of circuits is a special case of the more general representation from Balduccini, Gelfond, and Nogueira (2000), which deals with circuits with delays and possibly undefined signals. Reasoning about inheritance hierarchies has a long history, which probably started with Aristotle. Formalization of various forms of reasoning about hierarchies based on classical logic can be found in Baader et al. (2003).

Reasoning with inheritance hierarchies based on their graphical representation is described in Sowa (2000). For an approach to knowledge representation based on well-founded semantics of logic programs, one can consult Alferes and Pereira (1996). To get a better idea of a range of applications of ASP one can look at Nogueira et al. (2001) and Balduccini, Gelfond, and Nogueira (2006) (decision support for the space shuttle controllers), Ricca et al. (2012) (automation of the team-building process for the largest Italian seaport), Soininen and Niemela (1999) (product configuration), Manna et al. (2012) (information extraction from the WEB), Boenn et al. (2011) (music composition), Aker et al. (2011) (robotics), Inclezan (2013) (linguistics), and Balduccini and Girotto (2010) (psychology).

Exercises

1. Define and test relation
   $brothers(X, Y)$ — "X and Y are brothers".

2. Define and test relation
   $uncle(X, Y)$ — "X is an uncle of Y".
   To test this relation you will need to populate your world with relatives of John and/or Alice.

3. Consider the program obtained from our family knowledge base (lines 1–34) by removing rules on lines 28–31. Does this change the answers to our three queries from Section 4.1? Can you think of a reason to keep these rules? *Hint:* Consider (possibly erroneous) updates to the knowledge base.

4. Expand program `orphans.lp` from Section 4.1.2 to guarantee that input that violates the assumption concerning the completeness of information about a child's parents causes the program to become inconsistent.

5. Can statement `person(X)` be removed from the rule on line 15 in program `orphans.lp` from Section 4.1.2? Explain your answer.

6. Add a gate (with some input and output wires) to the configuration in Section 4.2 and test the program on some values.

7. A directed graph G can be described by a set of vertices, represented by facts $vertex(a), vertex(b), \ldots$ and a set of edges, represented by facts $edge(a, b), edge(a, c), \ldots$ Use ASP to define relation $connected(X, Y)$ that holds iff there is a path in G connecting vertices X and Y.

8. Consider a directed graph represented as in the previous exercise, but assume that some of its edges can be blocked (denoted as $blocked(X, Y)$). Redefine relation $connected(X, Y)$ as follows: Two vertices X and Y of the graph are *connected* iff there a path from X to Y such that no edge of this path is blocked.

9. "Jets are faster than birds. There is an eagle that is faster than every robin. The SR-71 Blackbird is a jet. Jo is a robin." Write a program to describe this story. Make sure that it can derive that the SR-71 is faster than Jo. *Hint:* Build a hierarchy of flying objects.

10. Modify the existing vehicle hierarchy to add the new subclasses and member shown in Figure 4.6. Add some property of water vehicles to your program and make sure that the *Narwhal* inherits this property and *Abby* does not.

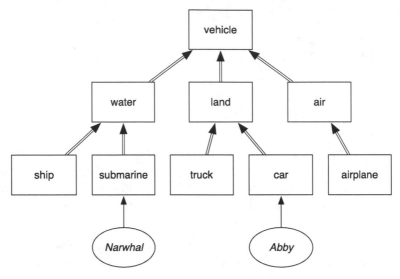

Figure 4.6. New Subclasses of Vehicles.

11. Consider a hierarchy where *is_a* is applicable only to members of leaf classes. Note that this would imply that information about membership is complete.

    (a) Give a recursive definition of membership using CWA. (Make sure $\neg member$ is part of your definition.)

    (b) The program in Exercise 11a still has the assumption that sibling classes are disjoint. Create a new program by removing this assumption. Compare the two programs. Do they have the same answer sets? Do they behave equivalently under updates? *Hint:* Consider the addition of an element that belongs to two subclasses of the program.

12. Consider the description of hierarchy as in Section 4.3 with the difference that we assume that we have complete information about the subdivision of subclasses (i.e., subclasses form a complete partition of the parent class, so that the sum of the parts forms a complete whole). This can be expressed by adding the following rules:

```
member(X,C) | -member(X,C) :- object(X),
                                 leaf(C).
in_a_leaf(X) :- object(X),
                leaf(C),
                member(X,C).
```

```
-in_a_leaf(X)  :-  object(X),
                   not in_a_leaf(X).
:-  object(X),  -in_a_leaf(X).
```

The first rule forces the agent to consider membership for each object and each leaf class, and the last three require an object to be in at least one leaf class.

(a) Define relation $leaf(C)$ that holds iff C is a leaf class of the hierarchy. *Hint:* Define $\neg leaf(C)$ first.

(b) Compare the answers that should be given by the hierarchy program that includes vehicle *Mystery* from Figure 4.5 with and without the above four rules on the following query:

$$sub(mystery) \ or \ car(mystery)$$

5

Representing Defaults

The closed world assumption introduced in the previous chapter is an example of a **default** – a statement of natural language containing words such as *"normally," "typically,"* or *"as a rule."* Defaults are very useful to humans because, in the absence of complete information, they allow us to draw conclusions based on knowledge of what is common or typical. However, these conclusions are tentative, and we may be forced to withdraw them when new information becomes available. In fact, a large part of our education seems to consist of learning various defaults, their exceptions, and the skill of reasoning with them. Defaults do not occur in the language of mathematics and, therefore, were not studied by classical mathematical logic. However, they play a very important role in everyday commonsense reasoning and present a considerable challenge to AI researchers. In this chapter we show how defaults and various forms of exceptions to them are represented in ASP and how this general representation can be used for reasoning in a variety of simple domains. After that, we show how defaults can be used to reason about knowledge bases with incomplete information, which is represented by so-called null values. Next, we demonstrate how defaults can be prioritized so that, in some cases, one default is preferred over another. Finally, we discuss the use of defaults when representing hierarchies of classes and the inheritance of class properties by subclasses and members.

5.1 A General Strategy for Representing Defaults

In this section we present the strategy for representing defaults and their exceptions in ASP.

5.1.1 Uncaring John

To illustrate the general idea of defaults, let us go back to our family example from Chapter 1. Suppose you are Sam's teacher and you strongly believe that Sam needs some extra help to pass the class. You convey this information to Sam's father, John, and expect some action on his part. Your reasoning probably goes along the following lines:

1. John is Sam's parent.
2. *Normally*, parents care about their children.
3. Therefore, John cares about Sam and will help him study.

The second statement is a typical example of a default.

To model this reasoning we introduce relation

$$cares(X, Y) - \text{``}X \text{ cares for } Y.\text{''}$$

The first inclination may be to ignore the word *normally* and simply expand the program

```
1  person(john).
2  person(sam).
3  person(alice).
4
5  father(john,sam).
6  mother(alice,sam).
7
8  parent(X,Y) :- father(X,Y).
9  parent(X,Y) :- mother(X,Y).
10
11 child(X,Y) :-  parent(Y,X).
```

by the new rule

```
% strict rule
cares(X,Y) :- parent(X,Y).
```

Program Π_1, consisting of lines 1–11 and the new strict rule, derives $cares(john, sam)$.

Assume now that in addition to the default "normally parents care about their children," you learn that "John is an exception to this rule. He does not care about his children." This new information can be represented by a rule:

```
12 -cares(john,X) :- child(X,john).
```

Unfortunately, the addition of this rule to Π_1 makes the program inconsistent, although in everyday reasoning this new information does not cause inconsistency. We simply withdraw our previous conclusion,

$cares(john, sam)$, and replace it by the new one, $\neg cares(john, sam)$. Representation of the default by a strict rule does not allow such nonmonotonic reasoning. We need another representation. This does not cause a difficulty. In ASP a default, d, stated as "Normally elements of class C have property P," is often represented by a rule:

$$p(X) \leftarrow c(X),$$
$$not\ ab(d(X)),$$
$$not\ \neg p(X).$$

Here, $ab(d(X))$ is read "X is abnormal with respect to d" or "a default d is not applicable to X" and $not\ \neg p(X)$ is read "$p(X)$ *may* be true."

The same technique can be used if X is a list of variables. For instance, the default d_{cares} "normally parents care about their children" can be represented as follows:

```
13  % default rule
14  cares(X,Y) :- parent(X,Y),
15                 not ab(d_cares(X,Y)),
16                 not -cares(X,Y).
```

Let Π_2 be the program given by lines 1–16. The new program is consistent and entails $\neg cares(john, sam)$ and $cares(alice, sam)$. As expected, the new information about John forces the program to withdraw one of its previous conclusions and replace it by the new one.

Defaults can have two types of exceptions – weak and strong. **Weak exceptions** render the default inapplicable (i.e., make our agent unable to use the default to come to a hasty conclusion). **Strong exceptions** refute the default's conclusion (i.e., they allow the agent to derive the opposite of the default). A weak exception $e(X)$ to a default d can be encoded by the so-called **cancellation axiom**

$$ab(d(X)) \leftarrow\ not\ \neg e(X). \tag{5.1}$$

which says that d is not applicable to X if X *may be* a weak exception to d. If e is a strong exception we need one more rule,

$$\neg p(X) \leftarrow e(X) \tag{5.2}$$

which allows us to defeat d's conclusion.

To illustrate the notion of weak exception, let us emulate a cautious reasoner who does not want to apply default d_{cares} to a parent of a child if that parent has never been seen at the school. We assume that the latter information is incomplete and is represented in our knowledge base by a collection of literals of the form $absent(p)$ or $\neg absent(p)$ where p is a person. An absent parent can be viewed as a weak exception to the default. Let's consider what we would expect in the three possible cases of the availability of knowledge about Alice's absence. If $\neg absent(alice)$ were in the knowledge base, then the reasoner would use the default and conclude that Alice cares about Sam. If the knowledge base were to contain $absent(alice)$, then the reasoner would not wish to apply d_{cares} to Alice. In this case her feelings about Sam would be unknown. Last, if the knowledge base had no information about Alice's absence (i.e., if it contained neither $absent(alice)$ nor $\neg absent(alice)$), then being cautious, the reasoner would not wish to apply the default either.

To model this reasoning we expand our program by the following cancellation axiom:

```
17  ab(d_cares(P,C))  :- person(P), person(C),
18                        not -absent(P).
```

The new program, Π_3 on lines 1–18, has no information on Alice's absence and, as expected, answers *no* to query $cares(john, sam)$ and *unknown* to query $cares(alice, sam)$. Similar behavior would be exhibited if the program contained

```
absent(alice).
```

If the knowledge

```
-absent(alice).
```

were available, then $cares(alice, sam)$ would be concluded. (Note that if definite information $cares(alice, sam)$ or $\neg cares(alice, sam)$ existed in our knowledge base, then the default would have no effect, regardless of Alice's absence.)

Now consider uncaring John, a strong exception to default d_{cares}. This exception was represented in the program by the rule on line 12. However, according to our general methodology, the fact that John does not care for his children should have been translated into ASP by two rules:

```
-cares(john,X)  :- parent(john,X).
ab(d_cares(john,X))  :- person(X),
                        not -parent(john,X).
```

It is easy to see, however, that addition of the second rule is unnecessary. (Indeed if John is a parent of X, then the first rule applies and defeats the default. If no information about $parent(john, X)$ is available, the default is not applicable anyway.) The existence of unnecessary rules is, of course, not surprising. The most general methodology does not necessarily lead to the simplest representation. As in any type of writing, additional editing may substantially improve the result.

To better understand the need for the cancellation axiom for strong exceptions, let's consider another strong exception to d_{cares}. Assume the existence of a mythical country, u, whose inhabitants do not care for their children. This exception is represented by the rule

```
19  -cares(P,X)  :- parent(P,X),
20                    born_in(P,u).
```

and the cancellation axiom

```
21  ab(d_cares(P,X)) :- person(P), person(X),
22                       not -born_in(P,u).
```

Suppose we have an extension of our family knowledge base that contains information about the national origin of most (but not all) recorded people. Assume, for instance, that, according to our records, Pit and Kathy are the father and mother of Jim. Kathy was born in Moldova, but the national origin of Pit is unknown. He could have been born in u. This can be represented by the following rules:

```
23  person(pit).
24  person(kathy).
25  person(jim).
26  father(pit,jim).
27  mother(kathy,jim).
28  country(moldova).
29  country(u).
30  born_in(kathy,moldova).
31  %% A person can only be born in one country
32  -born_in(P,X) :- country(X),
33                    born_in(P,Y),
34                    X != Y.
```

To simplify the discussion, we assume that both parents have been seen at the school:

```
35  -absent(pit).
36  -absent(kathy).
```

Let Π_4 be the program given by lines 1–36. The fact that neither Pit nor Kathy is absent allows us to ignore the cancellation axiom on lines 17–18 and concentrate on the effects of the cancellation axiom that we just introduced on lines 21–22. We can see that, as expected, Π_4 answers queries $cares(kathy, jim)$ and $cares(pit, jim)$ with *yes* and *unknown*, respectively. Without the new cancellation axiom, the program would have derived that Pit did care about Jim, even though his origin was unknown. If later we were to learn that Pit were indeed from u, then the second answer would be replaced by a definite *no*.

5.1.2 Cowardly Students

Let us consider another example that has both weak and strong exceptions. Consider the following information:

1. Normally, students are afraid of math.
2. Mary is not.
3. Students in the math department are not afraid of math.
4. Those in CS may or may not be afraid of math.

The first statement corresponds to a default, say d. The next two can be viewed as strong exceptions to it. The fourth is a weak exception.

We assume that we are given two sorts of objects, *student* and *dept*, containing names of all students and departments of the domain.

```
1  student(dave).student(mary).student(bob).student(pat).
2  dept(english).   dept(cs).   dept(math).
```

Suppose also that a (possibly incomplete) list

```
3  in(dave,english).
4  in(mary,cs).
5  in(bob,cs).
6  in(pat,math).
```

relates students to their unique departments. This uniqueness can be defined by rule

```
7  -in(S,D1)   :- dept(D1),
8                 in(S,D2),
9                 D1 != D2.
```

The default (statement 1 from the specification) is translated by the rule:

```
10  afraid(S,math) :- student(S),
11                    not ab(d(S)),
12                    not -afraid(S,math).
```

According to statement 2 from the specification, Mary is a strong exception to this default. According to our methodology, it can be represented as

```
13  -afraid(mary,math).
14  ab(d(mary)).
```

Note that, in this case, $ab(d(mary))$ is not necessary and can be removed.

The strong exception for math students (statement 3) is expressed as follows:

```
15  -afraid(S,math) :- in(S,math).
16  ab(d(S)) :- student(S),
17               not -in(S,math).
```

The following cancellation rule for CS students (statement 4) allow us to express the weak exception:

```
18  ab(d(S)) :- student(S),
19               not -in(S,cs).
```

It is easy to check that the program gives the following answers:

? $afraid(dave, math)$	Yes
? $afraid(mary, math)$	No
? $afraid(pat, math)$	No
? $afraid(bob, math)$	Unknown

Now consider another student, Jake, whose department affiliation is unknown. Given $person(jake)$, an agent using this program will correctly answer that it does not know whether Jake is afraid of math. Notice that this can only be done because of the cancellation axioms, which allow the expression of weak exceptions. However, if it was known that Jake was neither in the computer science nor in the math department, then the agent would correctly derive that Jake was afraid of math.

5.1.3 A Special Case

Let d be a default "Elements of class C normally have property P" and e be a set of exceptions to this default. If our information about membership in e is complete, then its representation can be substantially simplified. If e is a weak exception to d then cancellation axiom (5.1) can be written as

$$ab(d(X)) \leftarrow e(X). \tag{5.3}$$

If e is a strong exception then axiom (5.1) can be simply omitted.

For instance in our cowardly students example, if we had a complete list of students in the CS department, we could replace our original cancellation axiom for CS students by

```
ab(d(X))  :- in(X,cs).
```

If, in addition, we knew that our information about student membership in the math department is complete, then the cancellation axiom for math students could simply be dropped.

Similarly, if in the uncaring John example the place of birth for all parents were known, then the cancellation axiom on lines 21–22 could also be dropped. If information about which parents were never seen at school were complete, the axiom on lines 17–18 could be simplified to

```
ab(d_cares(P,C))  :- person(C),
                      absent(P).
```

5.2 Knowledge Bases with Null Values

Now let us look at the use of defaults for representing and reasoning about incomplete information in the presence of *null values* – constants used to indicate that the value of a certain variable or function is unknown. This technique is commonly used in relational databases, but due to the multiple and not always clearly specified meanings of these constants, it often leads to ambiguity and confusion. We now show how the use of defaults can alleviate this problem.

5.2.1 Course Catalog

Consider a database table representing a tentative summer schedule of a computer science department.

Professor	Course
mike	pascal
john	c
staff	prolog

Here "staff" is a null value that stands for an unknown professor. It expresses the fact that Prolog will be taught by *some* professor (possibly different from Mike or John).

To represent this information we assume that we are given two sorts, professors and courses

```
1  prof(mike).  prof(john).
2  course(pascal).  course(c).  course(prolog).
```

and introduce a relation $teaches(P, C)$ that says that professor P teaches a course C; the relation $teaches(staff, C)$ states that some professor teaches class C. The positive information from the table can be represented by a collection of facts:

```
3  teaches(mike,pascal).
4  teaches(john,c).
5  teaches(staff,prolog).
```

To represent negative information, we use default d: Normally, P teaches C only if this is listed in the schedule. Notice that d is not applicable to Prolog (or any other course taught by "staff"). This can be represented as follows:

```
6  -teaches(P,C)  :-  prof(P), course(C),
7                     not ab(d(P,C)),
8                     not teaches(P,C).
9  ab(d(P,C))  :-  teaches(staff,C).
```

Check that the resulting program produces correct answers (*no* and *unknown*) to queries $teaches(mike, c)$ and $teaches(mike, prolog)$, respectively.

There can be yet another type of incompleteness in database tables.

Professor	Course
mike	pascal
john	c
{mike, john}	prolog

Here {mike, john} represents the second type of nulls in which the value is unknown, but is one of a specified finite set. To represent this information we simply expand our program by

```
10  teaches(mike,prolog) | teaches(john,prolog).
```

With the new program, our agent's answers to queries $teaches(mike, c)$, $teaches(mike, prolog)$, and $teaches(mike, prolog) \land teaches(john, prolog)$ are *No*, *Unknown*, and *No*, respectively.

5.3 Simple Priorities between Defaults

In this section we examine a way to represent simple priorities between defaults. We start with assuming that the agent's knowledge base contains a database of records similar to that used in the orphan story from Section 4.1. To make the example slightly more realistic, we remove the assumptions that a child's record contains complete information about that child's parents. We still assume that the deaths of all people whose records are kept in our knowledge base are properly recorded, as is information about being a child.

In addition to these records let us supply our agent with knowledge about some fictitious legal regulations. The first regulation says that *orphans are entitled to assistance according to special government program 1*, and the second says that all *children are entitled to program 0*. The rules also say that *program 1 is preferable to program 0* (i.e., *a child qualified for receiving assistance from program 1 shall not receive assistance from program 0*), and that *no one can receive assistance from more than one program*.

Let us first represent these regulations and then define the records of the agent's knowledge base. Legal regulations usually come with exceptions and hence can be viewed as defaults. What follows is a complete representation. We use relation $record\_for(P)$ to indicate that the agent's knowledge base contains a record for person P. First we list the assistance programs; next we represent the first two regulations by standard default rules and by a rule prohibiting assistance from more than one program:

```
1   program(0).
2   program(1).
3
4   entitled(X,1)  :- record_for(X),
5                     orphan(X),
6                     not ab(d1(X)),
7                     not -entitled(X,1).
8   entitled(X,0)  :- record_for(X),
9                     child(X),
10                    not ab(d2(X)),
11                    not -entitled(X,0).
12  -entitled(X,N2) :- program(N1), program(N2),
13                     record_for(X),
14                     entitled(X,N1),
15                     N1 != N2.
```

The next two rules express preference for program 1 over program 0. Essentially we treat orphans (who are entitled to assistance from program 1) as strong exceptions to the second default. (In other circumstances preference can be expressed by weak exceptions.) The double negation in the last rule is needed because we may not know if a child is an orphan due to incompleteness of our record.

```
16  -entitled(X,0)  :- record_for(X),
17                        orphan(X).
18  ab(d2(X))  :- record_for(X),
19                   not -orphan(X).
```

There are also the following strong exceptions to both defaults:

```
20  -entitled(X,N)  :- record_for(X),
21                        dead(X),
22                        program(N).
23  -entitled(X,N)  :- record_for(X),
24                        -child(X),
25                        program(N).
```

(Since information about *dead* and *child* is complete, we do not need cancellation axioms for these strong exceptions.) Assuming that some person, say Joe, is alive, the rules guarantee that if Joe is an orphan, he will receive assistance from program 1. If Joe is a child who is not an orphan, he will be assisted by program 0. However, if Joe is a child and it is not known whether he is an orphan or not, Joe will receive no benefits at all. Of course this is not right. Something should be done about this case of insufficient documentation. The problem can be detected by the following rule:

```
26  check_status(X)  :- record_for(X),
27                        not -orphan(X),
28                        not orphan(X).
```

In other words, the person in charge of financial assistance will need to go to some extra trouble to check person X's status if the system does not know whether or not X is an orphan.

Let us now describe records from the agent's knowledge base. We use a slight modification of the database from the previous family example. As before, we assume that there is a sort *person* satisfied by any reasonable name we decide to use. But the rest of the information is more structured. For testing purposes let us assume that there are records for the following people:

```
29  record_for(bob).
30  father(rich,bob).
31  mother(patty,bob).
32  child(bob).
33
34  record_for(rich).
35  father(charles,rich).
36  mother(susan,rich).
37  dead(rich).
38
39  record_for(patty).
40  dead(patty).
41
42  record_for(mary).
43  child(mary).
44  mother(patty,mary).
```

To express the assumption that the deaths of all people whose records are kept in the knowledge base are properly recorded, we expand the above records by CWA for *dead*:

```
45  -dead(P) :- record_for(P),
46               not dead(P).
```

We do so similarly for the children.

```
47  -child(X) :- record_for(X),
48               not child(X).
```

Notice that our closed world assumptions only apply to people who have records in the agent's knowledge base. This is simply because we are not going to ask any questions about those who are not in it. If, by accident, such a question is asked, the answer will be *unknown*.

Now we are ready to define a notion of orphan. The positive part of the definition remains the same as before:

```
49  orphan(P) :- child(P),
50               parents_dead(P).
```

The negative part, however, undergoes a substantial change. The closed world assumption for orphans used in the previous example is replaced by a weaker statement:

```
51  -orphan(P) :- record_for(P),
52               not may_be_orphan(P).
```

where *may_be_orphan* is defined as follows:

```
53  may_be_orphan(P)  :-  record_for(P),
54                        child(P),
55                        not -parents_dead(P).
56
57  parent(X,P)  :-  father(X,P).
58  parent(X,P)  :-  mother(X,P).
59
60  parents_dead(P)  :-  father(X,P),
61                       dead(X),
62                       mother(Y,P),
63                       dead(Y).
64
65  -parents_dead(P)  :-  parent(X,P),
66                        -dead(X).
```

It is easy to check that the program entails $entitled(bob, 1)$, $\neg entitled(bob, 0)$, and $check\_status(mary)$.

Suppose that after checking the status of Mary, the administrator discovered that Mary has a father, Mike, who is alive. In that case, the record for Mary should be expanded by

```
67  father(mike,mary).
```

We also need a new record for Mike:

```
68  record_for(mike).
```

Now the program entails $entitled(bob, 1)$, $\neg entitled(bob, 0)$, $entitled(mary, 0)$, and $\neg entitled(mary, 1)$.

Of course the program also derives that no other person whose record is stored in the database is entitled to any of the assistance programs. (Note, however, that the system is not able to give a definite answer about entitlements for Charles and Susan, who have no such records. Moreover, the records for these people cannot be created because we do not know if they are dead or alive. The addition would violate our assumption about completeness of the death records.) This is one more example of the usefulness of discriminating between falsity and the mere absence of information. The distinction, together with the simple expression of preferences between defaults, allows our program to produce correct conclusions based on such absence.

5.4 Inheritance Hierarchies with Defaults

Whenever humans have a hierarchical organization of information, we make assumptions about certain properties that members of classes share with each other. For example, if we find out that something is an animal, we can assume that it eats, breathes, and so on. However, there can always be exceptions to such rules, and it is foolish to cling too tightly to conclusions we make based on class membership. Default reasoning is essential for making commonsense assumptions, but taking exceptions into account is essential to true intelligence.

5.4.1 Submarines Revisited

Now that we have the power to represent defaults, let's return to the hierarchical representation of our *Narwhal* example from Section 4.3. Instead of saying that all submarines are black, we can say that *normally* submarines are black. In accordance with our general methodology we simply replace

```
has_color(X,black) :- member(X,sub).
```

by

```
has_color(X,black) :- member(X,sub),
                      not ab(dc(X)),
                      not -has_color(X,black).
```

Suppose that we learned about a submarine named *Blue Deep*. In accordance with its name, this submarine is blue. (After all, it makes sense to use blue for better camouflage in case the screen door does not deter some of the fish.) The new information can be added as follows:

```
object(blue_deep).
color(blue).
is_a(blue_deep,sub).
has_color(blue_deep,blue).
```

Since colors of submarines are unique (see the rule on lines 29–31 from Section 4.3), the new blue submarine is a strong exception to our default. As expected the new program is consistent. It allows us to conclude that the *Blue Deep* is blue while retaining our ability to conclude that the *Narwhal* is black by default. If later we learn that the *Narwhal* is also blue, this would cause no contradiction.

5.4.2 Membership Revisited

Another lovely consequence of being able to add the word "normally" to our statements is that we can weaken our assumption that leaf classes of hierarchies are disjoint. The positive part of the definition of *member* and the definition of *sibling* remain unchanged:

```
member(X,C)  :- is_a(X,C).
member(X,C)  :- is_a(X,C0),
                subclass(C0,C).
siblings(C1,C2) :- is_subclass(C1,C),
                   is_subclass(C2,C),
                   C1 != C2.
```

The only change needed is the addition of a new line at the end of the old definition of $\neg member(X, C)$. Here is the new rule:

```
-member(X,C2)  :- member(X,C1),
                  siblings(C1,C2),
                  C1 != C2,
                  not member(X,C2).
```

Now we can introduce an amphibious vehicle called *Darling* owned by some great man of action. It belongs both to the car and the submarine class. This can be recorded by

```
object(darling).
is_a(darling, car).
is_a(darling, sub).
```

The resulting program allows our agent to deduce that the *Darling* is a member of both subclasses, but that the *Narwhal* is a sub and not a car.

5.4.3 The Specificity Principle

Let's consider another example that illustrates a classic problem that arose with the study of inheritance hierarchies. "Eagles and penguins are types of birds. Birds are a type of animal. Sam is an eagle, and Tweety is a penguin. Tabby is a cat." We represent this hierarchy exactly as before:

```
1  class(animal).
2  class(bird).
3  class(eagle).
```

```
4  class(penguin).
5  class(cat).
6
7  object(sam).
8  object(tweety).
9  object(tabby).
10
11 is_subclass(eagle,bird).
12 is_subclass(penguin,bird).
13 is_subclass(bird,animal).
14 is_subclass(cat,animal).
15
16 subclass(C1,C2) :- is_subclass(C1,C2).
17 subclass(C1,C2) :- is_subclass(C1,C3),
18                       subclass(C3,C2).
19
20 is_a(sam,eagle).
21 is_a(tweety,penguin).
22 is_a(tabby,cat).
23
24 member(X,C) :- is_a(X,C).
25 member(X,C) :- is_a(X,C0),
26                       subclass(C0,C).
27
28 siblings(C1,C2) :- is_subclass(C1,C),
29                       is_subclass(C2,C),
30                       C1 != C2.
31 -member(X,C2) :- member(X,C1),
32                       siblings(C1,C2),
33                       C1 != C2,
34                       not member(X,C2).
```

Our agent should now be able to answer correctly that Tweety is not an eagle but that Tweety is a penguin, a bird, and an animal. All these queries can be made using the *member* predicate.

Now we add default properties of classes. For example, *animals normally do not fly, birds normally fly, and penguins normally do not fly.* (The last default may look strange but we need it for illustrative purposes. After all, we may eventually want to consider penguins that fly because they are sprinkled with pixie dust.) What does the new theory allow us to conclude about Sam's ability to fly? Since Sam is both a bird and an animal, his flying abilities are defined by two contradictory defaults. The program has two answer sets containing $fly(sam)$ and $\neg fly(sam)$, respectively. Our common sense, however, tells us that only the first conclusion is justified. This is apparently the result of a broadly shared, commonsense **specificity principle** that states that *more specific information overrides less specific information.* The principle was first formalized by David S. Touretzky. The default "normally elements of class C_1 have property P" is preferred to the default "normally elements of class C_2 have property $\neg P$" if C_1 is a subclass of C_2. The following rules represent our defaults together with the specificity principle.

```
35  %% Animals normally do not fly.
36  -fly(X) :- member(X,animal),
37              not ab(d1(X)),
38              not fly(X).
39
40  %% Birds normally fly.
41  fly(X) :- member(X,bird),
42              not ab(d2(X)),
43              not -fly(X).
44
45  %% Penguins normally do not fly.
46  -fly(X) :- member(X,penguin),
47              not ab(d3(X)),
48              not fly(X).
49
50  %% X is abnormal w.r.t d2 if X might be a   penguin.
51  ab(d2(X)) :- not -member(X,penguin).
52
53  %% X is abnormal w.r.t d1 if X might be a   bird.
54  ab(d1(X)) :- not -member(X,bird).
```

The last rule, which prohibits the application of default d_1 to animals that might possibly be birds, expresses preference for default d_2 over default d_1. The previous rule does the same for defaults d_3 and d_2. We chose to express exceptions this way because our hierarchy allows objects for which the complete characterization of their membership relation is unknown. For example, if there is a bird that cannot be classified further, the agent should conclude "unknown" about its flying ability. After all, the bird might turn out to be a penguin.

Now our agent has no problem figuring out which animals and birds fly and which do not. Sam flies and Tweety and Tabby do not. And if we wanted to teach the program about baby eagles that do not fly, or penguins that do, we could.

Of course, the specificity principle is applicable to defaults with arbitrary incompatible conclusions, not just those of the form P and $\neg P$. For example, "Tucson is normally sunny" could be overridden by the more specific default that states, "Tucson is normally rainy during the monsoon season." The incompatibility of "sunny" and "rainy" may indirectly follow from other rules of the program.

Note that our formalization does not have a single rule expressing the specificity principle. Instead we need to write a separate rule for each pair of the corresponding contradictory defaults. This requirement is not surprising because to write such a rule we would need to reify defaults. There are commonsense theories in which defaults are reified and the specificity principle is stated as one rule, but they are beyond the scope of this book. You can give it a try in the last exercise.

5.5 (*) Indirect Exceptions to Defaults

In this section we consider yet another type of possible exceptions to defaults, sometimes referred to as **indirect exceptions**. Intuitively, these are rare exceptions that come into play only as a last resort, to restore the consistency of the agent's worldview when all else fails. The representation of indirect exceptions seems to be beyond the power of ASP. This observation led to the development of a simple but powerful extension of ASP called **CR-Prolog** (or ASP with consistency-restoring rules). To illustrate the problem let us look at the following example.

Consider an ASP representation of the default "elements of class c normally have property p":

$$p(X) \leftarrow c(X),$$
$$not\ ab(d(X)),$$
$$not\ \neg p(X).$$

together with the rule

$$q(X) \leftarrow p(X).$$

and two observations:

$$c(x).$$
$$\neg q(x).$$

where x is a constant denoting a particular object of the domain. It is not difficult to check that this program is inconsistent. No rules allow the reasoner to prove that the default is not applicable to x (i.e., to prove $ab(d(x))$) or that x does not have property p. Hence the default must conclude $p(x)$. The second rule implies $q(x)$, which contradicts the second observation.

There, however, seems to exists a commonsense argument that may allow a reasoner to avoid inconsistency and to conclude that x is an indirect exception to the default. The argument is based on the **Contingency Axiom** for default $d(X)$ that says, *"Any element of class c can be an exception to the default $d(X)$ above, but such a possibility is very rare and, whenever possible, should be ignored."* One may informally argue that since the application of the default to x leads to a contradiction, the possibility of x being an exception to $d(x)$ cannot be ignored and hence x must satisfy this rare property.

In what follows we give a brief description of CR-Prolog – an extension of ASP capable of encoding and reasoning about such rare events. We start with a description of the syntax and semantics of the language.

A program of CR-Prolog is a four-tuple consisting of

1. A (possibly sorted) signature.
2. A collection of regular rules of ASP.
3. A collection of rules of the form

$$l_0 \xleftarrow{+} l_1, \ldots, l_k, \; not \; l_{k+1}, \ldots, \; not \; l_n \qquad (5.4)$$

where ls are literals. Rules of type (5.4) are called **consistency-restoring rules (cr-rules)**.
4. A partial order, $\leq$, defined on sets of cr-rules. This partial order is often referred to as a **preference relation**.

Intuitively, rule (5.4) says that if the reasoner associated with the program believes the body of the rule, then it "may possibly" believe its head; however, this possibility may be used only if there is no way to obtain a consistent set of beliefs by using only regular rules of the program. The partial order over sets of cr-rules is used to select preferred possible resolutions of the conflict. Currently the inference engine of CR-Prolog supports two such relations. One is based on the set-theoretic inclusion ($R_1 \leq_1 R_2$ holds iff $R_1 \subseteq R_2$). Another is defined by the cardinality of the corresponding sets ($R_1 \leq_2 R_2$ holds iff $|R_1| \leq |R_2|$). To give the precise semantics we need some terminology and notation.

The set of regular rules of a CR-Prolog program Π is denoted by Π^r; the set of cr-rules of Π is denoted by Π^{cr}. By $\alpha(r)$ we denote a regular rule obtained from a consistency-restoring rule r by replacing $\xleftarrow{+}$ by $\leftarrow$; α is expanded in a standard way to a set R of cr-rules, i.e., $\alpha(R) = \{\alpha(r) : r \in R\}$. As in the case of ASP, the semantics of CR-Prolog is given for ground programs. A rule with variables is viewed as a shorthand for a schema of ground rules.

Definition 5.5.1. *(Abductive Support)*
A minimal (with respect to the preference relation of the program) collection R of cr-rules of Π such that $\Pi^r \cup \alpha(R)$ is consistent (i.e., has an answer set) is called an **abductive support** *of Π.*

Definition 5.5.2. *(Answer Sets of CR-Prolog)*
A set A is called an answer set *of Π if it is an answer set of a regular program $\Pi^r \cup \alpha(R)$ for some abductive support R of Π.*

Consider, for instance, the following CR-Prolog program:

$$p(a) \leftarrow not\ q(a).$$
$$\neg p(a).$$
$$q(a) \xleftarrow{+} .$$

It is easy to see that the regular part of this program (consisting of the program's first two rules) is inconsistent. The third rule, however, provides an abductive support that allows resolution of the inconsistency. Hence the program has one answer set $\{q(a), \neg p(a)\}$.

The previous example had only one possible resolution of the conflict, and hence its abductive support did not depend on the preference relation of the program. This is, of course, not always the case. Consider for instance the following collection of rules:

$$p_1 \leftarrow not\ \neg p_1.$$
$$\neg p_1 \xleftarrow{+} .$$
$$p_2 \leftarrow not\ \neg p_2.$$
$$\neg p_2 \xleftarrow{+} .$$
$$p_3 \leftarrow not\ \neg p_3.$$
$$\neg p_3 \xleftarrow{+} .$$

$$r \leftarrow p_1.$$

$$\neg r \leftarrow p_2.$$

$$\neg r \leftarrow p_3.$$

It is not difficult to see that a program consisting of these rules and set inclusion as the preference relation has two answer sets $\{\neg p_1, p_2, p_3, \neg r\}$ and $\{p_1, \neg p_2, \neg p_3, r\}$ corresponding to abductive supports $\{\neg p_1 \overset{+}{\leftarrow}\}$ and $\{\neg p_2 \overset{+}{\leftarrow}, \quad \neg p_3 \overset{+}{\leftarrow}\}$. (Note that the collection of all three cr-rules of the program does not provide a minimal conflict resolution.)

Consider now the program consisting of these rules and the cardinality-based preference relation. Observe that this program has only one abductive support and one answer set, $\{\neg p_1, p_2, p_3, \neg r\}$. Now let us show how CR-Prolog can be used to represent defaults and their indirect exceptions. The CR-Prolog representation of default $d(X)$ may look as follows:

$$p(X) \leftarrow c(X),$$
$$\qquad not \; ab(d(X)),$$
$$\qquad not \; \neg p(X).$$
$$\neg p(X) \overset{+}{\leftarrow} c(X).$$

The first rule is the standard ASP representation of the default, whereas the second rule expresses the contingency axiom for default $d(X)$.[1] Consider now a program obtained by combining these two rules with an atom

$$c(a).$$

The program's answer set is $\{c(a), p(a)\}$. Of course this is also the answer set of the regular part of our program. (Since the regular part is consistent, the contingency axiom is ignored.) Let us now expand this program by the rules

$$q(X) \leftarrow p(X).$$
$$\neg q(a).$$

The regular part of the new program is inconsistent. To save the day we need to use the contingency axiom for $d(a)$ to form the abductive support of the program. As a result the new program has the answer set $\{\neg q(a), c(a), \neg p(a)\}$. The new information does not produce inconsistency as in the analogous case of ASP representation. Instead the program

---

[1] In this form of the contingency axiom, we treat X as a strong exception to the default. Sometimes it may be useful to also allow weak indirect exceptions; this can be achieved by adding the rule: $ab(d(X)) \overset{+}{\leftarrow} c(X).$

withdraws its previous conclusion and recognizes a as a (strong) exception to default $d(a)$.

Here is another small example: Consider a reasoning agent whose knowledge base contains a default that says that "people normally keep their cars in working condition." A (slightly simplified) version of this default can be represented in CR-Prolog as follows:

$$\neg broken(X) \leftarrow car(X),$$
$$not\ ab(d(X)),$$
$$not\ broken(X).$$
$$broken(X) \overset{+}{\leftarrow} car(X).$$

Suppose also that the agent has some information about the normal operations of cars (e.g., it knows that turning the ignition key starts the car's engine). This knowledge can be represented by the rules:

$$starts(X) \leftarrow turn\_key(X),$$
$$\neg broken(X).$$
$$\neg starts(X) \leftarrow turn\_key(X),$$
$$broken(X).$$

(For simplicity we assume here that broken cars do not start.)

Given that the ignition key of car x was turned, i.e., statements

$$car(x).$$

$$turn\_key(x).$$

belong to the agent's knowledge base, the agent will be able to use regular rules to conclude $\neg broken(x)$ and $starts(x)$. If, however, in addition the agent learns

$$\neg starts(x)$$

both of the above conclusions will be withdrawn, and the cr-rule will be used to prove $broken(x)$, which, in turn, will imply $\neg starts(x)$.

The possibility of encoding rare events that may serve as unknown exceptions to defaults has proven to be very useful for various knowledge representation tasks, including planning, diagnostics, and reasoning about the agent's intentions. The later chapters contain a number of examples of such uses.

There are currently two ways to run CR-Prolog programs. One is to use a solver called CRModels, which can be found at http://www

`.mbal.tk/crmodels/`. The other is to use SPARC as described in Appendix C.

Summary

In this chapter we discussed the general strategy for representing defaults and their exceptions. The strategy explains how to translate natural-language statements of the form "normally, typically, as a rule," etc., into defeasible ASP rules and how to classify exceptions into strong, weak, and indirect. We showed how the first two types of exceptions could be recorded in ASP and gave a general representation of indirect exceptions in CR-Prolog. The nonmonotonicity of the ASP entailment was crucial for reasoning that allows the retraction of the defaults' conclusions after new information about exceptions to them became available. A number of examples illustrated the use of defaults for various knowledge representation tasks. In particular we showed how defaults could be used to specify negative information in databases containing incomplete knowledge expressed by null values – a task notoriously difficult in weaker languages. Another example dealt with inheritance hierarchies with default properties of classes. It showed how defaults could be blocked from being inherited by subclasses or objects using the general strategy for encoding exceptions. This allowed us to formalize the informal "specificity principle" used by people in their commonsense reasoning. A similar strategy could be used for specifying general preferences between defaults.

The ability to represent and reason about defaults is a very substantial achievement in KR. The design of logics and languages capable of doing this and gaining the ability to understand the correct ways of reasoning with defaults and their exceptions took many years of extensive research. Now, however, it has been honed enough to be included in a textbook.

References and Further Reading

A number of examples and techniques introduced in this chapter (including the representation of defaults with strong and weak exceptions) were first presented in Baral and Gelfond (1994). The "orphans" example was discussed in Gelfond (2002). The treatment of null values follows that of Taylor and Gelfond (1994). A rather general treatment of defaults including preferences between them can be found in Gelfond and Son (1997). In that paper defaults are reified and the preference relation can be defined by the context-dependent rules of the program. There is also a substantial amount of work on defining preferences between arbitrary logic programming rules as well as between answer sets of a logic program; see, for instance, Sakama and Inoue (2000), Delgrande, Schaub, and Tompits (2003), Delgrande et al. (2004), and Brewka and Eiter (1998). A general account of preferences and their role in nonmonotonic reasoning can be found in Brewka, Niemela, and Truszczynski (2008). The specificity principle is due to David Touretzky (1986). CR-Prolog was first introduced by Marcello Balduccini and Michael Gelfond in Doherty, McCarthy, and Williams (2003) and Balduccini (2007). An interesting application of CR-Prolog to planning can be found in Balduccini (2004); Balduccini (2007) contains the description of a CR-Prolog reasoning algorithm implemented in CRModels.

Exercises

Use the methodology for encoding defaults to represent the knowledge given in the following stories in ASP.

1. "Apollo and Helios are lions in a zoo. Normally lions are dangerous. Baby lions are not dangerous. Helios is a baby lion." Assume that the zoo has a complete list of baby lions that it maintains regularly. Your program should be able to deduce that Apollo is dangerous, whereas Helios is not. Make sure that (a) if you add another baby lion to your knowledge base, the program would derive that it is not dangerous, even though that knowledge is not explicit; and (b) if you add an explicit fact that Apollo is not dangerous, there is no contradiction and the program answers intelligently.

2. "John is married to Susan and Bob is married to Mary. Married people normally like each other. However, Bob hates Mary."
   (a) Make sure your program answers *yes* to queries
      $? \, likes(john, susan)$,
      $? \, likes(susan, john)$,
      $? \, likes(mary, bob)$,
      and *no* to $? \, likes(bob, mary)$.
   (b) Add the following knowledge to your program. "Arnold and Kate are also married, but Kate's behavior often does not follow predictable rules." Make sure your program can deduce that Arnold likes Kate, but it is unknown whether Kate likes Arnold. (Note that if you used the methodology properly, you should not need to change the first program but can just add to it.)

3. "American citizens normally live in the United States. American diplomats may or may not live in the United States. John, Miriam, and Caleb are American citizens. John lives in Italy. Miriam is an American diplomat."

   (a) Assume we do *not* have a complete list of American diplomats. (Note that your program should not be able to conclude that Caleb lives in the United States.)

   (b) Now assume we have a *complete* list of American diplomats. Add this information to the program. What does your new program say about Caleb's place of residence?

   (c) Rewrite the program from 3b by using the simplified form of the cancellation axiom.

4. "Adults normally work. Children do not work. Students are adults but they normally do not work. John and Betty are students. John works. Bob and Jim are adults who are not students. Bob does not work. Kate is an adult who may or may not be a student. Mary is a child." Make sure that your program is not only capable of answering questions about who works and does not work but also of who is or is not a child, an adult, and so on.

5. "A field that studies pure ideas does not study the natural world. A field that studies the natural world does not study pure ideas. Mathematics normally studies pure ideas. Science normally studies the natural world. As a computer scientist, Daniela studies both mathematics and science. Both mathematics and science study our place in the world." Make sure your program can deduce that Daniela studies our place in the world.

6. "Cars normally have four seats. Pick-up trucks are exceptions to this rule. They normally have two seats. Pick-up trucks with extended cab are exceptions to this rule. They have four seats." Your program should work correctly in conjunction with complete lists of facts of the form

$$car(a), car(b), car(c), \ldots$$

$$pickup(b), pickup(c), \ldots$$

$$extended\_cab(c), \ldots$$

7. You are given three complete lists of facts of the form

$$course(math), course(graphs), \ldots$$

$$student(john), student(mary), \ldots$$

$$took(john, math), took(mary, graphs), \ldots$$

Students can graduate only if they have taken all the courses in the first list. Write a program that, given the above information, determines which students can graduate. Make sure that, given the following sample knowledge base,

$$student(john).$$
$$student(mary).$$
$$course(math).$$
$$course(graphs).$$
$$took(john, math).$$
$$took(john, graphs).$$
$$took(mary, graphs).$$

your program is able to

$$conclude\ can\_graduate(john).$$
$$\neg can\_graduate(mary).$$

8. Consider the problem presented in Exercise 7. This time, however, the list of courses that the students took may be incomplete. Write a program that determines

   - which students can graduate
   - which students cannot graduate
   - which students' ability to graduate cannot be determined from the knowledge base; in this case, the program must recommend a review of the records of those students.

   Make sure that, given the following sample knowledge base,

$$student(john).$$
$$student(mary).$$
$$student(bob).$$
$$student(rick).$$
$$course(math).$$
$$course(graphs).$$
$$took(john, math).$$
$$took(john, graphs).$$
$$\neg took(mary, math).$$
$$took(mary, graphs).$$
$$\neg took(bob, math).$$

your program is able to conclude

$$can\_graduate(john).$$
$$\neg can\_graduate(mary).$$
$$\neg can\_graduate(bob).$$
$$review\_records(rick).$$

9. Using the notions of hierarchy and defaults as detailed in Section 5.4, write an ASP program to represent the following information. Be as general as you can.

   - A Selmer Mark VI is a saxophone.
   - Jake's saxophone is a Selmer Mark VI.
   - Mo's saxophone is a Selmer Mark VI.
   - Part of a saxophone is a high D key.
   - Part of the high D key is a spring that makes it work.
   - The spring is normally not broken.
   - Mo's spring for his high D key is broken.

   Make sure that your program correctly entails that Jake's saxophone works while Mo's is broken. For simplicity, assume that no one has more than one saxophone, and hence, saxophones can be identified by the name of their owner.

10. Consider the program from Section 5.4.3 in which lines 51 and 54 are replaced by

    ```
    ab(d2(X))  :- member(X,penguin).
    ab(d1(X))  :- member(X,bird).
    ```

    Given a bird, Squeaky, of unknown species, what would the agent answer about its flying ability?

11. (*) Encode the following story using CR-Prolog: Given the following program:

    ```
    day(d1).
    day(d2).
    % A day is considered to be a schoolday according to
    % the school calendar if it is not stated to be
    % otherwise:
    schoolday(D)  :- day(D),
                     not -schoolday(D).
    ```

```
% Schools are normally open on schooldays:
open_school(D) :- schoolday(D),
                  not ab(d(D)),
                  not -open_school(D).


% If school is open on day D, then D is not a
% snowday.
-snowday(D) :- open_school(D).


snowday(d1).
```

Add a cr-rule to resolve the inconsistency. It should express that, in rare cases, schools are closed on school days.

12. (**) We have noted before that to encode the specificity principle explicitly, we would have to reify the notion of default. Rewrite the program from Section 5.4.3 making the defaults objects of the domain and encode the specificity principle as a general rule about defaults.

6

The Answer-Set Programming Paradigm

So far we have used our ASP knowledge bases to get information about the truth or falsity of some statements or to find objects satisfying some simple properties. These types of tasks are normally performed by database systems. Even though the language's ability to express recursive definitions and the methodology of representing defaults and various forms of incomplete information gave us additional power and allowed us to construct rich and elaboration-tolerant knowledge bases, the types of queries essentially remained the same as in databases.

In this chapter we illustrate how significantly different computational problems can be reduced to finding answer sets of logic programs. The method of solving computational problems by reducing them to finding the answer sets of ASP programs is often called the **answer-set programming (ASP) paradigm**. It has been used for finding solutions to a variety of programming tasks, ranging from building decision support systems for the Space Shuttle and computer system configuration to solving problems arising in bio-informatics, zoology, and linguistics. In principle, any NP-complete problem can be solved in this way using programs without disjunction. Even more complex problems can be solved if disjunctive programs are used. In this chapter we illustrate the ASP paradigm by several simple examples. More advanced examples involving larger knowledge representation components are discussed in later chapters.

There are currently several ASP inference engines called *ASP solvers* capable of computing answer sets of programs with millions of ground rules. Normally, an ASP solver starts its computation by grounding the program (i.e., instantiating its variables by ground terms). The resulting program has the same answer sets as the original, but is propositional. The answer sets of the grounded program are then computed using generate-and-test algorithms, which we discuss in Chapter 7.[1]

---

[1] These algorithms have much in common with classical satisfiability algorithms for propositional logic.

You have, of course, already used an ASP solver if you used STUDENT to run examples or exercises in previous chapters; however, we kept the programs generic enough to run on any solver known to us. Different ASP solvers use various constructs not present in the original ASP discussed in this book. Some of the constructs are aimed at improving the efficiency of the solvers. Others provide useful syntactic sugar that saves programmer's time and may improve the readability of programs. For instance, popular ASP solvers such as **Smodels** and **ClaspD** use program grounders **Lparse** and **Gringo** whose input languages allow so-called choice rules not understood by another popular solver called **DLV**. In turn, DLV allows symbols for lists of terms, and other constructs not understood by Lparse/Gringo.[2]

There are currently efforts to standardize the input language. Meanwhile, we encourage readers to learn ASP programming by using their favorite ASP system. For standard ASP programs, this book focuses on two systems, clingo (Gringo + ClaspD) and DLV, to show the reader some useful features of both input languages. It is likely that, by the time this book is published, the features we mention will have become part of both systems and will be useful regardless of which system you choose. For a quick introduction and tips for using these systems, please see Appendix A. Both systems are good and have many elements that make them special; however, in our wish to keep things simple, we do not discuss all of their unique features.

6.1 Computing Hamiltonian Cycles

We start with describing an ASP solution of finding Hamiltonian cycles of a directed graph. Finding such cycles has applications to numerous important problems, including processor allocation and delivery scheduling. The general problem is stated as follows:

Given a directed graph G and an initial vertex v_0, find a path from v_0 to v_0 that enters each vertex exactly once.

For example, in Figure 6.1, if our initial vertex is a, the Hamiltonian cycle through the graph is a, b, c, d, e, a. Path a, b, c, d, a, e enters every vertex

---

[2] Gringo was originally based on Lparse, but is evolving. Since Gringo + Clasp D seems to be very efficient and is currently being actively developed and improved, we try to stay compatible with Gringo rather than with Lparse.

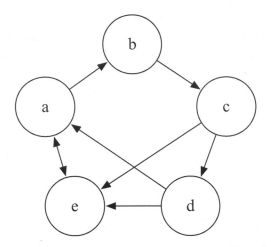

Figure 6.1. Directed Graph

exactly once, but is not a Hamiltonian cycle because it does not end at a. Path a, b, c, d, a is not a Hamiltonian cycle because it misses e.

We now show how the problem of finding a Hamiltonian cycle can be solved using ASP. The main idea is to construct an ASP program, $\Pi_H(G)$, whose answer sets correspond to Hamiltonian cycles of graph G. Once this is done, finding the cycles is reduced to finding answer sets of this program – a task that can be accomplished by an ASP solver. We first give our solution of the Hamiltonian cycle problem in DLV and clingo, then give an alternative solution using choice rules of clingo.

Not surprisingly, program $\Pi_H(G)$ contains the description of a graph G. The graph is represented by a sort $vertex(V)$ and a collection of atoms of the form $edge(V_1, V_2)$ describing its edges. The initial vertex is specified by atom $init(v_0)$. Note that the information about the input graph is complete, and strictly speaking, this fact should be indicated by the corresponding closed world assumptions. However, negative information about these relations is not relevant to our problem and is omitted for simplicity.

Now we are confronted with the problem of representing Hamiltonian cycles of G. The idea is to represent a cycle by a collection of statements of the form

$$in(v_0, v_1). \ \ldots \ in(v_k, v_0).$$

which belongs to an answer set of $\Pi_H(G)$. (Here $in(V_1, V_2)$ states that "the edge from vertex V_1 to vertex V_2 is in Hamiltonian cycle $\langle v_0, v_1, \ldots, v_k, v_0 \rangle$.")

We start by describing conditions on a collection P of atoms of the form $in(v_1, v_2)$ that will make P a Hamiltonian cycle:

1. P leaves each vertex at most once.
2. P enters each vertex at most once.
3. P enters every vertex of the graph.

The first and the second conditions are encoded by the rules:

```
1   -in(V,V2)  :- in(V,V1),
2                  vertex(V2),
3                  V1 != V2.
```

and

```
4   -in(V2,V)  :- in(V1,V),
5                  vertex(V2),
6                  V1 != V2.
```

For the third condition, we recursively define relation $reached(V)$, which holds if P enters vertex V on its way from the initial vertex:

```
7   reached(V2)  :- init(V1),
8                    in(V1,V2).
9
10  reached(V2)  :- reached(V1),
11                   in(V1,V2).
12
13  -reached(V)  :- vertex(V),
14                   not reached(V).
```

The constraint

```
15  :- -reached(V).
```

guarantees that every vertex of the graph is entered by our path.

To complete the solution we need to find some way to generate the collection of candidate paths and use these three conditions to select among them those that are Hamiltonian cycles. This can be done by the disjunctive *generation rule*

```
16  in(V1,V2) | -in(V1,V2) :- edge(V1,V2).
```

that states that every given edge is either in the path or is not in the path. The rule requires our answer sets to contain information about each edge's inclusion in the path. To see this more clearly, let us denote the program consisting of the representation of graph G (edges, vertices, and initial vertex) and the rule on line 16 by Π_0. Notice that there is a one-to-one correspondence between answer sets of Π_0 and arbitrary sets of edges of G. We sometimes say that Π_0 *generates* these sets. Now let Π be Π_0 expanded by the *testing rules* on lines 1–15. This time, there is a one-to-one correspondence between answer sets of Π and Hamiltonian cycles in G. They can be computed by clingo or DLV. Note that we are not really interested in all the information contained in the answer sets of the program – all we need is to display our Hamiltonian cycles (i.e., atoms formed by relation in). To make sure that DLV displays only atoms relevant to describing the Hamiltonian cycle, use option -filter=in. You can also use -pfilter=in to display only positive atoms formed by relation in. In the input language of clingo, display of relevant information is accomplished by a directive, #show included in the text of the program. In our case, we simply need to write

```
#show in/2.
```

where 2 refers to the arity of in.

To solve the problem in the example, we need to encode the graph from Figure 6.1 and initial vertex a:

```
17  vertex(a). vertex(b). vertex(c). vertex(d). vertex(e).
18  edge(a,b). edge(b,c). edge(c,d). edge(d,e).
19  edge(e,a). edge(a,e). edge(d,a). edge(c,e).
20  init(a).
```

Let's use hamgraph.lp to denote the program on lines 1–20. Calling DLV with

```
dlv -pfilter=in hamgraph.lp
```

we get the following output:

```
{in(a,b), in(b,c), in(c,d), in(d,e), in(e,a)}
```

which represents the only Hamiltonian cycle that starts at a.

There is another solution to the problem that uses a useful extension of the original ASP – the **Choice Rule**. This construct was first introduced in Smodels and is now implemented in all ASP solvers that use Lparse or Gringo as their grounder. Our description is informal; those interested in the formal definition should consult the related literature. A choice rule has two forms:

```
(a)   n1 {p(X)  :  q(X)} n2 :- body.
(b)   n1 {p(c1);...;p(ck)} n2 :- body.
```

where $n1$ and $n2$ are non-negative integers.[3] In this version of choice rules, both $n1$ and $n2$ can be omitted. Rules of type (a) allow inclusion in the program's answer sets of arbitrary collections S of atoms of the form $p(t)$ such that

1. $n1 \leq |S| \leq n2$
2. If $p(t) \in S$ then $q(t)$ belongs to the corresponding answer set.

If $n1$ is omitted then the above inequality turns into $0 \leq |S| \leq n2$; if $n2$ is omitted, it becomes $n1 \leq |S|$. Note that choice rule (a) can be viewed as a rule defining relation p in terms of previously defined relation q. Rules of type (b) allow selection of such an S from atoms listed in the head of the rule.

Example 6.1.1. *(Choice Rule (a))*
Program

```
q(a).
{p(X)  :  q(X)}1.
```

has answers sets $\{q(a)\}$ and $\{q(a), p(a)\}$. In the first case, the set S selected by the program is empty; in the second, $S = \{p(a)\}$. Note that both choices satisfy the cardinality constraints.

Example 6.1.2. *(Choice Rule (b))*
Program

```
q(b).
{p(a);p(b)}1.
```

has answers sets $\{q(b)\}$, $\{p(a), q(b)\}$, and $\{p(b), q(b)\}$. Replacing the 1 in the last rule by a 2 gives the original three answer sets, plus one more – $\{p(a), p(b), q(b)\}$.

Using the first form of the choice rule allows us to replace the disjunctive generation rule from line 16 by

---

[3] Actually `clingo` allows more general rules of the form
  (a) n1 OP1 {p(X) : q(X)} OP2 n2 :- body.
  (b) n1 OP1 {p(c1);...;p(ck)} OP2 n2 :- body.
  where the OPs are relations $<, >, =, !=, <=$ or $>=$ but we will not use it in this book.

```
{in(V1,V2) : edge(V1,V2)}.
-in(V1,V2) :- vertex(V1), vertex(V2),
              not in(V1,V2).
```

The first is the generation rule. (Note that the second rule is not really necessary for finding the solution to our puzzle and can be omitted.) To make sure that only relevant information is displayed we, of course, need to also include `#show in/2`.

You just saw your first example of a successful application of ASP methodology to solving a classical combinatorial problem. Now it may be prudent to spend some time reflecting on this experience. As you know, one of the main goals of computer science is to discover new ways of solving computational problems. (Think of the impact the discovery of recursion had on our ability to do that!) From this perspective, it is instructive to compare the *processes* of finding "procedural" versus "declarative" solutions to the Hamiltonian cycle problem. They are markedly different and lead to markedly different implementations. The first focuses on data structure and algorithm; the second on the appropriate encoding of the definition of the problem. We strongly encourage you to spend some time finding and implementing the procedural solution. But even without this exercise, one can probably see that the declarative solution is shorter, easier to implement (at least for those who had mastered both methodologies), more transparent, and more reliable. An important open question is "What are the limits of applicability of the second method?" (Perhaps some of you may decide to contribute to finding the answer to this question.)

Let us also mention that another declarative solution to the problem of finding Hamiltonian cycles had been discovered before ASP was even developed. In this solution a graph G and the definition of Hamiltonian cycle were encoded by a propositional formula F. There is a one-to-one correspondence between models of F and Hamiltonian cycles of G. A program, called a **satisfiability solver** finds the models. Computer scientists have been developing satisfiability solvers for propositional logic for more than 50 years and succeeded in producing remarkably efficient systems. So, why use ASP? There are two reasons to do so.

1. Often the ASP encoding is much shorter and easier to understand. Some recent mathematical results show that this feature is not an accident: Any equivalent translation from logic programs to propositional formulas involves a significant increase in size.
2. There are complexity results that prove that ASP with disjunction has more expressive power than propositional logic. Some problems

that can be solved by disjunctive ASP simply cannot be solved by satisfiability solvers.

The attractiveness of ASP does not mean that all the remarkable work on satisfiability solvers is in danger of becoming useless. The advantages and disadvantages of both methods are still under investigation. But more importantly the developers of ASP solvers are rapidly finding ways to use ideas from satisfiability theory, as well as actual, off-the-shelf satisfiability solvers, to build new and more efficient answer set solvers.

6.2 Solving Puzzles

The ability to solve puzzles is an important part of human intelligence. The skill with which students are able to do this is often used in decisions of whether to admit them to graduate school, offer them a job, and so on. Even though reasonable people can question the wisdom of such policies, few would argue that the ability to solve puzzles is at least one measure of intelligence. In this section we use ASP to design programs for solving several interesting puzzles.

6.2.1 Sudoku Puzzle

We start with a popular Japanese puzzle game called Sudoku. Our solution simply represents the Sudoku rules in ASP. The answer sets of the resulting program correspond to solutions of the puzzle.

Figure 6.2 shows a typical puzzle. As you can see, the game is played on a 9×9 grid that is further subdivided into nine 3×3 regions. Initially the grid contains numbers in some of its locations. A player must place the numbers 1 through 9 in the grid so that the following conditions are satisfied:

1. Each location contains a single number.
2. No row contains the same number twice.
3. No column contains the same number twice.
4. No 3×3 region contains the same number twice.

(Typically, for a given initial situation, the puzzle has exactly one solution.)

To describe the Sudoku puzzle's domain, we need names for the grid's locations and regions. We use coordinates – pairs of numbers from 1 to 9 – to name locations. Regions are numbered from 1 to 9. To describe numbers placed in the grid's locations, we use relation

$$pos(N, X, Y) - \text{"number } N \text{ is placed in location } (X, Y)\text{."}$$

	7		1					
9					3			
					7		2	5
	6							
		5		6		2	9	
3			4	5				6
1	2		8					
8		9				4		7
5								

Figure 6.2. Sudoku Puzzle

We also need a relation

$$in_region(X, Y, R) \text{ – “location } (X, Y) \text{ belongs to region } R.\text{”}$$

We are looking for a collection of atoms of the form $pos(N, X, Y)$ that satisfies the four conditions given earlier. For every coordinate (X, Y) there is a single number N such that $pos(N, X, Y)$ belongs to this collection. Using disjunction this can be expressed as follows:

```
1 num(1..9).
2 coord(X,Y) :- num(X), num(Y).
3 pos(1,X,Y) | pos(2,X,Y) | pos(3,X,Y) |
4 pos(4,X,Y)  | pos(5,X,Y) | pos(6,X,Y) |
5 pos(7,X,Y) | pos(8,X,Y) | pos(9,X,Y)  :-coord(X,Y).
```

The rule on lines 3–5 generates all possible assignments of numbers to locations. These assignments are tested against the remaining constraints by the following rules:
No row contains the same number twice:

```
6 -pos(N,X,Y2) :- pos(N,X,Y1),
7                 coord(X,Y2),
8                 Y1 != Y2.
```

No column contains the same number twice:

```
9   -pos(N,X2,Y)  :-  pos(N,X1,Y),
10                     coord(X2,Y),
11                     X1 != X2.
```

No region contains the same number twice:

```
12  -pos(N,X2,Y2)  :-  pos(N,X1,Y1),
13                     in_region(X1,Y1,R),
14                     in_region(X2,Y2,R),
15                     X1 != X2,
16                     Y1 != Y2.
```

Last, we define relation *in_region*. Given coordinates X and Y, their region R can be computed by the following formula:

$$R = ((X - 1)/3) * 3 + ((Y + 2)/3).$$

It is encoded in DLV by the following rule:

```
17  in_region(X,Y,R)  :-  num(X), num(Y), num(Z1), num(Z2),
18                         num(Z3), num(Z4), num(Z5), num(R),
19                         Z1 = X-1,
20                         Z2 = Z1/3,
21                         Z3 = Z2*3,
22                         Z4 = Y+2,
23                         Z5 = Z4/3,
24                         R = Z3 + Z5.
```

We can represent an initial position in the grid from Figure 6.2 by a collection of atoms of the form $pos(n, x, y)$, and compute answer sets of this program. These contain the solutions of the puzzle. For example, the puzzle in Figure 6.2 can be encoded as follows:

```
25  pos(7,2,1).   pos(1,4,1).   pos(9,1,2).   pos(3,6,2).
26  pos(7,6,3).   pos(2,8,3).   pos(5,9,3).   pos(6,2,4).
27  pos(5,3,5).   pos(6,5,5).   pos(2,7,5).   pos(9,8,5).
28  pos(3,1,6).   pos(4,4,6).   pos(5,5,6).   pos(6,9,6).
29  pos(1,1,7).   pos(2,2,7).   pos(8,4,7).   pos(8,1,8).
30  pos(9,3,8).   pos(4,7,8).   pos(7,9,8).   pos(5,1,9).
```

Let's call the program consisting of lines 1–30 sudokudlv.lp. Invoking DLV with

```
dlv -pfilter=pos sudokudlv.lp
```

produces the following output:

```
{pos(1,1,7), pos(1,4,1), pos(2,2,7),
 pos(2,7,5), pos(2,8,3), pos(3,1,6),
 pos(3,6,2), pos(4,4,6), pos(4,7,8),
 pos(5,1,9), pos(5,3,5), pos(5,5,6),
 pos(5,9,3), pos(6,2,4), pos(6,5,5),
 pos(6,9,6), pos(7,2,1), pos(7,6,3),
 pos(7,9,8), pos(8,1,8), pos(8,4,7),
 pos(9,1,2), pos(9,3,8), pos(9,8,5),
 pos(6,1,1), pos(4,1,3), pos(2,1,4),
 pos(7,1,5), pos(5,2,2), pos(1,2,3),
 pos(8,2,5), pos(9,2,6), pos(3,2,8),
 pos(4,2,9), pos(2,3,1), pos(8,3,2),
 pos(3,3,3), pos(4,3,4), pos(1,3,6),
 pos(7,3,7), pos(6,3,9), pos(2,4,2),
 pos(6,4,3), pos(9,4,4), pos(3,4,5),
 pos(5,4,8), pos(7,4,9), pos(9,5,1),
 pos(4,5,2), pos(8,5,3), pos(7,5,4),
 pos(3,5,7), pos(2,5,8), pos(1,5,9),
 pos(5,6,1), pos(8,6,4), pos(1,6,5),
 pos(2,6,6), pos(4,6,7), pos(6,6,8),
 pos(9,6,9), pos(3,7,1), pos(6,7,2),
 pos(9,7,3), pos(1,7,4), pos(7,7,6),
 pos(5,7,7), pos(8,7,9), pos(4,8,1),
 pos(7,8,2), pos(5,8,4), pos(8,8,6),
 pos(6,8,7), pos(1,8,8), pos(3,8,9),
 pos(8,9,1), pos(1,9,2), pos(3,9,4),
 pos(4,9,5), pos(9,9,7), pos(2,9,9)}
```

(If you wish to check the answer, note that the first four rows contain the input information, whereas the rest contain the solution numbers in a reasonable order.) Our solution can be viewed as a typical example of answer-set programming methodology.

The same problem can, of course, be solved using the choice rules of clingo. To do that we simply replace the generating disjunctive rule on lines 3–5 by the following choice rule:

```
1{pos(N,X,Y):num(N)}1 :- coord(X,Y).
```

Clingo allows us to simplify the rule from lines 17–24 by

```
in_region(X,Y,((X-1)/3)*3+((Y+2)/3)) :- num(X), num(Y).
```

For display purposes, we recommend inserting

```
#show pos/3.
```

6.2.2 Mystery Puzzle

A detective or mystery story can also be an interesting challenge for a rational agent. Unlike in Sudoku, it is not enough to know the puzzle's "rules" to find its solution. One normally also needs to make some assumptions that come from our general knowledge about the world. It means that programs solving such puzzles should possess some commonsense knowledge. Let us look at an example.

Vinny has been murdered, and Andy, Ben, and Cole are suspects. Andy says he did not do it. He says that Ben was the victim's friend but that Cole hated the victim. Ben says he was out of town the day of the murder, and besides he didn't even know the guy. Cole says he is innocent and he saw Andy and Ben with the victim just before the murder. Assuming that everyone – except possibly for the murderer – is telling the truth, use ASP to solve the case.

The story is about four people:

```
1 person(andy). person(ben). person(cole). person(vinny).
```

The next several statements record their testimony. Relation $says(P, S, 1)$ holds if person P says that statement S is true; $says(P, S, 0)$ holds if P says that S is false. The corresponding statements are represented by self-explanatory terms (e.g., $murderer(andy)$, $friends(ben, vinny)$, etc).

```
 2 %% Andy says:
 3 says(andy, murderer(andy), 0).      %% He didn't do it.
 4 says(andy, hated(cole,vinny), 1).  %% Cole hated Vinny.
 5 says(andy, friends(ben,vinny), 1). %% Ben and Vinny
 6                                     %% were friends.
 7 %% Ben says:
 8 says(ben, out_of_town(ben), 1).    %% He was out of town.
 9 says(ben, know(ben,vinny), 0).     %% He didn't know Vinny.
10 %% Cole says:
11 says(cole, innocent(cole), 1).      %% He is innocent.
12 says(cole, together(andy,vinny), 1). %% He saw Andy and
13 says(cole, together(ben,vinny), 1). %% Ben with victim.
```

The next two rules formalize the last statement of the puzzle, using relation $holds(F)$ – "statement F is true": Everyone, except possibly for the murderer, is telling the truth:

```
14  holds(S)  :- says(P,S,1),
15                -holds(murderer(P)).
16  -holds(S)  :- says(P,S,0),
17                -holds(murderer(P)).
```

The next rule states that one of the suspects is a murderer:

```
18  holds(murderer(andy)) | holds(murderer(ben)) |
    holds(murderer(cole)).
```

The next set of rules encodes some commonsense knowledge about the meaning of the relations used by the suspects. We start with proclaiming our belief that normally people are not murderers:

```
19  -holds(murderer(P))  :- person(P),
20                          not holds(murderer(P)).
```

Next we specify that some relations are symmetric and/or transitive: Relation *together* is symmetric and transitive:

```
21  holds(together(A,B))  :- holds(together(B,A)).
22  holds(together(A,B))  :- holds(together(A,C)),
23                           holds(together(C,B)).
```

Relation *friends* is symmetric:

```
24  holds(friends(A,B))  :- holds(friends(B,A)).
```

Several other properties express the mutual exclusivity of some of the relations mentioned in the story. Since these conditions are not used to *define* the corresponding relations, but rather relate two concepts to each other, they are represented by constraints.
Murderers are not innocent:

```
25  :- holds(innocent(P)),
26     holds(murderer(P)).
```

A person cannot be seen together with people who are out of town:

```
27  :- holds(out_of_town(A)),
28      holds(together(A,B)).
```

Friends know each other:

```
29  :- -holds(know(A,B)),
30      holds(friends(A,B)).
```

A person who was out of town cannot be the murderer:

```
31  :- holds(murderer(P)),
32      holds(out_of_town(P)).
```

To display the answer we introduce relation *murderer* defined as follows:

```
33  murderer(P)  :- holds(murderer(P)).
```

The only answer set of this program contains *murderer(ben)*, correctly concluding that Ben is the murderer. Clearly, enough commonsense knowledge was added to get the unique answer. Actually not all of this knowledge is even necessary – some of the constraints can be dropped without influencing the result. (We advise the reader to see which constraints can be safely eliminated.)

To rewrite the program for use with choice rules of clingo; we replace line 18 by the following choice rule:

```
1{holds(murderer(andy));holds(murderer(ben));
holds(murderer(cole))}1.
```

The rest of the program remains the same.

Summary

In this chapter we discussed the method of solving a computational problem P by writing an ASP program Π_P whose answer sets correspond to the problem's solutions and then using ASP solvers to find those solutions. Π_P normally consists of several parts: a knowledge base containing general knowledge related to the problem, a description of a particular instance of the problem, and a generator of possible solutions. Informally the last element is used to generate candidates for the solutions of the problem instance, whereas the first two parts are used to check if a candidate is indeed a solution. The general knowledge about the Hamiltonian cycles problem from Section 6.1 is recorded by the rules on lines 1–15. The candidate solution generation rule is given on line 16 (or by its choice rule alternative). The problem instance corresponding to Figure 6.1 is given on lines 17–20. It may be interesting to note that, in the Hamiltonian cycle example, relevant knowledge takes the form of the definition of Hamiltonian cycle and is completely separate from generation.

In the Sudoku examples the definition of a solution of the Sudoku puzzle consists of rules on lines 1–24. Note that it includes the generating rule (which says that such a solution must be a function assigning numbers to coordinates). The specific instance is given on lines 25–30.

In the mystery puzzle the precise mathematical definition of the solution does not exist. Instead the rules on lines 19–32 contain commonsense knowledge about the meaning of terms used in the story. As was mentioned earlier, these rules are not the definitions of the corresponding relations. They only contain partial knowledge about those relations represented by logic programming constraints. As a result a lot of negative information about them is missing. Fortunately, this lack of knowledge does not prevent us from correctly solving the problem.

The examples discussed in this chapter covered a number of different computational tasks. In the next few chapters, we use the same techniques to solve several classical AI problems including those related to planning and diagnostics. First, however, we present the basic algorithms for computing answer sets of a logic program.

References and Further Reading

Answer set programming as the method of solving nontrivial search problems was first advocated in Marek and Truszczynski (1999) and Niemela (1999). The method only became possible because of the development of a number of efficient answer set solvers Simons (1996), Smodels Web Page, Gebser et al. (n.d.), DLV Web Page, and Lierler and Marateo (n.d.). *Answer Set Solving in Practice* (Gebser et al. 2012) is a great introduction to practical applications of ASP with emphasis on efficiency and multiple advanced features of ASP languages not covered in our book. Results comparing the expressive power of Answer Set Prolog and propositional logic can be found in Lifschitz and Razborov (2006). A system solving puzzles formulated in natural language by translating them into formal ASP problems is described in Baral and Dzifcak (2012). Another ASP based "puzzle solver" that uses its own input language for formulating puzzles can be found in Truszczynski, Marek, and Finkel (2006).

Exercises

1. Run the Hamiltonian cycle program on graphs represented by the following statements. Give the answer set(s).

   (a) `vertex(a).    vertex(b).    vertex(c).`
       `edge(a,b).    edge(b,c).    edge(c,a).`
       `init(a).`

   (b) Same as exercise (1a) except replace `edge(c,a)` by `edge(a,c)`.

   (c) `vertex(a).    vertex(b).    vertex(c).    vertex(d).`
       `edge(a,b).    edge(b,c).    edge(c,d).    edge(d,a).`
       `edge(c,a).    edge(a,a).`
       `init(a).`

   (d) Same as exercise (1) except add

       `edge(b,a).    edge(c,b).    edge(d,c).    edge(a,d).`

2. Give the answer sets for the following program:

   ```
   q(a).
   q(b).
   1{p(X):q(X)}2.
   ```

3. Give the answer sets for the following program:

   ```
   {p(a);p(b)}2.
   ```

4. Suppose we wanted to separate the definition of the Sudoku problem rules from the generating part (lines 1–5). We could replace it by

   ```
   num(1..9).
   coord(X,Y) :- num(X), num(Y).
   pos(I,X,Y) | -pos(I,X,Y) :- num(I), coord(X,Y).
   ```

   What rules should be added to the program to complete the solution of the Sudoku problem? *Hint:* Encode the information necessary to describe the puzzle requirement that every location must be filled in with a unique number.

5. In the mystery puzzle, it is debatable whether the rule on lines 31–32 about murderers being in town is a valid assumption. Is it necessary to solve the crime?

6. Use a solver to find the answer set for the mystery program without suppressing the output of other predicates.

(a) Does the program correctly reject the rest of Ben's testimony?

(b) What would happen if anyone could be lying? Remove the rules on lines 14–17 and test whether the program conforms to your intuition.

(c) What if we were to assume that friends do not murder each other? For simplicity, just use rule

```
:- holds(friends(P,vinny)), murderer(P).
```

which states that a friend of Vinny's would not murder him. What happens when you add this rule to the original program? Why?

7. Given a round table with ten chairs and a group of ten people, some of whom are married and some of whom do not like each other, use ASP to find a seating assignment for members of this group such that husbands and wives are seated next to each other and no neighbors dislike each other.

7

Algorithms for Computing Answer Sets

In this chapter we give a short introduction to algorithms for computing answer sets of logic programs. These algorithms form the basis for the implementations of answer set solvers and query-answering systems used in previous chapters. For simplicity we limit ourselves to logic programs without classical negation $\neg$ and constraints (rules with an empty head). This is not a serious restriction because $\neg$ and constraints can always be eliminated from any program Π using Proposition 2.4.4.

The algorithms that we describe can be viewed as typical examples of generate-and-test reasoning algorithms. They have their roots in the Davis-Putnam procedure for finding models of propositional formulas. Understanding this procedure is a stepping-stone to understanding the generate-and-test algorithms implemented in ASP solvers.

7.1 Finding Models of Propositional Formulas

The Davis-Putnam procedure forms the basis of satisfiability solvers; it finds models of propositional formulas by traversing a tree of all possible truth assignments for the variables in that formula. For example, let F be a propositional formula, say

$$F = (X_1 \vee X_2) \wedge \neg X_2.$$

The tree in Figure 7.1 shows all possible assignments of truth values to variables of F. The algorithm traverses the tree looking for a path satisfying F. A simple depth-first search with backtracking allows us to find a path $\langle t, f \rangle$, which is a model of F.

It is clear that the efficiency of this algorithm depends on the ordering of variables and the efficiency of testing if a vector $\bar{X}$ of variables falsifies a propositional formula. For instance, a model of $F \vee (X_3 \vee \neg X_3)$ where F is an arbitrary formula could be found quickly if we were to start by assigning a value to X_3, and if our checking part were smart enough

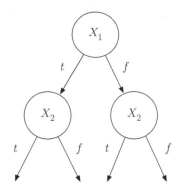

Figure 7.1. All Possible Truth Value Assignments for X_1 and X_2

to recognize that no other variable needs to be examined – an arbitrary
assignment of values to these variables would produce a model. Numerous
papers address the problem of finding an effective ordering, data structures,
and algorithms that would allow for efficient implementations of the Davis-
Putnam procedure. Here we describe a simple basic algorithm. Before we
go into the details of the algorithm, we define the necessary terminology:

- A *signature* is a set of propositional variables.
- A *clause* over signature Σ is a set $\{l_1, \ldots, l_n\}$ of literals of Σ denoting
  the disjunction $l_1 \vee \cdots \vee l_n$.
- A *formula* is a set $\{C_1, \ldots, C_m\}$ of clauses denoting the conjunction
  $C_1 \wedge \cdots \wedge C_m$.[1]
- A *partial interpretation* is a mapping of a set of propositional variables
  from Σ into truth values. We identify a partial interpretation I with
  the set of literals made true by I. For any variable p from the domain
  of I, if $p \in I$ we say that p is *true* in I; if $\neg p \in I$ then p is *false* in I.
- An *interpretation* is a partial interpretation defined on all variables of
  the language.
- A *model* of a formula F is an interpretation that makes the formula
  true.
- A formula is called *satisfiable* if it has a model.
- Partial interpretation I_2 is *compatible* with partial interpretation I_1 if
  $I_1 \subseteq I_2$.
- Variable p is *undefined* in partial interpretation I if it does not belong
  to the domain of I.

---

[1] Of course, the standard definition of a propositional formula is more general, but the restriction
is not overly strong because any such formula can be equivalently written as a conjunction of
clauses.

We are interested in the development of an algorithm $Sat(F)$ that takes a formula F as an input and returns a model of F if F is satisfiable and boolean value *false* otherwise. To define the algorithm recursively, we first describe a function $Sat(I, F)$ that searches for a model of formula F over signature Σ compatible with partial interpretation I. To find a model of F we then simply call $Sat(\emptyset, F)$. Here is the algorithm followed by a more detailed explanation.

function Sat
    input: partial interpretation I_0 and formula F_0;
    output: a pair $\langle I, true \rangle$ where I is a model of F_0 compatible with I_0;
            $\langle I_0, false \rangle$ if no such model exists;
var F : formula; I : partial interpretation; X : boolean;
begin
    $F := F_0$;
    $I := I_0$;
    $\langle F, I, X \rangle := Cons(F, I)$;
    if $X = false$ **then**
        return $\langle I_0, false \rangle$;
    if $F = \emptyset$ **then**
        return $\langle I, true \rangle$;
    select variable p undefined in I;
    $\langle I, X \rangle := Sat(I, F \cup \{p\})$;
    if $X = true$ **then**
        return $\langle I, true \rangle$;
    return $Sat(I, F \cup \{\overline{p}\})$;
end;

After initialization of F and I, Sat calls function $Cons$, which computes consequences of F and I, adds these consequences to I, and uses them to simplify F. If no contradiction is derived, the function returns *true* and the updated F and I; otherwise it returns *false* and the original formula and interpretation. (Later we describe a particular implementation of function $Cons$ that is called *unit propagation*.) Next we have two termination conditions. If $Cons$ finds a contradiction, Sat returns *false*. The second condition checks for success. Note that if $F = \emptyset$ then every element of F is vacuously satisfiable and so is F; thus, the function returns *true* together with the new I. It is not difficult to show that I is a desired model of F. If neither condition holds, Sat makes a nondeterministic choice of a yet undefined variable p of F and calls itself recursively.

Now we are ready to define our version of function $Cons$.

function $Cons$ [Unit Propagation];
    input: partial interpretation I_0 and formula F_0 with signature Σ_0;
    output: $\langle F, I, true \rangle$ where I is a partial interpretation such that $I_0 \subseteq I$

and F is a formula over signature Σ_0 such that
M is a model of F_0 compatible with I_0 iff
M is a model of F compatible with I;
$\langle F_0, I_0, false \rangle$ if no such model exists;
var F : formula; I : partial interpretation;
begin
   $F := F_0$;
   $I := I_0$;
   while F contains a unary clause $\{l\}$ **do**
        remove from F all clauses containing l;
        remove from F all occurrences of $\bar{l}$;
     $I := I \cup \{l\}$;
   if $\{\ \} \in F$ **then**
       return $\langle F_0, I_0, false \rangle$;
   return $\langle F, I, true \rangle$;
end;

Note that the condition $\{\ \} \in F$ is used to check if F is already shown to be unsatisfiable. To better understand this condition, note that to satisfy a clause we need to satisfy at least one element in it. Hence, the empty clause is unsatisfiable, and so is the collection F of clauses containing the empty clause. Note also that each call to $Cons$ eliminates occurrences of at least one literal from F, and hence Sat will eventually terminate.

Example 7.1.1. *(Tracing Sat)*
To illustrate the algorithm let us trace the computation of $Sat(I_0, F_0)$ where

$$I_0 = \emptyset$$

and

$$F_0 = \{\{X_1\}, \{\neg X_1, X_2, X_3\}, \{\neg X_1, X_4\}\}$$

First, function $Cons$ goes through two iterations of the loop and returns *true* together with

$$F = \{\{X_2, X_3\}\}$$

and

$$I = \{X_1, X_4\}.$$

It is easy to check that M is a model of F compatible with I iff it is a model of F_0 compatible with I_0. (This, of course, will be true after every iteration of the loop.) The termination conditions in Sat are not satisfied, so the algorithm selects a variable occurring in F and not occurring in I, say X_2, and calls

$$Sat(\{X_1, X_4\}, \{\{X_2, X_3\}, \{X_2\}\}).$$

The new call to $Cons$ returns $I = \{X_1, X_4, X_2\}$ and $F = \emptyset$. Now the second termination condition is satisfied and hence Sat returns $\langle\{X_1, X_4, X_2\}, true\rangle$.

Notice that I is a partial interpretation and hence, strictly speaking, is not a model of the original formula F_0. To make it a model we simply assign arbitrary values to variables that are not in I (in our case, to X_3).

The Sat algorithm is a typical example of the generate-and-test reasoning algorithms used for solving many complex problems in computer science. The practical efficiency of such algorithms depends on several factors including the following:

- The quality of the ordering of variables that determine the selection of an undefined variable in the Sat algorithm: Such orderings are frequently done by *heuristics* – rules of thumb proved to be useful by experience. One can, for instance, use the heuristic that selects the variable and its boolean value that satisfies the maximum number of yet unsatisfied clauses. Sometimes it may be useful to select a variable with the maximum number of occurrences in clauses of a minimum length – doing so increases our chances of arriving at an unsatisfiable clause or of obtaining a unary clause. In many cases the useful heuristics are much more complex and are based on the previous history of computation (e.g., a variable is selected from a clause that has caused the maximum number of conflicts). In all these cases the quality of a heuristic for a particular class of problems is normally determined by extensive experimentation.
- The quality of the procedure computing consequences of a program and a new partial interpretation: The procedure should balance the ability to compute a large number of consequences (which would of course allow a substantial decrease in the search space) and the efficiency of computing these consequences.
- The quality of data structures and the corresponding algorithms used in the actual implementation.

There is a substantial body of knowledge accumulated by computer scientists that allows the designers of solvers to make good choices related to these and other factors. In particular, the designers of answer set solvers have learned a great deal from the research on the design of Sat solvers.

We now describe two algorithms that adapt the basic ideas of Sat to the design of ASP solvers.

7.2 Finding Answer Sets of Logic Programs

Algorithms for computing answer sets of a logic program consist of two steps. In the first step of the computation, the algorithm replaces a program Π, which normally contains variables, by its ground instantiation $ground(\Pi)$. In practical systems $ground(\Pi)$ is not the full set of all syntactically constructible instances of the rules of Π; rather, it is an (often much smaller) subset having precisely the same answer sets as Π. The ability of the grounding procedure to construct small ground instantiation of the program may dramatically affect the performance of the entire system. The grounding techniques implemented by answer set solvers are rather sophisticated. Among other things, they use algorithms from deductive databases and require a good understanding of the relationship among various semantics of logic programming. Nevertheless, the grounding of a program containing variables over large domains can be prohibitively large, which has led to the recent development of answer set solvers that only do partial grounding.

Once the variables have been eliminated from Π, the heart of the computation is then performed by a function we call $Solver$. In this book we present two versions of the function, $Solver1$ and $Solver2$, which work for programs without $\neg$, *or*, and constraints. The first one uses a simple algorithm for computing consequences of the guessing decisions and is readily expandable to disjunctive programs. The second has a more sophisticated computation of consequences and is more efficient but is tailored toward non-disjunctive programs. Even though the structure of $Solver$ is very similar to that of Sat, it works on different objects with sightly different definitions of interpretation, consistency, and so on. Here is the corresponding terminology:

- By *program* we mean a ground logic program without $\neg$, *or*, and constraints.
- By *extended literal*, or simply *e-literal*, over signature Σ we mean a literal of Σ possibly preceded by default negation *not*. By *not l* we denote $not\ p(\bar{t})$ if $l = p(\bar{t})$ and $p(\bar{t})$ if $l = not\ p(\bar{t})$.
- A set of e-literals is called *consistent* if it contains no e-literals of the form l and *not l*.
- A *partial interpretation* of Σ is a consistent set of ground e-literals of Σ. If a partial interpretation I is complete (i.e., for any atom p of Σ either $p \in I$ or *not* $p \in I$), then I is called an *interpretation*.

- An atom p can be *true* $(p \in I)$, *false* $(not\ p \in I)$, or *undefined* $(p \notin I,\ not\ p \notin I)$ with respect to a partial interpretation I.
- An answer set A of a program Π will be represented as an interpretation I of the signature of Π such that

$$I = \{p(\bar{t}) : p(\bar{t}) \in A\} \cup \{not\ p(\bar{t}) : p(\bar{t}) \notin A\}.$$

- A set A of ground atoms is called *compatible* with partial interpretation I if for every ground atom $p(\bar{t})$, if $p(\bar{t}) \in I$ then $p(\bar{t}) \in A$ and if $not\ p(\bar{t}) \in I$ then $p(\bar{t}) \notin A$. A ground program Π is *compatible* with I if it has an answer set compatible with I.

Now we are ready to define our first answer set finding algorithm, $Solver1$.

7.2.1 The First Solver

The Main Program

```
function Solver1
    input: partial interpretation I₀ and program Π₀;
    output: ⟨I, true⟩ where I is an answer set of Π₀ compatible with I₀;
            ⟨I₀, false⟩ if no such answer set exists;
var Π : program; I : set of e-literals; X : boolean;
begin
    Π := Π₀;
    I := I₀;
    ⟨Π, I, X⟩ := Cons1(I, Π);
    if X = false then
        return ⟨I₀, false⟩;
    if no atom is undefined in I then
        if IsAnswerSet(I, Π₀) then
            return ⟨I, true⟩;
        return ⟨I₀, false⟩;
    select a ground atom p undefined in I;
    ⟨I, X⟩ := Solver1(I ∪ {p}, Π);
    if X = true then
        return ⟨I, X⟩;
    return Solver1((I \ {p}) ∪ {not p}, Π);
end;
```

$Solver1$ starts by initializing variables Π and I and calling a function $Cons1(\Pi, I)$, which expands I by a collection of e-literals that can be inferred from Π and I and uses it to simplify Π. If no contradiction is inferred in the process, $Cons1$ returns the new partial interpretation I and the simplified program, together with the boolean value *true*. Otherwise, it returns the original input together with *false*.

The call to $Cons1$ is followed by two termination conditions. First, $Solver1$ checks if $Cons1$ returns *false*. If so, I_0 is inconsistent with Π_0 and $Solver1$ returns *false*. Second, it checks whether partial interpretation I is complete (i.e., if for every atom p either p or *not* p belongs to I). If this is the case then $Solver1$ checks whether I is an answer set. If the answer is *yes* then the function returns *true* together with I. Otherwise, there is no answer set of Π_0 compatible with I_0 and the function returns *false*. If Π still contains some undefined atoms, the function selects such an atom p; $Solver1$ is (recursively) called to explore whether I can be expanded to an answer set of Π containing p. If this is impossible, then $Solver1$ searches for an answer set of Π containing *not* p. If one of these calls succeeds, then the function stops and returns *true* together with I. On the failure of both calls, the function returns *false*, because I cannot be expanded to any answer set. As in the case of Sat, an answer set of Π is computed by calling $Solver1(\emptyset, \Pi)$.

Lower Bound – First Refinement of the Consequence Function

Now let us discuss a comparatively simple version of function $Cons1$ traditionally called LB (where LB stands for *lower bound*). A different version of $Cons1$ is discussed later. In what follows we use the traditional name.

Function LB computes the consequences of its parameters, Π and I, using the following four *inference rules*:

(1) If the body of a rule is a subset of I, then its head must be in I.

(2) If atom $p \in I$ belongs to the head of exactly one rule of Π, then the e-literals from the body of this rule must be in I.

(3) If $(not\ p_0) \in I$, $(p_0 \leftarrow B_1, p, B_2) \in \Pi$, and $B_1, B_2 \subseteq I$, then *not* p must be in I.

(4) If Π contains no rule with head p_0, then *not* p_0 must be in I.

Let $1 \le i \le 3$ be one of the first three inference rules just defined, Π be a program, I be a partial interpretation, and r be a rule of Π. The set of i-consequences of Π, I, and r, denoted by $i\text{-}cons(i, \Pi, I, r)$, is defined as follows: If the *if part* of i is satisfied by Π, I, and r, then $i\text{-}cons(i, \Pi, I, r)$ is the set of e-literals from the i's *then part*. Otherwise, $i\text{-}cons(i, \Pi, I, r) = \emptyset$. (Notice that, for the first inference rule, function $i\text{-}cons$ does not require Π as a parameter, but we nevertheless include it for uniformity of notation.) If $i = 4$ then $i\text{-}cons(i, \Pi, I)$ is the set of literals that do not occur in the heads of rules of Π not falsified by I. Function $LB(I, \Pi)$ can be computed as follows:

function LB
    input: partial interpretation I_0 and program Π_0 with signature Σ_0;
    output: $\langle \Pi, I, true \rangle$ where I is a partial interpretation such that $I_0 \subseteq I$
              and Π is a program with signature Σ_0 such that for every A
              A is an answer set of Π_0 compatible with I_0 iff
              A is an answer set of Π compatible with I;
        $\langle \Pi_0, I_0, false \rangle$ if there is no answer set of Π_0 compatible with I_0;
var I, T : set of e-literals; Π : program;
begin
    $I := I_0$;
    $\Pi := \Pi_0$;
    repeat
        $T := I$;
        remove from Π all the rules whose bodies are falsified by I;
        remove from the bodies of rules of Π all e-literals of the form *not l* satisfied by I;
        select an inference rule i from (1)–(4);
        if $1 \le i \le 3$ **then**
            for every $r \in \Pi$ satisfied by the *if part* of inference rule i
                $I := I \cup i\text{-}cons(i, \Pi, I, r)$;
        else
            $I := I \cup i\text{-}cons(4, \Pi, I)$;
    until $I = T$;
    if I is consistent **then**
        return $\langle \Pi, I, true \rangle$;
    return $\langle \Pi_0, I_0, false \rangle$;
end;

First, function LB initializes variables I and Π and simplifies Π by removing from it any rules and e-literals made useless by I. Then LB selects an inference rule (1)–(4) and uses it to expand I by e-literals derived by this rule. The process continues until no more e-literals can be added. If the resulting set I is consistent, LB returns I, the simplified Π, and *true*; otherwise, it returns the original parameters and *false*.

The following example illustrates the function:

Example 7.2.1. *(Tracing LB)*
Consider program P_1:

$$p(a) \leftarrow not\ q(a).$$
$$p(b) \leftarrow not\ q(b).$$
$$q(a).$$

with the signature determined by the rules of the program, and trace the execution of $LB(\emptyset, P_1)$. Initially I and T are set to $\emptyset$, whereas Π is set to P_1. Application of the two simplifying rules of LB does not change Π. Now the function nondeterministically selects an inference rule. Suppose it selects inference rule (1). The bodies of the first two rules of the program are not satisfied by $\emptyset$. The body of the third rule is empty and hence is satisfied by any set of e-literals, including the empty one. Thus, applying inference rule (1) to the program produces one consequence, $q(a)$, which is added to I.

On the next iteration the simplification deletes the first program rule and hence Π consists of the second and third rule of P_1. Suppose that the inference rule selected next is (4). Since neither $p(a)$ nor $q(b)$ belongs to the heads of the rules of the simplified program, I becomes $\{q(a),\ not\ p(a),\ not\ q(b)\}$.

On the third iteration Π is further simplified to become $\{p(b).\quad q(a).\}$; LB again selects inference rule (1), applies it to the first rule of Π, and sets I to $\{q(a),\ not\ p(a),\ not\ q(b),\ p(b)\}$. Since the next iteration does not produce any new consequences and I is consistent, LB returns $\langle I, \Pi, true \rangle$.

Defining $IsAnswerSet$

Now we discuss a simple algorithm for computing function $IsAnswerSet(I, \Pi)$:

function $IsAnswerSet$
  input: interpretation I and program Π;
  output: *true* if I is an answer set of Π; *false* otherwise;
begin
  Compute the reduct, Π^I of Π with respect to I;
  Compute the answer set, A, of Π^I;
  Check whether $A = atoms(I)$ and return the result;
end;

The first and the last steps of the function are relatively straightforward, but the second one requires some elaboration. We need the following concept: A program Π is called **definite** if Π is a collection of rules of the form

$$p_0 \leftarrow p_1, \ldots, p_n$$

where ps are atoms of signature of Π. (In other words Π contains no default negation.)

Let Π be a definite program and T_Π be an operator defined on sets of atoms from the signature of Π as follows:

$$T_\Pi(A) = \{p_0 :\ p_0 \leftarrow p_1, \ldots, p_n \in \Pi,\ p_1, \ldots, p_n \subseteq A\}.$$

Intuitively, $T_\Pi(A)$ returns conclusions of all rules of Π whose bodies are satisfied by A. We use this operator to describe function $Least(\Pi)$, which takes as a parameter a finite definite program Π and returns its answer set. Since by definition of the reduct Π^I is obviously definite, this function can be used to find its answer set.

function *Least*
   input: a definite program Π;
   output: the answer set of Π;
var X, X_0 : set of atoms;
begin
  $X := \emptyset$;
  repeat
    $X_0 := X$;
    $X := T_\Pi(X)$;
  until $X = X_0$;
  return X;
end;

The following example illustrates the computation:

Example 7.2.2. *(Least)*
Consider a program

$$p(a) \leftarrow q(a).$$
$$q(a).$$

Its answer set is obtained as the result of the following computation:

$$T_\Pi(\emptyset) \Rightarrow T_\Pi(\{q(a)\}) \Rightarrow T_\Pi(\{q(a), p(a)\}) \Rightarrow \{q(a), p(a)\}.$$

It may be instructive to check that applying the same algorithm to $p(a) \leftarrow p(a)$ returns $\emptyset$.

This completes the refinement of $Solver1$. Now let us illustrate how it works by tracing several simple examples. (Remember that LB is just a different name for $Cons1$ from $Solver1$.)

Tracing *Solver1*

Example 7.2.3. *(A Simple Case)*
Consider program P_1 from the previous example:

$$p(a) \leftarrow not\ q(a).$$
$$p(b) \leftarrow not\ q(b).$$
$$q(a).$$

To compute the answer set of P_1, we call $Solver1(\emptyset, P_1)$, which starts by initializing Π and I and calling $LB(\emptyset, \Pi)$. As discussed in Example 7.2.1, function LB sets Π to

$$p(b).$$
$$q(a).$$

I to $\{q(a),\ not\ p(a),\ not\ q(b),\ p(b)\}$, and X to *true*. $Solver1$ discovers that, after the first application of LB, all the ground atoms from the signature of P_1 are defined. The last thing needed is to check if I is an answer set of Π. $Solver1$ calls $IsAnswerSet(I, P_1)$, which first computes the reduct P_1^I of P_1 with respect to I. By the definition of reduct we have, that P_1^I is

$$p(b).$$
$$q(a).$$

$Least(P_1^I) = \{q(a), p(b)\}$, which is equal to $atoms(I)$. Hence, $IsAnswerSet(I, P_1)$ returns *true* and the solver returns *true* together with the answer set I of the program.

It is easy to see that program P_1 from Example 7.2.3 is stratified (see Chapter 2) and hence has at most one answer set. The following example illustrates how $Solver1$ works on a program with multiple answer sets.

Example 7.2.4. *(Program with Multiple Answer Sets)*
Now let us compute an answer set of a program P_2:

$$p(a) \leftarrow\ not\ q(a).$$

$$q(a) \leftarrow\ not\ p(a).$$

$Solver1(\emptyset, P_2)$ initializes I and Π and calls $LB(\emptyset, \Pi)$. It is not difficult to see that Π cannot be simplified by $\emptyset$ and that no inference rule used by LB is applicable to the program. Hence LB returns *true* without changing I and Π. $I = \emptyset$, no atom is yet defined, and $Solver1$ starts the selection process. Let us assume that $Solver1$ selects $p(a)$ and makes the recursive call $Solver1(\{p(a)\}, \Pi)$, which, in turn, calls $LB(\{p(a)\}, \Pi)$. After the simplification Π becomes

$$p(a) \leftarrow\ not\ q(a).$$

Suppose that LB selects inference rule (2). It is applicable to the rule of the program, so LB computes a new consequence, $not\ q(a)$; I becomes $\{p(a),\ not\ q(a)\}$ and Π becomes

$$p(a).$$

(Another possibility is to select inference rule (4) instead of (2); this would lead to the same result.) Next, function $IsAnswerSet(\{p(a),\ not\ q(a)\}, P_2)$ computes P_2^I:

$$p(a).$$

and discovers that $Least(P_2^I) = atoms(I)$; hence, $\{p(a)\}$ is an answer set of P_2. A different choice of a selected e-literal would lead to finding another answer set of the program, $\{q(a)\}$.

Now let us consider a program without answer sets.

Example 7.2.5. *(Detecting Inconsistency)*
Consider a program P_3:

$$p(a) \leftarrow\ not\ p(a).$$

and trace the execution of $Solver1(\emptyset, P_3)$. After the initialization the function calls $LB(\emptyset, \Pi)$. Since no simplification is possible and no inference rule is applicable to Π, $LB(\emptyset, \Pi)$ returns *true* without changing $I = \emptyset$ and $\Pi = P_3$, and $Solver1$ starts its selection process. If $p(a)$ is selected first, then the solver recursively calls $Solver1(\{p(a)\}, \Pi)$. This, in turn, calls $LB(\{p(a)\}, \Pi)$. After the simplification $\Pi = \emptyset$. By inference rule (4) LB concludes *not* $p(a)$, detects inconsistency, and returns *false* together with $\{p(a)\}$. The next call is $Solver1(\{not\ p(a)\}, \Pi)$. This time $LB(\{not\ p(a)\}, \Pi)$ simplifies Π to $p(a)$. Using rule (1) LB obtains inconsistency and $Solver1$ returns *false*. The program has no answer sets.

So far in all our examples $IsAnswerSet$ always returned *true*. In the next example this is not the case.

Example 7.2.6. *(The Importance of $IsAnswerSet$)*
Consider a program P_4:

$$p(a) \leftarrow p(a).$$

and call $Solver1(\emptyset, P_4)$. The program cannot be simplified by $\emptyset$ and none of the four inference rules of LB are applicable to this program, so $LB(\emptyset, \Pi)$ returns *true* without changing I and Π. Now $Solver1$ may select $p(a)$ and call $Solver1(\{p(a)\}, \Pi)$. $LB(\{p(a)\}, \Pi)$ sets I to $\{p(a)\}$, does not change Π and returns *true*. All atoms of P_4 are now defined and $Solver1$ calls $IsAnswerSet(\{p(a)\}, P_4)$. The reduct $P_4^I = \Pi$. Obviously, $Least(\Pi) = \emptyset$. Now $IsAnswerSet(\{p(a)\}, P_4)$ compares $\emptyset$ and $\{p(a)\}$, discovers that they are not equal, and returns *false*. $Solver1$ tries another choice, selects $not\ p(a)$, and eventually correctly returns $\{not\ p(a), true\}$.

7.2.2 The Second Solver

In this section we give a different algorithm for computing answer sets of a program. The new algorithm, called $Solver2$, uses a more powerful method for computing consequences than the one used by function LB. In fact, the method is so powerful that checking whether the computed interpretation is indeed an answer set of the program is no longer necessary.

The new consequences-computing function $Cons2$ expands $Cons1$ by computing more negative consequences of the program. (For example, $Cons2$ is able to compute $not\ p$ as a consequence of a program $p(a) \leftarrow p(a)$ with respect to $I = \emptyset$, whereas $Cons1$ cannot.) The computation of these new consequences is done by a new function, $UB(I, \Pi)$, called the **upper bound** of I with respect to Π. Eventually we define $Cons2$ in terms of both functions, LB and UB.

function UB
    input: partial interpretation I_0 and program Π_0 with signature Σ_0;
    output: A set N of e-literals of the form $not\ p$ such that for every A
        A is an answer set of Π_0 compatible with I_0 iff
        A is an answer set of Π_0 compatible with $N \cup I_0$;
var M : partial interpretation; Π : program;
begin
    Let Π be the definite program obtained from Π_0 by
        removing from Π_0 all the rules whose bodies are falsified by I_0 and then
        removing all other occurrences of e-literals of the form $not\ p$;
    $M := Least(\Pi)$;
    $M := \{not\ p : p \in \Sigma_0 \text{ and } p \notin M\}$;
    return M;
end;

Example 7.2.7. *(Upper Bound 1)*
Let us trace $UB(\emptyset, P_4)$ where P_4 is

$$p(a) \leftarrow p(a).$$

First Π is set to P_4. It is easy to see that no simplification of Π by $\emptyset$ is possible and that $Least(\Pi) = \emptyset$. Since the only atom in the signature of Π is $p(a)$, function $UB(\emptyset, \Pi)$ returns $\{not\ p(a)\}$.

Example 7.2.8. *(Upper Bound 2)*
Consider now a program P_5

$$p(a) \leftarrow s(a),\ not\ q(a).$$

This time Π is set to P_5 and $UB(\emptyset, \Pi)$ simplifies Π. Now Π is

$$p(a) \leftarrow s(a).$$

$Least(\Pi)$ returns $\emptyset$. There are three atoms in the signature of P_5: $p(a)$, $q(a)$, and $s(a)$. Hence UB returns $\{not\ p(a), not\ q(a), not\ s(a)\}$.

Now we are ready to define $Cons2$. The function computes consequences of I with respect to Π using both LB and UB.

function $Cons2$
    input: partial interpretation I_0 and program Π_0 with signature Σ_0;
    output: $\langle \Pi, I, true \rangle$ where I is a partial interpretation such that $I_0 \subseteq I$
                 and Π is a program with signature Σ_0 such that
                 A is an answer set of Π_0 compatible with I_0 iff
                 A is an answer set of Π compatible with I;
            $\langle \Pi_0, I_0, false \rangle$ if there is no answer set of Π_0 compatible with I_0;
var I, T : set of e-literals; Π : program; X : boolean;
begin
    $I := I_0$;
    $\Pi := \Pi_0$;
    $\langle \Pi, I, X \rangle := LB(I, \Pi)$;
    if $X = true$ **then**
        $T := UB(I, \Pi)$;
        $I := I \cup T$;
        if I is consistent **then**
            return $\langle \Pi, I, true \rangle$;
        return $\langle \Pi_0, I_0, false \rangle$;
end;

Example 7.2.9. *(Cons2 1)*
Consider program P_4 from Example 7.2.7 and trace $Cons2(\emptyset, P_4)$. Recall that P_4 consists of rule

$$p(a) \leftarrow p(a)$$

and that $LB(\emptyset, \Pi)$ where Π is set to P_4 returns $\langle \Pi, \emptyset, true \rangle$. As shown earlier, T is set to $\{not\ p(a)\}$ and the function returns

$$\langle \Pi, \{not\ p(a)\}, true \rangle.$$

Example 7.2.10. *(Cons2 2)*
Consider now a program P_6

$$p(a) \leftarrow s(a), p(a),\ not\ q(a).$$
$$s(a).$$

and trace $Cons2(\emptyset, P_6)$. As usual Π is set to P_6. This time LB returns $\langle \Pi, \{s(a), \ not \ q(a)\}, true \rangle$ where Π consists of the rules

$$p(a) \leftarrow s(a), p(a).$$
$$s(a).$$

and has the signature of P_6. UB sets T to $\{not \ p(a), not \ q(a)\}$ and $Cons2$ returns

$$\langle \Pi, \{s(a), \ not \ q(a), \ not \ p(a)\}, true \rangle.$$

Now we can give the new answer set finding algorithm $Solver2$:

function $Solver2$
    input: partial interpretation I_0 and program Π_0;
    output: $\langle I, true \rangle$ where I is an answer set of Π_0 compatible with I_0;
            $\langle I_0, false \rangle$ if no such answer set exists;
var Π : program; I : set of e-literals; X : boolean;
begin
    $\Pi := \Pi_0$;
    $I := I_0$;
    $\langle \Pi, I, X \rangle := Cons2(I, \Pi)$;
    if $X = false$ **then**
        return $\langle I_0, false \rangle$;
    if no atom is undefined in I **then**
        return $\langle I, true \rangle$;
    select a ground atom p undefined in I;
    $\langle I, X \rangle := Solver2(I \cup \{p\}, \Pi)$;
    if $X = true$ **then**
        return $\langle I, X \rangle$;
    return $Solver2(I \cup \{not \ p\}, \Pi)$;
end;

In comparing the efficiency of the two answer set solvers, one can see that $Solver1$ spends less time computing the consequences of the program, but pays for this by spending additional time checking if the computed interpretation is an answer set. $Solver2$ spends more time computing consequences, but does not need the additional checking. Extensive experimentation has shown that the second method of computing this function is usually more efficient. In this case spending more time in computing consequences and avoiding the checking increase the efficiency of the solver. Note, however, that the correctness of the second solver is much less obvious than that of the first. In fact the theorem showing that the interpretation computed by $Solver2$ is an answer set of the program is rather nontrivial.

Another way to improve performance of answer set solvers is to employ a good heuristic for the selection of undefined ground atoms. Selection of a good heuristic is an interesting and important topic for any generate-and-test algorithm. There is a substantial body of research related to the subject. In fact, the area of search and heuristics deserves its own course. In this section we only briefly mention a particular heuristic used in some answer set solvers. The heuristic is rather application-independent and leads to good performance across a range of applications. It can be taken as a starting point for developing more-refined heuristics for particular application areas. First, we replace the selection of an atom by selection of an e-literal. There is no reason to try an atom p first. Sometimes *not* p can do as well or better. Next we try to select an e-literal that has the greatest possibility of changing current partial interpretation I, thereby helping the algorithm discover conflicts or find complete sets of e-literals with a minimal number of choices. For illustrative purposes we give a simple refinement of this idea. First we need a definition. A rule

$$p_0 \leftarrow p_1, \ldots, p_m, \ not \ p_{m+1}, \ldots \ not \ p_n$$

is called *applicable* with respect to a partial interpretation I if

1. $\{p_1, \ldots, p_m\} \subseteq I$,
2. there is no k such that $m + 1 \leq k \leq n$ and $p_k \in I$, and
3. $p_0 \notin I$.

The heuristic *selects an e-literal* not p *from the body of an applicable rule with the least number of negated atoms not belonging to* I. For instance, if $I = \{b, \ not \ f\}$ and Π consists of two rules

$$a \leftarrow b, \ not \ c, \ not \ d$$
$$a \leftarrow b, \ not \ e, \ not \ f$$

the heuristic selects *not* e. The selection ensures that a is immediately added to I. If we were to select, say, *not* c, the expansion of I would have to wait for the next selection of an atom.

7.2.3 Finding Answer Sets of Disjunctive Programs

So far we have only discussed solvers for logic programs not containing disjunction. Dealing with disjunctive programs requires some additional ideas that we briefly discuss in this section. This additional difficulty is not surprising because it follows from the theoretical analysis of the complexity of these two tasks. Finding answer sets of programs not containing epistemic disjunction is an NP-complete problem; therefore, testing (in our case done by $IsAnswerSet$) can be performed in polynomial time (or even eliminated altogether). The problem of computing answer sets for disjunctive programs belongs to a higher complexity class, and hence, checking if a given set of literals is an answer set cannot always be done in polynomial time. (There are, however, large classes of disjunctive logic programs for which the complexity of computing answer sets is NP-complete. Actually *all* of the disjunctive programs we considered so far belong to such a class.) This complexity consideration implies that $Solver2$, which does not check if a computed interpretation is an answer set of a program, cannot be easily adapted to deal with disjunction. $Solver1$, however, is more amenable to change. All we need to do is to replace function $IsAnswerSet$ by a more complex version that works for disjunctive programs. Instead of using a simple computation incorporated in $Least$, we need to check that I satisfies all the rules of the program and, more importantly, that there is no I' such that $atoms(I') \subset atoms(I)$ that also satisfies these rules. This second condition is exactly the one that adds complexity to the algorithm.

7.2.4 Answering Queries

The method for computing answer sets of ASP programs illustrated in the previous section can be used to implement STUDENT-like query-answering systems of ASP. Suppose, for instance, that we are given a consistent program Π and would like to know the answer to a ground query q where q is a literal. The following algorithm allows us to answer this question. (Note that by the call to $Solver$ in this algorithm, we mean $Solver1$ or $Solver2$, whichever implementation is appropriate.)

function $Query$
    input: ground literal l and consistent program Π;
    output: *yes* if l is true in all answer sets of Π,
           no if $\bar{l}$ is true in all answer sets of Π,
           unknown otherwise;
begin
if $Solver(\emptyset, \Pi \cup \{\leftarrow \ not\ l\}) = false$ **then**
    return *yes*
if $Solver(\emptyset, \Pi \cup \{\leftarrow \ not\ \bar{l}\}) = false$ **then**
    return *no*;
return *unknown*;
end;

Of course the consistency of Π can be checked in advance by a single call to $Solver(\emptyset, \Pi)$.

To answer a query $q_1 \wedge \cdots \wedge q_n$ where qs are ground literals, we expand Π by rules:

$$
\begin{aligned}
q &\leftarrow q_1, \ldots, q_n \\
\neg q &\leftarrow \neg q_1 \\
&\vdots \\
\neg q &\leftarrow \neg q_n
\end{aligned}
$$

where q is a new atom. Denote the new program by Π'. Now the question can be answered by a single call to $Query(q, \Pi')$. A similar technique can be used to answer disjunctive query q_1 *or* $\ldots$ *or* q_n. In this case Π should be expanded by rules:

$$
\begin{aligned}
q &\leftarrow q_1 \\
&\vdots \\
q &\leftarrow q_n \\
\neg q &\leftarrow \neg q_1, \ldots, \neg q_n
\end{aligned}
$$

Not surprisingly, the approach does not apply to nonground queries. They can be answered by a simple (but not always efficient) algorithm that computes and stores all the answer sets of Π. The analysis of these answer sets allows to return all ground terms t such that query $q(t)$ is true in all the answer sets.

Summary

In this chapter we started by outlining a SAT algorithm for finding models of formulas of propositional logic. This algorithm can be viewed as a typical example of the generate-and-test reasoning algorithm used for solving many complex problems in computer science. We briefly discussed the general structure of such algorithms and several methods for improving their efficiency. Next we showed how the basic ideas of SAT could be adapted to the problem of computing answer sets of nondisjunctive logic programs. In particular we presented two versions of such an algorithm that differ primarily by the functions they use for computing consequences of a program and its new partial interpretation. A short discussion explained how these algorithms can be used to answer simple queries and how the first one could be adapted to work for disjunctive programs. Of course this is only a brief introduction. Serious study of SAT-like methods used to solve problems of non-polynomial complexity requires much more time. Moreover, we are far from fully understanding these algorithms. Many unanswered and fascinating questions remain – after all, many computational problems that need solutions are not polynomial. Discovering methods that allow us to find practical solutions to such problems is crucial for our understanding of computation and for many applications.

References and Further Reading

The Davis-Putnam algorithm for testing satisfiability of propositional formulas was introduced in Davis and Putnam (1960) and further elaborated in Davis, Logemann, and Loveland (1962). Marek (2009) gives a nice introduction and overview of the mathematics of satisfiability. Empirical evaluation of various SAT heuristics can be found, for instance, in Hoos and Stützle (2000). Our presentation of algorithms for computing answer sets of logic programs follows the basic ideas implemented in Smodels and early versions of DLV. See, for instance, Niemela, Simons, and Soininen (2002) and Leone et al. (2006). Recent work establishing close connections between computing answers sets and the SAT algorithms can be found in Lin and Zhao (2004) and Giunchiglia, Lierler, and Maratea (2006). Other approaches investigate computing answer sets via reasoning in difference logic (Janhunen, Niemela, and Sevalnev 2009), mixed integer programming (Liu, Janhunen, and Niemela 2012), and the like. There are also attempts to, at least partially, avoid grounding by integrating ASP-based techniques with that developed in constraint logic programming in Mellarkod, Gelfond, and Zhang (2008), Balduccini (2011), and Ostrowski and Schaub (2012). (See also a solver (Balduccini 2012) that gains efficiency by expanding ASP with non-herbrand functions.) Smart grounders, such as Lparse (Syrjanen 1998), `gringo` (Gebser, Schaub, and Thiele 2007), and DLV's grounder (Alviano et al. 2012) use techniques from deductive databases (Abiteboul, Hull, and Vianu, 1995) and research on logic programming semantics Fitting (1985) and Van Gelder, Ross, and Schlipf (1991). Information on complexity and expressive power of logic programs can be found in Dantsin et al. (2001). A state of the art of design and implementation of ASP solvers can be found in Gebser et al. (2012). Pearl (1984) gives a comprehensive overview of heuristic search theory.

Exercises

1. Given a formula $\{\{a, b, \neg c\}, \{a, \neg b\}, \{\neg b, c, d\}\}$ use the satisfiability algorithm to prove that the formula is satisfiable. *Hint:* Use a reasonable heuristic to order variables of the formula.

2. Given a program

$$\Pi \begin{cases} c \leftarrow a, \ not \ d. \\ a \leftarrow \ not \ b. \\ b \leftarrow \ not \ a. \end{cases}$$

trace the computation of
(a) $LB(\{a\}, \Pi)$
(b) $Solver1(\{a\}, \Pi)$
(c) $UB(I, \Pi)$ for I returned by LB from (a)
(d) $Cons2(\{a\}, \Pi)$
(e) $Solver2(\emptyset, \Pi)$

3. (a) Use Solver1 to compute answer set(s) of program Π shown next. (Assume that a and b are the only constants of the signature of Π.) Do not forget to first modify Π to eliminate classical negation $\neg$ and the constraints.

$$\Pi \begin{cases} p(a) \leftarrow \ not \ \neg p(b). \\ \neg p(b) \leftarrow \ not \ p(a). \\ p(a) \leftarrow \ not \ r(a). \\ r(a) \leftarrow \ not \ p(a). \\ q(X) \leftarrow \ not \ p(X). \\ \neg p(X) \leftarrow \ not \ p(X). \\ \leftarrow r(a). \\ r(b). \end{cases}$$

(b) How does Π answer queries

$?q(a) \qquad ?q(b)$
$?r(a) \qquad ?r(b)$

4. Modify $Solver2$ to find *all* answer sets of a given program.

5. Design an algorithm to answer nonground query $Q(X)$.

8

Modeling Dynamic Domains

So far, we have limited our attention to *static* domains – no attempt was made to represent a domain's evolution in time. Recall from the introduction that we are interested in agents that are intended to populate *dynamic*, changing domains and should therefore be able to plan, explain unexpected observations, and do other types of reasoning requiring the ability to predict effects of series of complex actions. This can be done only if the agent has sufficient knowledge about actions and their effects. In this chapter we discuss one of several current approaches to representing and reasoning with such knowledge. We start by looking at an extended example that illustrates some of the issues that arise when we attempt to represent actions and their effects on the world. Once some of these issues become clear, we present a general, formal theory of actions and change, with further examples on how to apply it to various domains. The theory views the world as a dynamic system whose states are changed by actions, and provides an "action language" for describing such systems. This language allows concise and mathematically accurate descriptions of the system's states and of possible state-action-state transitions; it allows us to represent dynamic domains and their laws. Such representations can be translated into ASP programs that are used to give the precise semantics of the language. Later, we show how this and similar translations can be used to answer queries about the effects of actions in a given situation. In keeping with our plan to separate the representation of our world from using that representation to perform intelligent tasks, we save the discussion of planning and other types of reasoning for later chapters in which we apply the knowledge of answer set programming that we presented previously.

8.1 The Blocks World – A Historic Example

In 1966 a group of researchers at SRI International (then known as the Stanford Research Institute) decided to build a reasoning robot. The result was Shakey (named for its jerky motions). The robot could receive a description of a goal from a human, make a plan, and execute the necessary actions to achieve the goal.

One task that the researchers believed a robot should be able to perform was to move blocks and create various configurations with them. This blocks world became what some have termed the "Drosophila of AI"[1] because this simple domain provided so much research potential. It has been especially popular in the planning community because of its simplicity and its search space that grows rapidly with the addition of blocks.

The work on Shakey that continued through 1972 brought to light many of the challenges involved in building and programming such a machine. Naturally, there were many hardware challenges. For example, making a robotic arm actually capable of picking something up turned out to be very difficult. Vision is also a very complex topic. A robot may have an onboard camera, but how does it parse out the necessary images? Shakey had to settle for pushing blocks around, and it could not evaluate whether it achieved the goal by seeing the result of its actions.

The software challenge turned out to be no less difficult. Many questions arose, such as the following:

- How do we represent knowledge?
- How do we teach a robot to use this knowledge to make plans?
- How do we teach a robot to evaluate if its execution of a plan was successful?
- How should the robot re-plan if there are changes?

Shakey used LISP and a theorem-proving planner called STRIPS. Its planning was domain-specific. Many planners that followed were also domain-specific, difficult to modify, and slow. Huge progress has been made since then, both in efficiency of the planners and in the kind of information they were able to represent. The approach we present separates representation of a domain from the reasoning done in that domain (i.e., teaching a computer about the laws of a world is separate from teaching it how to use this information for various tasks). This separation allows us to use the same method of representation for whatever domain we wish and

---

[1] The Drosophila fly, commonly known as the fruit fly, was chosen as a subject of study by geneticists because it was so easy to take care of and reproduced so quickly. It turned out that studying this little fly, so seemingly unlike humans, unlocked many secrets of our own genetic code. The blocks world, often criticized as a "toy" example so unlike the real world, nonetheless allowed scientists to learn much about commonsense reasoning in a changing world.

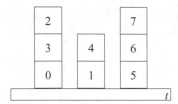

Figure 8.1. Initial Configuration

to use whatever reasoning algorithm we choose with our domain.[2] With the same information, an agent can plan its actions, attempt to explain unexpected events in the world, and so on. Separating the representation from the reasoning component allows for clearer and much more elaboration-tolerant programs.

Let's consider how a blocks-world problem can be encoded in ASP. First, let us define the particular version of the blocks world that we will use:

The **basic blocks world** consists of a robotic arm that can manipulate configurations of same-sized cubic blocks on a table. There are limitations to what the robotic arm can do. It can move *unoccupied* blocks, one at a time, onto other unoccupied blocks or onto the table. (An unoccupied block is one that does not have another block stacked on it.) At any given step, a block can be in at most one location; in other words, a block can be directly on top of one other block, or on the table. We do not impose a limit on how tall our towers can be. Our table is big enough to hold all the blocks, even if they are not stacked. We do not take into account spatial relationships of *towers*, just which *blocks* are on top of each other and which blocks are on the table.

Figures 8.1 and 8.2 illustrate an example problem in this domain. Blocks 0–7 are stacked on table t as shown in Figure 8.1. Our robot could, for example, turn this configuration into the one shown in Figure 8.2 by putting block 2 on the table and block 7 on block 2.

We would like to be able to write a program to model the transformation of the domain caused by the robotic arm's activity; that is, given an

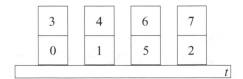

Figure 8.2. Final Configuration

---

[2] This does not mean that we cannot use domain-specific information to guide our reasoning. We show how we can do this with the logic-programming approach in Chapter 9.

initial position of blocks and a sequence of actions, our program should be able to answer queries about the positions of blocks after the execution of these actions. You should recall that writing a declarative program involves identifying the objects and the relations between the objects that you are interested in. The blocks and the table are some obvious objects. We would also like to talk about possible locations, so that we do not always have to distinguish between blocks and the table. We will denote blocks by $b0 \ldots b7$ and locations will be blocks plus the table (named t). To describe a configuration of blocks, we will use terms of the form $on(b, l)$ where b is a block and l is a location; the term states that block b is on location l. Thus, a configuration S is a set of terms $on(b, l) \in S$ if and only if b is on l. For instance, the configuration from Figure 8.1 can be described by a collection of terms

$$\sigma_0 = \{on(b0, t), on(b3, b0), on(b2, b3), on(b1, t), on(b4, b1),$$
$$on(b5, t), on(b6, b5), on(b7, b6)\}.$$

The action of the robotic arm moving block B to location L will be denoted by terms of the form $put(B, L)$. Action $put(b2, t)$ changes our initial configuration into

$$\sigma_1 = \{on(b0, t), on(b3, b0), on(b1, t), on(b4, b1), on(b2, t),$$
$$on(b5, t), on(b6, b5), on(b7, b6)\}.$$

Action $put(b7, b2)$ transforms block configuration σ_1 into configuration

$$\sigma_2 = \{on(b0, t), on(b3, b0), on(b1, t), on(b4, b1), on(b2, t),$$
$$on(b5, t), on(b6, b5), on(b7, b2)\}.$$

This matches Figure 8.2. The execution of a sequence of these two actions in configuration σ_0 determines the system's trajectory[3]

$$\langle \sigma_0, put(b2, t), \sigma_1, put(b7, b2), \sigma_2 \rangle$$

that describes its behavior.

    To describe the changes our system undergoes, we use integers from 0 to some finite n to denote *steps* of the corresponding trajectories. (We limit the length of the trajectory for computational reasons.) We also distinguish between **fluents** – properties that can be changed by actions (such as one

---

[3] By a trajectory of a dynamic system we mean a sequence $\langle \sigma_0, a_0, \sigma_1, \ldots, \sigma_{n-1}, a_{n-1}, \sigma_n \rangle$ where $\langle \sigma_i, a_i, \sigma_{i+1} \rangle$ is a state-action-state transition of the system.

block being on top of another), and **statics** – properties that cannot (such as the state of something being a block). Blocks, locations, configurations, steps, actions, and fluents are the objects in our domain. Now it's time to consider the relationships between them. Let $\langle \sigma_0, a_0, \sigma_1, \ldots, a_n, \sigma_{n+1} \rangle$ be a trajectory of our system. Two new predicates, $holds(fluent, step)$ and $occurs(action, step)$, can be used to describe what fluents are true and what actions occurred at any given step. In our example, we define relation $holds(on(B, L), I)$, which says that block B is on location L at step I. When we want to say that block B was put on location L at step I, we simply say $occurs(put(B, L), I)$.[4]

We begin our program by defining the objects of the domain. Note that in our definition of steps, we use a new construct `#const` to define a constant n, which is then used in a range declaration `step(0..n)` to specify the maximum number of steps.

```
1  %% blocks:
2  block(b0).   block(b1).   block(b2).   block(b3).
3  block(b4).   block(b5).   block(b6).   block(b7).
4
5  %% A location can be a block or the table.
6  location(X) :- block(X).
7  location(t).
8
9  #const n = 2.
10  step(0..n).
11
12  %% "Block B is on location L" is a property that
13  %% changes with time.
14  fluent(on(B,L)) :- block(B), location(L).
15
16  %% "Put block B on location L" is a possible action
17  %% provided we don't try to put a block onto itself.
18  action(put(B,L)) :- block(B), location(L),
19                      B != L.
```

---

[4] We could have made our time steps part of our fluent and action predicates and just said $on(B, L, I)$ and $put(B, L, I)$ instead of using *holds* and *occurs*. However, reifying actions and fluents allows us to introduce rules involving these concepts themselves, rather than their specific instances. We see examples of such rules later in the chapter.

To illustrate the behavior of our program, we fix the initial configuration to the one shown in Figure 8.1. We can describe it by specifying the locations of the blocks at step 0 and including the closed world assumption for the *holds* relation for the initial situation:

```
20  %% holds(on(B,L),I):block B is on location L at step I.
21  holds(on(b0,t),0).
22  holds(on(b3,b0),0).
23  holds(on(b2,b3),0).
24  holds(on(b1,t),0).
25  holds(on(b4,b1),0).
26  holds(on(b5,t),0).
27  holds(on(b6,b5),0).
28  holds(on(b7,b6),0).
29
30  %% If block B is not known to be on location L at
31  %% step 0, then we assume it is not.
32  -holds(on(B,L),0) :- block(B), location(L),
33                       not holds(on(B,L),0).
```

Note that the logic program on lines 1–33 completely defines the initial configuration of the blocks (i.e., we know the values of all the fluents of the domain at step 0 of our trajectory).

Now let's define the theory of the blocks world. To do this, we describe the effects of its actions. Since each action takes one step, the following rule describes an effect of action $put(B, L)$:

```
34  holds(on(B,L),I+1) :- occurs(put(B,L),I),
35                        I < n.
```

It states that putting block B on location L at step I causes B to be on L at step $I + 1$. We assume for now that the robot never drops a block and is otherwise perfect in its execution of actions.

This rule can be viewed as a special case of a **causal law** – a statement of the form

$$a \textbf{ causes } f \textbf{ if } p_0, \ldots, p_m$$

that says that action a executed in a state of the domain satisfying conditions $p_0, \ldots, p_m$ causes fluent f to become true in the resulting state. Such general laws are discussed in the next section.

The new location of block B can be viewed as a "direct" effect of action put. There are also "indirect" effects caused by relationships between fluents. For example, performing action $put(b2, t)$ in the initial situation has the direct effect of placing $b2$ on the table and the indirect effect of $b3$ being removed from $b3$. This type of indirect conclusions can often be obtained from direct ones by using relations between fluents. In this case, it is sufficient to know that a block occupies a single location. This can be expressed by the following rule:

```
36  -holds(on(B,L2),I) :- holds(on(B,L1),I),
37                        location(L2),
38                        L1 != L2.
```

The fact that no block can support more than one block directly on top can be expressed by the following rule[5]:

```
39  -holds(on(B2,B),I) :- block(B),
40                        holds(on(B1,B),I),
41                        block(B2),
42                        B1 != B2.
```

Later we show that both of these rules can be viewed as special cases of **state constraints** – statements of the form

$$f \textbf{ if } p_0, \ldots, p_m$$

that say that every state satisfying $p_0, \ldots, p_m$ must also satisfy f.

As usual, we test the success of our representation by inputting it into STUDENT and checking what it knows. Of course, we gave a complete initial situation, so it knows which blocks are where at step 0. Now let's expand our program by a new statement:

```
occurs(put(b2,t),0).
```

This statement allows us to ask the agent questions about what is true at step 1. Try giving STUDENT the program on lines 1–42 and the $occurs$ statement above and asking it query $holds(on(b2, t), 1)$. It should be able to figure out the answer on its own, based on the laws we encoded, and say yes. Now try query $holds(on(b0, t), 1)$. What do you expect? What does STUDENT answer?

---

[5] It is worth noting that statements $block(B)$ and $block(B2)$ in the body of the rule play substantially different roles. The latter is simply added for safety. The former, however, is necessary to correctly convey the meaning. If this statement were omitted, the rule would claim that not only a block but also a table cannot support more than one block.

A person would assume that $b0$ is still on the table because it was not moved, but STUDENT will answer "maybe." Is STUDENT not smart enough, or does it not have enough information? In most cases, unless they are told otherwise, humans live with an operative assumption that *things normally stay as they are*. Picking up an object does not normally affect properties of every other thing around us. We go on with our lives, feeling pretty safe that bunnies are still furry and the ocean is still big. It seems reasonable to assume that moving a single block does not cause other blocks to move so much that their locations change. At least for purposes of this example, we had assumed that our robot is good at manipulating blocks, so we would like STUDENT to believe that the only change that occurred is that $b2$ is now on the table and no longer on $b3$. We must teach it that, lacking evidence to the contrary, it should assume that *normally things stay as they are*. This principle is known as the **Inertia Axiom** and can be expressed by two rules:

```
43  holds(F,I+1)  :- holds(F,I),
44                     not -holds(F,I+1),
45                     I < n.
46
47  -holds(F,I+1)  :- -holds(F,I),
48                     not holds(F,I+1),
49                     I < n.
```

The rules state that without explicit evidence to the contrary, the value of fluent F remains constant at step $I + 1$. This is a typical representation of defaults as in Chapter 5. Note that $not\ ab(d(F, I))$ is not included, which simplifies the program. Since our states are complete and the rule has no weak exceptions, the omission is justified. (Recall from Section 5.1.1 that a strong exception refutes the default's conclusion and a weak one renders the default inapplicable.)

The rules on lines 34–49 give a complete description of a configuration σ_1 that results from executing action $put(B, L)$. Create a program consisting of lines 1–49 and the *occurs* statement and ask STUDENT some questions about its new configuration. Its answers should be more intuitive now. Later we show how to define "successor" states in more complex dynamic domains.

Is our description of the blocks world complete? To answer this question, change the *occurs* statement of the program to contain an action that should not be executable:

```
occurs(put(b6,t),0).
```

Since $b6$ is occupied, this action should not be allowed. Ask STU-DENT to describe the next state by asking it for all answers to query $holds(on(B, L), 1)$. You will see that the program derives that block $b6$ is on the table at step 1 and that $b7$ is still on top of it. This answer does not match our intuition unless we believe the robot arm to be very co-ordinated. Once again, we see that STUDENT needs more information; namely, we need to tell it which actions are not allowed. The next two rules are restrictions on the executability of actions.

```
50  -occurs(put(B,L),I) :- location(L),
51                              holds(on(B1,B),I).
52
53  -occurs(put(B1,B),I) :- block(B1),
54                              block(B),
55                              holds(on(B2,B),I).
```

The first rule says that it is impossible to move a block that is occupied. The second says that it is impossible to move a block onto an occupied block. These rules are examples of **executability conditions** whose general form is

$$\textbf{impossible } a_1 \ldots a_k \textbf{ if } p_0, \ldots, p_m.$$

Intuitively, the law states that it is impossible to execute actions $a_1 \ldots a_k$ simultaneously in a state satisfying conditions $p_0, \ldots, p_m$.

Add these rules and ask STUDENT to describe again what is true at Step 1. It should answer that there are no models, which indicates that the suggested scenario is inconsistent with the rules of the program, as we would expect.

The rules on lines 34–55 constitute a simple theory of the blocks world. Let's see how well STUDENT does if we add another step. To ask questions about the state of the world after block $b2$ is moved on the table and $b7$ is put on $b2$, we need to get rid of our bad *occurs* statement and write the following two statements instead:

```
56  occurs(put(b2,t),0).
57  occurs(put(b7,b2),1).
```

Let us name lines 1–57 blocks1.lp. Querying it with $holds(on(B, L), 2)$ gives us everything that is true after the two actions have been executed. Finally our representation mirrors what we expect the program to know, and it can answer our queries intelligently. For practice, run STU-DENT with blocks1.lp. Try changing the two *occurs* statements in the program to the nonexecutable statements $occurs(put(b2, b4), 0)$ and $occurs(put(b7, b4), 1)$. What is the result? Is the rule on lines 53–55 necessary for STUDENT to give the right answers?

Thus far our model of the blocks world contained only fluents formed by relation on. Let us now see if we can expand our model by introducing a new fluent, $above(B, L)$ – "block B is located above location L." This can be done by adding the line

```
58  fluent(above(B,L))  :-  block(B), location(L).
```

and the following recursive definition:

```
59  holds(above(B,L),I)  :-  holds(on(B,L),I).
60  holds(above(B,L),I)  :-  holds(on(B,B1),I),
61                           holds(above(B1,L),I).
62  %% CWA
63  -holds(above(B,L),I) :-  block(B), location(L), step(I),
64                           not holds(above(B,L),I).
```

This is very similar to other recursive definitions we discussed in Chapter 4, such as the definition of ancestors in Section 4.1.3 or subclasses in Section 4.3. But definitions of fluents in dynamic domains are slightly more subtle. To see the problem, let us consider program `blocks2.lp` given by lines 1–64 and the following statement:

```
:-  -holds(above(b2,b0),1).
```

Since intuitively $\neg holds(above(b2, b0), 1)$ should be true, the resulting program should be inconsistent. But this is not what happens: The solver returns an answer set containing $holds(above(b2, b0), 1)$. The problem is caused by the unintended interplay between the inertia axiom and the CWA part of the definition of *above*. Informal reasoning that corresponds to this answer set goes as follows: $b2$ is above $b0$ at step 0. The inertia axiom allows us to conclude that $b2$ is still above $b0$ even after $b2$ is put on the table. The CWA from the definition is blocked, the constraint is satisfied, and the answer set is found. Of course, if in the attempt to construct an answer set we were to apply the CWA first, then the inertia axiom would be blocked, and we would not be able to satisfy the constraint. (It may be instructive to check that program `blocks2.lp` without the constraint has two answer sets: one that contains $holds(above\ (b2,\ b0),\ 1)$ and one that contains $\neg holds(above\ (b2,\ b0),\ 1)$.

To remedy the problem, it is sufficient to notice that the new fluent, *above*, is uniquely defined by the values of fluent *on* and therefore should not be made subject to the inertia axiom. This observation suggests a division of fluents of our domain into two classes – **inertial** and **defined**. Intuitively, an inertial fluent is subject to the law of inertia; its value can be (directly or indirectly) changed by an action. If no such action occurs, the value of the fluent remains unchanged. A defined fluent is not subject to the inertia axiom and cannot be directly caused by any action; instead it is defined in terms of other fluents.

To reflect the division of fluents into two types, let's create `blocks3.lp` by modifying `blocks2.lp` as follows:

1. Replace the definition of fluent on line 14 by

   ```
   fluent(inertial,on(B,L)) :- block(B), location(L).
   ```

2. Change the rules stating the inertia axiom (lines 43–49) to allow their application only to inertial fluents by adding condition

   ```
   fluent(inertial,F)
   ```

   to their bodies.

3. List *above* as a defined fluent in our list of fluents by replacing line 58 with

   ```
   fluent(defined,above(B,L)) :- block(B), location(L).
   ```

Now the notion of *above* is properly introduced. Run `blocks3.lp` and check that the results correspond to our intuition.

8.2 A General Solution

The knowledge base from the example in the previous section defines a dynamic system containing all possible trajectories of the blocks world. In our general theory of actions and change, a dynamic system is modeled by a **transition diagram** – a directed graph whose nodes correspond to physically possible states of the domain and whose arcs are labeled by actions. Such models are called Markovian.

A transition $\langle \sigma_0, \{a_1, \ldots, a_k\}, \sigma_1 \rangle$ of the diagram, where $\{a_1, \ldots, a_k\}$ is a set of actions executable in state σ_0, indicates that σ_1 may be a result of simultaneous execution of these actions in σ_0. Our representation guarantees that the effect of an action depends only on the state in which that action was executed. The way in which this state was reached is irrelevant.

A path $\langle \sigma_0, a_0, \sigma_1, \ldots, a_{n-1}, \sigma_n \rangle$ of the diagram represents a possible trajectory of the system with initial state σ_0 and final state σ_n. The transition diagram for a system contains all possible trajectories of that system.

In the dynamic system from the blocks-world example, states correspond to configurations of blocks satisfying the constraints from lines 36–42. Actions are of the form $put(Block, Location)$. Program rules on lines 34–55 define the corresponding state transitions.

A system may often have a large and complex diagram. The problem of finding its concise and mathematically accurate description is not trivial and has been a subject of research for more that 30 years. Its solution requires a good understanding of the nature of causal effects of actions in the presence of complex interrelations between fluents. An additional level of complexity is added by the need to specify *what is not changed by actions*. As noted by John McCarthy, the problem of finding a concise and accurate representation of this statement in a formal language, known as the **Frame Problem**, can be reduced to finding a representation of the inertia axiom – a default that states that things normally stay as they are. In our blocks-world example, we represented this axiom by logic programming rules on lines 43–49. Notice that the methodology of representing defaults from Chapter 5 was instrumental in solving this problem.

As we have seen, causal effects of actions can be defined by causal laws of the form:

$$a \textbf{ causes } f \textbf{ if } p_0, \ldots, p_m.$$

The law says that *action a, executed in a state satisfying conditions $p_0, \ldots, p_m$, causes fluent f to become true in the resulting state.* We saw the use of such laws in our blocks-world example when we defined the effect of action $put(Block, Location)$.

Consider another, simpler example of a dynamic system whose states are described by two Boolean inertial fluents, f and g, and whose arcs are labeled by one action a whose effect is described by a single causal law, $a \textbf{ causes } \neg f \textbf{ if } f$. We denote this description of our system by $\mathcal{D}_0$. Common sense suggests that if a is executed in $\sigma_0 = \{f, g\}$, the new, successor state will contain $\neg f$ implied by the causal law. Note also that g will remain true by the inertia axiom. Figure 8.3 shows the transition diagram for $\mathcal{D}_0$.

Causal and other relations between fluents can be described by state constraints – statements of the form

$$f \textbf{ if } p_0, \ldots, p_m$$

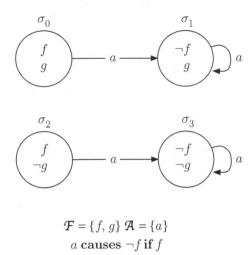

$$\mathcal{F} = \{f, g\}\ \mathcal{A} = \{a\}$$
$$a \text{ causes } \neg f \text{ if } f$$

Figure 8.3. Transition Diagram of System $\mathcal{D}_0$

that say that *every state satisfying conditions* $p_0, \ldots, p_m$ *must also satisfy* f. They are used to define indirect effects of actions. Finding concise ways of defining these effects is called the **Ramification Problem**. Together with the frame problem discussed earlier the ramification problem caused substantial difficulties for researchers in their attempts to precisely define transitions of discrete dynamic systems.

As we have seen, blocks-world rules on lines 36–42 are examples of state constraints. Note that they are not dependent on actions.

To illustrate this feature, let us expand description $\mathcal{D}_0$ by adding an inertial fluent h and state constraint $\neg h$ **if** $\neg f$. Figure 8.4 shows the transition diagram of $\mathcal{D}_1$. State σ_1 contains direct effect $\neg f$ of a derived by the causal law, g derived by inertia, and indirect effect $\neg h$ of a derived by the new state constraint.

Executability conditions are represented by laws of the form

$$\textbf{impossible } a_0, \ldots, a_k \textbf{ if } p_0, \ldots, p_m$$

that say that *it is impossible to execute actions* $a_0, \ldots, a_k$ *simultaneously in a state satisfying conditions* $p_0, \ldots, p_m$. To illustrate, let's create $\mathcal{D}_2$ by expanding $\mathcal{D}_1$ by executability condition **impossible** a **if** $\neg f$, which says that it is impossible to perform action a in any state that contains fluent $\neg f$. Its transition diagram is shown in Figure 8.5. The diagram differs from Figure 8.4 in that it has fewer transitions; namely, the cycles in σ_1 and σ_5 have been eliminated.

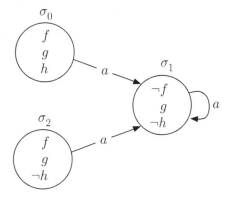

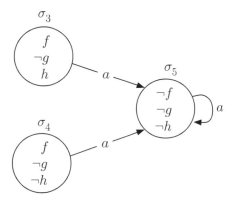

$$\mathcal{F} = \{f, g, h\} \quad \mathcal{A} = \{a\}$$
$$a \textbf{ causes } \neg f \textbf{ if } f$$
$$\neg h \textbf{ if } \neg f$$

Figure 8.4. Transition Diagram of System $\mathcal{D}_1$

Descriptions $\mathcal{D}_0$, $\mathcal{D}_1$, and $\mathcal{D}_2$ can be viewed as theories in action language $\mathcal{AL}$. **Action languages** are formal models of parts of natural language used for describing the behavior of dynamic systems. Another way to look at them is as tools for describing transition diagrams. These examples have given a brief introduction to the syntax of these languages. The semantics was given by our intuitive understanding of what these laws might mean. Now we give a formal, mathematical definition of the syntax and semantics of $\mathcal{AL}$.

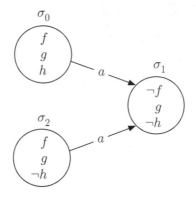

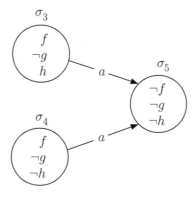

$$\mathcal{F} = \{f, g, h\} \quad \mathcal{A} = \{a\}$$
$$a \textbf{ causes } \neg f \textbf{ if } f$$
$$\neg h \textbf{ if } \neg f$$
$$\textbf{impossible } a \textbf{ if } \neg f$$

Figure 8.5. Transition Diagram of System $\mathcal{D}_2$

8.3 $\mathcal{AL}$ Syntax

Let us begin with some basic terminology. Action language $\mathcal{AL}$ is parametrized by a sorted signature containing three special sorts: *statics*, *fluents*, and *actions*. The fluents are partitioned into two sorts: *inertial* and *defined*. We refer to both statics and fluents as **domain properties**. A **domain literal** is a domain property p or its negation $\neg p$. If domain literal l is formed by a fluent, we refer to it as a **fluent literal**; otherwise it is a **static literal**.

A set S of domain literals is called **complete** if for any domain property p either p or $\neg p$ is in S; S is called **consistent** if there is no p such that $p \in S$ and $\neg p \in S$.

Definition 8.3.1. *(Statements of $\mathcal{AL}$)*
Language $\mathcal{AL}$ allows the following types of statements:

1. *Causal Laws:*

$$a \textbf{ causes } l_{in} \textbf{ if } p_0, \ldots, p_m$$

2. *State Constraints:*

$$l \textbf{ if } p_0, \ldots, p_m$$

3. *Executability Conditions:*

$$\textbf{impossible } a_0, \ldots, a_k \textbf{ if } p_0, \ldots, p_m$$

where a is an action, l is an arbitrary domain literal, l_{in} is a literal formed by an inertial fluent, $p_0, \ldots, p_m$ are domain literals, $k \geq 0$, and $m \geq -1$.[6]
Moreover, no negation of a defined fluent can occur in the heads of state constraints.

The collection of state constraints whose head is a defined fluent f is referred to as the *definition* of f. As in logic programming definitions, f is true if it follows from the truth of the body of at least one of its defining rules. Otherwise, f is false.

Definition 8.3.2. *(System Description)*
A **system description** *of $\mathcal{AL}$ is a collection of statements of $\mathcal{AL}$.*

8.4 $\mathcal{AL}$ Semantics – The Transition Relation

A system description $\mathcal{SD}$ serves as a specification of the transition diagram $\mathcal{T}(\mathcal{SD})$ defining all possible trajectories of the corresponding dynamic system. Therefore, to define the semantics of $\mathcal{AL}$, we have to precisely define the states and legal transitions of this diagram.

8.4.1 States

We start with the states. If $\mathcal{SD}$ does not contain defined fluents, the definition of a state is simple – a state is simply a complete and consistent set of domain literals satisfying state constraints of $\mathcal{SD}$. This definition was used earlier

---

[6] If $m = -1$, keyword **if** is omitted.

in examples $\mathcal{D}_0$, $\mathcal{D}_1$, and $\mathcal{D}_2$. For system descriptions with defined fluents the situation is more subtle. The following simple example illustrates the problem.

Example 8.4.1. *(State)*
Let us consider a system description $\mathcal{D}_3$ with two inertial fluents, f and g, and a fluent h defined by the following rules:

$$h \text{ if } f$$
$$h \text{ if } \neg g.$$

Clearly, $\{f, g, h\}$ is a state of $\mathcal{D}_3$ and $\{f, g, \neg h\}$ is not. But what about $\{\neg f, g, h\}$? It does not seem to satisfy the definition of h since the truth of h does not follow from any of its defining rules. So the intended answer to our question seems to be *no*. But $\{\neg f, g, h\}$ satisfies the constraints! The suggested definition does not work. It may be tempting to consider an additional condition requiring a defined fluent to be true *iff* at least one of its defining rules is satisfied. This would give the correct answer to our example, but would not work if we were to expand the definition by an extra rule:

$$h \text{ if } h.$$

The tautological rule should not change the states of $\mathcal{D}_3$, but it does. According to the suggested modification, $\{\neg f, g, h\}$ is a state. An attentive reader will notice the similarity between this situation and the use of Clark's completion for defining semantics of logic programs. This similarity led to *the idea of defining states via logic programming under answer set semantics*, as shown later.

We now need the following notation. By $\Pi_c(\mathcal{SD})$ (where c stands for constraints) we denote the logic program defined as follows:

1. For every state constraint

$$l \text{ if } p$$

$\Pi_c(\mathcal{SD})$ contains

$$l \leftarrow p.$$

2. For every defined fluent f, $\Pi_c(\mathcal{SD})$ contains the CWA:

$$\neg f \leftarrow \text{ not } f.$$

For any set σ of domain literals let σ_{nd} denote the collection of all domain literals of σ formed by inertial fluents and statics. (The $_{nd}$ stands for nondefined.)

Definition 8.4.1. *A complete and consistent set σ of domain literals is a* **state** *of the transition diagram defined by a system description $\mathcal{SD}$ if σ is the unique answer set of program $\Pi_c(\mathcal{SD}) \cup \sigma_{nd}$.*

In other words, a state is a complete and consistent set of literals σ that is the unique answer set of the program that consists of the nondefined literals from σ, the encoding of the state constraints, and the CWA for each defined fluent. *Note that (a) every state of system description $\mathcal{SD}$ satisfies the state constraints of $\mathcal{SD}$ and (b) if the signature of $\mathcal{SD}$ does not contain defined fluents, a state is simply a complete, consistent set of literals satisfying the state constraints of $\mathcal{SD}$.*

Example 8.4.2. *(Example 8.4.1 Revisited)*
Let us consider the system description $\mathcal{D}_3$ from Example 8.4.1. Program $\Pi_c(\mathcal{SD})$ consists of these rules:

$$h \leftarrow f.$$
$$h \leftarrow \neg g.$$
$$\neg h \leftarrow \ not\ h.$$

It is easy to check that the transition diagram defined by $\mathcal{D}_3$ has the following states: $\{f, g, h\}, \{f, \neg g, h\}, \{\neg f, \neg g, h\}, \{\neg f, g, \neg h\}$. To check that $\sigma_0 = \{f, \neg g, h\}$ is a state, it is sufficient to check that σ_0 is the only answer set of $\Pi_c(\mathcal{SD}) \cup \{f, \neg g\}$. The process is similar for other states. To see that $\sigma = \{\neg f, g, h\}$ is not a state, it suffices to see that σ is not the answer set of $\Pi_c(\mathcal{SD}) \cup \{\neg f, g\}$.

The next example explains the importance of the uniqueness requirement of the definition.

Example 8.4.3. *(Mutually Recursive Laws)*
Let us consider a system description $\mathcal{D}_4$ with two defined fluents, f and g, which are defined by the following mutually recursive laws:

$$g \ \textbf{if} \ \neg f.$$
$$f \ \textbf{if} \ \neg g.$$

Let us check if $\{f, \neg g\}$ is a state of $\mathcal{T}(\mathcal{D}_4)$. Program $\Pi_c(\mathcal{D}_4)$ from Definition 8.4.1 consists of these rules:

$$g \leftarrow \neg f.$$
$$f \leftarrow \neg g.$$
$$\neg g \leftarrow \ not\ g.$$
$$\neg f \leftarrow \ not\ f.$$

Since all the fluents of $\mathcal{D}_4$ are defined, $\sigma_{nd} = \emptyset$ and program $\Pi_c(\mathcal{D}_4) \cup \sigma_{nd}$ has two answer sets, $\{f, \neg g\}$ and $\{g, \neg f\}$. This violates the uniqueness condition of Definition 8.4.1, and hence $\mathcal{T}(\mathcal{D}_4)$ has no states. This result is intended. Mutually recursive laws of $\mathcal{D}_4$ are not strong enough to uniquely define f and g; thus, the definition is rejected.

We conclude our definition of state by giving a sufficient condition that guarantees that defined fluents of a system description are uniquely defined by the system's statics and inertial fluents. To mathematically capture this property we use the following definition:

Definition 8.4.2. *(Well-Founded System Description)*
A system description $\mathcal{SD}$ of $\mathcal{AL}$ is called **well founded** *if for any complete and consistent set of fluent literals σ satisfying the state constraints of $\mathcal{SD}$, the program*

$$\Pi_c(\mathcal{SD}) \cup \sigma_{nd} \qquad\qquad (8.1)$$

has at most one answer set.

We now also need the following notions:

Definition 8.4.3. *(Fluent Dependency Graph)*
The **fluent dependency graph** *of a system description $\mathcal{SD}$ is the directed graph such that*

- *Its vertices are arbitrary domain literals.*
- *It has an edge*
  - *from l to l' if l is formed by a static or an inertial fluent and $\mathcal{SD}$ contains a state constraint with the head l and the body containing l',*
  - *from f to l' if f is a defined fluent and $\mathcal{SD}$ contains a state constraint with the head f and the body containing l' and not containing f.*
  - *from $\neg f$ to f for every defined fluent f.*

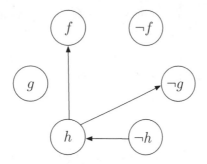

Figure 8.6. Fluent Dependency Graph for Example 8.4.2

The fluent dependency graphs for Examples 8.4.2 and 8.4.3 are given in Figures 8.6 and 8.7, respectively. Recall that h is the defined fluent in the first example, whereas f and g are the defined fluents in the second.

Definition 8.4.4. *(Weak Acyclicity)*
A fluent dependency graph is **weakly acyclic** *if it does not contain paths from defined fluents to their negations. By extension, a system description with a weakly acyclic fluent dependency graph is also called* weakly acyclic.

Consequently, as expected, the graph in Figure 8.6 is weakly acyclic, whereas the one in Figure 8.7 is not.

Proposition 8.4.1. *(Sufficient Condition for Well-Foundedness)*
If a system description SD of AL is weakly acyclic then SD is well-founded.

8.4.2 Transitions

Our *definition of transition relation of $T(SD)$ is also based on the notion of the answer set of a logic program.* To describe a transition $\langle \sigma_0, a, \sigma_1 \rangle$ we construct a program $\Pi(SD, \sigma_0, a)$ consisting of logic programming encodings of the system description SD, initial state σ_0, and set of actions

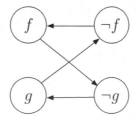

Figure 8.7. Fluent Dependency Graph for Example 8.4.3

a, such that answer sets of this program determine the states the system can move into after the execution of a in σ_0.

Definition 8.4.5. *The encoding $\Pi(\mathcal{SD})$ of system description $\mathcal{SD}$ consists of the encoding of the signature of $\mathcal{SD}$ and rules obtained from statements of $\mathcal{SD}$.*

- **Encoding of the Signature**
  We start with the encoding $sig(\mathcal{SD})$ of the signature of $\mathcal{SD}$.
  - *For each constant symbol c of sort $sort\_name$ other than $fluent$, static or action, $sig(\mathcal{SD})$ contains*

  $$sort\_name(c). \tag{8.2}$$

  - *For every static g of $\mathcal{SD}$, $sig(\mathcal{SD})$ contains*

  $$static(g). \tag{8.3}$$

  - *For every inertial fluent f of $\mathcal{SD}$, $sig(\mathcal{SD})$ contains*

  $$fluent(inertial, f). \tag{8.4}$$

  - *For every defined fluent f of $\mathcal{SD}$, $sig(\mathcal{SD})$ contains*

  $$fluent(defined, f). \tag{8.5}$$

  - *For every action a of $\mathcal{SD}$, $sig(\mathcal{SD})$ contains*

  $$action(a). \tag{8.6}$$

- **Encoding of Statements of $\mathcal{SD}$**
  For this encoding we only need two steps, 0 and 1, which stand for the beginning and the end of a transition. This is sufficient for describing a single transition; however, later, we describe longer chains of events and let steps range over $[0, n]$ for some constant n. To allow an easier generalization of the program we encode steps by using constant n for the maximum number of steps, as follows:

  $$\#const\ n = 1. \tag{8.7}$$

  $$step(0..n). \tag{8.8}$$

As in our blocks-world example, we introduce a relation $holds(f, i)$ that says that fluent f is true at step i. To simplify the description of the encoding, we also introduce a new notation, $h(l, i)$ where l is a domain literal and i is a step. If f is a fluent then by $h(l, i)$ we denote $holds(f, i)$ if $l = f$ or $\neg holds(f, i)$ if $l = \neg f$. If l is a static *literal then $h(l, i)$ is simply l. We also need relation $occurs(a, i)$ that says that action a occurred at step i; $occurs(\{a_0, \ldots, a_k\}, i) =_{def} \{occurs(a_i) : 0 \le i \le k\}$.*

We use this notation to encode statements of $\mathcal{SD}$ as follows:

− *For every causal law*

$$a \text{ causes } l \text{ if } p_0, \ldots, p_m$$

$\Pi(\mathcal{SD})$ *contains*

$$
\begin{aligned}
h(l, I + 1) \leftarrow{} & h(p_0, I), \ldots, h(p_m, I), \\
& occurs(a, I), \\
& I < n.
\end{aligned}
\tag{8.9}
$$

− *For every state constraint*

$$l \text{ if } p_0, \ldots, p_m$$

$\Pi(\mathcal{SD})$ *contains*

$$h(l, I) \leftarrow h(p_0, I), \ldots, h(p_m, I). \tag{8.10}$$

− $\Pi(\mathcal{SD})$ *contains the CWA for defined fluents:*

$$
\begin{aligned}
\neg holds(F, I) \leftarrow{} & fluent(defined, F), \\
& not\ holds(F, I).
\end{aligned}
\tag{8.11}
$$

− *For every executability condition*

$$\text{impossible } a_0, \ldots, a_k \text{ if } p_0, \ldots, p_m$$

$\Pi(\mathcal{SD})$ *contains*

$$
\begin{aligned}
\neg occurs(a_0, I)\ or\ & \ldots\ or\ \neg occurs(a_k, I) \leftarrow h(p_0, I), \ldots, \\
& h(p_m, I).
\end{aligned}
\tag{8.12}
$$

− $\Pi(\mathcal{SD})$ *contains the inertia axiom:*

$$
\begin{aligned}
holds(F, I + 1) \leftarrow{} & fluent(inertial, F), \\
& holds(F, I), \\
& not\ \neg holds(F, I + 1), \\
& I < n.
\end{aligned}
\tag{8.13}
$$

$$\neg holds(F, I + 1) \leftarrow fluent(inertial, F),$$
$$\neg holds(F, I),$$
$$not\ holds(F, I + 1), \quad (8.14)$$
$$I < n.$$

- $\Pi(\mathcal{SD})$ *contains CWA for actions:*

$$\neg occurs(A, I) \leftarrow not\ occurs(A, I). \quad (8.15)$$

This completes the construction of encoding $\Pi(\mathcal{SD})$ of system description $\mathcal{SD}$.

To continue with our definition of transition $\langle \sigma_0, a, \sigma_1 \rangle$ we describe the two remaining parts of program $\Pi(\mathcal{SD}, \sigma_0, a)$ – the encoding $h(\sigma_0, 0)$ of initial state σ_0 and the encoding $occurs(a, 0)$ of action a:

$$h(\sigma_0, 0) =_{def} \{ h(l, 0) : l \in \sigma_0 \}$$

and

$$occurs(a, 0) =_{def} \{ occurs(a_i, 0) : a_i \in a \}.$$

To complete program $\Pi(\mathcal{SD}, \sigma_0, a)$ we simply gather our description of the system's laws, together with the description of the initial state and the actions that occur in it.

Definition 8.4.6.

$$\Pi(\mathcal{SD}, \sigma_0, a) =_{def} \Pi(\mathcal{SD}) \cup h(\sigma_0, 0) \cup occurs(a, 0).$$

Now we are ready to define the notion of transition of $\mathcal{T}(\mathcal{SD})$.

Definition 8.4.7. *Let a be a nonempty collection of actions and σ_0 and σ_1 be states of the transition diagram $\mathcal{T}(\mathcal{SD})$ defined by a system description $\mathcal{SD}$. A state-action-state triple $\langle \sigma_0, a, \sigma_1 \rangle$ is a **transition** of $\mathcal{T}(\mathcal{SD})$ iff $\Pi(\mathcal{SD}, \sigma_0, a)$ has an answer set A such that $\sigma_1 = \{ l : h(l, 1) \in A \}$.*

We now have a program that, like a rational human reasoner, can predict what the state of the world will be once an action is performed in a given state. In the next section, we give examples of specific domains that can be described by $\mathcal{AL}$ and how they can be translated into ASP programs using Definition 8.4.6.

8.5 Examples

As we have seen, to model a dynamic domain, we need to describe what actions cause what effects under what conditions. To do this, we need to identify

1. the objects, properties, and actions of the domain;
2. the relationships between the properties;
3. the executability conditions and causal effects of actions.

In other words, we must come up with an $\mathcal{AL}$ system description for our domain. In this section we give several examples of such descriptions and walk through the steps of constructing the corresponding transition diagrams.

8.5.1 The Briefcase Domain

Consider a briefcase with two clasps. We have an action, toggle, which moves a given clasp into the up position if the clasp is down, and vice versa. If both clasps are in the up position, the briefcase is open; otherwise, it is closed. Create a (simple) model of this domain.

The signature of the briefcase domain consists of sort $clasp = \{1, 2\}$, inertial fluent $up(C)$ that holds iff clasp C is up, defined fluent $open$ that holds iff both clasps are up, and action $toggle(C)$ that toggles clasp C.

The system description $\mathcal{D}_{bc}$ of our domain consists of axioms

$$toggle(C) \textbf{ causes } up(C) \textbf{ if } \neg up(C)$$
$$toggle(C) \textbf{ causes } \neg up(C) \textbf{ if } up(C)$$
$$open \textbf{ if } up(1), up(2)$$

where C ranges over the sort *clasp*. Since these laws contain variables, they are not, strictly speaking, proper statements of our action language; such laws are often referred to as **schemas**. Individual laws can be obtained from schemas by grounding the variables. Since our signature is sorted and variable C ranges over clasps, the grounding will respect this sorting information and replace C by 1 and 2. For instance, the first schema can be viewed as shorthand for two laws:

$$toggle(1) \textbf{ causes } up(1) \textbf{ if } \neg up(1)$$
$$toggle(2) \textbf{ causes } up(2) \textbf{ if } \neg up(2).$$

Now let us figure out what the states of our domain look like. According to Definition 8.4.1 we need a program $\Pi_c(\mathcal{D}_{bc})$ that consists of the following two rules:

$$open \leftarrow up(1), up(2) \tag{1}$$

$$\neg open \leftarrow not\ open. \tag{2}$$

Consider a collection

$$\sigma = \{\neg up(1), up(2), \neg open\}.$$

Is this a state? First we need to check if it is complete and consistent. By definition, it is. Next we need to consider

$$\sigma_{nd} = \{\neg up(1), up(2)\}$$

and check if σ is the only answer set of the program $\Pi_c(\mathcal{D}_{bc}) \cup \sigma_{nd}$ consisting of rules (1) and (2) given earlier, and facts $\neg up(1)$ and $up(2)$. Clearly, it is, and hence, as expected, σ is a state of our transition diagram.

Now let σ be $\{\neg up(1), up(2), open\}$. According to the description of the briefcase, this is a physical impossibility and hence should not be a state. Indeed this is the case according to our definition. Although it is complete and consistent, it is not the answer set of the program consisting of rules (1) and (2) and facts $\neg up(1)$ and $up(2)$. Therefore, σ is not a state.

Moving on to defining transitions of our system, we construct program $\Pi(\mathcal{D}_{bc})$, which will be written in the syntax of Gringo and named bc.lp. In its construction we slightly deviate from the standard encoding in Definition 8.4.5 to avoid a long listing of fluents, actions, and other sorts. Instead we define sorts using logic programming rules with variables. Definitions of fluents and actions in the following program can serve as an example of this technique. Of course, the use of rules is just a matter of convenience; they can be eliminated and replaced by collections of atoms. Here is the translation of our system description $\mathcal{D}_{bc}$ into a logic program:

```
1  %% Domain Signature
2  clasp(1).
3  clasp(2).
4
5  fluent(inertial, up(C)) :- clasp(C).
6  fluent(defined, open).
7  action(toggle(C)) :- clasp(C).
```

Clearly the definition of inertial fluent

```
fluent(inertial, up(C)) :- clasp(C).
```

can be replaced by two atoms

```
fluent(inertial, up(1)).
fluent(inertial, up(2)).
```

The same can be done for actions. This completes our definition of sort *clasp* and the fluents and actions of the domain.

Next, we translate our axioms. The first two axioms of our system description are causal laws with variables. It is not difficult to see that rule (8.9) from Definition 8.4.5 can be adapted to apply to such laws. As the result we obtain the following encoding where C ranges over sort *clasp*:

```
8  #const n = 1.
9  step(0..n).
10
11 %% toggle(C) causes up(C) if -up(C)
12 holds(up(C),I+1) :- occurs(toggle(C),I),
13                    -holds(up(C), I),
14                    I < n.
15
16 %% toggle(C) causes -up(C) if up(C)
17 -holds(up(C),I+1) :- occurs(toggle(C),I),
18                     holds(up(C),I),
19                     I < n.
```

The last law of $\mathcal{D}_{bc}$ is a state constraint. Using rule (8.10) we get

```
20 %% open if up(1), up(2).
21 holds(open,I) :- holds(up(1),I),
22                 holds(up(2),I).
```

We add the closed world assumption for defined fluents as dictated by rule (8.11):

```
23 %% CWA for Defined Fluents
24 -holds(F,I) :- fluent(defined,F),
25               step(I),
26               not holds(F,I).
```

(Notice that, in accordance with the general translation, this rule encodes the CWA for all defined fluents. Currently, we only have one such fluent, but we might wish to add more. The CWA for defined fluents is taken care of once and for all.)

Then we add the inertia axiom as defined by rules (8.13) and (8.14), allowing us to derive values of inertial fluents, even if no action explicitly dictated their change.

```
27  %% General Inertia Axiom
28  holds(F,I+1)  :- fluent(inertial,F),
29                    holds(F,I),
30                    not -holds(F,I+1),
31                    I < n.
32  -holds(F,I+1) :- fluent(inertial,F),
33                    -holds(F,I),
34                    not holds(F,I+1),
35                    I < n.
```

Last we add the closed world assumption for actions as given by rule (8.15):

```
36  %% CWA for actions
37  -occurs(A,I)  :- action(A), step(I),
38                    not occurs(A,I).
```

This concludes our encoding of the briefcase domain.

Figure 8.8 shows the transition diagram for this system. Using this program one can check, for instance, that the system contains transitions

$$\langle\{\neg up(1), up(2), \neg open\}, toggle(1), \{up(1), up(2), open\}\rangle,$$
$$\langle\{up(1), up(2), open\}, toggle(1), \{\neg up(1), up(2), \neg open\}\rangle,$$
$$\langle\{\neg up(1), \neg up(2), \neg open\}, \{toggle(1), toggle(2)\}, \{up(1), up(2), open\}\rangle,$$
etc.

Simply add the appropriate information about the initial state and the action that occurred in it as in Definition 8.4.7. For example, to check the first transition, add these statements:

```
%% Initial Situation
-holds(up(1),0).
holds(up(2),0).
-holds(open,0).
%% Action
occurs(toggle(1),0).
%% Display
#show holds/2.
#show -holds/2.
```

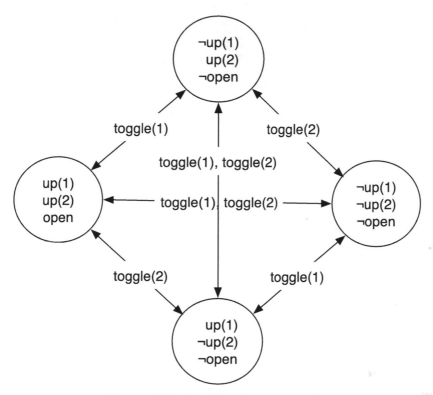

Figure 8.8. The Two-Clasp Briefcase Domain

and invoke the program to get the values of the fluents. The transition with $toggle(1)$ and $toggle(2)$ occurring simultaneously can be tested in the same manner by using two actions, $occurs(toggle(1), 0)$ and $occurs(toggle(2), 0)$.

Note that the encoding of our initial state can be simplified by omitting -holds(open,0). This is true because *open* is a defined fluent and its value is computed by the corresponding default of $\Pi(\mathcal{D}_{bc})$. This property, of course, holds in general, and from now on we do not include the encoding of the values of defined fluents in the encoding of a state.

8.5.2 The Blocks World Revisited

Let's go back to our basic blocks-world example from Section 8.1, with two fluents *on* and *above*, and construct a system description $\mathcal{D}_{bw}$ in $\mathcal{AL}$ representing the blocks-world transition diagram.

The signature of $\mathcal{D}_{bw}$ consists of sorts $block = \{b_0 \ldots b_7\}$ and $location = \{t\} \cup block$, inertial fluent $on(block, location)$, defined fluent

$above(block, location)$, and action $put(block, location)$. We assume that $put(B, L)$ is an action only if $B \neq L$.

The laws of the blocks world are

1. $put(B, L)$ **causes** $on(B, L)$
2. $\neg on(B, L_2)$ **if** $on(B, L_1), L_1 \neq L_2$
3. $\neg on(B_2, B)$ **if** $on(B_1, B), B_1 \neq B_2$
4. $above(B, L)$ **if** $on(B, L)$
5. $above(B, L)$ **if** $on(B, B1), above(B1, L)$
6. **impossible** $put(B, L)$ **if** $on(B_1, B)$
7. **impossible** $put(B_1, B)$ **if** $on(B_2, B)$

where (possibly indexed) Bs and Ls stand for blocks and locations, respectively.

Now let us translate $\mathcal{D}_{bw}$ into the corresponding logic program bw.lp. The collection of blocks is represented by

```
1  block(b0).    block(b1).    block(b2).    block(b3).
2  block(b4).    block(b5).    block(b6).    block(b7).
```

Instead of listing the collection of facts defining sort *location*, we save ourselves some typing and define locations using logic programming rules

```
3  location(X)  :- block(X).
4  location(t).
```

We also define fluents, actions, and steps:

```
5  fluent(inertial,  on(B,L))  :- block(B), location(L).
6  fluent(defined, above(B,L))  :- block(B), location(L).
7  action(put(B,L))  :- block(B), location(L),
8                              B != L.
9
10 #const n = 1.
11 step(0..n).
```

Now let's use the encoding from Definition 8.4.5 to encode the blocks-world laws. As in the briefcase example, we modify this encoding for dealing with variables. In doing so we assume that Bs and Ls range over blocks and locations, respectively, and that $put(B, L)$ occurring in the rules represents actions (i.e., $B \neq L$). Note that, strictly speaking, these conditions should be enforced by adding sort information (including $action(put(B, L))$ in the bodies of our rules. Otherwise, the ground instances of the rule may express meaningless statements about the results of putting a table on a block, for example, which may lead to misleading answers if the program is used together with statements expressing impossible actions. The same goes for fluents. To simplify the presentation we assume that the program will always be used with meaningful input. Doing so allows us to ignore sorts for actions and fluents in rules of the translation. Of course, we will add sort information, including that about blocks and locations, to some rules to reflect the meaning of the laws and the usual considerations about the rules' safety.

Law 1 is a causal law with fluent $on(B, L)$ and action $put(B, L)$. Following the directions for causal laws, we use encoding (8.9) :

```
12  holds(on(B,L),I+1)  :- occurs(put(B,L),I),
13                          I < n.
```

Laws 2–5 are typical state constraints, and we translate them using (8.10) as follows:

```
14  -holds(on(B,L2),I)  :- holds(on(B,L1),I),
15                         location(L2),
16                         L1 != L2.
17
18  -holds(on(B2,B),I)  :- holds(on(B1,B),I),
19                         block(B),
20                         block(B2),
21                         B1 != B2.
22
23  holds(above(B2,B1),I)  :- holds(on(B2,B1),I).
24
25  holds(above(B2,B1),I)  :- holds(on(B2,B),I),
26                            holds(above(B,B1),I).
```

Using (8.12), executability conditions from Laws 6 and 7 become

```
27  -occurs(put(B,L),I)  :-  location(L),
28                           holds(on(B1,B),I).
29
30  -occurs(put(B1,B),I)  :- block(B1), block(B),
31                           holds(on(B2,B),I).
```

Last, we add the rules needed for all domains: the CWA for defined fluents (8.11), the inertia axiom (8.13 and 8.14), and the CWA for actions (8.15):

```
32  %% CWA for Defined Fluents
33
34  -holds(F,I)  :- fluent(defined,F), step(I),
35                  not holds(F,I).
```

```
36
37  %% General Inertia Axiom
38
39  holds(F,I+1) :- fluent(inertial,F),
40                  holds(F,I),
41                  not -holds(F,I+1),
42                  I < n.
43
44  -holds(F,I+1) :- fluent(inertial,F),
45                   -holds(F,I),
46                   not holds(F,I+1),
47                   I < n.
48
49  %% CWA for Actions
50
51  -occurs(A,I) :- action(A), step(I),
52                  not occurs(A,I).
```

This concludes the encoding bw.lp of system description $\mathcal{D}_{bw}$. The resulting program (lines 1–52) defines the transition diagram of the dynamic system associated with the blocks world.

You might have noticed that our translation algorithm produces the same encoding as that in blocks3.lp. This is, of course, not an accident – insights obtained by researchers representing the blocks world and similar problems in ASP led them to the development of $\mathcal{AL}$ and its translation given in Definition 8.4.5. So why use $\mathcal{AL}$? Notice that the description of the blocks world in $\mathcal{AL}$ is substantially shorter than that in ASP. The former does not explicitly mention steps and contains neither inertia axioms nor defaults. These details are hidden in the translation, which can easily be automated. The statements of $\mathcal{AL}$ have a rather clear, intuitive meaning and can be used by knowledge engineers who do not have a clear notion of default negation and other nontrivial ASP concepts. This abstraction should not come as a surprise to computer scientists who are by now very familiar with the idea of high-level languages and language translators.

8.5.3 Blocks World with Concurrent Actions

So far we have dealt with a one-arm blocks-world domain. Suppose that we have two robotic arms capable of avoiding collisions in the air. Now that two blocks can be moved simultaneously, we must make sure that our robot can behave sensibly. Clearly the new system description $\mathcal{D}_{tbw}$ must contain all the statements of $\mathcal{D}_{bw}$, but we may also need some additional executability conditions. Let's think about what problems our new system might encounter. For example, consider what would happen if both arms were to try to move the same block to two separate locations at the same time; that is, we should not allow $occurs(put(b2, t), 0)$ and $occurs(put(b2, b4), 0)$, even though each individual action is perfectly legal. It can be easily seen, however, that the laws of $\mathcal{D}_{bw}$ already prohibit those two actions from occurring simultaneously. If the two actions were executed in parallel, then by causal law (1), $b2$ would be located on both $b4$ and the table. This would contradict constraint (2), and hence, such a parallel execution is already prohibited. Indeed, if we combine bw.lp with the initial situation described in Figure 8.1 (encoded on lines 21–33 of the program in Section 8.1) and actions $occurs(put(b2, t), 0)$ and $occurs(put(b2, b4), 0)$, the program will be inconsistent. So far so good. Now suppose we instead want to simultaneously execute actions $put(b2, t)$ and $put(b7, b2)$. Replacing the previous actions by these ones would produce a program with the answer set containing $b2$ on the table and $b7$ on $b2$. Is this the answer you expected? If you assumed that our robot arms were coordinated in such a way as to be able to stack blocks while moving them and then to put them down, then you answered "yes." But if you, like us, are not as confident in the state of the art of robotics and considered the concurrent execution of these two actions to be physically impossible, then the program's answer is wrong. However, this incorrect answer is to be expected because nothing in $\mathcal{D}_{bw}$ prevents this from happening. To avoid the problem, let's teach the system that actions that put B_1 on B_2 and simultaneously move B_2 are impossible:

$$\textbf{impossible } put(B_1, L), put(B_2, B_1).$$

Translating into ASP we get

```
53  -occurs(put(B1,L),I) | -occurs(put(B2,B1),I)  :-
54                                 step(I),
55                                 action(put(B1,L)),
56                                 action(put(B2,B1)).
```

(The sorts in the body of the rule are added for safety.)

To test the new system description let's add lines 53–56 to bw.lp, denote the resulting program by twoarms.lp, and compute the answer sets of twoarms.lp combined with the usual initial situation (lines 21–33 from Section 8.1) and statements

```
occurs(put(b2,t),0).
occurs(put(b7,b2),0).
```

The program should say that there are no models.

If instead we use the program together with concurrent actions

```
occurs(put(b2,t),0).
occurs(put(b4,b7),0).
```

we obtain the expected results. But what would happen if we were to attempt to simultaneously move $b4$ to $b7$ and $b2$ to $b1$? Physically, of course, these actions also depend on the degree of coordination of the robot's arms, but this degree of coordination seems reasonable. Our program, however, will not believe so. Not surprisingly it will tell us that such a move is impossible. This happens because constraint (7) does not allow us to stack a block on top of a block occupied at the beginning of the action. Can we allow such a move? Fortunately, the answer is yes. It is simply sufficient to remove constraint (7) from $\mathcal{D}_{bw}$. Of course we need to make sure that doing so would not allow some impossible moves. After all, the constraint was added for the purpose of prohibiting such moves. Some thought will show that no impossible moves will be allowed after all. Indeed this constraint was unnecessary from the beginning. Moving blocks B_1 and B_2 onto block B would cause two blocks to be located on the same block, which is prohibited by law (3) of $\mathcal{D}_{bw}$.

What happened is a typical and rather frequently occurring problem called **overspecification**. The condition, which was simply unnecessary in the original situation, caused an unexpected problem when the domain was expanded. In other words overspecification can decrease the degree of elaboration tolerance of the program.

Experience in many areas of computer science shows that programmers must be careful to avoid unwanted side effects when allowing concurrent actions, but the payoff may be substantial. The discussion in this section demonstrates that our approach incorporates concurrent actions and restrictions on them naturally and intuitively. It requires no special accommodations to be made for concurrency other than those required by the nature of the domain. These accommodations, in turn, can be incorporated within the original framework by adding the required executability conditions.

8.6 Nondeterminism in $\mathcal{AL}$

A transition diagram $\mathcal{T}$ is called **deterministic** if for every state σ and action a there is at most one state σ' such that $\langle \sigma, a, \sigma' \rangle \in \mathcal{T}$. Perhaps somewhat surprisingly, system descriptions of $\mathcal{AL}$ are capable of describing non-deterministic diagrams. Consider, for instance, the system described by the following laws:

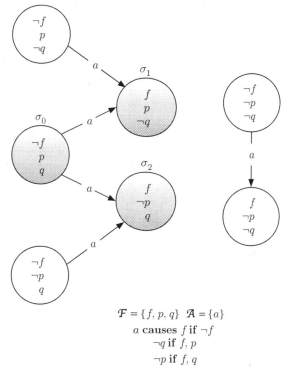

$\mathcal{F} = \{f, p, q\}$ $\mathcal{A} = \{a\}$
a causes f if $\neg f$
$\neg q$ if f, p
$\neg p$ if f, q

Figure 8.9. Nondeterministic System Description

1. a **causes** f **if** $\neg f$
2. $\neg q$ **if** f, p
3. $\neg p$ **if** f, q

where f, q, and p are inertial fluents. Suppose action a is executed in state
$\sigma_0 = \{\neg f, p, q\}$. What would be the states the system can move into as a
result of this execution? It is clear that every such state must contain f.
But what about p? One may notice that there are two possibilities: First, p
may maintain its value by inertia. In this case the system will move into
state $\sigma_1 = \{f, p, \neg q\}$ (where q is false due to the second law of our system
description). Symmetrically, q may be preserved by inertia, and the system
may move into $\sigma_2 = \{f, \neg p, q\}$. Figure 8.9 shows the possible transitions
in the system; the nondeterministic transitions are shaded. One can easily
check that these are exactly the transitions produced by our semantics.

The nondeterminism of the resulting system can be attributed to the
incompleteness of our specification and not to the real nondeterminism of
causal effects of action a. Yet experts disagree whether actions are really

nondeterministic or whether the impression of nondeterminism is caused by our lack of knowledge. We do not discuss these issues here. Instead we simply advise users of $\mathcal{AL}$ to make sure that their descriptions are sufficiently complete and, hence, the corresponding systems are deterministic.

8.7 Temporal Projection

In this chapter we introduced the syntax and semantics of action language $\mathcal{AL}$ that allow a concise and accurate description of transition diagrams of dynamic systems. The fact that the semantics of the language was given in terms of the semantics of ASP allows us to reduce answering questions about the values of fluents of the domain along a given trajectory to computing answer sets of simple logic programs. The task of predicting such values is often referred to as **temporal projection**. We already encountered this task in Section 8.1 where we dealt with predicting positions of blocks after a sequences of moves. The method is rather general. Given a system description $\mathcal{D}$, an initial state σ_0, and a sequence of consecutive occurrences of actions $\alpha = \langle a_0, \dots, a_{n-1} \rangle$, one can compute the trajectories of the system by combining $\Pi^n(\mathcal{D}) \cup h(\sigma_0, 0)$ with the encoding

$$occurs(a_0, 0).$$
$$\vdots$$
$$occurs(a_{n-1}, n-1).$$

of the sequence and computing the answer sets of the resulting program $\Pi^n(\mathcal{D}, \sigma_0, \alpha)$. It is not difficult to show that a sequence

$$\langle \sigma_0, a_0, \dots, a_{n-1}, \sigma_n \rangle$$

is a trajectory of $\mathcal{D}$ defined by sequence α iff there is an answer set A of $\Pi^n(\mathcal{D}, \sigma_0, \alpha)$ such that for every $0 \leq i \leq n$

$$\sigma_i = \{l : h(l, i) \in A\}.$$

Consider the briefcase example. To predict what will happen in the state where neither clasp is up if we toggle the first clasp and then toggle the second clasp, we construct $\Pi^2(\mathcal{D}_{bc}, \sigma_0, \langle toggle(1), toggle(2) \rangle)$. This is done by replacing #const n = 1 by #const n = 2 and combining $\Pi^2(\mathcal{D}_{bc})$ with the encoding of the initial state

```
-holds(up(1),0).
-holds(up(2),0).
```

and the encoding of the action sequence

```
occurs(toggle(1),0).
occurs(toggle(2),1).
```

The answer set of the resulting program will uniquely define the resulting state.

The following chapters show how we can use material introduced here to do more complex reasoning tasks including planning and diagnostics. It is worth noting that this approach to reasoning about actions and change could not have been possible without a good understanding of the representation of defaults in ASP.

Summary

In this chapter we discussed an ASP-based methodology for representing knowledge about discrete dynamic systems. Mathematically, such a system is represented by a transition diagram whose states correspond to physically possible states of the domain and whose arcs are labeled by actions. A transition $\langle \sigma_0, a, \sigma_1 \rangle$ belongs to the diagram iff the execution of action a in state σ_0 can move the system to state σ_1. Even for simple systems the corresponding diagrams may be huge and difficult to represent. In this chapter we showed how this problem can be solved using a simple action language $\mathcal{AL}$. We showed how transition diagrams can be described by collections of $\mathcal{AL}$ statements called system descriptions. These representations are concise (a comparatively small system description can define a very large diagram), have intuitive informal semantics, and a comparatively high degree of elaboration tolerance. The formal mathematical semantics of $\mathcal{AL}$ was given in terms of logic programs under answer set semantics. The ability of ASP to represent defaults and direct and indirect effects of actions helped solve the frame and ramification problems that, for a long time, prevented researchers from finding precise mathematical definitions of transitions of discrete dynamic systems. We also described some simple but useful mathematical properties of system descriptions of $\mathcal{AL}$ and illustrated how translations of its system descriptions can be used to solve an important computational task, called temporal projection, consisting of computing the states that the system can move into after the execution of a sequence of actions in a given initial state. In the following chapters we show how this connection between system descriptions and logic programs allows answer set programming to be used to solve a number of more complex computational problems. The problem of representing dynamic systems is an active and important area of knowledge representation and artificial intelligence. There are by now a number of action languages that differ from each other by underlying fundamental assumptions, the type of dynamic systems they are meant to model, and their ability to combine knowledge into modules. For instance, whereas $\mathcal{AL}$ is based on the inertia axiom, another action language called $\mathcal{C}$ uses a different fundamental assumption called the Law of Universal Causation, which says that everything that is true in the world must have a cause. Language H is an extension of $\mathcal{AL}$ that allows representation of so-called hybrid dynamic system (i.e., systems with both discrete and continuous change). Another extension of $\mathcal{AL}$, called $\mathcal{ALM}$, supplies $\mathcal{AL}$ with modular structure, which supports reusability and simplifies the development of knowledge representation libraries. This is, of course, a very incomplete list. Development of action languages and the study of relationships between them are important topics for future research.

References and Further Reading

Information about Shakey the robot and STRIPS can be found in Nillson (1984) and Fikes and Nilsson (1971). There are several early influential approaches to formalization of reasoning about actions and change. The first such formalism, called situation calculus, was introduced by John McCarthy (1983) and later developed by a large number of researchers; see, for instance, Lin and Reiter (1994), Lin (1995), Pinto (1998), Pinto and Reiter (1995), and Gelfond (1991). The calculus reifies actions and fluents and expresses their properties in the language of classical logic. The underlying semantics of the formalism was given by circumscription. A mathematically precise and intuitively clear account of reasoning about dynamic domains based on a modern version of this formalism can be found in Ray Reiter's book (2001). Another early approach to reasoning about actions and change is based on event calculus. Its original version, formulated in the framework of logic programming, was first introduced by Robert Kowalski and Marek Sergot (1986). A later work (Shanahan 1995) reformulated the logic programming axioms in the logic of circumscription. For more information on event calculus see, for instance, Kowalski (1992), Kakas and Miller (1997), and Kakas, Miller, and Toni (2001). The formalism is covered in detail by Murray Shanahan (1997) and Erik Mueller (2006). Another interesting approach to reasoning about dynamic domains that is based on a form of preferential entailment and combines differential equations and logic is summarized in Sandewall (1994). The formalism gave rise to temporal action logics; see, for instance, Doherty et al. (1998).

Action languages have their roots in STRIPS that evolved into action description language (ADL; Pednault 1994) and planning domain definition language (PDDL; McDermott et al. 1998). The latter language and its variants are commonly used in the planning community. The language $\mathcal{AL}$ used in this book is an extension of action language $\mathcal{B}$ (Gelfond and Lifschitz 1998), which is essentially a subset of the action language from Turner (1997). The investigation of the relationship between these languages and logic programming started in Gelfond and Lifschitz (1993) and continued in a number of papers including Turner (1997), Baral and Lobo (1997), and Balduccini and Gelfond (2003). Action language $\mathcal{C}$, based on the Principle of Universal Causation (Leibniz, 1951), was introduced in Giunchiglia and Lifschitz (1998). Its popular generalization $\mathcal{C}^+$ can be found in Giunchiglia et al. (2004). In a number of respects $\mathcal{C}$-based languages are more general than those based on $\mathcal{B}$. In other respects the situation is reversed. For instance, in $\mathcal{C}$ and its extensions causal laws may contain arbitrary propositional formulas, be defeasible, and so on. In contrast, causal laws in these languages cannot be recursive, which is allowed in $\mathcal{B}$. For comparison of $\mathcal{B}$ and $\mathcal{C}$ one can see Gelfond and Lifschitz (2012). Languages $\mathcal{ALM}$ and H were introduced in Gelfond and Inclezan (2009) and Chintabathina, Gelfond, and Watson (2005), respectively. For a different perspective, one can consult Thielscher (2008). The frame problem was first described by Patrick Hayes and John McCarthy (1969); our formulation of the ramification problem goes back to Ginsberg and Smith (1988). Proposition 8.4.1 and the related definitions are from Gelfond and Inclezan (2013).

Exercises

1. Prove that
   (a) Every state of system description $\mathcal{SD}$ satisfies the state constraints of $\mathcal{SD}$.
   (b) If the signature of $\mathcal{SD}$ does not contain defined fluents, a state is a complete, consistent set of literals satisfying the state constraints of $\mathcal{SD}$.

2. Given the following $\mathcal{AL}$ system description where fluents f and g are inertial and h is defined,

$$a \textbf{ causes } f \textbf{ if } g$$

$$h \textbf{ if } f, g$$

   (a) Show its translation into the corresponding ASP program.

(b) Check if each of the following is a valid state:

    i. $\sigma = \{f, \neg g, \neg h\}$
    ii. $\sigma = \{\neg f, \neg g, \neg h\}$
    iii. $\sigma = \{\neg f, g, h\}$
    iv. $\sigma = \{f, g, \neg h\}$

(c) Draw the transition diagram for the system.

3. Consider the system description presented in Section 8.6.
   (a) Explain why $\{f, p, q\}$ is not a valid state of this system description.
   (b) Add causal law b **causes** $\neg f$ **if** f to the system description and draw the corresponding transition diagram.

4. Given the following story: *Jenny painted the wall white.*
   (a) Represent the story in $\mathcal{AL}$. Assume that to paint a wall a given color, one must have paint of the appropriate color. Initially the wall is yellow and Jenny has the white paint. Jenny paints the wall at step 0. Make sure that your theory entails that at the end of the story the wall is white and not yellow.
   (b) Translate the representation to ASP and run it using an ASP solver to predict the values of fluents if Jenny paints the wall white.
   (c) Now suppose Jenny has black paint as well and, after painting the wall white, decides to paint it black. Use ASP to do some temporal projection about the values of the fluents after both actions are performed sequentially.
   (d) Now go back to the original story, but add another person, say Jill. Jenny and Jill have white paint. Jenny painted a wall white. Jill painted another wall white. Assume two people cannot paint the same wall at the same time, but they can paint different walls concurrently. Modify your $\mathcal{AL}$ representation to accommodate the new law, initial situation, and trajectory. Translate to ASP and run the program to compute the answer set after Jill and Jenny painted concurrently. Make sure that if you told the program that they painted the same wall concurrently, there would be no answer set.

5. Given the following story: *Claire always carries her cell phone with her. Claire is at the library.*
   (a) Represent the story in $\mathcal{AL}$. Include any commonsense knowledge necessary to answer the question, "Where is Claire's cell phone?" Make the representation general enough so that when you add the fact that Claire went home, her cell phone's location changed

accordingly. Also make it general enough that if we change the cell phone to a pet chihuahua, your program will still make the proper conclusions. Assume locations are distinct. *Hint:* Use the inertial fluent $carried(Obj, Person)$ – the object is carried by the person.

(b) Translate the representation to ASP and run it using an ASP solver to predict the values of fluents after Claire returns home.

(c) Modify your program to include that Rod carries a towel with him everywhere and that Claire and Rod are never at the same place at the same time. Make sure that your program can conclude that Claire's cell phone and Rod's towel are also not at the same place at the same time, even when it does not know where Rod is initially.

6. Given the following story: *Amy, Bruce, Carrie, and Don are vendors at a farmers' market. Amy sells apples and carrots, Bruce sells lettuce, Carrie sells apples, and Don sells cabbage and pears. For simplicity, assume that when a customer buys a type of produce from a vendor, he buys the whole quantity that the vendor has to offer.*

(a) Suppose that *Sally goes to the farmers' market and buys all the lettuce that Bruce sells and all the apples that Carrie sells. Peter goes to the farmers' market afterward.* Represent both parts of the story in $\mathcal{AL}$. Make sure that the temporal projection on your representation entails that Peter cannot buy lettuce but can buy apples.

(b) Translate the representation to ASP and run it using an ASP solver to answer the questions.

7. Given the following story: *Jonathan has requirements for playing the Wii: He should make sure that his homework is done, the bed is made, and he has practiced Tae Kwon Do. He can only do one thing at a time. Of course, he cannot make the bed if it already made or do his homework if it is already done or if none was assigned.*

(a) Select an initial situation and a sequence of Jonathan's actions that would allow him to play the Wii. Represent the resulting story in $\mathcal{AL}$. *Hint:* Create a sort $activity$ for homework, make_bed, TKD, and Wii. Then use actions $do(hw)$, $do(make\_bed)$, $do(tkd)$, and $do(wii)$ to make it easy to express the requirement that actions be mutually exclusive.

(b) Translate the representation to ASP and run it using an ASP solver to answer questions about whether a boy may play the Wii at various future moments. Make sure that the system description part of your program works for other variants of this story.

9

Planning Agents

In the next several chapters we discuss the application of the methodology for representing knowledge about dynamic domains and ASP programming to the design of intelligent agents capable of acting in a changing environment. The design is based on the agent architecture from Section 1.1. In this chapter we address *planning* – one of the most important and well studied tasks that an intelligent agent should be able to perform (see step 3 of the agent loop from Section 1.1).

9.1 Classical Planning with a Given Horizon

We start with **classical planning** in which a typical problem is defined as follows:

- A **goal** is a set of fluent literals that the agent wants to become true.
- A **plan** for achieving a goal is a sequence of agent actions that takes the system from the current state to one that satisfies this goal.
- **Problem**: Given a description of a deterministic dynamic system, its current state, and a goal, find a plan to achieve this goal.

A sequence α of actions is called a *solution* to a classical planning problem if the problem's goal becomes true at the end of the execution of α.

In this chapter we show how to use ASP programming techniques to solve a special case of the classical planning problem in which the agent has a limit on the length of the allowed plans. The limit is often referred to as the **horizon** of the planning problem.

To solve a classical planning problem $\mathcal{P}$ with horizon n, we construct a program $plan(\mathcal{P}, n)$ such that solutions of $\mathcal{P}$ whose length do not exceed n correspond to answer sets of $plan(\mathcal{P}, n)$. The program consists of ASP encodings of the system description of $\mathcal{P}$, the current state, and the goal, together with a small, domain-independent ASP program called the **simple**

planning module. The encoding of the system description is identical to the one used for temporal projection (meaning that, variable I for steps ranges over integers from 0 to n). (In the original encoding, it was enough for us to consider $n = 1$.) The encoding of the current state is identical to the encoding of the initial state from Chapter 8.

To encode the goal, we first introduce a new relation $goal(I)$ that holds if and only if all fluent literals from the problem's goal G are satisfied at step I of the system's trajectory. This relation can be defined by a rule:

```
goal(I) :- holds(f_1,I), ..., holds(f_m,I),
              -holds(g_1,I), ..., -holds(g_n,I).
```

where $G = \{f_1, \ldots, f_m\} \cup \{\neg g_1, \ldots, \neg g_n\}$.

Now let us describe the domain-independent part of the program (i.e., the simple planning module). The first two rules define the success of the search for a plan:

```
1  success :- goal(I),
2                I <= n.
3  :- not success.
```

The first rule defines success as the existence of a step in the system's trajectory that satisfies the relation $goal$. The second states that failure is not acceptable – a plan satisfying the goal should be found.

The second part of the planning module generates sequences of actions of the appropriate length that can possibly be the desired plans. One can imagine that the consequences of the execution of such a sequence in the current state are computed by the encoding of the system description of the problem. If these consequences include *success*, a plan is found. (Actual computation of plans is, of course, quite different – this is just one possible way to think about the program's behavior.)

In Gringo syntax, the corresponding generator can be written as a simple choice rule:

```
4  1{occurs(A,I): action(A)}1 :- step(I),
5                                 not goal(I),
6                                 I < n.
```

This guarantees that every answer set of our program includes an action sequence containing exactly one occurrence of an action at each step prior to the goal being achieved, and no occurrences of actions after the goal has been achieved. Note that if n is equal to the length of the shortest plan, then the planner will produce all plans of length n. For n larger than the length of the shortest plan, some of the plans produced will be longer than necessary – they may include irrelevant actions executed before the goal is achieved.

A similar effect can be achieved with DLV as shown next. The choice rule is replaced by several new rules where, as before, n stands for the horizon.

```
1  success  :- goal(I),
2                  I <= n.
3  :- not success.
4
5  occurs(A,I) | -occurs(A,I) :- action(A), step(I),
6                                  not goal(I),
7                                  I < n.
8
9  %% Do not allow concurrent actions:
10 :- action(A1), action(A2),
11    occurs(A1,I),
12    occurs(A2,I),
13    A1 != A2.
14
15 %% An action occurs at each step before
16 %% the goal is achieved:
17
18 something_happened(I) :- occurs(A,I).
19
20 :- step(J),
21    goal(I), not goal(I-1),
22    J < I,
23    not something_happened(J).
```

The encoding of the simple planning module is the last step in the construction of our program $plan(\mathcal{P}, n)$. The following proposition establishes the relationship between answer sets of this program and the solutions of $\mathcal{P}$.

Proposition 9.1.1. *Let $\mathcal{P}$ be a classical planning problem with a deterministic system description and let $0 < n$. A sequence of actions $a_0, \ldots, a_k$ where $0 \leq k < n$ is a solution of $\mathcal{P}$ with the horizon n iff there is an answer set S of $plan(\mathcal{P}, n)$ such that*

(i)   For any $0 < i \leq k$, $occurs(a_i, i-1) \in S$,
(ii) S contains no other atoms formed by occurs.

As mentioned earlier, if a horizon n is larger than the shortest plan needed to satisfy our goal, the planner may find that the plans contain irrelevant, unnecessary actions. To avoid this problem, we can use the planner to look for plans of lengths 1,2, and so on, until a plan is found. This can be accomplished by finding answer sets of programs $plan(\mathcal{P}, k)$ with $k = 1, 2, \ldots, n$. If $k = m$ is the smallest number for which this program is consistent, the shortest solutions of the planning problem $\mathcal{P}$ are given by answer sets of $plan(\mathcal{P}, k)$. If $plan(\mathcal{P}, k)$ is inconsistent for every $1 \le k \le n$, then problem $\mathcal{P}$ has no solution. There is no known way of automatically finding a minimal-length plan without multiple calls; however, Section 9.5 describes two simple extensions of ASP that achieve the task.

9.2 Examples of Classical Planning

9.2.1 Planning in the Blocks World

Let us start with considering the blocks world from Section 8.5.2. The ASP encoding of the system description of this domain is given by program bw.lp from that section. Our goal is to create a new program, bwplan.lp, which will find plans for the blocks world. The main thing we have to do is add one of the simple planning modules we just defined to bw.lp. Since our transition system in bw.lp was only defined for steps 0 and 1, we need to set the horizon by changing the value of n from 1 to 8:

```
1 #const n=8.
2 step(0..n).
```

As an added convenience, gringo (and therefore clingo) allows us to override the constant definition from the command line. Therefore, whenever we wish to run the program with a different horizon, we could simply change our call. For example, the call

```
clingo 0 -c n=9 bwplan.lp
```

would set the horizon to 9.

Further, we wish to format the output by adding a show statement to display only the positive *occurs* statements.

```
3 #show occurs/2.
```

These extract the plans from the corresponding answer sets. If the program is written in DLV, use option -pfilter=occurs.

We now have our blocks world planner, `bwplan.lp`. Try giving it a variety of initial states and goals. For example, you can use the initial state as encoded in Section 8.1 on lines 21–33, and the goal defined by the following rule:

```
4  goal(I) :-
5     holds(on(b4,t),I), holds(on(b6,t),I),
6     holds(on(b1,t),I), holds(on(b3,b4),I),
7     holds(on(b7,b3),I), holds(on(b2,b6),I),
8     holds(on(b0,b1),I), holds(on(b5,b0),I).
```

Let the horizon of our planning problem be $n = 8$. Now we have a planning problem and its logic programming encoding.

The call,

```
clingo 0 bwplan.lp
```

will find the problem's solutions. For instance, one of the answer sets of the program contains the following sequence:

```
occurs(put(b2,t),0)
occurs(put(b4,b1),1)
occurs(put(b3,b4),2)
occurs(put(b7,b3),3)
occurs(put(b6,t),4)
occurs(put(b2,b6),5)
occurs(put(b0,b1),6)
occurs(put(b5,b0),7)
```

To make the output more readable, we normally sort the predicates with respect to the second parameter. This may or may not be done by the solver, which knows nothing about the significance of this order.

If we try to run the same program with $n = 7$, we discover that the program is inconsistent. Hence, the earlier sequence is a shortest solution of our problem.

Now let's change n to 9 and ask our solver for all possible answer sets. It outputs quite a few. Some of them only have eight steps. Here is one with nine steps:

```
occurs(put(b2,t),0)
occurs(put(b7,t),1)
occurs(put(b6,t),2)
occurs(put(b4,t),3)
```

```
occurs(put(b3,b4),4)
occurs(put(b0,b1),5)
occurs(put(b5,b0),6)
occurs(put(b7,b3),7)
occurs(put(b2,b6),8)
```

Notice that this plan contains a wasteful action; by putting $b2$ on the table first, the planner misses the opportunity to put it directly on $b6$ at a later time. As we noted earlier, there is nothing in the code that insists that the planner find *only* the shortest plan – just that it not exceed the horizon. Therefore, it finds all plans that meet the conditions – shortest and otherwise.

Program bwplan.lp is a typical example of **Answer Set Planning**. It consists of the theory of the blocks world, the description of the initial state, the goal, the horizon, and the planning module. Our solution is completely independent of the problem description. We can change the initial state, the goal, and the horizon at will, without changing the rest of the program. Note that just because the theory is independent of the planning module does not mean that we cannot use specific domain knowledge to guide a planner. *The separation between domain knowledge and search strategy makes it easy to write domain-specific rules describing actions that can be ignored in the search.* This is covered in Section 9.3. As we see later, the blocks theory is also completely independent of planning – it can be used for multiple purposes.

Answer set planning does not require any specialized planning algorithm. The "planning" query is answered by the same reasoning mechanism used for other types of queries. *Therefore, the planning program can be easily generalized and improved.*

To illustrate, we begin by giving a few more examples of planning in the blocks world, followed by examples in a variety of other domains.

Example 9.2.1. *(Multiple Goal States)*
Note that each block of our domain is accounted for in the previous goal and there is only one possible goal state. Having only one goal state is certainly not a requirement, and it is perfectly fine to have multiple goal states. For example, we may only wish to require that $b3$ be on the table, in which case we write:

```
goal(I) :- holds(on(b3,t),I).
```

We let $n = 2$ and call the new program bwplanb3.lp. The solutions of the new problem can be found by calling an ASP solver. For example,

```
clingo 0 bwplanb3.lp
```

```
Answer: 1
occurs(put(b2,b4),0) occurs(put(b3,t),1)
Answer: 2
occurs(put(b2,b7),0) occurs(put(b3,t),1)
Answer: 3
occurs(put(b2,t),0) occurs(put(b3,t),1)
```

Example 9.2.2. *(Using Defined Fluents in the Goal)*
Let us now consider an extension of the system description of the blocks world by a new defined fluent, *occupied*(*block*). The corresponding definition is given by the following state constraint:

$$occupied(B) \textbf{ if } on(B_1, B)$$

We create a new program, occupied.lp, that incorporates this concept into our current blocks-world planner as specified by bwplan.lp. First, we expand our planner by the logic programming translation of this law; i.e., we add statements

```
1 fluent(defined, occupied(B)) :- block(B).
2 holds(occupied(B),I) :- block(B),
3                          holds(on(B1,B),I).
```

Note that rule

```
-holds(occupied(B),I) :- block(B), step(I),
                         not holds(occupied(B),I).
```

is not necessary because we already have the CWA for defined fluents in bwplan.lp.

Suppose now that we want blocks $b0$ and $b1$ to be unoccupied, but we do not care about the rest of the blocks. We state the goal as follows:

```
4 goal(I) :- -holds(occupied(b0),I),
5            -holds(occupied(b1),I).
```

Running program occupied.lp (bwplan.lp plus lines 1–5) with horizon 3 and the usual initial state, we get 45 answer sets corresponding to the shortest plans. Here are three examples:

```
Answer: 1
occurs(put(b4,t),0) occurs(put(b2,b7),1)
    occurs(put(b3,b2),2)
Answer: 2
```

```
occurs(put(b4,t),0) occurs(put(b2,b4),1)
    occurs(put(b3,b2),2)
Answer: 3
occurs(put(b4,t),0) occurs(put(b2,t),1)
    occurs(put(b3,b2),2)
```

Note that setting the horizon to 2 correctly produces no answer sets and setting it to 4 gives 837 answer sets, most of which contain a useless action.

This example shows that defined fluents can be useful in stating our goals. In fact, we may wish to define fluents specifically for this purpose.

Example 9.2.3. *(Defining Complex Goals)*
Further extension of the basic blocks-world domain can be obtained by supplying blocks with colors. This can be done by simply expanding our blocks-world $\mathcal{AL}$ system description from the previous example by a new sort, say *color*, with values *white* and *red* and a new static relation

$$is\_colored(B, C)$$

that holds iff block B is of color C. We assume that each block can have at most one color; i.e., the states of our domain should satisfy the following requirement:

$$\neg is\_colored(B, C_1) \text{ if } is\_colored(B, C_2), C_1 \neq C_2.$$

A possible goal for such a domain could be the general requirement that all towers must have a red block on top of them. To express this we use a defined fluent $wrong\_config$ (wrong configuration) that holds iff there is an unoccupied block B that is not red. (Of course, a block is unoccupied if and only if it is located on top of some (possibly empty) tower.) This can be specified using the fluent *occupied* from Example 9.2.2:

$$fluent(defined, wrong\_config(B))$$
$$wrong\_config \text{ if } \neg occupied(B), \neg is\_colored(B, red).$$

The goal of our problem is of the form:

```
goal(I) :- -holds(wrong_config,I).
```

All these examples show that our planning methods have a reasonable degree of elaboration tolerance with respect to possible extensions of the initial planning domain and modifications of goals and initial situations. Note also that our translation of system descriptions into ASP programs is modular (i.e., an extension of a system description is simply translated into ASP and added to the original program without necessitating further changes).

The next two examples show the application of our planning methodology to very different domains:

9.2.2 Igniting the Burner

Consider the following domain:

A burner is connected to a gas tank through a pipeline. The gas tank is on the left-most end of the pipeline and the burner is on the right-most end (see Fig. 9.1). The pipeline is made up of sections connected with each other by valves. The pipe sections can be either pressurized by the tank or unpressurized. Opening a valve causes the section on its right side to be pressurized if the section to its left is pressurized. Moreover, for safety reasons, a valve can be opened only if the next valve in the line is closed. Closing a valve causes the pipe section on its right side to be unpressurized.

We associate this domain with a planning problem of starting a flame in the burner. We start by describing an $\mathcal{AL}$ representation of this domain. The signature contains names for sections of the pipeline, $s_1, s_2, \ldots$, and for valves $v_1, v_2, \ldots$. The pipeline is described by static relations $connected\_to\_tank(S)$, $connected\_to\_burner(S)$, and $connected(S_1, V, S_2)$. (The latter holds if sections S_1 and S_2 are connected by valve V and the flow of gas is directed from S_1 to S_2.) Relation $connected$ defines the pipeline as the directed graph with source s_0 and sink s_n where s_0 is connected to the tank and s_n is connected to the burner. We also need inertial fluents – $opened(V)$ and $burner\_on$ – and defined fluent $pressurized(S)$. The actions are $open(V)$, $close(V)$, and $ignite$ – open and close the corresponding valves and ignite the burner. The state of the domain and its actions are characterized by the following system description:

$$pressurized(S) \textbf{ if } connected\_to\_tank(S).$$
$$pressurized(S2) \textbf{ if } connected(S1, V, S2),$$
$$opened(V),$$
$$pressurized(S1).$$
$$\neg burner\_on \textbf{ if } connected\_to\_burner(S),$$
$$\neg pressurized(S).$$
$$open(V) \textbf{ causes } opened(V).$$
$$\textbf{impossible } open(V) \textbf{ if } opened(V).$$
$$\textbf{impossible } open(V1) \textbf{ if } connected(S1, V1, S2),$$
$$connected(S2, V2, S3),$$
$$opened(V2).$$
$$close(V) \textbf{ causes } \neg opened(V).$$
$$\textbf{impossible } close(V) \textbf{ if } \neg opened(V).$$
$$ignite \textbf{ causes } burner\_on.$$
$$\textbf{impossible } ignite \textbf{ if } connected\_to\_burner(S),$$
$$\neg pressurized(S).$$

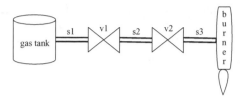

Figure 9.1. Pipeline Configuration

We use this description in conjunction with the specification of a pipeline that includes the pipeline configuration satisfying the above conditions and the status of the pipeline valves. We also assume that initially the burner is off.

Suppose the pipeline looks like the one modeled in Figure 9.1. Then an example initial situation could be

$$\{\neg burner\_on, \neg opened(v1), opened(v2)\}.$$

A goal can be defined as

$$burner\_on.$$

This completes the $\mathcal{AL}$ system description. The translation into ASP is straightforward. Please see Appendix D.1 for the ASP encoding; we call the program `ignite.lp`. The result of invoking `clingo` with the program is

```
occurs(close(v2),0)
occurs(open(v1),1)
occurs(open(v2),2)
occurs(ignite,3)
```

9.2.3 Missionaries and Cannibals

Another classical planning problem is stated as follows:

Three missionaries and three cannibals come to a river and find a boat that holds at most two people. If the cannibals ever outnumber the missionaries on either bank, the missionaries will be eaten. How can they all cross?

Here is one possible implementation. Our objects are missionaries, cannibals, a boat, and two locations corresponding to the two banks. We use variables $N, N1, N2, NC, NM, NCSource$, and $NMSource$ to stand for the number of cannibals or missionaries; they are integers in range 0 to 3.

Similarly, variable names starting with NB stand for the number of boats and can have values of either 0 or 1. We choose to represent the number

of missionaries, cannibals and boats at a location with inertial fluents as
follows:

$$m(Loc, N)$$

$$c(Loc, N)$$

$$b(Loc, NB)$$

where Loc is location $bank1$ or $bank2$. Letters m, c, and b stand for missionaries, cannibals, and the boat, respectively. For example, $m(bank1, 3)$
means that there are three missionaries on $bank1$; $b(bank1, 0)$ states that
there is no boat at $bank1$. Another important inertial fluent is

$$casualties$$

which is true if the cannibals outnumber the missionaries on the same bank.

Possible actions in this story are ones having to do with the movements
of missionaries and cannibals. We use

$$move(NC, NM, Dest)$$

to represent moving, by boat, NC cannibals and NM missionaries to
destination $Dest$. For example, $move(0, 1, bank2)$ means to move one
missionary to $bank2$.

To define some of our laws, we need to know the source of the movement,
not just the destination. We know that the source is always the opposite bank,
so we define a static relation:

$$opposite(bank1, bank2)$$

$$opposite(bank2, bank1).$$

The $\mathcal{AL}$ system description consists of the following laws:

- Moving objects increases the number of objects at the destination by
  the amount moved:

  $move(NC, NM, Dest)$ **causes** $m(Dest, N + NM)$ **if** $m(Dest, N)$
  $move(NC, NM, Dest)$ **causes** $c(Dest, N + NC)$ **if** $c(Dest, N)$
  $move(NC, NM, Dest)$ **causes** $b(Dest, 1)$

- The number of missionaries/cannibals at the opposite bank is 3 −
  number_on_this_bank. The number of boats at the opposite bank is

1 – number_of_boats_on_this_bank:
$$m(Source, 3 - N) \text{ if } m(Dest, N),$$
$$opposite(Source, Dest)$$
$$c(Source, 3 - N) \text{ if } c(Dest, N),$$
$$opposite(Source, Dest)$$
$$b(Source, 1 - NB) \text{ if } b(Dest, NB),$$
$$opposite(Source, Dest)$$

- There cannot be different numbers of the same type of person at the same location:
$$\neg m(Loc, N1) \text{ if } m(Loc, N2), N1 \neq N2$$
$$\neg c(Loc, N1) \text{ if } c(Loc, N2), N1 \neq N2$$

- A boat cannot be in and not in a location:
$$\neg b(Loc, NB1) \text{ if } b(Loc, NB2), NB1 \neq NB2$$

- A boat cannot be in two places at once:
$$\neg b(Loc1, N) \text{ if } b(Loc2, N), Loc1 \neq Loc2$$

- There will be casualties if cannibals outnumber missionaries:
$$casualties \text{ if } m(Loc, NM),$$
$$c(Loc, NC),$$
$$NM > 0, NM < NC$$

- It is impossible to move more than two people at the same time; it is also impossible to move less than one person:
$$\textbf{impossible } move(NC, NM, Dest) \text{ if } (NC + NM) > 2$$
$$\textbf{impossible } move(NC, NM, Dest) \text{ if } (NM + NC) < 1$$

- It is impossible to move objects without a boat at the source:
$$\textbf{impossible } move(NC, NM, Dest) \text{ if } opposite(Source, Dest),$$
$$b(Source, 0)$$

- It is impossible to move N objects from a source if there are not at least N objects at the source in the first place:
$$\textbf{impossible } move(NC, NM, Dest) \text{ if } opposite(Source, Dest),$$
$$m(Source, NMSource),$$
$$NMSource < NM$$
$$\textbf{impossible } move(NC, NM, Dest) \text{ if } opposite(Source, Dest),$$
$$c(Source, NCSource),$$
$$NCSource < NC$$

The ASP encoding is called `crossing.lp` and is in Appendix D.2. Invoking it with

```
clingo 0 crossing.lp
```

gives four answer sets, one of which we show next:

```
occurs(move(1,1,bank2),0)
occurs(move(0,1,bank1),1)
occurs(move(2,0,bank2),2)
occurs(move(1,0,bank1),3)
occurs(move(0,2,bank2),4)
occurs(move(1,1,bank1),5)
occurs(move(0,2,bank2),6)
occurs(move(1,0,bank1),7)
occurs(move(2,0,bank2),8)
occurs(move(0,1,bank1),9)
occurs(move(1,1,bank2),10)
```

9.3 Heuristics

The efficiency of ASP planners can be substantially improved by expanding a planning module by domain-dependent heuristics represented by ASP rules. As an example consider our blocks-world planning problem. Note that plans produced by the planning module in `bwplan.lp` may contain actions of the form $put(B, L)$ even when B is already located at L. Such an action can be executed by the robot's arm by lifting B up and putting it back on L or by simply doing nothing. In any case the action is completely unnecessary and can be eliminated from consideration by the planner. This can be done by the following heuristic rule:

```
1  :- holds(on(B,L),I),
2      occurs(put(B,L),I).
```

The additional information guarantees that the program will not generate plans containing this type of useless action.

The planning module can be expanded by another useful heuristic that tells the planner to only consider moving those blocks that are out of place. Notice that this heuristic is defined naturally in terms of subgoals because our towers are defined in terms of individual block placement. However, in our current encoding, this information is hidden in the rule defining relation $goal(I)$. To make it explicit we introduce a new relation

$$subgoal(fluent, boolean)$$

and expand our program by the following:

```
1  subgoal(on(b4,t),true).
2  subgoal(on(b6,t),true).
3  subgoal(on(b1,t),true).
4  subgoal(on(b3,b4),true).
5  subgoal(on(b7,b3),true).
6  subgoal(on(b2,b6),true).
7  subgoal(on(b0,b1),true).
8  subgoal(on(b5,b0),true).
```

This idea can be generalized for all heuristics that are based on knowledge of subgoal interaction.

Now the heuristic can be defined by the following rules:

```
9   in_place(B,I) :- subgoal(on(B,B1),true),
10                    holds(on(B,B1),I),
11                    in_place(B1,I).
12  in_place(t,I) :- step(I).
13
14  :- in_place(B,I),
15     occurs(put(B,L),I).
```

Again the heuristic allows the elimination of some "nonoptimal" plans. More importantly, it may have a substantial positive effect on the efficiency of the planning program. This is especially true if achieving the agent's goal does not require disassembling some of the towers located on the table. To see the effect of our two heuristics let us look at the following example.

Consider a blocks world with 17 blocks, $b0, \ldots, b16$, an initial block configuration represented by Figure 9.2, and a goal represented by Figure 9.3. The initial configuration is represented by the following collection of facts:

$$holds(on(b0, t), 0). \ holds(on(b3, b0), 0). \ \ldots$$

The goal configuration is given by this rule:

$$goal(I) \leftarrow holds(on(b4, t), I), holds(on(b1, b4), I), \ldots$$

and a collection of subgoals:

$$subgoal(on(b4, t), true). \ subgoal(on(b1, b4), true). \ \ldots$$

It may be instructive to run this input with and without the two heuristics described earlier for $n = 7$ (no solution), $n = 8$ (shortest solutions), and

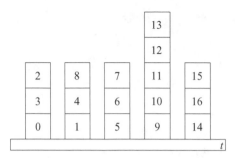

Figure 9.2. Initial Configuration

$n = 9$. Of course the result will depend on the solver you use, but most likely, you will be able to see that addition of the heuristics improves performance of the program. On our computer we have an approximately fivefold increase in efficiency of the planner tested with `clingo`. There is, however, only a slight improvement in the quality of plans. For $n = 8$ both planners (with and without heuristics) find five best plans of length 8. If $n = 9$ then the planner without heuristics finds 2,041 plans whereas the one with the heuristics finds 2,014 plans. Only 27 nonoptimal plans are eliminated.

Additional heuristics may help further improve efficiency and eliminate a much larger number of nonoptimal plans. Consider, for instance, another domain-dependent heuristic that gives priority to actions that increase the number of blocks placed in the right position. This can be written as follows:

```
1  good_move(B,L,I) :- subgoal(on(B,L),true),
2                      in_place(L,I),
3                      -occupied(L,I),
4                      -occupied(B,I).
5
6  occupied(B,I) :- block(B),
```

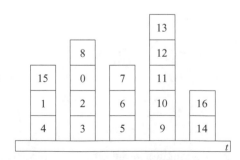

Figure 9.3. Goal Configuration

```
 7                    holds(on(B1,B),I).
 8  -occupied(t,I)  :- step(I).
 9  -occupied(B,I)  :- block(B), step(I),
10                     not occupied(B,I).
```

The first rule suggests that, if possible, it is good to move block B onto its required position L. The last three simply define relation *occupied*.

Note that it may be tempting to express our heuristic by a rule requiring an agent to execute a good move. This can be done by the rule

```
occurs(put(B,L),I)  :- good_move(B,L,I).
```

Unfortunately, this rule may lead to inconsistency. Remember that the domain has only one robotic arm and hence can execute only one action at a time. There are, however, situations with more than one good move.

We need to find another representation. The following, slightly more complex rules will do the job:

```
11  exists_good_move(I)  :- good_move(B,L,I).
12
13  :- exists_good_move(I),
14     occurs(put(B,L),I),
15     not good_move(B,L,I).
```

Instead of requiring good moves to be executed, these rules prohibit the execution of "bad" moves.

Let us now try a new planner containing all three heuristics on instances of the blocks-world problem from the previous example. This planner yields not only further improvement in efficiency but also in the number of nonoptimal plans eliminated by the heuristics. Instead of finding $2,014$ plans using the first two heuristics for $n = 9$, the planner that uses all three heuristics finds 42 plans. With the increase of n the advantages of using all three heuristics become even more obvious.

It is difficult to overestimate the importance of heuristic information for our ability to solve difficult search problems. There is, of course, a substantial amount of work related to heuristics. Among other things researchers are trying to discover criteria allowing us to estimate the usefulness of a heuristic and to find algorithms to automatically derive heuristics that are good for a given problem. Much of this work is done for planners based on specialized procedural planning algorithms. As previous examples show, heuristics can also be expressed declaratively, but much more work is needed to fully understand how to evaluate and automatically learn heuristics in the context of declarative planning methods.

9.4 Concurrent Planning

If our domain allows the simultaneous execution of several actions, we may want to look for so-called concurrent plans in which more than one action can be executed at each step. To adapt our $plan(\mathcal{P}, n)$ to this situation, all we need to do is change the planner's "generator" rule as follows:

```
1   1 {occurs(Action,I): action(Action)} m :- step(I),
2                                              not goal(I),
3                                              I < n.
```

Here m is the maximum number of actions that can be performed simultaneously. That's it. Answer sets of this new planning module, used together with the problem description, produce concurrent plans for achieving the problem's goal.

To better understand the behavior of concurrent planners, let us again look at the blocks world but now assume that the domain contains two robotic arms that are able to operate independently. We construct a new program, twoarmplan.lp, from bwplan.lp by changing the generator rule as described earlier (i.e., we simply set $m = 2$). As discussed in Section 8.5.3, we need to prohibit the program from putting something on a moving block. To achieve this, we add rule

```
4   -occurs(put(B1,L),I) | -occurs(put(B2,B1),I) :-
5                                   step(I),
6                                   action(put(B1,L)),
7                                   action(put(B2,B1)).
```

to twoarmsplan.lp, just as we did in Section 8.5.3.

We set the horizon to 5 and run clingo as follows:

```
clingo twoarmsplan.lp
```

The program returns one of the possible plans, say,

```
occurs(put(b7,t),0)
occurs(put(b4,t),0)
occurs(put(b2,t),1)
occurs(put(b6,t),1)
occurs(put(b2,b6),2)
occurs(put(b3,b4),2)
occurs(put(b0,b1),3)
occurs(put(b7,b3),3)
occurs(put(b5,b0),4)
```

The plan contains nine actions executed in five steps. The goal cannot be reached in four steps (i.e., the program with $n = 4$ is inconsistent). Note, however, that this plan is not optimal because there are plans containing a smaller number of actions. For example, the plan

```
occurs(put(b4,t),0)
occurs(put(b2,t),0)
occurs(put(b3,b4),1)
occurs(put(b0,b1),2)
occurs(put(b7,b3),2)
occurs(put(b6,t),3)
occurs(put(b5,b0),4)
occurs(put(b2,b6),4)
```

consist of eight actions. In the next section we show how to find optimal plans for this and similar problems.

9.5 (*) Finding Minimal Plans

It is, of course, desirable not to be forced to make multiple calls to a solver or to be able to make very good guesses about the horizon of planning problems in order to find minimal plans. Unfortunately, there is no known simple way to reduce the automatic discovery of minimal plans to computing answer sets of ASP programs. In this section we discuss how finding minimal plans can be done using two extensions of ASP – CR-Prolog introduced in Section 5.5 and ASP with minimality statements implemented on top of many ASP systems such as Smodels and `clingo`.

To use CR-Prolog to find minimal solutions to planning problems, we use the following rules instead of the original simple planning module of ASP:

```
1  success :- goal(I),
2              I <= n.
3  :- not success.
4
5  r1(A,I):occurs(A,I) +-.
6
7  something_happened(I) :- occurs(A,I).
8  :- step(I),
9     not something_happened(I),
10    something_happened(I+1).
```

```
11
12  -occurs(A2,I) :- occurs(A1,I),
13                   action(A2),
14                   A1 != A2.
```

The first two rules should be familiar. The next rule simply says that during the planning process the agent may consider occurrences of its actions if they are needed to resolve a contradiction (i.e., to achieve "success"). The next two rules guarantee that the agent does not plan to procrastinate (i.e., to remain idle at some time steps and continue actions afterward). The last rule is used to limit our planner to finding plans that allow the execution of at most one action per step.

The **Simple Planning Module of CR-Prolog** then consists of the above rules and the cardinality-based preference relation of CR-Prolog. It allows us to find the shortest one-action-per-step solutions of the planning problem with horizon n without resorting to multiple calls to ASP solvers. To obtain the concurrent version of the planner, we simply remove the planner's last rule. The new planner will find solutions of a planning problem that involve the minimal number of actions.

For example, let's replace the simple planning module of `bwplan.lp` with the CR-Prolog simple planning module to create program `crbwplan.lp`. Recall that running `bwplan.lp` with n=9 gave us plans with useless actions. To run `crbwplan.lp` with horizon 9, use the following command:

```
crmodels -m 0 -c n=9 --min-card --smodels clasp crbwplan.lp
```

- `-m 0` means "find all models"
- `-c n=9` means "set program constant n to 9"
- `--min-card` means "use the cardinality-based preference relation"
- `--smodels clasp` means "use clasp as the solver"

You will see that `crmodels` correctly finds the plans with eight actions, not nine.

Similarly, we can create `crtwoarmsplan.lp` from `twoarmsplan.lp` from the previous section. In this case, we replace the planning module with the CR-Prolog simple planning module without the last rule. Running `crmodels` to find minimal cardinality plans gives us only 2 models, as opposed to the 298 models for `twoarmsplan.lp`, even when the horizon is minimal ($n = 5$). Note also that because of the concurrency, minimal plans can be of different lengths. For example, if we use `crmodels` to run `crtwoarmsplan.lp` with the horizon set to 6, we get 20 models. Each one has only eight actions, but some have five steps and some have six.

We can also compute minimal plans by using a special form of the minimize statement of Lparse and `gringo`. Syntactically, the statement has the form

$$\#minimize\{q(X_1, \ldots, X_n) : s_1(X_1) : \cdots : s_n(X_n)\}$$

where $s_1, \ldots, s_n$ are sorts of parameters of q. The statement, which can be viewed as a directive to an ASP solver, instructs it to compute only those answer sets of the program that contain the smallest number of occurrences of atoms formed by predicate symbol q. To use this for planning, we simply add the statement:

```
#minimize{occurs(Action, K) : action(Action) : step(K)}.
```

to our programs. To get all optimizations, we need to call `clingo` with the command option `--opt-all`. To see how this affects the computations, try running `bwplan.lp` with and without the minimize statement as follows:

```
clingo 0 -c n=9 bwplan.lp --opt-all
```

Summary

In this chapter, we described declarative methodology for solving classical planning problems. Its main steps are as follows:

1. Use an action language (in our case $\mathcal{AL}$) to represent information about an agent and its domain.
2. Automatically translate this representation into a program of Answer Set Prolog.
3. Expand the program by the description of the initial state and the goal.
4. Use answer set solvers to compute the answer sets of the resulting program combined with a small program called the planning module. The maximum number of steps in plans computed by this program is parametrized by non-negative integer n.
5. A collection of facts formed by relation *occurs* that belong to such an answer set corresponds to a plan for achieving the goal in at most n steps.

This methodology was demonstrated by several examples.

The chapter is of interest for at least two reasons. First, it explains how to declaratively implement one of the most important reasoning steps in the agent loop – searching for plans to achieve the agent's goal. Second, it can be viewed as another typical example of answer set programming. Intuitively the task is solved by generating sequences of actions and testing if their execution satisfies the goal. This basic generate-and-test procedure is independent of the domain. Of course, real generate-and-test is done by answer set solvers and is much smarter than the "blind" generate-and-test of our theoretical models. We also discussed how additional knowledge given in terms of logic programming rules containing heuristic information can further increase the efficiency of the search.

Our solution has the typical advantages of ASP. It has a reasonably high level of elaboration tolerance. We do not need to alter an existing knowledge base of an agent to add planning capability. Very small changes allow us to go from one-action-at-a-time planning to planning allowing concurrent actions. The resulting programs are provably correct – they are shown to find plans that guarantee success (assuming of course that the world does not change in some unexpected way to interfere with our plans). Existing answer set solvers are sufficiently efficient to provide acceptable solutions for a substantial number of nontrivial planning problems. In many cases they successfully compete with specialized planners. In other cases no procedural solutions are known. This is especially true in domains where planning requires a large amount of knowledge.

There are, of course, a number of remaining problems. First, ASP-based planners may be inefficient if the required plans are very long because grounding programs with a large number of steps can be too costly. There is extensive ongoing work on efficient grounding in the ASP community that may help alleviate this problem (see, for instance, a new incremental ASP solver called iClingo). Second, ASP solvers may produce plans with a number of redundant, unnecessary actions. A short discussion in the last section of this chapter described several ways of finding optimal plans that do not contain such actions.

Finally, it is worth mentioning that the chapter only dealt with classical planning. There are many different types of planning undergoing extensive study in AI. For instance, if the initial information of the agent is incomplete or some actions in the domain are nondeterministic, the limited approach given in this chapter is not enough. In this situation the transition diagram of our domain may have multiple trajectories that start at possible initial states and are labeled by the same actions. Some of them will lead to the goal, whereas others will not. Our method allows us to find paths leading to the goal, but cannot guarantee that the execution of the corresponding actions will always do so. A sequence of actions such that *all paths* in the diagram that start in possible initial states and are labeled by actions of the sequence lead to states satisfying the goal is called a *conformant* plan. Finding conformant plans is computationally more difficult than simple planning but, when successfully solved, can be very useful. There are also planning and scheduling problems, the problem of finding plans that succeed with a high degree of probability, and so on. There are substantial advances in these areas as well. Both procedural and declarative methods for solving such problems (including those based on ASP) have been developed, but much more remains to be done.

Planning is a fascinating and important part of human reasoning, and of course, it is not surprising that it is not yet fully understood and automated. We hope, however, that this chapter gives some insight into a number of problems related to planning and outlines a feasible solution to the simplest (but nontrivial) form of this problem.

References and Further Reading

A good introduction to various planning methods can be found in Geffner and Bonet (2013). The earliest declarative planning program known to the authors is due to Cordell Green (1969). In this work knowledge is represented in situation calculus, and planning is reduced to theorem proving. The origins of declarative planning discussed in this chapter can be found in Kautz and Selman (1992). In this paper Henry A. Kautz and Bart Selman show how the classical planning problem can be reduced to checking satisfiability of a propositional formula. The use of ASP in planning can be traced to Subrahmanian and Zaniolo (1995) and Dimopoulos, Koehler, and Nebel (1997). A good exposition can be found in Lifschitz (2002). For information about various forms of procedural planning see, for instance, Poole and Mackworth (2010) and Ghallab, Nau, and Traverso (2004). Conformant planning is described in Tu et al. (2011) and Tran et al. (2013). More information about the use of heuristics in ASP can be found in Son et al. (2006), Gebser et al. (2013), and Balduccini (2011); Nogueira et al. (2001) contains an example of the practical use of planning with heuristics knowledge. The minimality and other optimization statements were first introduced in ASP by Ilkka Niemela and Patrik Simons (1997). To learn more about solving optimization problems using ASP one can consult Brewka, Niemela, and Truszczynski (2003). A new ASP solver, called iClingo (Gebser et al. 2008), grounds and solves problems incrementally; this avoids some of the grounding difficulties related to a large horizon.

Exercises

1. Replace rules

   ```
   success :- goal(I).
   :- not success.
   ```

   in program bwplan.lp by the single statement

   ```
   :- step(I), not goal(I).
   ```

   What happens? Why?

2. Add the planning module to the briefcase program, bc.lp, from Section 8.5.1 and set the horizon. Run the program to find a plan to unlock the briefcase from an initial situation in which both clasps are locked.

3. Create a new program, colorplan.lp, that extends bwplan.lp by incorporating logic programming translations of the laws defined in Examples 9.2.2 and 9.2.3. Test this program with the following colors of blocks in the initial situation: blocks 0, 3, 4, and 5 are red; the rest are white. Use the new goal and find a minimal plan. (Adjust the horizon accordingly.)

4. Modify the basic system description presented in Example 9.2.3 and use it to write a program that finds a minimal plan to have at least one tower consisting of only red blocks. The program must work with an arbitrary initial configuration (although you can adjust the horizon accordingly).

5. Expand the basic blocks-world system description $\mathcal{D}_{bw}$ by information on which blocks are heavy and which are light. Define a tower of blocks to be "uniform" if it consists entirely of one type of block, either all heavy or all light. Use the new system description to write an ASP program to find a minimal plan to create configurations of only uniform towers. The program must work with an arbitrary initial configuration (although you can adjust the horizon accordingly).

6. Give a simple $\mathcal{AL}$ action theory of shooting and use it to write an ASP program that finds a plan for shooting a turkey. Assume that the theory has actions *load* and *shoot* and fluents *loaded* and *alive*.

7. Give an $\mathcal{AL}$ action theory and use it to create an ASP program to solve the following classic puzzle:

A farmer needs to get a chicken, some seed, and a fox safely across a river. He has a boat that will carry him and one "item" across the river. The chicken cannot be left with the seed or with the fox without the farmer's presence. How can the farmer get everything across intact? Note: Don't get cute – there is no bridge, the river is not dry or frozen, there is no cage he can build, etc. The farmer must use the boat to ferry one thing/creature at a time.

8. Create a new system description by extending that given in Example 9.2.3 by adding a new action, $paint(B, C)$, which changes the color of block B to color C. Painting actions can be executed concurrently, but it is impossible to paint a moving block. Use the new theory to create a program with block colors in the initial situation as follows: Blocks 0, 3, 4, and 5 are red; the rest are white. Use the "towers must have a red block on top" goal. What is the shortest plan that the program comes up with if action "paint" is allowed? What is the shortest plan if action "paint" does not exist?

9. Convert the program from Exercise 7 in Chapter 8 to a planner that can find a plan for Jonathan to play the Wii.

10. Consider the farmers' market story from Exercise 6 in Chapter 8. Add the knowledge that customers will not buy a product from a vendor if they already have that product. Let us assume that Evaline is the first customer of the day and she knows what every vendor sells. For each of the following goals, write a program to find a plan to achieve it.
    (a) Evaline wants to buy something from every vendor.
    (b) She wants to buy one kind of fruit and two different kinds of vegetables.
    (c) Expand the problem's knowledge base by a new action $make\_coleslaw(P)$, which is executable if person P has carrots and cabbage. Evaline wants to make coleslaw.
    (d) She wants to buy apples, carrots and lettuce from the vendors closest to the entrance who carry these products. Amy has the closest stand followed by Bruce, Carrie, and Don.

10

Diagnostic Agents

In this chapter we discuss how to build agents capable of finding explanations of unexpected observations. To do that we divide actions of our domain into two disjoint classes: **agent actions** and **exogenous actions**. As expected the former are those performed by the agent associated with the domain, and the latter are those performed by nature or by other agents.[1] As usual we make two simplifying assumptions:

1. The agent is capable of making correct observations, performing actions, and recording these observations and actions.
2. *Normally* the agent is capable of observing all relevant exogenous actions occurring in its environment.

Note that the second assumption is defeasible – some exogenous actions can remain unobserved. These assumptions hold in many realistic domains and are suitable for a broad class of applications. In other domains, however, the effects of actions and the truth-values of observations can only be known with a substantial degree of uncertainty, which cannot be ignored in the modeling process. We comment on such situations in Chapter 11, which deals with probabilistic reasoning.

In our setting a typical **diagnostic problem** is informally specified as follows:

- A **symptom** consists of a recorded history of the system such that its last collection of observations is unexpected (i.e., it contradicts the agent's expectations).
- An **explanation** of a symptom is a collection of unobserved past occurences of exogenous actions that may account for the unexpected observations.

---

[1] If our agent is part of a multi-agent system, it is convenient to view actions of other agents as exogenous, just as we would view the occurrence of any other naturally occurring action.

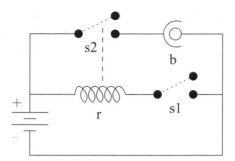

Figure 10.1. Circuit $\mathcal{AC}$

This notion of explanation is closely connected with our second simplifying assumption. Recall that, although assumptions about the agent's ability to perform and observe, as well as its knowledge of causal laws, are not defeasible, the completeness of its observations of exogenous actions is defeasible. Accordingly, the agent realizes that it may miss some of the exogenous actions and attributes its wrong prediction to such an omission. A collection of missing occurrences of exogenous actions that may account for the discrepancy is therefore viewed as an explanation.

- **Diagnostic Problem:** Given a description of a dynamic system and a symptom, find a possible explanation of the latter.

We illustrate this intuition by the following example.

Example 10.0.1. *(A Diagnostic Problem)*
Consider an agent controlling a simple electrical system consisting of circuit $\mathcal{AC}$ (see Fig. 10.1). We assume that switches s_1 and s_2 are mechanical components that cannot become damaged. Relay r is a magnetic coil. If not damaged, it is activated when s_1 is closed, causing s_2 to close. An undamaged bulb b emits light if s_2 is closed. The agent is aware of two exogenous actions relevant to its work: *break*, which causes the circuit bulb to become faulty, and *surge*, which damages the relay and also the bulb if the latter is not protected.

Suppose that at the beginning of the agent's activity the system is in the state depicted by Figure 10.1: The bulb is protected, both the bulb and the relay are known to be OK, and the agent closes switch s_1. The agent expects that this action will activate relay r and that, as a consequence, switch s_2 will become closed and bulb b will emit light. Assume now that the agent is surprised by an unexpected observation – the light is not lit. There are three natural explanations for this phenomenon: The bulb broke, the relay broke, or both broke. In other words one or both of the actions $break$ and $surge$ occurred in parallel with the agent's closing the switch. It seems that the commonsense reasoner usually ignores the third explanation and only concentrates on the first two. This is probably due to some notion of a minimal or best explanation that usually depends on ordering explanations as determined by the domain. In our case the first two explanations are minimal with respect to set-theoretic and cardinality-based orderings of explanations.

If, in addition to the initial observations, the agent was to observe that the bulb was OK, then the only possible minimal explanation of our unexpected observation would be the occurrence of $surge$. If the bulb was observed to be broken, then the only possible minimal explanation would be the occurrence of $break$. Of course, if initially the bulb was not protected, then both minimal explanations would still be valid. To find out the correct one, the agent would need to perform more "testing" actions (e.g., replace the bulb, etc).

In what follows we make this intuition precise. We start by presenting the syntax and semantics of the system's recorded history and show how it can be used to predict the current state of the system and to discover and explain unexpected observations.

10.1 Recording the History of a Domain

As mentioned earlier, we assumed that, in addition to a description of the transition diagram that represents possible trajectories of the system, the knowledge base of a diagnostic agent contains the system's **recorded history** – observations made by the agent together with a record of its own actions.

The recorded history defines a collection of paths in the diagram that, from the standpoint of the agent, can be interpreted as the system's possible pasts. If the agent's knowledge is complete (i.e., contains complete information about the initial state and the occurrences of actions) and the system's actions are deterministic, then there is only one such path. The following definitions describe the syntax and semantics of the recorded history of a dynamic system $\mathcal{SD}$ up to the current step n.

Definition 10.1.1. *(Recorded History – Syntax)*
*The **recorded history** Γ_{n-1} of a system up to a current step n is a collection of **observations** that come in one of the following forms:*

1. $obs(f, true, i)$ – *fluent f was observed to be true at step i; or*
2. $obs(f, false, i)$ – *fluent f was observed to be false at step i; or*
3. $hpd(a, i)$ – *action a was performed by the agent or observed to happen at step i*

where i is an integer from the interval $[0, n)$.

Definition 10.1.2. *(Recorded History – Semantics)*
A path $\langle \sigma_0, a_0, \sigma_1, \ldots, a_{n-1}, \sigma_n \rangle$ in the transition diagram $\mathcal{T}(\mathcal{SD})$ is a **model of a recorded history** Γ_{n-1} *of dynamic system $\mathcal{SD}$ if for any $0 \leq i < n$*

1. $a_i = \{a : hpd(a, i) \in \Gamma_{n-1}\}$;
2. *if $obs(f, true, i) \in \Gamma_{n-1}$ then $f \in \sigma_i$;*
3. *if $obs(f, false, i) \in \Gamma_{n-1}$ then $\neg f \in \sigma_i$.*

We say that Γ_{n-1} is **consistent** *if it has a model.*

Definition 10.1.3. *(Entailment)*

- *A fluent literal l* **holds** *in a model M of Γ_{n-1} at step $i \leq n$ (denoted by $M \models h(l, i)$) if $l \in \sigma_i$;*
- Γ_{n-1} **entails** $h(l, i)$ *(denoted by $\Gamma_{n-1} \models h(l, i)$) if, for every model M of Γ_{n-1}, $M \models h(l, i)$.*

Example 10.1.1. *(Recorded History in the Briefcase Domain)*
Let's look back at our briefcase example from Section 8.5.1. The system description, $\mathcal{D}_{bc}$, contains the agent's knowledge about the domain.

$$toggle(C) \textbf{ causes } up(C) \textbf{ if } \neg up(C)$$
$$toggle(C) \textbf{ causes } \neg up(C) \textbf{ if } up(C)$$
$$open \textbf{ if } up(1), up(2)$$

Suppose that, initially, clasp 1 was fastened and the agent unfastened it. The corresponding recorded history is

$$\Gamma_0 \begin{cases} obs(up(1), false, 0). \\ hpd(toggle(1), 0). \end{cases}$$

There are two models of Γ_0 that satisfy this history. In both models, our action, a_0, is $toggle(1)$, but our states, σ_0 and σ_1, are different. Path $\langle \sigma_0, toggle(1), \sigma_1 \rangle$ is a model of Γ_0 if

$$M_1 \begin{cases} \sigma_0 = \{\neg up(1), \neg up(2), \neg open\} \\ \sigma_1 = \{up(1), \neg up(2), \neg open\} \end{cases}$$

or

$$M_2 \begin{cases} \sigma_0 = \{\neg up(1), up(2), \neg open\} \\ \sigma_1 = \{up(1), up(2), open\} \end{cases}$$

Since Γ_0 has models, it is consistent with respect to the transition diagram for the briefcase domain in Figure 8.8. Although we have a consistent history, our knowledge is not complete. There are two possible trajectories consistent with the agent's recorded history Γ_0. At the end of one trajectory, the briefcase is open; at the end of the other, it is not. An intelligent agent would need more information to come up with a conclusion about the state of the briefcase. But, because $\Gamma_0 \models holds(up(1), 1)$, the agent knows that currently the first clasp is unlocked.

Consider another example where

$$\Gamma_0 \begin{cases} obs(up(1), true, 0) \\ obs(up(2), true, 0) \\ hpd(toggle(1), 0) \\ obs(open, true, 1) \end{cases}$$

This history is not consistent with the transition diagram in Figure 8.8 because it has no model. Note that there is no path in our diagram that we can follow in this situation. This makes sense since the briefcase is open iff both clasps are up, but the first clasp must be down at step 1 as the result of *toggle*.

10.2 Defining Explanations

Now let us consider an agent that completed the execution of its nth action. We denote the recorded history of the system up to this point by Γ_{n-1}. In accordance with our agent loop, the agent now observes the values of a collection of fluents at current step n. Let us denote these observations by O^n. The pair $\mathcal{C} = \langle \Gamma_{n-1}, O^n \rangle$ is often referred to as the **system configuration**. If new observations are consistent with the agent's view of the world (i.e., if $\mathcal{C}$ is consistent[2]), then O^n simply becomes part of the recorded history. Otherwise, the agent needs to start seeking the explanation(s) of

---

[2] Note that syntactically $\mathcal{C}$ can be viewed as the recorded history of the system, but unlike recorded history, it is not yet stored in the agent's memory. However, let us slightly abuse our terminology and talk about the inconsistency of system configuration $\mathcal{C}$ understood as the absence of a model of $\mathcal{C}$ viewed as a recorded history.

the mismatch. As mentioned earlier, the only possible explanation for un-expected observations would be that *some exogenous action(s) occurred that the agent did not observe*. This intuition is captured by the following definition:

Definition 10.2.1. *(Possible Explanation)*

- *A configuration $\mathcal{C} = \langle \Gamma_{n-1}, O^n \rangle$ is called a* **symptom** *if it is incon-sistent (i.e., has no model).*
- *A* **possible explanation** *of a symptom $\mathcal{C}$ is a set $\mathcal{E}$ of statements $occurs(a, k)$ where a is an exogenous action, $0 \leq k < n$, and $\mathcal{C} \cup \mathcal{E}$ is consistent.*

Example 10.2.1. *(Diagnosing the Circuit-1)*
To illustrate these definitions let us go back to the diagnostic problem from Example 10.0.1. To model the dynamic system from this example, we first need to define its transition diagram. This is done by the following system description, $\mathcal{D}_{ec}$:

Signature

Components:

$$comp(r)$$
$$comp(b)$$

Switches:

$$switch(s_1)$$
$$switch(s_2)$$

Fluents:

$$fluent(inertial, prot(b))$$
$$fluent(inertial, closed(SW)) \leftarrow switch(SW)$$
$$fluent(inertial, ab(X)) \leftarrow comp(X)$$
$$fluent(defined, active(r))$$
$$fluent(defined, on(b))$$

Actions:

$$action(agent, close(s_1))$$
$$action(exogenous, break)$$
$$action(exogenous, surge)$$

Laws

The causal laws, state constraints, and executability conditions describing the normal functioning of our system are encoded as follows:

$$close(s_1) \textbf{ causes } closed(s_1)$$
$$active(r) \textbf{ if } closed(s_1), \neg ab(r)$$
$$closed(s_2) \textbf{ if } active(r)$$
$$on(b) \textbf{ if } closed(s_2), \neg ab(b)$$
$$\textbf{impossible } close(s_1) \textbf{ if } closed(s_1)$$

The information about the system's malfunctioning is given by

$$break \textbf{ causes } ab(b)$$
$$surge \textbf{ causes } ab(r)$$
$$surge \textbf{ causes } ab(b) \textbf{ if } \neg prot(b)$$

This concludes our system description.

Next consider a history of the system:

$$\Gamma_0 \begin{cases} hpd(close(s_1), 0) \\ obs(closed(s_1), false, 0) \\ obs(closed(s_2), false, 0) \\ obs(ab(b), false, 0) \\ obs(ab(r), false, 0) \\ obs(prot(b), true, 0) \end{cases}$$

It is easy to see that the path $\langle \sigma_0, close(s_1), \sigma_1 \rangle$ where

$$\sigma_0 = \{prot(b)\}^3$$

$$\sigma_1 = \{prot(b), closed(s_1), active(r), closed(s_2), on(b)\}$$

is the only model of Γ_0 and hence

$$\Gamma_0 \models h(on(b), 1).$$

In other words, the agent expects the bulb to be lit.

To illustrate the notion of possible explanation, let us now assume that the agent observes that the bulb is not lit (i.e., its prediction differs from reality).

---

[3] Here, for simplicity, we show only positive literals in the description of states.

In our terminology it means that the configuration

$$\mathcal{C} = \langle \Gamma_0, obs(on(b), false, 1) \rangle$$

is a symptom. As discussed informally in Example 10.0.1 the symptom is expected to have three possible explanations:

$$\mathcal{E}_1 = \{occurs(surge, 0)\},$$
$$\mathcal{E}_2 = \{occurs(break, 0)\},$$
$$\mathcal{E}_3 = \{occurs(surge, 0), occurs(break, 0)\}.$$

Two of them are minimal with respect to set-theoretic and cardinality-based orderings of possible explanations. Our formal analysis leads to the same conclusion. Actions *break* and *surge* are the only exogenous actions available in our language, and $\mathcal{E}_1, \mathcal{E}_2$, and $\mathcal{E}_3$ are the only sets such that $\mathcal{C} \cup \mathcal{E}_i$ is consistent (for every $1 \leq i \leq 3$). Hence $\mathcal{E}_1, \mathcal{E}_2, \mathcal{E}_3$ are the only possible explanations of the symptom. If the agent was to observe that the bulb was OK, $\mathcal{E}_2$ would be the only possible explanation.

It is possible, in fact probable, that the system we would be modeling would be much more complex than the one we have here. Therefore, it is logical to assume that there may be many, possibly irrelevant, exogenous actions in our system. If we were to expand our circuit example by another exogenous action, $make\_coffee$, the addition of this action alone would add three new possible explanations of our original symptom:

$$\mathcal{E}_4 = \{occurs(surge, 0), \ occurs(make\_coffee, 0)\},$$
$$\mathcal{E}_5 = \{occurs(break, 0), \ occurs(make\_coffee, 0)\},$$
$$\mathcal{E}_6 = \{occurs(surge, 0), \ occurs(break, 0), occurs(make\_coffee, 0)\}.$$

Notice that, although we might want an explanation that includes both *break* and *surge*, we are probably not at all interested in knowing that some other agent made coffee.[4]

It is clear that no rational agent would be interested in finding all possible explanations of a symptom. Normally, different explanations can be compared with each other using various criteria. This comparison can be represented by an ordering relation between explanations. $\mathcal{E}_1$ can be viewed to be *better* than $\mathcal{E}_2$ if $\mathcal{E}_1$ is a proper subset of $\mathcal{E}_2$, or if the cardinality of $\mathcal{E}_1$ is less then the cardinality of $\mathcal{E}_2$, or if $\mathcal{E}_1$ contains actions that are more

---

[4] Of course, in the great scheme of things, we may not be able to dismiss this action lightly; it is possible that plugging in the coffee pot might have caused the surge in the first place.

likely to occur or are more relevant to the symptom than those in $\mathcal{E}_2$, and so on. The following definition makes this idea precise.

Definition 10.2.2. *(Best Explanation)*
*Let C be a symptom and $<$ be a partial linear order defined on possible explanations of C (where $\mathcal{E}_1 < \mathcal{E}_2$ is read as $\mathcal{E}_1$ is better than $\mathcal{E}_2$). Possible explanation $\mathcal{E}$ of C is called a **best explanation** with respect to $<$ if there is no possible explanation $\mathcal{E}_0$ of C such that $\mathcal{E}_0 < \mathcal{E}$.*

If the partial linear order on which we base our definition of best explanation is either cardinality-based or subset-based, the best explanations for the circuit problem would be $\{occurs(break, 0)\}$ and $\{occurs(surge, 0)\}$. In some situations one may want to also allow explanation $\{occurs(break, 0), occurs(surge, 0)\}$, but certainly no "best" explanation of our symptom will contain information about occurrences of $make\_coffee$. This result can be achieved by considering explanations consisting of actions "relevant" to the symptom. These actions can be defined as ones that in some way may, directly or indirectly, cause the corresponding fluent (in our case $on(b)$) to become false. Since no law in our system description links making coffee to problems with the circuit, this action can be considered irrelevant. Our best explanations would then be $\{occurs(break, 0)\}$, $\{occurs(surge, 0)\}$, and $\{occurs(break, 0), occurs(surge, 0)\}$ because, by our definition, they are better than the ones containing action $make\_coffee$.

10.3 Computing Explanations

Let us now consider a system with current configuration

$$C = \langle \Gamma_{n-1}, O^n \rangle.$$

The agent associated with the system just performed its nth action and observed the values of some fluents. Now the agent needs to check that this *configuration is consistent with the expectations* (i.e., that C is not a symptom). As in the case of planning, the problem can be reduced to reasoning with answer sets. To do that we construct program **all_clear** (with parameters $\mathcal{SD}$ and C) consisting of the encoding $\Pi(\mathcal{SD})$ of system description $\mathcal{SD}$, configuration C, and the following axioms:

$$holds(F, 0) \ or \ \neg holds(F, 0) \leftarrow fluent(inertial, F).$$
$$occurs(A, I) \leftarrow hpd(A, I).$$
$$\leftarrow obs(F, true, I), \neg holds(F, I).$$
$$\leftarrow obs(F, false, I), holds(F, I).$$

with I ranging over $[0, n]$. If program $all\_clear(\mathcal{SD}, \mathcal{C})$ is consistent, then the agent's expectations are consistent with its observations. Otherwise, diagnostics are required.

Each of these axioms deserves some explanation. We begin by briefly introducing them and then elaborating on each one in the examples that follow. The first axiom, sometimes called the **Awareness Axiom**, guarantees that the agent takes into consideration all the fluents of the system. Recall that this is not a tautology. Under the answer set semantics, the disjunction is epistemic, and the statement simply asserts that, during the construction of an agent's beliefs, the value of the fluent in question cannot be unknown; i.e., any answer set of the program must contain either $holds(F, 0)$ or $\neg holds(F, 0)$.

The second axiom establishes the relationship between two similar relations – $occurs$ and hpd. The latter is used to record actions that were actually observed to have happened, whereas the former holds even if the corresponding action is only hypothetical (as, for instance, in planning). As you can see, $occurs$ is a superset of hpd. The rule ensures that, in the process of hypothetical reasoning, we take into account actions that actually happened.

The last two rules, often called the **Reality Check Axioms**, guarantee that the agent's expectations agree with its observations. If they do not, we want the program to realize that there is an inconsistency between what it believes should logically be true versus what it has observed. Note that, despite the apparent similarity between the pair of relations hpd and $occurs$ and that of obs and $holds$, the actual axioms representing these relationships are different. The reason for this difference is discussed in Section 10.5.

The following proposition reduces detection of symptoms to ASP reasoning.

Proposition 10.3.1. *(Symptom Checking)*
A configuration $\mathcal{C}$ is a symptom iff program all$\_$clear$(\mathcal{SD}, \mathcal{C})$ *is inconsistent (i.e., has no answer set).*

Example 10.3.1. *(Briefcase)*
Let us again consider the briefcase domain from Section 8.5.1. One can easily check that for configuration $\mathcal{C}_0 = \langle \Gamma_0, obs(open, true, 1) \rangle$ where Γ_0 is

$$\Gamma_0 \begin{cases} obs(up(1), false, 0) \\ obs(up(2), true, 0) \\ hpd(toggle(1), 0) \end{cases}$$

program $all\_clear(\mathcal{D}_{bc}, \mathcal{C}_0)$ is consistent, and hence $\mathcal{C}_0$ is not a symptom. If $\mathcal{C}_1 = \langle \Gamma_0, obs(open, false, 1) \rangle$ then $all\_clear(\mathcal{D}_{bc}, \mathcal{C}_1)$ is inconsistent, and as expected, $\mathcal{C}_1$ is a symptom.

Now let us consider the problem of computing explanations of a symptom $\mathcal{C} = \langle \Gamma_{n-1}, O^n \rangle$. Again, this problem can be reduced to computing answer sets of an ASP program. The program, called **diagnose** (with parameters $\mathcal{SD}$ and $\mathcal{C}$), consists of

- the rules of $all\_clear(\mathcal{SD}, \mathcal{C})$
- the **explanation generation** rule

$$occurs(A, I) \ or \ \neg occurs(A, I) \leftarrow 0 \leq I < n,$$
$$action(exogenous, A)$$

or, alternatively,

$$\{occurs(A, I) : action(exogenous, A)\} \leftarrow 0 \leq I < n.$$

- and the following rule, which defines the new relation $expl(A, I)$: The relation holds iff an exogenous action A is hypothesized to occur at I, but there is no record of this occurrence in the agent's history.

$$expl(A, I) \leftarrow action(exogenous, A),$$
$$occurs(A, I),$$
$$not \ hpd(A, I).$$

The following proposition reduces computation of a possible explanation of a symptom to extracting atoms formed by relation $expl$ from an answer set of $diagnose(\mathcal{SD}, \mathcal{C})$.

Proposition 10.3.2. *(Computing Possible Explanations)*
A set $\mathcal{E}$ is a possible explanation of a symptom $\mathcal{C}$ iff there is an answer set A of diagnose($\mathcal{SD}, \mathcal{C}$) such that

$$\mathcal{E} = \{occurs(a, i) : expl(a, i) \in A\}.$$

Example 10.3.2. *(Diagnosing the Circuit–2)*
To illustrate the proposition let us again go back to the electrical circuit domain and history Γ_0 from Example 10.2.1. Initially both switches are open, the bulb and the resistor are normal, the bulb is protected, and the agent closes switch s_1. In Example 10.2.1 we showed that a configuration

$$\mathcal{C} = \langle \Gamma_0, obs(on(b), false, 1) \rangle$$

is a symptom with three possible explanations:

$$\mathcal{E}_1=\{occurs(surge,0)\},$$
$$\mathcal{E}_2=\{occurs(break,0)\},$$
$$\mathcal{E}_3=\{occurs(surge,0),occurs(break,0)\}.$$

One can easily check that, using Proposition 10.3.2, these explanations can be extracted from answer sets of program $diagnose(\mathcal{D}_{ec},C)$. Please see Appendix D.3 for the complete program, $diagnose(\mathcal{D}_{ec},C)$; we call it circuit.lp. Note that, in the presence of complete information for the initial state, it is often convenient to use a CWA to specify the inertial fluents that are false:

```
obs(F, false, 0) :- fluent(inertial,F),
                    not obs(F,true,0).
```

If we had added the above line to circuit.lp, then the recorded history could have simply been coded as

```
obs(prot(b),true,0).
hpd(close(s1),0).
obs(on(b),false,1).
```

Defined fluents are taken care of by their CWA.

As expected, invoking this program with, say, clingo 0 circuit.lp yields the following:

```
Answer: 1
expl(break,0)
Answer: 2
expl(surge,0)
Answer: 3
expl(break,0) expl(surge,0)
```

Note that the last explanation is not minimal and may or may not be viewed as desirable. At the end of the previous section we discussed an extension of our system by a new action, *make_coffee*, and showed that it substantially increased the number and length of explanations. All these explanations are found by our method. Possibly the simplest way to limit this number would be to put restrictions on the number of exogenous actions that may be unnoticed by the agent. This can be done by the addition of a simple constraint

```
%% The agent could miss at most one exogenous action.
:- action(exogenous,X1),
   action(exogenous,X2),
   X1 != X2,
   occurs(X1,I),
   not hpd(X1,I),
   occurs(X2,I1),
   not hpd(X2,I1).
```

This constraint eliminates explanation $\{expl(break, 0), expl(surge, 0)\}$, as well as all explanations containing action $make\_coffee$. If we wanted to preserve explanation $\{expl(break, 0), expl(surge, 0)\}$ but still eliminate those that contain irrelevant actions, we could replace the above constraint by

```
:- action(exogenous,X),
   occurs(X,I),
   not hpd(X,I),
   not relevant(X,on(b)).

relevant(break,on(b)).
relevant(surge,on(b)).
```

where $on(b)$ is the fluent whose unexpected value we are trying to explain.

The next section describes other ways of computing best explanations by using existing extensions of ASP. These methods are very similar to those used to find minimal plans in Section 9.5.

10.4 (*) Finding Minimal Explanations

So far we only discussed the way to compute possible explanations of unexpected observations. As seen in the coffee example from Section 10.2, there are normally too many such explanations, often containing completely irrelevant actions. So it would be natural to limit ourselves to computing minimal possible explanations (with respect to cardinality, set-theoretic, or some other type of explanation ordering). Unfortunately, as with the problem of finding minimal plans, there is no known simple way to reduce this to computing answer sets of ASP programs. Therefore, as in Section 9.5 of the chapter on planning, we rely on CR-Prolog or the `minimize` statement.

To reduce the problem of computing minimal explanations to finding answer sets of programs of CR-Prolog, we can simply replace the earlier explanation-generation rule by cr-rule

$$occurs(A, I) \xleftarrow{+} 0 \leq I < n,$$
$$action(exogenous, A).$$

The rule says that an observed exogenous action could possibly have occurred in the past, but is a rare event that should be ignored by the agent whenever possible. Accordingly, if a current configuration is not a symptom, these rules are ignored. However, if it is a symptom, then a minimal collection of such rules is used to restore consistency and provide the symptom's diagnosis. (Recall that minimality can refer to set-theoretic or cardinality ordering depending on the options used in the invocation of the CR-Prolog inference engine.) Try adding exogenous action $make\_coffee$ to `circuit.lp`, changing the explanation-generation rule, and running the new program with CR-Prolog.

The `minimize` statement of Gringo that came in so handy for finding minimal plans in Section 9.5 can also be used to compute minimal explanations. Let us consider a program $min\_diagnose(\mathcal{SD}, \mathcal{C})$ obtained by expanding $diagnose(\mathcal{SD}, \mathcal{C})$ with

$$minimize\{occurs(A, S) : action(exogenous, A) : step(S)\}.$$

It is clear that the resulting program is going to compute only the diagnosis of $\mathcal{C}$ that is minimal with respect to the cardinality ordering of explanations. Try adding this `minimize` statement to the circuit program that includes exogenous action $make\_coffee$. You will need to use the `--opt-all` option with `clingo` to direct it to return all possible optimizations.

10.5 Importance of New Predicates hpd and obs

The attentive reader may wonder why our language of recorded history (and consequently the program $diagnose$) uses new predicate symbols obs and hpd instead of the old $holds$ and $occurs$ used in the previous chapter. Of course, part of the explanation lies in these symbol's intuitive meaning. In accordance with assumptions about our agent's ability made at the beginning of this chapter, $obs(f, true, i)$ guarantees the truth of f at step i of the corresponding trajectory, whereas $holds(f, i)$ can also stand for expressing our hypothesis about the value of f at i. (This is exactly how $holds$ was used in planning.) The same goes for hpd and $occurs$. One can still wonder why this distinction is important. What, if anything, will be lost if we stick with our old vocabulary?

To answer this question for *obs* and *holds*, it is enough to notice that our definition of a symptom depends on the agent's ability to distinguish between observations and hypotheses, and hence, the distinction does not look too surprising. One can still ask, however, why the reality check (which is based on the distinction between observation and prediction) is not written in a way similar to the axiom for *hpd* and *occurs* as follows:

$$holds(F, I) \leftarrow obs(F, true, I). \qquad\qquad (*)$$

$$\neg holds(F, I) \leftarrow obs(F, false, I). \qquad\qquad (**)$$

To see the difficulty let us consider the following history of some domain

$$obs(f, true, 0)$$

$$hpd(a, 0)$$

where action a does not change the value of inertial fluent f. What would be the value of f at 1? From the observation of f, the awareness axiom, and the original reality check, we have $holds(f, 0)$. From the inertia axiom, the axiom relating hpd and $occurs$, and the independence of f from a, we have $holds(f, 1)$. What would happen now if we were to expand our history by

$$obs(f, false, 1)?$$

Clearly, this observation will contradict our (default) prediction $holds(f, 1)$, and hence the reality check will, as expected, cause a contradiction.

Let's now see how this reasoning would change if we were to replace the reality check by rules (*) and (**) mentioned earlier, which can be viewed as expansions of the agent's definition of *holds*. Suppose there is no observation at step 1, yet f is still true at 0. As before, inertia leads us to believe $holds(f, 1)$. However, the addition of $obs(f, false, 1)$ together with the new axiom (**) allows the reasoner to defeat the inertia axiom and conclude $\neg holds(f, 1)$. This new power of prediction allows the agent to conclude too much – f mysteriously becomes false. This clearly contradicts our general assumption about dynamic domains from Chapter 8 that insists that change is the result of action. Therefore, we defined the reality check in terms of constraints and used the awareness axiom to resolve any possible incompleteness of the initial state.

Summary

In this chapter, we described declarative methodology for solving the basic diagnostics problem – finding possible explanations for discrepancies between what an agent expects and what it observes. As in the case of classical planning, we used a mathematical model that views a dynamic domain as a transition system represented by a system description of $\mathcal{AL}$. The description contains axioms specifying normal behavior of the system together with those describing actions that can cause the system's malfunctioning. These axioms, however, are not enough. In addition, the agent must maintain the recorded history of actions and observations that describes past trajectories of the system possible from the standpoint of the agent. Given this information the agent can determine a symptom – a new observation not compatible with any of these trajectories. The symptom is explained by assuming the existence of past occurrences of exogenous actions that escaped the agent's attention and remain unobserved. The precise definition of a recorded history and its models, as well as the notions of symptom and possible explanation that were presented in this chapter, capture this intuition. To compute possible explanations of symptoms, we expanded our translation of a system description of $\mathcal{AL}$ into logic programs by using several additional axioms including the awareness and reality check axioms. The new translation allowed us to introduce the basic diagnostics module, which is very similar to the simple planning module discussed in the previous chapter. (Instead of hypothesizing about future actions by the agent, the diagnostics module makes hypotheses about past exogenous actions.) The chapter continued with a short discussion of ways to limit our computation to explanations that do not contain irrelevant actions. As in the case of planning, we showed how this can be done in extensions of Answer Set Prolog by consistency-restoring rules and by minimization constructs. The chapter ended with some comments explaining several subtle points related to the language used to record the history of the domain.

The ability to find explanations of unexpected events is another important reasoning task that has been reduced to the computation of answer sets. Even though much more work is needed to fully understand diagnostic reasoning, the material presented in the chapter can serve as the basis for declarative design of intelligent agents. It is especially important to notice that both planning and diagnostic reasoning use the same knowledge of the domain.[5]

---

[5] Even though this may not be surprising to the readers of this book, historically substantially different knowledge bases were used for each task.

References and Further Reading

The account of diagnosis presented in this chapter is based on Balduccini and Gelfond (2003). The approach has its roots in the early work of Reiter (1987), de Kleer, Mackworth, and Reiter (1992), and Poole (1994), which laid the foundations of logic based diagnosis. Readers interested in learning more about this period may want to consult Hamscher, Console, and de Kleer (1992). Most of the early work on diagnosis was limited to static domains and defined diagnosis in terms of a collection of faulty components that could explain unexpected behavior of the system. In Thielscher (2008) and Baral, McIlraith, and Son (2000), these ideas were applied to dynamic domains, and diagnosis became related to exogenous actions causing the corresponding faults. In Balduccini and Gelfond (2003), the authors simplified these ideas and established the relationship between diagnosis and answer set programming presented in this chapter. Of course our account of diagnostic reasoning only touches on this vast and important area of research. A rather comprehensive panorama of different diagnosis-related problems and solutions can be found in the proceedings of the annual International Workshop on Principles of Diagnosis that started in 1989.

Exercises

1. (a) Give causal laws of $\mathcal{AL}$ for action $receive(X, N, P)$ – person X receives N units of produce P. Use a fluent $has(X, N, P)$ that holds iff person X has N units of produce P.
   (b) Describe a recorded history Γ_1 in which Ray, who initially has three apples, receives two more of them.
   (c) Show logic program $all\_clear(\mathcal{SD}, \mathcal{C})$ for system description $\mathcal{SD}$ from (a) and configuration $\mathcal{C} = \langle \Gamma_1, \emptyset \rangle$.
   (d) Check if $\mathcal{C}$ is a symptom.

2. You are given the following story:
   Mixing baking soda with lemon juice produces foam, unless the baking soda is stale. Joanna mixed baking soda with lemon juice, but there was no foam as a result.

   (a) Represent the story by a system description of $\mathcal{AL}$ and a recorded history.
   (b) Translate this representation into ASP and check if the resulting configuration is a symptom. What knowledge does the agent have about the quality of Joanna's baking soda?

3. You are given the following story:
Arnold needs to get the book he left in his room. The room is locked and dark, but Arnold has the key and can turn on the light.

  (a) Represent this domain in ASP and write a program that finds a plan that allows Arnold to get the book. *Hint*: Do not forget to tell the planner that one cannot go into a room if one is already in it, etc.

  (b) Suppose that *after Arnold turned on the light switch, the room remained dark*. Add a history to your program that records that the steps in Arnold's plan have been executed and that the room was observed to still be dark. Assume that there are two relevant exogenous actions, $break(switch)$ and $break(power\_line)$.
  Replace your planning module with an explanation module that comes up with a minimal explanation of this unexpected observation.

4. Consider the farmers' market story from Exercise 10 in Chapter 9. Suppose that Fred, Georgina, and Harry are the first customers to arrive at the farmers' market. Fred wants to buy apples, pears, and lettuce. He knows what each of the vendors sells, so he decides to buy apples from Amy first, then lettuce from Bruce, and finally pears from Don. However, when he arrives at Don's booth he learns that Don is out of pears. Write an ASP program that models this domain and its history and comes up with a diagnosis. Note that, because Fred is the one doing the shopping, his actions are considered agent actions, whereas the actions of other customers are exogenous. Natural concurrent actions should be allowed, but obvious restrictions should also apply. To limit possible answer sets, also add the assumption that two customers cannot buy from the same vendor at the same time.

5. You are given the following story:
Millie is a teenager. She felt fine when she was at school but when she came home she observed that she had a fever and a severe, coated sore throat. She knows that, in teenagers, these are symptoms of both strep throat and mononucleosis. She concludes that she has one of these diseases.

  (a) Represent Millie's medical knowledge in $\mathcal{AL}$ and her knowledge about her actions and observations as a recorded history. Use exogenous actions $infect(strep, Person)$ or $infect(mono, Person)$ that cause a person to have strep or mono, respectively. The symptoms of these diseases can be viewed as indirect effects of these actions.

(b) Translate your representation into ASP, and add the explanation module and rules limiting the number of unobserved exogenous actions to model Millie's reasoning.

(c) *A day later, Millie develops jaundice, which is a symptom of mono, but not strep. She concludes that she has mononucleosis.* Add the new knowledge to you program and run it to find the new explanation. Use action *wait* to represent that Millie waited a day before observing her new symptom.

11

Probabilistic Reasoning

The knowledge representation languages and reasoning algorithms discussed in previous chapters allowed an agent to reason with various forms of incomplete knowledge. Defaults gave agents the ability to make assumptions about completeness of their knowledge and to withdraw these assumptions if they contradicted new information. Incompleteness of the agent's knowledge was manifested by multiple answer sets, some of which contained proposition p whereas others contained its negation. This was the case for, say, the program consisting of the awareness axiom,

$$p(a) \ or \ \neg p(a)$$

for $p(a)$. Another form of incompleteness, exhibited by program

$$q(a). \quad q(b). \quad p(b).$$

corresponded to the case when the agent associated with the program was simply not aware of $p(a)$. Technically, the program has one answer set containing neither $p(a)$ nor $\neg p(a)$. In both these cases, propositions could only have three truth values: *true*, *false*, and *unknown*. In this chapter we discuss an augmentation of our knowledge representation languages with constructs for representing a finer gradation of the strength of an agent's beliefs. The resulting language preserves all the power of ASP, including the ability to represent defaults, nonmonotonically update the knowledge base with new information, define rules recursively, and so on, while allowing an agent to do sophisticated probabilistic reasoning.

11.1 Classical Probabilistic Models

Mathematicians and computer scientists have developed a number of mathematical models capturing various aspects of quantifying the beliefs of a rational agent. The oldest and most developed collection of such models can be found in probability theory – a branch of mathematics with a several hundred year history of development and applications. Even though probability theory is a well-developed branch of mathematics, the methodology of its use for knowledge representation and even the intuitive meaning of basic notions of the theory are still matters of contention. In this book we view probabilistic reasoning as *commonsense reasoning about the degree of an agent's beliefs in the likelihood of different events*. In what follows we clarify the meaning of this statement. Let us start with a simple example.

Example 11.1.1. *(Lost in the Jungle)*

Imagine yourself lost in a dense jungle. A group of natives has found you and offered to help you survive, provided you can pass their test. They tell you they have an Urn of Decision from which you must choose a stone at random. (The urn is sufficiently wide for you to easily get access to every stone, but you are blindfolded so you cannot cheat.) You are told that the urn contains nine white stones and one black stone. Now you must choose a color. If the stone you draw matches the color you chose, the tribe will help you; otherwise, you can take your chances alone in the jungle. (The reasoning of the tribe is that they do not wish to help the exceptionally stupid or the exceptionally unlucky.)

It does not take knowledge of probability theory to realize that you will have a much better chance of obtaining their help if you choose white for the color of the stone. All that is required is common sense. Your line of reasoning may be as follows: "Suppose I choose white. What would be my chances of getting help? They are the same as the chances of drawing a white stone from the urn. There are nine white stones out of a possible ten. Therefore, my chances of picking a white stone and obtaining help are $\frac{9}{10}$." The number $\frac{9}{10}$ can be viewed as the degree of belief that help will be obtained if you select white. To double-check yourself (since your life may depend on your choice), you might consider what would happen if you choose black. In this case, to get help you need to draw the black stone. The chances of that are one out of ten ($\frac{1}{10}$). Clearly, you should choose white.

To mathematically study this type of reasoning, one may use the classical notion of a **probabilistic model**. Such models consist of

- a finite set Ω whose elements are referred to as **possible worlds**. Intuitively possible worlds correspond to possible outcomes of random experiments we attempt to perform (such as drawing a stone from the urn);

- a function μ from possible worlds of Ω to the set of real numbers such that

$$\text{for all } W \in \Omega \; \mu(W) \geq 0 \text{ and}$$

$$\sum_{W \in \Omega} \mu(W) = 1.$$

Function μ is referred to as a **probabilistic measure**. Intuitively $\mu(W)$ quantifies the agent's degree of belief in the likelihood of the outcomes of random experiments represented by W.

A function

$$P : 2^{\Omega} \to [0, 1]$$

such that

$$P(E) = \sum_{W \in E} \mu(W)$$

for any $E \subseteq \Omega$ is called a **probability function** induced by μ; it characterizes the degree of belief in the likelihood of the actual outcome of the agent's experiment belonging to E.

Of course, this simple definition only works for situations in which there is only a finite number of possible worlds. Modern probability theory generalizes this notion to the infinite case and discovers many nontrivial properties of probability and other similar measures. But even the simple definition described earlier allows us to obtain nontrivial properties of probability and to successfully use the resulting calculus to reason about the likelihood of a particular outcome of random events.

In logic-based probability theory, possible worlds are often identified with logical interpretations, and a set E of possible worlds is often represented by a formula F such that $W \in E$ iff W is a model of F. In this case the probability function may be defined on propositions

$$P(F) =_{def} P(\{W : W \in \Omega \text{ and } W \text{ is a model of } F\}).$$

Now let us go back to our traveler saying, "Suppose I choose white," and performing the mental experiment of randomly drawing a stone from the urn. To understand a mathematical model that predicts his chances of getting help, we need to come up with a collection Ω of possible worlds that correspond to possible outcomes of this random experiment. There are, of course, many ways of doing this task. We start with a fairly detailed representation that includes individual stones. To be able to refer to stones, we enumerate them by integers from 1 to 10 starting with the black stone. The possible world describing the effect of the traveler drawing stone number 1 from the urn looks like this:

$$W_1 = \{select\_color = white, draw = 1, \neg help\}.$$

Drawing the second stone results in possible world

$$W_2 = \{select\_color = white, draw = 2, help\}$$

etc. We will have 10 possible worlds, 9 of which contain *help*. To define a probabilistic measure μ on these possible worlds, we use the so-called **Principle of Indifference** – a commonsense rule that states that *possible outcomes of a random experiment are assumed to be equally probable if we have no reason to prefer one of them to any other.* This rule suggests that $\mu(W) = 0.1$ for any possible world $W \in \Omega$. According to our definition of probability function P, the probability that the outcome of the experiment contains *help* is 0.9. A similar argument for the case in which the traveler selects black gives 0.1. The probabilistic model allowed us to produce the expected result.

The reader, of course, noticed that the most difficult part of this argument was setting up a probabilistic model of our domain – especially the selection of possible worlds. This observation raises a typical computer science question: *"How can possible worlds of a probabilistic model be found and represented?"* In what follows we discuss one of the possible ways of doing this: We simply encode the knowledge presented to us in a story by a program in knowledge representation language **P-log** – an extension of ASP and/or CR-Prolog that allows us to combine logical and probabilistic knowledge. Answer sets of a program of the new language are identified with possible worlds of the domain.

11.2 The Jungle Story in P-log

We now show how to encode the jungle story in P-log. (We call the resulting program Π_{jungle}.) The syntax of P-log is similar to that of ASP but unlike standard ASP, the signature of a P-log program is sorted – each function symbol comes with sorts for its parameters and its range. Π_{jungle} has two sorts, *stones* and *colors*, consisting of objects of our domain. The sorts are defined by the following P-log statements:

$$stones = \{1, 2, 3, 4, 5, 6, 7, 8, 9, 10\}.$$

$$colors = \{black, white\}.$$

For the sake of making it easy to talk about the stones, we assume that the first one is black and the others are white. (It really does not matter which one is black.) This is exactly what we did in setting up our first model. To record this we introduce a function *color* mapping stones into colors:

$$color : stones \rightarrow colors.$$

(The usual mathematical notation is used for the function declarations.) The values of the function are given by the following P-log rules.

$$color(1) = black.$$
$$color(X) = white \leftarrow X \neq 1.$$

Note that the only difference between rules of P-log and ASP is the form of the atoms.

To proceed, let us call the random process of selecting one of these stones from the urn *draw*. In P-log this process corresponds to the following declaration:

$$draw : stones.$$
$$random(draw).$$

The first statement says that *draw* is a zero-arity function that takes its values from the sort *stones*. The second statement, referred to as a **random selection rule**, states that *normally*, in a (mental or physical) experiment conducted by the reasoner, the values for *draw* are selected at random. Random processes of P-log are often referred to as **random attributes**. Finally we need to declare two zero-arity functions

$$select\_color : colors$$

and

$$help : boolean$$

where *boolean* is a predefined sort with the usual values *true* and *false*. The tribal laws are then represented by these rules:

$$help \leftarrow draw = X,$$
$$color(X) = C,$$
$$select\_color = C.$$
$$\neg help \leftarrow draw = X,$$
$$color(X) = C,$$
$$select\_color \neq C.$$

Here *help* and $\neg help$ are used as shorthand for $help = true$ and $help = false$, respectively. Also, $select\_color \neq C$ is understood as shorthand for $\neg(select\_color = C)$.

This concludes the construction of our first P-log program, Π_{jungle}. It represents the traveler's knowledge about his situation. Recall that informally the traveler starts by asking himself the following question: *"Suppose I choose white. What would be my chances of getting help?"* To answer this question the reasoner first expands the program Π_{jungle} by the statement

$$select\_color = white.$$

The resulting program, $\Pi_{jungle}(white)$, contains one random attribute, $draw$.

Each possible outcome of random selection for $draw$ defines one possible world. The precise definition of possible worlds of the program is given in the next section, but intuitively one should be able to compute them. If the result of our random selection were 1, then this world would be

$$W_1 = \{draw = 1, select\_color = white, \neg help\}.^1$$

(Since $color(1) = black$ and $select\_color = white$ are facts of the program, the result follows immediately from the definition of $help$.) If the result of our random selection were 2, then the world determined by this selection would be

$$W_2 = \{draw = 2, select\_color = white, help\}.$$

Similarly for stones from 3 to 10. Possible worlds defined by our program are exactly those introduced in our previous solution. The new representation, however, is more elaboration tolerant and is closer to the informal description of the story. The semantics of P-log uses the indifference principle to automatically compute the probabilistic measure of every possible world and hence the probabilities of the corresponding events. Since in this case all worlds are equally plausible, the ratio of possible worlds in which arbitrary statement F is true to the number of all possible worlds gives the probability of F. Hence the probability of $help$ defined by the program $\Pi_{jungle}(white)$ is $\frac{9}{10}$.

Now the reasoner considers a program $\Pi_{jungle}(black)$ obtained from Π_{jungle} by adding the statement

$$select\_color = black.$$

A similar argument shows that the probability of getting help in this situation is $\frac{1}{10}$. Clearly, the first choice is preferable.

---

[1] Actually this possible world also contains other atoms that do not depend on the value of $draw$ such as sorts, statements of the form $color(1) = black$, $color(2) = white$, etc. However, they are the same in all the possible worlds, and we do not show them in our representation.

11.3 Syntax and Semantics of P-log

In this section we use the jungle program to informally explain the syntax and semantics of P-log. Since P-log is a sorted language, its programs contain definitions of sorts and declarations of functions. The atoms of P-log are properly typed expressions of the form $a(\bar{t}) = y$, where y is a constant from the range of a function symbol a or a variable. A term of the form $a(\bar{t})$ is called an **attribute**. The negation of an atom, $\neg(a(\bar{t}) = y)$, is written as $a(\bar{t}) \neq y$. As usual, atoms and their negations are referred to as literals. In addition to declarations and the regular ASP rules formed from P-log literals, the P-log programmer may declare some of the attributes to be random.

It is not difficult to show that program Π_{jungle}, as well as any other P-log program Π, can be translated into a regular ASP program, say $\tau(\Pi)$, with the same logical meaning. In fact the logical semantics of Π are defined via the semantics of $\tau(\Pi)$.

Definition 11.3.1. *($\tau(\Pi)$)*
For every attribute $a(\bar{t})$ with $range(a) = \{y_1, \ldots, y_n\}$, the mapping τ

- *represents the sort information by a corresponding set of atoms; e.g., $s = \{1, 2\}$ is turned into facts $s(1)$ and $s(2)$;*
- *replaces every occurrence of an atom*

$$a(\bar{t}) = y$$

by

$$a(\bar{t}, y),$$

and expands the program by rules of the form

$$\neg a(\bar{t}, Y_2) \leftarrow a(\bar{t}, Y_1), Y_1 \neq Y_2;$$

- *replaces every occurrence of $a(\bar{t}, true)$ and $a(\bar{t}, false)$ by $a(\bar{t})$ and $\neg a(\bar{t})$, respectively, and removes double negation $\neg\neg$, which might have been introduced by this operation;*
- *replaces every rule of the form*

$$random(a(\bar{t})) \leftarrow body$$

by

$$a(\bar{t}) = y_1 \ or \ \ldots \ or \ a(\bar{t}) = y_n \leftarrow body, \ not \ intervene(a(\bar{t}))$$
$$(11.1)$$

where intervene *is a new predicate symbol;*

The translation is justified by the intuitive reading of $random(a(\bar{t}))$
that says that, under normal circumstances, during the construction
of a possible set of beliefs, the reasoner associated with the program
must randomly select exactly one value of $a(\bar{t})$ from a's range.
*Actually, P-log allows more-general random selection rules that have
the form:*

$$random(a(\bar{t}) : \{X : p(X)\}) \leftarrow body.$$

The set $\{X : p(X)\}$ *is often referred to as the* **dynamic range** *of*
$a(\bar{t})$. *The rule limits the selection of the value of* $a(\bar{t})$ *to elements of*
a's *range that satisfy property* p. *For each such rule,* τ *creates an
additional ASP rule:*

$$\leftarrow a(\bar{t}, Y), \; not \; p(Y), \; not \; intervene(a(\bar{t})). \qquad (11.2)$$

- *grounds the resulting program by replacing variables with elements
  of the corresponding sorts.*

This completes the construction of $\tau(\Pi)$.

Last, we note that P-log's random selection rules may be preceded by
terms used as rule names. In fact, because of technical reasons, some P-log
solvers require such names. They are not, however, used in this book.

Definition 11.3.2. *Collections of atoms from answer sets of* $\tau(\Pi)$ *are
called* **possible worlds** *of* Π. *(We use the new term simply to stay close to
the traditional terminology of probability theory.)*

Declarations and rules of the form described so far form the logical
part of a P-log program Π. This part defines sets of beliefs of a rational
reasoner associated with Π or, in the language of probability, possible worlds
of Π.

In addition, program Π may contain so-called pr-atoms[2] describing the
likelihood of particular random events, as well as constructs describing
observations and actions of the reasoner associated with the program. The
syntax and semantics of these constructs are defined later.

Meanwhile we proceed with defining the probabilistic semantics of a P-
log program. We first define a probabilistic measure on its possible worlds.
This measure, a real number from the interval $[0, 1]$, represents the degree
of a reasoner's belief that a possible world W matches a true state of the

---

[2] Here pr stands for *probabilistic.*

world. Zero means that the agent believes that the possible world does not correspond to the true state; one corresponds to the certainty that it does. *The probability of a set of possible worlds is the sum of the probabilistic measures of its elements.* This definition is easily expanded to define the probability of propositions.[3]

Definition 11.3.3. *The **probability of a proposition** is the sum of the probabilistic measures of possible worlds in which this proposition is true.*

Our next task is to explain the definition of a probabilistic measure of possible worlds of a P-log program. The jungle example shows how this can be done using the indifference principle for a program with one random selection rule. The following example demonstrates how the indifference principle is used to define a probabilistic measure for programs with multiple random selection rules.

Example 11.3.1. *(Dice)*

Mike and John each own a die. Each die is rolled once. We would like to estimate the chance that the sum of the rolls is high (i.e., greater than 6).

To do that we construct a P-log program Π_{dice} encoding our knowledge of the domain. (The program contains some knowledge that is not necessary for making the desired prediction, but is useful for further modifications of the example.) Π_{dice} has a signature Σ containing the sort *dice* consisting of the names of the two dice, d_1 and d_2; a (random) attribute *roll* mapping each die to the value it indicates when thrown, which is an integer from 1 to 6; an attribute *owner* mapping each die to a person; relation *high*, which holds when the sum of the rolls of the two dice is greater than 6. The corresponding declarations look like this:

$$die = \{d_1, d_2\}.$$
$$score = \{1, 2, 3, 4, 5, 6\}.$$
$$person = \{mike, john\}.$$
$$roll : die \to score.$$
$$random(roll(D)).$$
$$owner : die \to person.$$
$$high : boolean.$$

---

[3] Here by "proposition" we mean ground atoms or formulas obtained from these atoms using connectives $\neg$, $\wedge$, and or .

The regular part of the program consists of the following rules:

$$owner(d_1) = mike.$$
$$owner(d_2) = john.$$
$$high \leftarrow roll(d_1) = Y_1,$$
$$roll(d_2) = Y_2,$$
$$(Y_1 + Y_2) > 6.$$
$$\neg high \leftarrow roll(d_1) = Y_1,$$
$$roll(d_2) = Y_2,$$
$$(Y_1 + Y_2) \leq 6.$$

The translation, $\tau(\Pi_{dice})$, of our program into ASP looks like this:

$$die(d_1).$$
$$die(d_2).$$
$$score(1..6).$$
$$person(mike).$$
$$person(john).$$
$$roll(D, 1) \ or \ \ldots \ or \ roll(D, 6) \leftarrow \ not \ intervene(roll(D)).$$
$$\neg roll(D, Y_2) \leftarrow roll(D, Y_1),$$
$$Y_1 \neq Y_2.$$
$$owner(d_1, mike).$$
$$owner(d_2, john).$$
$$\neg owner(D, P_2) \leftarrow owner(D, P_1),$$
$$P_1 \neq P_2.$$
$$high \leftarrow roll(d_1, Y_1),$$
$$roll(d_2, Y_2),$$
$$(Y_1 + Y_2) > 6.$$
$$\neg high \leftarrow roll(d_1, Y_1),$$
$$roll(d_2, Y_2),$$
$$(Y_1 + Y_2) \leq 6.$$

Notice that, in accordance with the definition of τ, function declarations are simply omitted.

By computing answer sets of $\tau(\Pi_{dice})$ we obtain 36 possible worlds of our program – with each world corresponding to a possible selection of values for random attributes $roll(d_1)$ and $roll(d_2)$; i.e.,

$$W_1 = \{roll(d_1) = 1, roll(d_2) = 1, high = false, \ldots\},$$
$$\vdots$$
$$W_{36} = \{roll(d_1) = 6, roll(d_2) = 6, high = true, \ldots\}.$$

(The possible worlds only differ by atoms formed by $roll(d_1)$, $roll(d_2)$, and $high$; other atoms, such as $die(d_1)$ and $owner(d_1, mike)$, are the same in all possible worlds and are not listed.) The selection for d_1 has six possible outcomes that, by the principle of indifference, are equally likely. The same goes for d_2. *The mechanisms controlling the way the agent selects the values of $roll(d_1)$ and $roll(d_2)$ during the construction of his beliefs are independent from each other.* This independence justifies the definition of the probabilistic measure of a possible world containing $roll(d_1) = i$ and $roll(d_2) = j$ as the product of the agent's degrees of belief in $roll(d_1) = i$ and $roll(d_2) = j$.[4] Hence the measure of a possible world containing $roll(d_1) = i$ and $roll(d_2) = j$ for every possible i and j is $\frac{1}{6} \times \frac{1}{6} = \frac{1}{36}$. The probability $P_{\Pi_{dice}}(high)$ is the sum of the measures of the possible worlds that satisfy $high$. Since $high$ holds in 21 worlds, the probability $P_{\Pi_{dice}}(high)$ of $high$ being true is $\frac{7}{12}$. If the reasoner associated with Π_{dice} had to bet on the outcome of the game, betting on $high$ would be better.

Note that the jungle example did not require the use of the product rule because it contained only one random selection rule. Since the dice example has two such rules, the product rule is necessary.

Suppose now that we learned from a reliable source that, although the die owned by John is fair, the die owned by Mike is biased. The source conducted multiple statistical experiments that allowed him to conclude that, on average, Mike's die will roll a 6 in one out of four rolls. To incorporate this type of knowledge in our program, we need some device allowing us to express the numeric probabilities of possible values of random attributes. This is expressed in P-log through **causal probability statements**, or pr-**atoms**. A pr-atom takes the form

$$pr_r(a(\overline{t}) = y|_c B) = v \tag{11.3}$$

where $a(\overline{t})$ is a random attribute, B is a conjunction of literals, r is the name of the random selection rule used to generate the values of $a(\overline{t})$, $v \in [0, 1]$, and y is a possible value of $a(\overline{t})$. If the rule generating the values of $a(\overline{t})$ is uniquely determined by the program, then its name, r, can be omitted. The

---

[4] In probability theory two events A and B are called independent if the occurrence of one does not affect the probability of another. Mathematically, this intuition is captured by the following definition: Events A and B are independent (with respect to probability function P) if $P(A \wedge B) = P(A) \times P(B)$. For example, the event d_1 *shows a 5 is independent of d_2 shows a 5*, whereas the event *the sum of the scores on both dice shows a 5* is dependent on the event d_1 *shows a 5*.

"causal stroke" '$|_c$' and the "rule body" B may also be omitted in case B is empty.

The statement has a rather sophisticated informal reading. First it says that *if the value of* $a(\bar{t})$ *is generated by rule* r, *and* B *holds, then the probability of the selection of* y *for the value of* $a(\bar{t})$ *is* v. In addition, it indicates the potential *existence of a direct causal relationship between* B *and the possible value of* $a(\bar{t})$. Sometimes relations expressed by causal probability statements of P-log are referred to as causal probabilities. In this book we only briefly discuss causal probability and its properties. For an in-depth study of this relation, defined in terms of acyclic directed graphs and probability tables, one can consult Judea Pearl's book on causality (2000). This remarkable book contains a wealth of information about causality, probability, and their applications to various types of causal and probabilistic reasoning.

Example 11.3.2. *(Biased Dice)*
Information about the fairness of Mike's die after the bias was discovered is expressed by pr-atom

$$pr(roll(D) = 6 \mid_c owner(D) = mike) = \frac{1}{4}.$$

Let us now demonstrate how these statements can be used to define the probabilistic measures of possible worlds of the resulting program Π_{biased}. Clearly programs Π_{dice} and Π_{biased} have the same possible worlds. First consider a possible world

$$W = \{roll(d_1) = 6, roll(d_2) = 1, high = true, \dots\}$$

Die d_1 belongs to Mike, and hence, by the earlier causal probability statement, the likelihood of this die showing 6 as the result of the corresponding selection is $\frac{1}{4}$. By the principle of indifference the likelihood of d_2 showing 1 is $\frac{1}{6}$. As explained before, the measure of W is the product of our degrees of belief in $roll(d_1) = 6$ and $roll(d_2) = 1$. Hence the measure of W_1 is $\frac{1}{24}$. Similarly for other worlds in which $roll(d_1) = 6$. What about the measure of each world in which Mike's die shows 5 or less? Since we have no information about the likelihood of these five possible outcomes of Mike's die, by the principle of indifference, we have that our degree of belief in each such outcome is $\frac{(1-\frac{1}{4})}{5} = \frac{3}{20}$. So the measure of each such world is $\frac{3}{20} \times \frac{1}{6} = \frac{1}{40}$. Now we know the probabilistic measure of every possible world of Π_{biased}. To compute the probability of the sum of the points on both dice being greater than 6, we need to sum up the measures of the worlds satisfying $high$. It is easy to check that $P_{\Pi_{biased}}(high) = \frac{5}{8}$.

To better understand the intuition behind our definition of a probabilistic measure, it may be useful to consider an intelligent agent associated with the program in the process of constructing possible worlds. Suppose the agent has already constructed a part V of a (not yet completely constructed) possible world W, and suppose that V satisfies the precondition of some random selection rule r defining the value of some random attribute $a(\bar{t})$. The agent can continue construction by considering a mental experiment associated with r – a random selection of the possible value of $a(\bar{t})$. If y is a possible outcome of this experiment, then the agent may continue construction by adding the atom $a(\bar{t}) = y$ to V. To define the probabilistic measure μ of the possible world W under construction, we need to know the likelihood of y being the outcome of r, which we call the **causal probability of atom** $a(t) = y$ **in** W. The agent can obtain this information from a pr-atom $pr(a(\bar{t}) = y \mid_c B) = v$ of our program with B satisfied by W or compute it by using the principle of indifference. In the former case the corresponding causal probability is v. In the latter case the agent needs to consider the collection R of possible outcomes of experiment r. For example if $y \in R$, there is no pr-atom assigning probability to outcomes of R, and $|R| = n$, then the causal probability of $a(\bar{t}) = y$ in W will be $\frac{1}{n}$.

In general, to compute the probabilistic measure of W, one needs to consider values $y_1, \ldots, y_n$ of random attributes $a_1(\bar{t}_1), \ldots, a_n(\bar{t}_n)$ that determine a possible world W. The **unnormalized probabilistic measure**, $\hat{\mu}$ of W, is defined as the product of causal probabilities of atoms $a_1(\bar{t}_1), \ldots, a_n(\bar{t}_n)$ in W. The probabilistic measure $\mu(W)$ of a possible world W is the unnormalized probabilistic measure of W divided by the sum of the unnormalized probabilistic measures of all possible worlds of Π, i.e.,

$$\mu(W) =_{def} \frac{\hat{\mu}(W)}{\sum_{W_i \in \Omega} \hat{\mu}(W_i)}.$$

For this definition to be correct, program Π must satisfy several natural conditions. There should be possible worlds (i.e., program $\tau(\Pi)$ should be consistent). In the process of construction of a possible world, a random attribute $a(\bar{t})$ should be defined by a unique random selection rule. There are a few others. It is not difficult to show that if these conditions are satisfied then the function μ defined earlier is indeed a probabilistic measure.

Finally, we introduce the two remaining syntactic constructs of P-log – statements recording observations of the results of random experiments

$$obs(a(\bar{t}) = y) \tag{11.4}$$

$$obs(a(\bar{t}) \neq y) \tag{11.5}$$

and of deliberate interventions in these experiments, setting the value of the corresponding attribute to some given y,

$$do(a(\bar{t}) = y). \tag{11.6}$$

Here $a(\bar{t})$ is a random attribute, and y is a possible value of $a(\bar{t})$. For instance, statement $obs(roll(d_1) = 6)$ says that the random experiment consisting of rolling the first die shows 6; $do(roll(d_1) = 6)$ says that, instead of throwing the die at random, it was deliberately put on the table showing 6. To give formal semantics of these statements we need to expand our translation $\tau(\Pi)$. This is done as follows. First, for every atom of the form (11.4), (11.5), and (11.6), we write, respectively,

$$obs(a(\bar{t}, y))$$
$$\neg obs(a(\bar{t}, y))$$
$$do(a(\bar{t}, y)).$$

Next, we add the following rules:

$$\leftarrow obs(a(\bar{t}, y)), \neg a(\bar{t}, y) \tag{11.7}$$

$$\leftarrow \neg obs(a(\bar{t}, y)), a(\bar{t}, y) \tag{11.8}$$

$$a(\bar{t}, y) \leftarrow do(a(\bar{t}, y)) \tag{11.9}$$

$$intervene(a(\bar{t})) \leftarrow do(a(\bar{t}, y)). \tag{11.10}$$

The first two rules eliminate possible worlds of the program that fail to satisfy the observation. The third rule makes sure that interventions affect their intervened-on variables in the expected way. The fourth rule defines the relation $intervene$ that, for each intervention, cancels the randomness of the corresponding attribute (see rule [11.1]). This completes the definition of $\tau(\Pi)$ for programs with observations and deliberate interventions.

As before, possible worlds of Π are defined as collections of atoms from answer sets of $\tau(\Pi)$. The definition of probability does not change either, but one should pay careful attention to the process of normalization and the possible change of an attribute from random to deterministic.

We illustrate the semantics of the new statements by revisiting our dice example.

Example 11.3.3. *(Dice Revisited)*
Consider the P-log program from Example 11.3.1 expanded by the observation that John rolled a 3:

$$obs(roll(d_2) = 3).$$

It is not difficult to see that the resulting program $\Pi_{dice} \cup \{obs(roll(d_2) = 3)\}$, has six possible worlds, which are obtained from possible worlds of Π_{dice} by removing those containing $roll(d_2) = y$ where $y \neq 3$. For each such world W, the unnormalized probabilistic measure is

$$\hat{\mu}(W) = \frac{1}{6} \times \frac{1}{6} = \frac{1}{36}$$

After normalization we have

$$\mu(W) = \frac{1/36}{6/36} = \frac{1}{6}$$

and hence, because $high$ is true in three worlds, we have

$$P_{\Pi_{dice}}(high) = \frac{3}{6} = \frac{1}{2}$$

(We hope the reader noticed the importance of normalization.)

Conditioning on observations has been extensively studied in classical probability theory. If P is a probability function, then the conditional probability $P(A|B)$ is defined as $P(A \wedge B)/P(B)$, provided $P(B)$ is not 0. Intuitively, $P(A|B)$ is understood as the probability of a formula A with respect to the background theory and a set B of all of the agent's additional observations of the world. The new evidence B simply eliminates the possible worlds that do not satisfy B. It can be shown that, under reasonable conditions on program Π, the same formula can be used to compute the corresponding P-log probability, i.e., we have

$$P_\Pi(A|B) = P_{\Pi \cup obs(B)}(A).$$

Let us now consider program $\Pi_{dice} \cup \{do(roll(d_2) = 3)\}$, which is identical to $\Pi_{dice} \cup \{obs(roll(d_2) = 3)\}$ except that the observation is replaced by the deliberate action of putting John's die on the table showing three dots. Possible worlds of the new program are the same as that of $\Pi_{dice} \cup \{obs(roll(d_2) = 3)\}$, but now, by rule (11.10), $intervene(roll(d_2))$ is true and hence the value of attribute $roll(d_2)$ is not selected at random by rule (11.1). Instead it is deterministically assigned the value 3, and is not used in the computation of the probabilistic measure. For each such world W, the normalized probabilistic measure

$$\mu(W) = \frac{1}{6}.$$

With d_2 deliberately set to 3, *high* holds in three out of six possible worlds; hence,

$$P_{\Pi_{dice} \cup \{do(roll(d_2)=3)\}}(high) = \frac{1}{2}.$$

Even though the computations of the corresponding probabilities for observations and deliberate actions were different, they led to the same results. This is not always the case. The substantial differences between the results of updating your knowledge base by observations and interventions are discussed in later examples.

There is one more concept left to demonstrate, and that is the effect of the dynamic range on possible worlds. When an attribute has a dynamic range, it means that the sample from which its values are drawn can change with time. For example, if we draw a card from a deck and then draw another card without replacing the first, our sample has changed.

Example 11.3.4. *(Aces in Succession)*
Suppose we are interested in the probability that two consecutive draws from a deck of 52 cards result in both cards being aces. We begin by representing the relevant knowledge. One possible way to do that is to enumerate our cards

$$card = \{1 \ldots 52\}.$$

Without loss of generality we can assume that the first four cards are aces:

$$ace = \{1, 2, 3, 4\}.$$

We also need two tries and a random attribute *draw* that maps each try into the card selected by this draw:

$$try = \{1, 2\}.$$
$$draw : try \rightarrow card.$$

If we were to simply draw a card from the deck and then put it back, we could define *draw* as random $(random(draw(T)))$. However, because the card we drew is not returned to the deck, the second selection is made from a smaller deck. To encode this we use a dynamic range and define the randomness of *draw* as follows:

$$draw(T) : \{C : available(C, T)\}.$$

We define $available(C, T)$ to be the set of cards without the one we drew in the previous try:

$$available(C, 1) \quad \leftarrow card(C).$$
$$available(C, T+1) \leftarrow available(C, T),$$
$$draw(T) \neq C.$$

Finally we add

$$two\_aces \leftarrow draw(1) = Y1,$$
$$draw(2) = Y2,$$
$$1 \leq Y1 \leq 4,$$
$$1 \leq Y2 \leq 4.$$

Note that because of the dynamic range of our selection the two cards chosen by the two draws cannot be the same. Possible worlds of the program are of the form

$$W_k = \{draw(1) = c_1, draw(2) = c_2, \ldots\}$$

where $c_1 \neq c_2$. There are 52 possible outcomes of the first draw and 51 possible outcomes of the second. Thus, the program has 52×51 possible worlds – each world corresponding to outcomes of the two successive draws. By the Principle of Indifference the unnormalized probabilistic measure of each such world is equal to $\frac{1}{52} \times \frac{1}{51} = \frac{1}{2652}$. One can easily check that, as expected, the unnormalized measure is equal to the normalized one. To compute the number of possible worlds containing two_aces, let us notice that the number of aces that may be selected by the first draw is 4, whereas the number of aces that may be selected by the second draw is 3. Thus, there are 12 possible worlds containing two_aces, and the probability of this event is $12 \times \frac{1}{2652} = \frac{12}{2652} = \frac{1}{221}$.

11.4 Representing Knowledge in P-log

The previous examples addressed rather simple probabilistic problems, which could be easily solved without building a knowledge base of the corresponding domain. In this section we consider several examples where the use of P-log allows substantial clarification of the modeling process.

11.4.1 The Monty Hall Problem

This example, known as the Monty Hall Problem, is a nontrivial puzzle that is frequently solved incorrectly even by people with some knowledge of probability theory. The problem gets its name from the TV game show, *Let's Make a Deal*, hosted by Monty Hall. Here is a description of the problem:

Monty's show involves a player who is given the opportunity to select one of three closed doors, behind one of which there is a prize. Behind the other two doors are empty rooms. Once the player has made a selection, Monty is obligated to open one of the remaining closed doors that does not contain the prize, showing that the room behind it is empty. He then asks the player if she would like to switch her selection to the other unopened door or stay with her original choice. Does it matter if she switches?

The answer is *yes*. In fact switching doubles the player's chance to win. This problem is quite interesting, because many people – often including mathematicians – feel the answer to be counter-intuitive. These people almost immediately come up with a (wrong) negative answer and are not easily persuaded that they made a mistake. We believe that part of the reason for the difficulty is that there is some disconnect between modeling probabilistic and nonprobabilistic knowledge about the problem. Let us show that in a P-log solution this disconnect disappears.

We start writing the P-log program representing knowledge about the show by declaring the set of three doors and three zero-arity attributes *selected*, *open*, and *prize*:

$$(1) \quad doors = \{1, 2, 3\}.$$
$$(2) \quad open, selected, prize : doors.$$

(The numbers are not part of the program; we number statements so that we can refer back to them.)

The regular part of the program contains rules that state that Monty can open any door to a room that is not selected by the player and that does not contain the prize.

$$(3) \quad \neg can\_open(D) \leftarrow selected = D.$$
$$(4) \quad \neg can\_open(D) \leftarrow prize = D.$$
$$(5) \quad can\_open(D) \leftarrow not \neg can\_open(D).$$

The first two rules are self-explanatory. The last rule, which uses both classical and default negations, is a typical ASP representation of the closed world assumption – Monty can open any door except those that are explicitly prohibited.

We assume that both Monty and the player act randomly. This information is expressed as follows:

(6) $random(prize).$
(7) $random(selected).$
(8) $random(open : \{X : can\_open(X)\}).$

Notice that rule (8) uses a dynamic range; this guarantees that Monty
selects only those doors that can be opened according to rules (3)–(5). The
logical knowledge expressed by these rules (which can be extracted from
the specification of the problem) is not explicitly represented in standard
probabilistic formalisms that lack the expressive power to do that. The
absence of this explicit knowledge may explain mistakes that are sometimes
made in the process of solving the problem by traditional methods.

P-log program Π_{monty0} consisting of logical rules (1)–(8) represents our
general knowledge of the problem domain. To proceed with our particular
story, let us encode the results of random events that occurred before the
player was asked if she wanted to change her selection. Without loss of
generality we can assume that the player has already selected door 1 and
that Monty opened door 2, revealing that it did not contain the prize. This
is recorded by the following statements:

$obs(selected = 1).$
$obs(open = 2).$
$obs(prize \neq 2).$

Let us denote the resulting P-log program by Π_{monty1}. The program represents the player's complete knowledge relevant to her behavior in the game.
To make an informed decision about switching, the player should compute
the probability of the prize being behind door 1 and the prize being behind
door 3. To do that, she must consider the possible worlds of Π_{monty1} and
find their measures. Once the measures are found, she must sum up the
measures of the worlds in which the prize is behind door 1 and do the same
for worlds where the prize is behind door 3.

Because of the observations, Π_{monty1} has two possible worlds:

$W_1 = \{selected = 1, prize = 1, open = 2, can\_open(2), can\_open(3)\}.$

$W_2 = \{selected = 1, prize = 3, open = 2, can\_open(2)\}.$

In W_1 the player would lose if she switched; in W_2 she would win. Note that
the possible worlds contain information not only about where the prize is
but also which doors Monty can open. This is the key to correct calculation!

Now the player is ready to compute the probabilistic measures of W_1 and W_2. To do that she needs to compute the likelihood of random events within each world. In this case, these random events are which door is selected, where the prize is, and which door is opened by Monty. By the principle of indifference the causal probability of selecting particular values of *prize* and *selected* during the construction of both possible worlds is $\frac{1}{3}$ each. The situation, however, is different for the random attribute *open*. Recall that Monty can only open a door satisfying relation *can_open*. There are two such doors in W_1; hence the causal probability of selecting the second door in W_1 is $\frac{1}{2}$. But because Monty can open only one door in W_2, the causal probability of his choosing door 2 in W_2 is 1. The probabilistic measure of a possible world is the product of likelihoods of the random events that it comprises. It follows that

$$\hat{\mu}(W_1) = \frac{1}{3} \times \frac{1}{3} \times \frac{1}{2} = \frac{1}{18}$$
$$\hat{\mu}(W_2) = \frac{1}{3} \times \frac{1}{3} \times 1 = \frac{1}{9}.$$

Normalization gives us

$$\mu(W_1) = \frac{1/18}{1/18 + 1/9} = \frac{1}{3}$$

$$\mu(W_2) = \frac{1/9}{1/18 + 1/9} = \frac{2}{3}.$$

Finally, since *prize* $= 1$ is true in only W_1,

$$P_{\Pi_{monty1}}(prize = 1) = \mu(W_1) = \frac{1}{3}.$$

Similarly for *prize* $= 3$:

$$P_{\Pi_{monty1}}(prize = 3) = \mu(W_2) = \frac{2}{3}.$$

Changing doors doubles the player's chance to win.

Now consider a situation when the player assumes (either consciously or without consciously realizing it) that Monty could have opened any one of the doors not selected by her (including the one that contains the prize). Then the corresponding program has a new definition of *can_open*. Rules (3)–(5) are replaced by

$$\neg can\_open(D) \leftarrow selected = D.$$
$$can\_open(D) \leftarrow not \ \neg can\_open(D).$$

The resulting program Π_{monty2} also has two possible worlds containing $prize = 1$ and $prize = 3$, respectively, each with an unnormalized probabilistic measure of $\frac{1}{18}$, and therefore, $P_{\Pi_{monty2}}(prize = 1) = \frac{1}{2}$ and $P_{\Pi_{monty2}}(prize = 3) = \frac{1}{2}$. In that case, changing the door does not increase the probability of getting the prize. Since the rules are explicitly written, it makes the discussion about correctness of the answer much easier.

Program Π_{monty1} has no explicit probabilistic information, and so the possible results of each random selection are assumed to be equally likely. If we learn, for example, that given a choice between opening doors 2 and 3, Monty opens door 2 four times out of five, we can incorporate this information by the following statement:

$$(9) \; pr(open = 2 \mid_c can\_open(2), can\_open(3)) = \frac{4}{5}.$$

A computation similar to this one shows that changing doors still increases the player's chances of winning. (In fact changing doors is advisable as long as each of the available doors can be opened with some positive probability.)

The next example demonstrates the causal character of probabilistic statements of P-log.

11.4.2 Death of a Rat?

Consider the following program Π_{rat} representing knowledge about whether a certain rat will eat arsenic today and whether it will die today.

$$arsenic, death : boolean.$$
$$random(arsenic).$$
$$random(death).$$
$$pr(arsenic) = 0.4.$$
$$pr(death \mid_c arsenic) = 0.8.$$
$$pr(death \mid_c \neg arsenic) = 0.01.$$

This program tells us that the rat eating arsenic and the rat dying are viewed as random events and that the rat is more likely to die if it eats arsenic. In addition, the intuitive semantics of the pr-atoms expresses that the rat's consumption of arsenic carries information about the cause of its death (as opposed to, say, the rat's death being informative about the causes of its eating arsenic).

An intuitive consequence of this reading is that seeing the rat die raises our suspicion that it has eaten arsenic, whereas killing the rat (say, with a pistol) does not affect our degree of belief that arsenic has been consumed.

The following computations show that this implication is reflected in the probabilities computed under our semantics.

The possible worlds of this program, with their unnormalized probabilistic measures, are as follows (we show only *arsenic* and *death* literals):

$$W_1 : \quad \{arsenic, death\}. \qquad \hat{\mu}(W_1) = 0.4 \times 0.8 = 0.32$$
$$W_2 : \quad \{arsenic, \neg death\}. \qquad \hat{\mu}(W_2) = 0.4 \times 0.2 = 0.08$$
$$W_3 : \quad \{\neg arsenic, death\}. \qquad \hat{\mu}(W_3) = 0.6 \times 0.01 = 0.006$$
$$W_4 : \quad \{\neg arsenic, \neg death\}. \quad \hat{\mu}(W_4) = 0.6 \times 0.99 = 0.594$$

Since the unnormalized probabilistic measures add up to 1, they are the same as the normalized measures. Hence,

$$P_{\Pi_{rat}}(arsenic) = \mu(W_1) + \mu(W_2) = 0.32 + 0.08 = 0.4.$$

To compute the probability of *arsenic* after the observation of *death*, we consider the program created from Π_{rat} and the statement *obs(death)*. The resulting program has two possible worlds, W_1 and W_3, with their unnormalized probabilistic measures shown earlier. Normalization yields

$$P_{\Pi_{rat} \cup \{obs(death)\}}(arsenic) = \frac{0.32}{0.32 + 0.006} = 0.982.$$

Notice that the observation of death raised our degree of belief that the rat had eaten arsenic.

To compute the effect of deliberately killing the rat on the agent's belief in *arsenic*, we augment the original program with the literal *do(death)*. The resulting program has the same two possible worlds, W_1 and W_3. However, the action of deliberate killing defeats the randomness of death so that W_1 has the unnormalized probabilistic measure 0.4 and W_3 has the unnormalized probabilistic measure 0.6. These sum up to 1, so the measures are also 0.4 and 0.6, respectively, and we get

$$P_{\Pi_{rat} \cup \{do(death)\}}(arsenic) = 0.4.$$

Note that this is identical to the initial probability $P_{\Pi_{rat}}(arsenic)$ computed earlier.

This last example shows that, in contrast to the case when the effect was passively observed, deliberately bringing about the effect did not change our degree of belief about the propositions relevant to its cause. On the other hand, propositions relevant to a cause, give equal evidence for the attendant effects whether they are forced to happen or are passively observed. For example, if we feed the rat arsenic, this increases its chance of death, just as if we had observed the rat eating the arsenic on its own. The conditional probabilities computed under our semantics bear this out. Similarly to the above example, we can compute

$$P_{\Pi_{rat}}(death) = 0.362$$

$$P_{\Pi_{rat} \cup \{do(arsenic)\}}(death) = 0.8$$

$$P_{\Pi_{rat} \cup \{obs(arsenic)\}}(death) = 0.8$$

11.4.3 The Spider Bite

Here is another example of subtle probabilistic reasoning that can be done in P-log with the help of interventions. The story we would like to formalize follows:

In Stan's home town there are two kinds of poisonous spiders – the creeper and the spinner. Bites from the two are equally common in Stan's area, although spinner bites are more common on a worldwide basis. An experimental antivenom has been developed to treat bites from either kind of spider, but its effectiveness is questionable.

One morning Stan wakes to find he has a bite on his ankle and drives to the emergency room. A doctor examines the bite and concludes it is from either a creeper or a spinner. In deciding whether to administer the antivenom, the doctor examines the data he has on bites from the two kinds of spiders: Of 416 people bitten by the creeper worldwide, 312 received the antivenom and 104 did not. Among those who received the antivenom, 187 survived, whereas 73 survived among those who did not receive antivenom. The spinner is more deadly and tends to inhabit areas where the treatment is less available. Of 924 people bitten by the spinner, 168 received the antivenom, 34 of whom survived. Of the 756 spinner bite victims who did not receive the experimental treatment, only 227 survived. Should Stan take the antivenom treatment?

Let us formalize relevant parts of the story in a P-log program Π_{spider} from the point of view of the doctor. We use boolean attributes *survive* – a random patient survived, *antivenom* – a random patient was administered antivenom, and attribute *spider* where *spider* = *creeper* indicates that a random person was bitten by *creeper*; we do so similarly for *spinner*. From the standpoint of the doctor all three attributes (including *antivenom*) are random. Hence we have

$$survive, antivenom : boolean.$$
$$spider : \{creeper, spinner\}.$$

$$random(spider).$$
$$random(survive).$$
$$random(antivenom).$$

Since bites from the two spiders are equally common in the area, the doctor assumes that

$$pr(spider = creeper) = 0.5.$$

Statistical information available in the story allows the doctor to estimate the corresponding probabilities:

$pr(antivenom|spider = creeper) = 312/416 = 0.75$

$pr(antivenom|spider = spinner) = 168/924 = 0.18$

$pr(survive \mid_c spider = creeper, antivenom) = 187/312 = 0.6$

$pr(survive \mid_c spider = creeper, \neg antivenom) = 73/104 = 0.7$

$pr(survive \mid_c spider = spinner, antivenom) = 34/168 = 0.2$

$pr(survive \mid_c spider = spinner, \neg antivenom) = 227/756 = 0.3$

How should the doctor decide whether giving the antivenom to Stan would be beneficial? A natural answer is to compare the result of the deliberate action of taking the antivenom on Stan's chance of survival with that of not taking the antivenom. To do that let us first compute $P_{\Pi_{spider} \cup \{do(antivenom)\}}(survive)$. The program $\Pi_{spider} \cup \{do(antivenom)\}$ has the following possible worlds:

$$W_1 = \{spider = creeper, antivenom, survive\}$$
$$W_2 = \{spider = creeper, antivenom, \neg survive\}$$
$$W_3 = \{spider = spinner, antivenom, survive\}$$
$$W_4 = \{spider = spinner, antivenom, \neg survive\}$$

To compute the probabilistic measures of the possible worlds, let us first notice that, because of the intervention, each possible world contains only two random attributes, *spider* and *survive*. Accordingly,

$$\mu(W_1) = 0.5 \times 0.6 = 0.3$$
$$\mu(W_2) = 0.5 \times 0.4 = 0.2$$
$$\mu(W_3) = 0.5 \times 0.2 = 0.1$$
$$\mu(W_4) = 0.5 \times 0.8 = 0.4$$

(Note that, because the measures sum up to 1, unnormalized and normalized measures coincide.)

It follows that the probability of survival after the treatment is

$$P_{\Pi_{spider} \cup \{do(antivenom)\}}(survive) = 0.4.$$

Now let us compute $P_{\Pi_{spider} \cup \{do(\neg antivenom)\}}(survive)$. Possible worlds of the associated program are

$$W_5 = \{spider = creeper, \neg antivenom, survive\}$$

$$W_6 = \{spider = creeper, \neg antivenom, \neg survive\}$$

$$W_7 = \{spider = spinner, \neg antivenom, survive\}$$

$$W_8 = \{spider = spinner, \neg antivenom, \neg survive\}$$

The measures are

$$\mu(W_5) = 0.5 \times 0.7 = 0.35$$

$$\mu(W_6) = 0.5 \times 0.3 = 0.15$$

$$\mu(W_7) = 0.5 \times 0.3 = 0.15$$

$$\mu(W_8) = 0.5 \times 0.7 = 0.35$$

and the probability of survival without the treatment is

$$P_{\Pi_{spider} \cup \{do(\neg antivenom)\}}(survive) = 0.5.$$

Thus, to maximize Stan's chance of survival, it is better not to administer the antivenom.

But what would happen if, instead of conditioning on intervention, the doctor decided to use what he believes to be a more traditional approach and condition on observations; i.e., compare $P_{\Pi_{spider} \cup \{obs(antivenom)\}}(survive)$ and $P_{\Pi_{spider} \cup \{obs(\neg antivenom)\}}(survive)$? The program $P_{\Pi_{spider} \cup \{obs(antivenom)\}}$ would have the possible worlds $W_1, \ldots, W_4$ as defined earlier, but the measures would be different. In this case, $antivenom$ would be a random attribute, so the likelihood of antivenom being given would be taken into account.

The unnormalized probabilistic measures induced by $P_{\Pi_{spider} \cup \{obs(antivenom)\}}$ are

$$\hat{\mu}(W_1) = 0.5 \times 0.75 \times 0.6 = 0.225$$

$$\hat{\mu}(W_2) = 0.5 \times 0.75 \times 0.4 = 0.15$$

$$\hat{\mu}(W_3) = 0.5 \times 0.18 \times 0.2 = 0.018$$

$$\hat{\mu}(W_4) = 0.5 \times 0.18 \times 0.8 = 0.072$$

The normalized measures are

$$\mu(W_1) = 0.225/0.465 = 0.484$$
$$\mu(W_2) = 0.15/0.465 = 0.322$$
$$\mu(W_3) = 0.018/0.465 = 0.039$$
$$\mu(W_4) = 0.072/0.465 = 0.155$$

and the probability is

$$P_{\Pi_{spider} \cup \{obs(antivenom)\}}(survive) = \mu(W_1) + \mu(W_3) = 0.523.$$

Similarly, we can compute the unnormalized probabilistic measures for $P_{\Pi_{spider} \cup \{obs(\neg antivenom)\}}$:

$$\hat{\mu}(W_5) = 0.5 \times 0.25 \times 0.7 = 0.088$$
$$\hat{\mu}(W_6) = 0.5 \times 0.25 \times 0.3 = 0.038$$
$$\hat{\mu}(W_7) = 0.5 \times 0.82 \times 0.3 = 0.123$$
$$\hat{\mu}(W_8) = 0.5 \times 0.82 \times 0.7 = 0.287$$

Normalization gives us

$$P_{\Pi_{spider} \cup \{obs(\neg antivenom)\}}(survive) = \mu(W_5) + \mu(W_7) = 0.164 + 0.229$$
$$= 0.393.$$

This different computation suggests that taking antivenom would increase Stan's chance of survival; i.e., it would lead to a different (and wrong) conclusion. We hope that this example shows how conditioning on interventions – a possibility not available in classical probability – helps avoid an unpleasant and costly mistake caused by the confusion between observations and interventions.

11.4.4 The Bayesian Squirrel

In this section we consider an example from Hilborn and Mangel (1997) used to illustrate the notion of Bayesian learning. One common type of learning problem consists of selecting from a set of models of a random phenomenon by observing repeated occurrences of that phenomenon. The Bayesian approach to this problem is to begin with a "prior density" on the set of candidate models and update it in light of our observations.

As an example, Hilborn and Mangel describe the Bayesian squirrel. The squirrel has hidden its acorns in one of two patches, say Patch 1 and Patch 2, but cannot remember which. The squirrel is 80% certain that the food is hidden in Patch 1. Also, it knows there is a 20% chance of finding food per day when it is looking in the right patch (and, of course, a 0% chance if it is looking in the wrong patch).

To represent this knowledge in P-log program Π_{sq}, we introduce sorts

$$patch = \{p1, p2\}.$$
$$day = \{1 \ldots n\}.$$

(where n is some constant, say, 5) and attributes

$$hidden\_in : patch.$$
$$found : day \rightarrow boolean.$$
$$look : day \rightarrow patch.$$

Attribute $hidden\_in$ is always random. Hence we include

$$random(hidden\_in).$$

Attribute $found$, however, is random only if the squirrel is looking for food in the right patch; i.e., we have

$$random(found(D)) \leftarrow hidden\_in = P,$$
$$look(D) = P.$$

Otherwise we have

$$\neg found(D) \leftarrow hidden\_in = P_1,$$
$$look(D) = P_2,$$
$$P_1 \neq P_2.$$

The value of attribute $look(D)$ is decided by the squirrel's deliberation. Hence this attribute is not random.

Probabilistic information of the story is given by these statements:

$$pr(hidden\_in = p1) = 0.8.$$
$$pr(found(D)) = 0.2.$$

This knowledge, in conjunction with the description of the squirrel's activity, can be used to compute probabilities of possible outcomes of the next search for food.

Consider, for instance, program $\Pi_{sq1} = \Pi_{sq} \cup \{look(1) = p_1\}$, which represents that the squirrel decided to look for food in Patch 1 on the first day.

The program has three possible worlds

$$W_1^1 = \{look(1) = p_1, hidden\_in = p_1, found(1), \dots\}$$
$$W_2^1 = \{look(1) = p_1, hidden\_in = p_1, \neg found(1), \dots\}$$
$$W_3^1 = \{look(1) = p_1, hidden\_in = p_2, \neg found(1), \dots\}$$

with probabilistic measures

$$\mu(W_1^1) = 0.16$$
$$\mu(W_2^1) = 0.64$$
$$\mu(W_3^1) = 0.2$$

As expected,

$$P_{\Pi_{sq1}}(hidden\_in = p_1) = 0.16 + 0.64 = 0.8$$

and

$$P_{\Pi_{sq1}}(found(1)) = 0.16.$$

Suppose now that the squirrel failed to find its food during the first day and decided to continue its search in Patch 1 the next morning. Failure to find food on the first day should decrease the squirrel's degree of belief that the food is hidden in Patch 1 and, consequently, decrease its degree of belief that it will find food by looking in the first patch again. This is reflected in the following computation:

Let $\Pi_{sq2} = \Pi_{sq1} \cup \{obs(\neg found(1)), look(2) = p_1\}$.

The possible worlds of Π_{sq2} are

$$W_1^2 = \{look(1) = p_1, \neg found(1), hidden\_in = p_1,$$
$$look(2) = p_1, found(2) \dots\}$$
$$W_2^2 = \{look(1) = p_1, \neg found(1), hidden\_in = p_1,$$
$$look(2) = p_1, \neg found(2) \dots\}$$
$$W_3^2 = \{look(1) = p_1, \neg found(1), hidden\_in = p_2,$$
$$look(2) = p_1, \neg found(2) \dots\}$$

Their probabilistic measures are

$$\mu(W_1^2) = 0.128/0.84 = 0.152$$
$$\mu(W_2^2) = 0.512/0.84 = 0.61$$
$$\mu(W_3^2) = 0.2/0.84 = 0.238$$

Consequently,

$$P_{\Pi_{sq2}}(hidden\_in = p_1) = 0.762$$

and

$$P_{\Pi_{sq2}}(found(2)) = 0.152$$

and so on.

After a number of unsuccessful attempts to find food in the first patch, the squirrel can come to the conclusion that the food is probably hidden in the second patch and can change its search strategy accordingly. Notice that each new experiment changes the squirrel's probabilistic model in a nonmonotonic way. That is, the set of possible worlds resulting from each successive experiment is not merely a subset of the possible worlds of the previous model. The program, however, is changed only by the addition of new actions and observations. Distinctive features of P-log such as the ability to represent observations and actions, as well as conditional randomness, play an important role in allowing the squirrel to learn new probabilistic models from experience.

11.5 (*) P-log + CR-Prolog and the Wandering Robot

There is no reason why P-log must be limited to standard ASP. In fact, its semantics is naturally defined on top of CR-Prolog, with the only difference being that possible worlds correspond to CR-Prolog answer sets instead of to ASP ones. In this section we give an example of a P-log program with a cr-rule.

A robot is located in a circular hall connected to three rooms, say r_0, r_1, r_2. The robot can enter any room. Normally this works pretty well, but in a rare case the robot might have a malfunction and end up in any of the three rooms. If it does malfunction, the probability of the robot ending up in the intended room is $\frac{1}{2}$.

The formalization of this domain in P-log requires the initial and final moments of time

$$time = \{0, 1\}.$$

three rooms

$$room = \{r_0, r_1, r_2\}.$$

and four places

$$position = \{h, r_0, r_1, r_2\}.$$

where h stands for the hall.

There are two attributes that we refer to as actions:

$$enter : room.$$

$$break : boolean.$$

The value of action $enter$ is R if at time 0 the robot *attempts* to enter room R. This action succeeds unless exogenous action $break$, which corresponds to the robot's malfunctioning, occurs at the same time. Since the value of $enter$ is determined by the deliberating robot, the attribute is not random. We know that $break$ normally does not happen, and we have no information on the likelihood of this rare event. Hence $break$ is not random either.

An attribute in

$$in : time \to postion.$$

returns the position of the robot at a given point in time. Initially, the robot is in the hall:

$$in(0) = h.$$

The following rules govern changes in the domain:

1. If no malfunction occurs, the robot gets to where it is going:

$$in(1) = R \leftarrow enter = R, \neg break.$$

2. A malfunction can cause the robot to end up in any of the rooms:

$$random(in(1) : room) \leftarrow enter = R, break.$$

3. If there is a malfunction, the probability of the robot winding up in the room it intended to enter is $\frac{1}{2}$:

$$pr(in(1) = R \mid_c enter = R, break) = \frac{1}{2}.$$

4. We assume that normally the robot does not malfunction:

$$\neg break \leftarrow not\ break.$$

However, if no other consistent state of the world exists, we must assume that the robot malfunctioned:

$$break \overset{+}{\leftarrow} .$$

(For the sake of brevity, we also assume that the program is used in conjunction with collections of atoms that make sense. For example, we do not allow a robot to be in two rooms at once, to try to enter more than one room at a time, and so on.)

Let's consider some inputs and the corresponding possible worlds of the program. Let's add the line

$$enter = r_0$$

to our program. In this case, there is a unique possible world that contains $\neg break$ and $in(1) = r_0$. Since we do not consider malfunctions unless we are told about them or there is some sort of inconsistency, we have this expected result. Now let's tell the program that a malfunction occurred by adding this line:

$$break.$$

The program with the two new inputs has three possible worlds:

$$W_0 = \{in(1) = r_0, \dots\}$$
$$W_1 = \{in(1) = r_1, \dots\}$$
$$W_2 = \{in(1) = r_2, \dots\}$$

According to P-log semantics, the first world is assigned the probability of $\frac{1}{2}$, whereas the next two get $\frac{1}{4}$. Notice that the addition of $break$ changed the reasoner's degree of belief in the robot's being in r_0 from 1 to $\frac{1}{2}$ – a feat not possible in classical Bayesian updating.

Let's return to the original program and assume no given knowledge of a break occurring. Given CR-Prolog semantics, we can have inputs such as

$$enter = r_0.$$
$$obs(in(1) = r_2).$$

without contradiction because the program will simply fire the CR-rule and deduce $break$. (Note, that we have $obs(in(1) = r_2)$ instead of $in(1) = r_2$ because the value of $in(1)$ can be selected randomly.)

Consider another situation. Suppose we learn that the robot tried to enter r_0, but failed to do so. This knowledge can be recorded by adding the following lines to the original program:

$$enter = r_0.$$
$$obs(in(1) \neq r_0).$$

Now there are two possible worlds:

$$W_0 = \{in(1) = r_1, break, \dots\}$$

$$W_1 = \{in(1) = r_2, break, \dots\}$$

each with probability $\frac{1}{2}$, which conforms to intuition. We hope this example demonstrates the utility of combining CR-Prolog and P-log and the simplicity with which this can be done.

Summary

In this chapter we defined the syntax and semantics of knowledge representation language P-log, which is capable of combining logical and probabilistic reasoning. The logical part of the language is based on ASP and its extensions. The probabilistic part adopts the idea of causal probability from Pearl (2000). The interpretation of the probability of an event as a measure of the degree of a rational agent's belief in the truth of that event allows for a natural combination of the two formalisms. Several examples showed how the language can be used to formalize subtle forms of reasoning including both probability and logic.

There has been a substantial number of other attempts to combine logical and probabilistic reasoning. However, P-log programs have a collection of properties that are not seen together in other languages. These include the following:

- P-log probabilities are defined with respect to an explicitly stated knowledge base. In many cases this greatly facilitates the creation of probabilistic models.
- In addition to logical nonmonotonicity, P-log is "probabilistically nonmonotonic" – the addition of new information can add new possible worlds and substantially change the original probabilistic model, allowing for Bayesian learning.
- Possible knowledge base updates include defaults, rules introducing new terms, observations, and deliberate actions in the sense of Pearl (2000).

The language is comparatively new and is currently the subject of extensive investigation. In particular, we can expect substantial progress in the automation of P-log reasoning.

References and Further Reading

The material in this chapter is based primarily on Baral, Gelfond, and Rushton (2009) and Gelfond and Rushton (2010). Some information on P-log inference engines and applications can be found in Gelfond, Rushton, and Zhu (2006), Zhu (2010, 2012), Anh et al. (2008), Pereira and Ramli (2010), and Baral and Hunsaker (2007). The reader may be especially interested in the use of P-log for finding most probable diagnosis discussed in Zhu (2012), which combines logical knowledge about dynamic systems in the style presented in this book with some probabilistic information about the likelihood of possible faults. Our understanding of the nature of probability and causality, their role in AI, and the importance of the representation of probability distributions by Bayesian nets was greatly influenced by Pearl (1988, 2000). E.T. Jaynes (2003) gives an account of probability that views probabilistic reasoning as commonsense reasoning of a rational agent. There are numerous attempts to combine logical and probabilistic knowledge via logic programming; see, for instance, Poole (2008), Sato and Kameya (1997), and Vennekens, Denecker, and Bruynooghe (2009). A more traditional approach to combining logic and probability uses classical logic. For an early example of this approach one can see Nilsson (1986). A contemporary review can be found in Domingos and Lowd (2009). The recent book by Koller and Friedman (2009) is a good example of approaches that combine classical logic with graphical probabilistic models.

Exercises

1. Consider the following P-log program Π:

$$num = \{1, 2, 3, 4\}.$$
$$draw : num.$$
$$random(draw).$$
$$success : boolean.$$
$$even(N) \leftarrow N \bmod 2 = 0.$$
$$success \leftarrow draw = N, even(N).$$

   (a) Construct possible worlds of Π and compute probability P_Π of *success*.

   (b) Expand the program by statement

$$pr(draw = 1) = \frac{1}{2}.$$

      What is the probability of *success* now?

2.   Expand the program Π_{dice} from Example 11.3.1 by a new boolean attribute *max_score*, which holds iff each die shows 6. Compute the probability of *max_score* defined by the new program.

3.   Consider a P-log program Π:

$$p : \{y_1, y_2\}.$$
$$random(p).$$
$$q : boolean.$$
$$q \leftarrow p = y_1.$$
$$\neg q \leftarrow not\ q.$$

Show possible worlds of programs Π, $\Pi \cup \{obs(q)\}$, and $\Pi \cup \{q\}$. Compute and compare probabilities of q defined by each one of the programs.

4.   Consider a game of Russian roulette with two six-chamber guns. Each of the guns is loaded with a single bullet. Write a P-log program to represent this knowledge. What is the probability of the player dying if he fires both guns simultaneously? (*Hint:* Use the following attributes: *pull_trigger*(G), which says that the player pulls the trigger of gun G; *fatal*(G), which says that the bullet from gun G is sufficient to kill the player, and *is_dead*, which says that the player is dead.)

5.   A parallel system (see Fig. 11.1) consists of three components, and it functions if at least one component works. The probability that each component works is independent of the others.

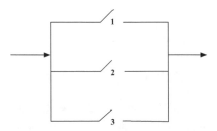

Figure 11.1. Parallel System

(a) Write a P-log program to describe this system. Use the notion of probabilistic measure defined by this program to compute the probability that the system functions.

(b) How would you use P-log to write that the first component was observed to be broken?

(c) How would you use P-log to write that the first component was broken on purpose?

(d) Suppose the system consists of components a, b, and c. Part a works $\frac{1}{2}$ of the time, part b works $\frac{1}{3}$ of the time, and part c works $\frac{2}{5}$ of the time. Write statements that would allow the program to take this new information into account. Compute the probability that the system functions.

(e) Change the program to describe a serial system (see Fig. 11.2). Compute the probability that the system functions. (A serial system requires all components to work.)

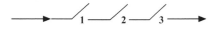

Figure 11.2. Serial System

6. Write a P-log program to represent the information about cards from Example 11.3.4 that does not require the use of a dynamic range. *Hint:* Use attribute

$$draw\_ace : try \rightarrow boolean.$$

and define pr-atoms for $draw\_ace(1)$ and $draw\_ace(2)$.

7. At a party names of dance partners are drawn at random from two hats. The first hat contains the names of all the boys, and the second contains those of the girls. There are three names in each hat. Write a P-log program to compute the odds that boy 1 and girl 1 will end up as dance partners.

8. Write a P-log program (with cr-rules) to represent the following information: A circuit has a motor, a breaker, and a switch. The switch may be open or closed, the breaker may be tripped or not, and the motor may be turning or not. The operator may toggle the switch or reset the breaker. If the switch is closed and the system is functioning normally, the motor turns. The motor never turns when the switch is open, the breaker is tripped, or the motor is burned out. The system may break,

and if so the break could consist of a tripped breaker, a burned-out motor, or both, with respective probabilities 0.9, 0.09, and 0.01. Breaking, however, is rare, and should be considered only in the absence of other explanations. Design several scenarios to test your representation.

9. Prove that for any disjoint subsets E_1 and E_2 of Ω, $P(E_1 \cup E_2) = P(E_1) + P(E_2)$.

12

The Prolog Programming Language

We complete the book by a short discussion of an inference mechanism that is very different from the one presented in Chapter 7. It is only applicable to normal logic programs (*nlp*s),[1] and although sound with respect to answer set semantics of *nlp*s, it is not complete and might not even terminate; however, it has a number of advantages. In particular, it is applicable to *nlp*s with infinite answer sets, and it does not require grounding. The algorithm is implemented in interpreters for programming language Prolog. The language, introduced in the late 1970s, is still one of the most popular universal programming languages based on logic. Syntactically, Prolog can be viewed as an extension of the language of *nlp*s by a number of nonlogical features. Its inference mechanism is based on two important algorithms called *unification* and *resolution*, implemented in standard Prolog interpreters. **Unification** is an algorithm for matching atoms; **resolution** uses unification to answer queries of the form "find X such that $q(X)$ is the consequence of an *nlp* Π."

We end this chapter with several examples of the use of Prolog for finding declarative solutions to nontrivial programming problems. Procedural solutions to these problems are longer and much more complex.

12.1 The Prolog Interpreter

We start with defining unification and **SLD resolution** – an algorithm used by Prolog interpreters to answer queries to definite programs (i.e., *nlp*s without default negation). Then we look at an example of computing answers

---

[1] Recall from Chapter 3 that an *nlp* is a logic program without classical negation and disjunction; i.e., a program consisting of rules of the form

$$a_0 \leftarrow a_1, \ldots, a_m, \; not \; a_{m+1}, \ldots, \; not \; a_n$$

where as are atoms.

to queries to an *nlp* with default negation using **SLDNF resolution**.[2] (The accurate description of the algorithm is nontrivial, but we believe that the example is sufficient to illustrate the process for its practical understanding.)

12.1.1 Unification

The unification algorithm forms the core of resolution. Given a collection of atoms it checks if these atoms can be made identical by substitutions of terms for variables. For instance, atoms $p(X, a)$ and $p(b, Y)$ can be made identical by substitution $\alpha = [X{=}b, Y{=}a]$, which replaces X by b and Y by a; atoms $p(a)$ and $p(b)$ cannot be made identical by any substitution. Unexpectedly this seemingly simple procedure becomes nontrivial in more complex examples. Before giving a general unification algorithm we need the following definitions.

Definition 12.1.1. *A* **substitution** *is a finite mapping from variables to terms. We only consider substitutions α such that for any variable X, X does not occur in $\alpha(X)$.*

A substitution α defines a mapping on arbitrary expressions: For any expression A, $\alpha(A)$ is defined as the result of simultaneously applying α to all occurrences of variables in A. For instance, if $\alpha = [X{=}b, Y{=}a]$ and $A = p(X, Y, f(X))$, then $\alpha(A) = p(b, a, f(b))$.

Definition 12.1.2. *A substitution α is called a* **unifier** *of expressions A and B if $\alpha(A) = \alpha(B)$.*

Definition 12.1.3. *A substitution α is called a* **most general unifier (mgu)** *of A and B if*

1. *$\alpha(A) = \alpha(B)$ (i.e., α is a unifier).*
2. *α is more general than any other unifier β of A and B; i.e., there is a substitution γ such that for any variable X from the domain of α, $\beta(X) = \gamma(\alpha(X))$.*

It is possible to prove that most general unifiers only differ by the names of variables, but we do not do this here for the sake of brevity. Due to this result, we sometimes say "the" mgu instead of "an" mgu.

Here are a few examples to illustrate the definitions.

---

[2] The NF in SLDNF resolution stands for negation as failure – an alternative name for default negation.

1. Mappings $\beta = [X=a, Y=a]$ and $\alpha = [X=Y]$ are unifiers of expressions $f(X)$ and $f(Y)$. Mapping β says that you can unify $f(X)$ and $f(Y)$ by replacing X by a and Y by a. Mapping α says that you can unify these expressions by simply replacing X in $f(X)$ by Y; it requires one less step. It is easy to see that α is more general than β since $\beta(X) = \gamma(\alpha(X))$ for $\gamma = [Y=a]$. In fact (as we show later), α is a most general unifier.
2. Mapping $[X=a, Y=f(b)]$ is an mgu of expressions $f(X, f(b))$ and $f(a, Y)$.
3. Expressions $f(X)$ and $f(f(X))$ are not unifiable.

Theorem 3. *(Unification Theorem)*
(Herbrand, Robinson, Martelli, and Montanari)
There exists an algorithm that for any two atoms produces their most general unifier if they are unifiable and otherwise reports nonexistence of a unifier.

Proof: Notice that atoms are unifiable only if they start with the same predicate symbol. Therefore it suffices to describe a unification method for atoms $p(t_1, \ldots, t_n)$ and $p(s_1, \ldots, s_n)$; i.e., to find a unifier for a set of equations

$$S_0 = \{t_1 = s_1, \ldots, t_n = s_n\}.$$

This can be done by the following algorithm. For the purpose of this algorithm, treat constants as function symbols of arity 0. Nondeterministically select the appropriate form of equation from the following table and perform the associated action:

	Equation	**Action**
(1)	$f(t_1, \ldots, t_n) = f(s_1, \ldots, s_n)$	replace by the set $\{t_i = s_i : i \in [1..n]\}$
(2)	$f(t_1, \ldots, t_n) = g(s_1, \ldots, s_m)$	stop with failure
(3)	$X = X$	delete the equation
(4)	$t = X$ where t is not a variable	replace by $X = t$
(5)	$X = t$ where t is not X, and X has another occurrence in the set of equations	if X occurs in t, then stop with failure else replace X by t in every other equation

Let $X_1, \ldots, X_n$ be the set of variables occurring in S_0. We now show that the algorithm stops with failure or produces a substitution of the form

$[X_1=t_1,\ldots,X_n=t_n]$. The key is to show that the algorithm always terminates.

Consider a trace of the algorithm consisting of sets $S_0, S_1, S_2, \ldots$ where S_i is obtained from S_{i-1} by an application of one of the rules in the table. Notice that a successful application of rule (5) to variable X_i reduces the number of occurrences of X_i to one and that application of no other rule increases this number. Since S_0 contains a finite number of variables and since rule (5) is not applicable to a set with no multiple occurrences of variables, we can conclude that rule (5) can only occur in a trace a finite number of times. Let S_n be the set obtained by the last application of rule (5). Since an application of rule (1) to a set S decreases the number of occurrences of function symbols in S and no other rule except (5) increases this number, there can only be a finite number of applications of rule (1) in a trace after S_n. A similar argument can be used for other rules, and hence any trace of the algorithm is finite. From the definition of the algorithm's rules it is clear that for every rule r, substitution α is a unifier of a set E of equations iff α is a unifier of the result of applying r to E. This implies that if the two atoms are unifiable, the last collection of equations is their most general unifier. As mentioned earlier, such a unifier is unique modulo renaming of variables.

Let's apply the algorithm to our previous examples.

Example 12.1.1.

- Unify $p(f(X))$ and $p(f(Y))$.

We record the trace of the algorithm by listing equations in each set formed by the iterations.

$$S_0 \ \{ f(X) = f(Y) $$

Rule (1) gives us

$$S_1 \ \{ X = Y $$

No other rules are applicable. Hence, S_1 is an mgu of $p(f(X))$ and $p(f(Y))$.

Example 12.1.2.

- Unify $p(f(X, f(b)))$ and $p(f(a, Y))$.

$$S_0 \ \{ f(X, f(b)) = f(a, Y) $$

Rule (1) gives us

$$S_1 \ \begin{cases} X = a \\ f(b) = Y \end{cases}$$

Rule (4) requires that we flip the second equation:

$$S_2 \begin{cases} X = a \\ Y = f(b) \end{cases}$$

S_2 is the mgu.

Example 12.1.3.

- Unify $p(f(X))$ and $p(f(f(X)))$.

The algorithm forms equation $X=f(X)$ by rule (1) and stops with failure by rule (5).

A few other examples follow.

Example 12.1.4.

- Unify $p(a)$ and $p(b)$.

Applying rule (1) of the algorithm forms equation $a = b$. Since the algorithm treats constants as function symbols of arity 0, it stops with failure by rule (2).

Example 12.1.5.

- Unify $p(X, f(f(a,b), X))$ and $p(g(c), f(Y, Z))$.

(The equation selected for the next step is indicated by an arrow.)

$$S_0 \begin{cases} X = g(c) \\ f(f(a,b), X) = f(Y, Z) \quad \longleftarrow \end{cases}$$

Rule (1) gives us the following set of equations:

$$S_1 \begin{cases} X = g(c) \quad \longleftarrow \\ f(a, b) = Y \\ X = Z \end{cases}$$

Rule (5) applied to $X = g(c)$ tells us to replace other occurrences of X by $g(c)$:

$$S_2 \begin{cases} X = g(c) \\ f(a, b) = Y \\ g(c) = Z \quad \longleftarrow \end{cases}$$

Rule (4) makes $g(c) = Z$ into $Z = g(c)$:

$$S_3 \begin{cases} X = g(c) \\ f(a,b) = Y \quad \longleftarrow \\ Z = g(c) \end{cases}$$

and $f(a,b) = Y$ into $Y = f(a,b)$:

$$S_4 \begin{cases} X = g(c) \\ Y = f(a,b) \\ Z = g(c) \end{cases}$$

The equations in S_4 describe the mgu.

12.1.2 SLD Resolution

The Prolog interpreter uses resolution-based algorithms as its method for finding answers to queries to a logic program. In this section we define **SLD resolution** used by Prolog interpreters to answer queries to definite programs. We give definitions of the basic notions of SLD resolution – SLD inference rule and SLD derivation. Theorems 4 and 5 show soundness and completeness of SLD derivation with respect to answer-set semantics of definite programs, thereby showing the correctness of answers to queries derived using SLD derivation.

We start with basic definitions:

Definition 12.1.4. *Let* $Q = [q_0, \ldots, q_m]$ *(where the qs are atoms) be a* **query** *to a definite program* Π. *An* **answer** *to* Q *by* Π *is a substitution* α *such that*

$$\Pi \models \forall\, \alpha(Q)$$

(i.e., every ground instance of $\alpha(Q)$ *belongs to the answer set of* Π*).*

For example, consider Π_1:

$$p(a).$$
$$q(a).$$
$$q(b).$$

and query $Q = [p(X), q(X)]$. An answer to Q by Π is $[X{=}a]$. You can see that the ground instance of $\alpha(Q)$ is $\{p(a), q(a)\}$ and that it belongs to the answer set of Π.

Now we describe the SLD resolution method for answering queries to definite programs. For the purpose of our resolution algorithm, we represent the original query Q by a rule

$$yes(X_1, \ldots, X_k) \leftarrow Q \qquad (12.1)$$

where $X_1, \ldots, X_k$ is the list of variables of Q and yes is a new predicate symbol not appearing in the program. (In our later discussion we refer to rules containing the yes predicate symbol in the head as **query rules**.) It is easy to see that α is an answer to a query Q by Π_1 iff α is an answer to a query $yes(X_1 \ldots, X_k)$ by $\Pi_1 \cup$ (12.1).

A solution α to a query Q is then found by a series of consecutive transformations of the initial query rule, which leads to a single atom $yes(t_1, \ldots, t_k)$ where $\alpha = [X_1{=}t_1, \ldots, X_k{=}t_k]$.

For example, consider program Π_2 consisting of three rules

$$p(X, Y) \leftarrow q(X, b), r(f(X), Y). \qquad (\Pi_2{:}1)$$

$$q(a, b). \qquad (\Pi_2{:}2)$$

$$r(f(a), b). \qquad (\Pi_2{:}3)$$

and query $Q = [p(X, Y)]$. The initial query rule, denoted by r_1, has the form

$$yes(X, Y) \leftarrow p(X, Y). \qquad (r_1)$$

Rule $(\Pi_2{:}1)$ is used to transform r_1 into another query rule r_2 of the form

$$yes(X, Y) \leftarrow q(X, b), r(f(X), Y). \qquad (r_2)$$

The new rule is obtained by replacing $p(X, Y)$ by the body of $(\Pi_2{:}1)$. Intuitively it is clear that if α is a solution to query $yes(X, Y)$ with respect to program $\Pi_2 \cup \{r_2\}$, then it is a solution to the same query with respect to program $\Pi_2 \cup \{r_1\}$. The second rule of Π_2 is used to transform r_2 into the next query rule r_3

$$yes(a, Y) \leftarrow r(f(a), Y). \qquad (r_3)$$

This time the transformation is slightly more involved. It consists of two steps. During the first step, query $q(X, b)$ is unified with $q(a, b)$ – the head of rule $(\Pi_2{:}2)$. The corresponding substitution is applied to the whole rule, transforming it into $yes(a, Y) \leftarrow q(a, b), r(f(a), Y)$. The second step replaces $q(a, b)$ by the body of rule $(\Pi_2{:}2)$ – in our case the empty set. Finally, a similar transformation that uses the last rule $(\Pi_2{:}3)$ is applied to transform r_3 into r_4:

$$yes(a, b). \qquad (r_4)$$

Clearly $\alpha = [X{=}a, Y{=}b]$ is a solution of Q with respect to the original program Π_2.

In general, each step of this process is accomplished by the following rule called the **Resolution Rule**:

Definition 12.1.5. *(Resolution Rule)*
Consider a query rule r_q

$$yes(t_1, \ldots, t_k) \leftarrow q_0, \Delta$$

where q_0 *is the first atom in the body and* Δ *represents the rest of the query atoms, and a program rule* r_p

$$p_0 \leftarrow \Gamma$$

such that q_0 *and* p_0 *are unifiable and* r_q *and* r_p *do not have common variables.*

Rule r

$$\alpha(yes(t_1, \ldots, t_k) \leftarrow \Gamma, \Delta).$$

where α *is the mgu of* p_0 *and* q_0 *is called the* **resolvent** *of rules* r_q *and* r_p. *A triple* $\langle r_q, r_p, r \rangle$ *is referred to as the* **SLD resolution inference rule** *with premises* r_q, r_p *and conclusion* r.

It can be shown that if α is a solution to query $yes(X, Y)$ with respect to program $\Pi \cup \{r_q\}$, then it is a solution to the same query with respect to program $\Pi \cup \{r\}$.

The following is an example of the application of the resolution inference rule. Consider a query rule r_q,

$$yes(X, Y) \leftarrow p(X, Y), s(X)$$

and a program Π_3 consisting of a single rule r_p,

$$p(a, Y_1) \leftarrow r(f(a), Y_1).$$

The first rule, r_q, has the form

$$yes(X, Y) \leftarrow q_0, \Delta$$

where q_0 is $p(X, Y)$ and Δ is $s(X)$. The second, r_p, is of the form

$$p_0 \leftarrow \Gamma$$

where p_0 is $p(a, Y_1)$ and Γ is $r(f(a), Y_1)$. Clearly, the two rules have no common variables, and $\alpha = [X{=}a, Y{=}Y_1]$ is an mgu of q_0 and p_0. Hence the resolvent of r_q and r_p is r:

$$yes(a, Y_1) \leftarrow r(f(a), Y_1), s(a).$$

Now we define the notion of SLD derivation, which serves as the basis of the resolution algorithm.

Note that a rule r_2 obtained from a rule r_1 by renaming its variables is called a **variant** of r_1.

Definition 12.1.6. *(SLD Derivation)*
An **SLD derivation** *of Q from Π is a sequence $r_0, \ldots, r_n$ of query rules such that*

- $r_0 = \{yes(X_1, \ldots, X_k) \leftarrow Q\}$ *where $X_1, \ldots, X_k$ is the list of variables in Q.*
- r_i *is obtained by resolving r_{i-1} with a variant r of some rule of Π such that r and r_{i-1} have no common variables.*
- r_n *has the empty body.*

The following theorems explain the importance of SLD derivation.

Theorem 4. *Soundness of SLD Derivation*
If $yes(t_1, \ldots, t_k)$ is the last rule in the SLD derivation of $Q(X_1, \ldots, X_k)$ from Π, then the substitution $[X_1{=}t_1, \ldots, X_k{=}t_k]$ is an answer to Q by Π.

Theorem 5. *Completeness of SLD Derivation*
If a ground query $Q(c_1, \ldots, c_k)$ is true in the answer set of Π, then there is an SLD derivation of $Q(X_1, \ldots, X_k)$ from Π with the last rule $yes(t_1, \ldots, t_k)$, such that $Q(c_1, \ldots, c_k)$ is a ground instantiation of $Q(t_1, \ldots, t_k)$.

Clearly the sequence of rules r_q, r_p, r given earlier is an SLD derivation of query $[p(X, Y), s(X)]$ from program Π_3. Similarly, the sequence r_1, r_2, r_3 of rules illustrates the derivation of query $p(X, Y)$ from program Π_2. There is a subtle point we need to make here. Even though r_1, r_2, r_3 is an SLD derivation, our explanation of its construction is not, strictly speaking, accurate. A careful reader will notice that, in this construction, something similar to the resolution rule was applied to rules $(\Pi_2{:}1)$ and r_1 that have common variables – this action is prohibited by the definition of SLD derivation. Of course, the problem can be easily remedied by renaming variables of one of the rules. So why does the definition include such a requirement? The next example gives an answer to this question and shows that such renaming is indeed necessary.

Consider a program Π_4 that consists of the rule

$$p(f(X)).$$

Suppose we have query $p(X)$. If we ignore the requirement and attempt to apply the resolution to the program's rule and the first query rule

$$yes(X) \leftarrow p(X). \tag{r_1}$$

we fail. (This, of course, happens because $p(X)$ and $p(f(X))$ are not unifiable.) However, $p(X)$ and $p(f(Y))$ are unifiable. Resolving query rule r_1 with variant $p(f(Y))$ of the program rule produces resolvent r_2

$$yes(f(Y)). \tag{r_2}$$

Since this rule has an empty body, r_1, r_2 is our SLD derivation. The answer to query $p(X)$ is substitution $[X{=}f(Y)]$. Without renaming variables we would fail to produce this answer.

12.1.3 Searching for SLD Derivation – Prolog Control

An algorithm implemented in the interpreter for definite Prolog programs can be viewed as a depth-first search for an SLD derivation of Q from Π in the space of "candidate derivations." In this search a "candidate rule" r_i of this derivation is always obtained by resolving the candidate rule r_{i-1} with the topmost available rule of Π. For example, let Π be a program consisting of the following three rules:

$$p(a). \tag{1}$$

$$p(b). \tag{2}$$

$$q(b). \tag{3}$$

To answer query $Q(X) = [p(X), q(X)]$ the Prolog interpreter creates the first query rule r_0

$$yes(X) \leftarrow p(X), q(X) \tag{r_0}$$

and resolves it with the topmost rule (1) of the program. The body, $q(a)$, of the resulting query rule

$$yes(a) \leftarrow q(a) \tag{r_1}$$

is, however, not unifiable with any rule of the program. Hence, no further resolution is possible. Since the body of (r_1) is not empty, the algorithm **backtracks**. Now (r_0) is resolved with rule (2) because it is the first untried rule of the program. The resulting query rule

$$yes(b) \leftarrow q(b) \qquad (r_2)$$

is further resolved with rule (3), which obtains

$$yes(b). \qquad (r_3)$$

Clearly, $(r_0), (r_2), (r_3)$ is an SLD derivation, and the answer to our query is

$$X = b.$$

The use of depth-first search allows the Prolog interpreter to find answers without using a large amount of memory (as opposed to the use of breadth-first search). It is, however, responsible for the nontermination of programs, which causes substantial problems for beginning Prolog programmers.

Consider, for instance, a program

$$\Pi_1 \left\{ \begin{array}{l} p \leftarrow p. \\ p. \end{array} \right.$$

and a query p. Clearly the answer to the query according to Prolog semantics is *yes*. However, it is not difficult to see that the search mechanism implemented in the Prolog interpreter cannot produce this answer. After producing the query rule

$$yes \leftarrow p$$

the interpreter resolves it with the topmost possible rule $p \leftarrow p$ of the program. The result is again

$$yes \leftarrow p.$$

The interpreter is unable to find its way out of this loop.

There, of course, is an SLD derivation of a rule

$$yes$$

that can be obtained by resolving the query rule with the second rule of the program, but this derivation is never found.

The same query to the semantically equivalent program

$$\Pi_2 \left\{ \begin{array}{l} p. \\ p \leftarrow p. \end{array} \right.$$

will return *yes*, but will go into the loop if the interpreter is forced to backtrack.

The limited control strategy of Prolog does not allow it to be viewed as a fully declarative language. If it were, termination properties of its programs would not be dependent on the rules' order or other semantically equivalent transformations.

There are modifications of control strategies implemented in Prolog interpreters that try to alleviate this problem. For instance, the interpreter of the XSB logic programming system tables information about the query-answering process. Given the program Π_1 described earlier and a query p, the XSB interpreter resolves the query rule with the first rule of the program and records this fact in a table. If the backtracking requires resolution of the same query rule (as in our example), XSB will consult the table, discover that this query rule has already been resolved with the first rule of Π_1 and will not attempt to repeat the process. Instead it will resolve the query rule with the second rule p of Π_1, obtaining the desired answer *yes*.

If the program contains variables and negation, the tabling mechanism is deeply nontrivial, but even in this case XSB manages to avoid a large number of potential loops. It is important to realize, however, that the complete elimination of loops is impossible. This follows immediately from the fact that Prolog is a universal programming language and can therefore represent any algorithm. Hence, according to the famous undecidability result by Turing, it is impossible to design an algorithm capable of detecting all the loops in an arbitrary program.

12.1.4 SLDNF Resolution

In this section we discuss the Prolog interpreter for programs containing default negation *not*. Let us first expand the definition of a query from the section on SLD resolution. Now by a **query** we mean a sequence $Q = [q_0, \ldots, q_m]$ where qs are atoms or atoms preceded by the default negation *not*. To answer queries for *nlp*s with *not*, the Prolog interpreter implements a version of an extension of SLD resolution. The precise definition of this algorithm, called SLDNF resolution, is somewhat complex so we explain it by way of example.

Let us consider a program Π consisting of the following four rules:

$$p(a). \tag{Π:1}$$

$$p(b). \tag{Π:2}$$

$$q(a). \tag{Π:3}$$

$$r(X) \leftarrow p(X), \; not \; q(X). \tag{Π:4}$$

and a query $r(X)$ represented as a rule:

$$yes(X) \leftarrow r(X). \tag{r_0}$$

The resolution rule from Definition 12.1.5 can be naturally expanded to rules in which atoms in the body can be preceded by *not*. SLDNF resolution uses this rule to resolve query r_0 with program rule (Π:4). The resulting query rule,

$$yes(X) \leftarrow p(X), \; not \; q(X) \tag{r_1}$$

is resolved with program rule (Π:1) to obtain the next query rule

$$yes(a) \leftarrow \; not \; q(a). \tag{r_2}$$

The first atom in the body of this rule is preceded by default negation, and hence the resolution rule is not applicable. To proceed we need a new inference rule called **Negation as Finite Failure (NAF)**: *A query rule*

$$yes(t_1, \dots, t_k) \leftarrow \; not \; q, \Delta$$

where q is a ground atom derives a query rule

$$yes(t_1, \dots, t_k) \leftarrow \Delta$$

if SLDNF resolution can consider all possible ways to prove q and demonstrate that all of them fail.[3]

If we go back to our example we see that SLDNF's attempt to prove $q(a)$ immediately succeeds. Neither the resolution rule nor NAF can use rule r_2, and hence the algorithm is forced to backtrack to rule (r_1). By resolving (r_1) and (Π:2) it finds another candidate rule:

$$yes(b) \leftarrow \; not \; q(b). \tag{r_3}$$

It is easy to see that the query $q(b)$ cannot be resolved with anything else and cannot therefore be proven by SLDNF resolution. At this point the resolution algorithm uses NAF and removes $not \; q(b)$ from the body of (r_3),

---

[3] This description is admittedly vague. Since NAF is used in the definition of SLDNF resolution, the description is circular and requires clarification. It is exactly this problem that makes the precise description of SLDNF resolution nontrivial. In most cases, however, this circularity does not cause any problem.

producing the rule

$$yes(b) \qquad\qquad (r_4)$$

which contains the answer to the initial query.

Notice that the algorithm only works if the corresponding negated query is ground. Otherwise the interpreter is said to **flounder**, and its actual behavior depends on the implementation.

It can be shown that *if the algorithm does not flounder then it is sound with respect to the answer set semantics*. It is also shown to be complete for a comparatively large class of programs.

12.2 Programming in Prolog

In this section we briefly discuss data representation in Prolog and give examples of using the language for solving several nontrivial programming problems. It is not our purpose to teach Prolog programming; many good books have already been written on that subject. Rather, we want to give readers a feel for the language and the types of solutions its use can produce. We use actual Prolog programming systems (such as SICStus, SWI, GNU, etc.) that include several "meta-level" constructs that do not fit into the syntax of *nlp* rules we discussed so far. We give intuitive explanations of these Prolog features without going deeply into the precise definition of the semantics so as not to digress from the main goal with a lengthy discussion. As examples of Prolog use, we present solutions to two classical problems. The first one, referred to as the *parts inventory problem*, consist of finding the type and quantity of basic parts needed to assemble a given number of products (in this case, bicycles). The second is that of *computing derivatives of polynomials*.

Note that many versions of Prolog use the built-in operator \+ to denote default negation.

12.2.1 The Basics of Prolog Programming

We start with a simple program stating that two terms, a and b, satisfy property p.

```
1 % First Prolog Program
2 p(a).
3 p(b).
```

Let us assume that the program is stored in file `first.pl`.

Let's run the program in Prolog. You can use any Prolog system mentioned earlier. After installing the system, invoke it from the command line. (Make sure you are in the directory where your program resides.) You should see a question mark prompt. For instance, if you type

```
swipl
```

for SWI Prolog, this prompt appears:

```
?-
```

You then need to tell the interpreter to load the program. This is called "consulting" the file. If you use extension .pl in naming your file, you can omit it when consulting and just type

```
?- [first].
```

Prolog should respond with a message telling you that it has compiled your program. (If you do not use .pl but some other extension, say .ext, you have to type ['first.ext'].

Next, type in the following query to Prolog and hit return. It will respond with true and return you to a Prolog prompt.

```
?- p(a).
true
?-
```

The query $p(X)$ produces the following:

```
?- p(X).
X = a
```

At this point you have a choice. If you hit the return/enter key, Prolog will say true, return to the Prolog prompt, and wait for further input. Sometimes, however, you will want to force the interpreter to backtrack to see if there are any more possible answers to the query. If you type in a semicolon, you will do just that. If there is another answer, Prolog will return the first one it finds and, again, wait to see if you want more. In our case we have

```
?- p(X);
X = a ;
X = b ;
false
```

Answer false indicates that there is no other correct answer to the query. To exit the Prolog environment, type halt.

Consider now program

```
1  % Second Prolog Program
2  p(a).
3  p(f(X)) :-
4      p(X).
```

stored in file second.pl. If you consult this program and ask it query $p(X)$, Prolog will return X = a. If prompted to backtrack, it will return p(f(a)), p(f(f(a))), etc. Since the answer set of the program contains an infinite set of answers to our query, it will be up to you to stop the process.

For the next example, consider a directed acyclic graph represented by relation $edge(X, Y)$ and relation $connected(X, Y)$, which holds if there is a path in the graph from node X to node Y.

```
1  % Graph Connectivity
2  edge(a,b).
3  edge(a,c).
4  edge(b,d).
5  connected(X,Y) :-
6      edge(X,Y).
7  connected(X,Y) :-
8      edge(X,Z),
9      connected(Z,Y).
```

The program will respond to query $connected(X, Y)$ as follows:

```
X = a,
Y = b ;

X = a,
Y = c ;

X = b,
Y = d ;

X = a,
Y = d ;

true
```

correctly returning all the pairs satisfying our relation. Note, however, that if we replace the last rule of the program by equivalent rule

```
connected(X,Y) :-
    connected(Z,Y),
    edge(X,Z).
```

and force Prolog to backtrack, it will quickly run out of memory. (In our experiments, Prolog found the four answers, but instead of answering *false*, it returned an error message.) This happens because, due to the control strategy of the Prolog interpreter, it will go into an infinite loop. As we mentioned in Section 12.1.3, Prolog programmers cannot fully rely on the declarative meaning of Prolog statements and need to firmly keep in mind the basic strategy of Prolog control.

In addition to terms, Prolog has another useful datatype called the **list**. A list of objects can be formed by using square brackets. An expression $[a, b, c]$ defines a list of three terms, a, b, and c; [ ] denotes the empty list. A special expression $[F|T]$ denotes a list with head F and tail T. Here F is the first element of the list, and T is the list consisting of the rest of the elements. For instance, list $[a, b, c]$ can be written as $[a|[b, c]]$; list $[a]$ as $[a|[]]$, and so on. This definition is reflected in the unification algorithm. For instance, list $[F|T]$ is unified with a list $[a, b, c]$ by substitution $F=a, T=[b, c]$. The head and tail notation for lists is very convenient for writing recursive definitions of list properties and relations. For example, the following program tests the membership relation in lists:

```
1 % Program in1.pl
2 is_in(X,[X|_]).
3 is_in(X,[Y|T]) :-
4     is_in(X,T),
5     diff(X,Y).
6 eq(X,X).
7 diff(X,Y) :-
8     \+ eq(X,Y).   % i.e., not eq(X,Y)
```

In the first rule '_' stands for an arbitrary term and is often called an "anonymous variable." (Any variable except X can be used instead, but it is easier to write '_'.)

The definition can be used to check if a ground term t belongs to a ground list l. For instance, to check membership of a in $[a, b, c]$ we ask a query $is\_in(b, [a, b, c])$, which, as expected, will be answered by `true`; query $is\_in(d, [a, b, c])$ will be answered by `false`.

In addition to checking if an element belongs to a list, the definition of
is_in can be used to find list members. This can be done by a query of the
form $is\_in(X, list)$ where *list* is ground. For example,

```
?- is_in(X,[a,b,a]).
X = a ;
X = b ;
false.
```

Sometimes it is useful to use a more complex nonground term as the
first parameter. For instance, to answer query $is\_in([X, b], [[a, b], c, [d, b]])$
Prolog does the necessary matching and responds as follows:

```
?- is_in([X,b],[[a,b],c,[d,b]]).
X = a ;
X = d ;
false.
```

These examples show that the program is capable of answering queries
whose parameters are an arbitrary term and a ground term, respectively.
(In fact, it can be proven that such queries are always correctly answered
by the program.) But such good behavior is not guaranteed if the second
parameter is not ground.

For instance, a query $is\_in(a, X)$ will be answered by X = [a|_A]?,
read as "any list that starts with a'. This is, of course, a correct answer, but
if prompted for another answer, the program will go into an infinite loop
(which, most likely, will be indicated by a message mentioning "insufficient
memory").

To avoid using a Prolog definition for answering unintended queries,
Prolog programmers are strongly advised to mention the type of expected
queries in documentation. In what follows we use symbol + if the corresponding parameter must be ground, − if it contains variables, and ? if
the parameter is arbitrary (i.e., if it may or may not contain variables). For
instance, the definition of *is_in* in program in1.pl would be preceded by
a comment line

```
% is_in(?,+).
```

which indicates that the second parameter of the query formed by *is_in*
must be ground. Sometimes a mapping of parameters into $\{+, -, ?\}$ is
called the **mode** of a definition.

One might ask why we did not use a definition of *is_in* given by the
following rules:

```
1  % Program in2.pl
2  is_in(X,[X|_]).
3  is_in(X,[Y|T]) :-
4      is_in(X,T).
```

This would work too, but there would be slight differences between the two definitions. For instance, let us run Prolog on the new program with query $is\_in(X, [a, b, a])$

```
?- is_in(X,[a,b,a]).
X = a ;
X = b ;
X = a ;
false.
```

The last answer is redundant and was not produced by the first program. To understand the difference let us trace the execution of both programs. For simplicity we drop the extension pl and refer to the programs as in1 and in2. On the first call to program in2, Prolog instantiates X with a using the first rule. It does so similarly for in1. When asked to backtrack in in2, Prolog uses the second rule of in2, instantiates Y with a and T with $[b, a]$, and calls $is\_in(X, [b, a])$. Backtracking in in1 is almost identical except the last call is $is\_in(X, [b, a]), diff(X, a)$. Both programs return the second answer $X = b$. One more backtrack shows us the difference: in2 backtracks to $is\_in(X, [b, a])$ and returns the third answer $X = a$; in1 backtracks to $is\_in(X, [b, a]), diff(X, a)$. As in in2, the call to $is\_in(X, [b, a])$ returns $X = a$, but $diff(a, a)$ fails and in1 exits without returning a redundant answer.

This happens because the two rules in the definition of in2 are not mutually exclusive, whereas the corresponding rules of in1 are. It is good programming practice to keep rules in the definition of a relation mutually exclusive to avoid unintended consequences.

Note also that, although it would be logical to write

```
is_in(X,[Y|T]) :-
    diff(X,Y),    % causes floundering!
    is_in(X,T).
```

we cannot, because doing so would cause floundering as mentioned in Section 12.1.4. (Recall that \+ is used in the definition of $diff$.) This undesirable behavior of the interpreter can be avoided if we put the is_in predicate first because it would serve to ground the variable and $diff$ would no longer be called incorrectly. Relation is_in is similar to relation $member$, which is predefined in some Prologs and is part of a list library in others.

There are many other useful relations on lists that have been implemented as part of the Prolog systems in various ways; e.g.,

$length(L, N)$ iff N is the length of list L.
$append(L_1, L_2, L_3)$ iff L_3 is the result of appending L_1 and L_2.

Others can be defined by the programmer; e.g., relation $rm\_dupl(L_1, L_2)$ with mode $rm\_dupl(+, -)$ finds a list L_2 that is obtained from a ground list L_1 by removing duplicate elements. The relation is defined by the following rules:

```
1  % rm_dupl(+,-)
2  rm_dupl([],[]).
3  rm_dupl([X|T], L2) :-
4      is_in(X,T),
5      rm_dupl(T,L2).
6  rm_dupl([X|T],[X|T1]) :-
7      \+ is_in(X,T),
8      rm_dupl(T,T1).
```

The program answers query $rm\_dupl([a, a, b, c, b], X)$ as follows:

```
?- rm_dupl([a,a,b,c,b],X).
X = [a, c, b] ;
false
```

In other words the above definition allows us to find only one answer to that query. Another valid answer, [a,b,c], will not be found. If one desires to get all the answers, one can modify the definition using relation $permutation$, which is available in the list libraries of most Prologs, as follows:

```
1  % rm_dupl1(+,?)
2  rm_dupl1(L1,L2) :-
3      rm_dupl(L1,L),
4      permutation(L,L2).
```

Lists in Prolog can be created with the help of several important 'meta-level' relations. When relation $findall(Obj, Goal, Res)$ is called, it produces a list Res of all the objects Obj that satisfy goal $Goal$. It is a built-in predicate in many Prolog systems.

Consider a knowledge base containing the test grades of students $s1, s2, s3$:

```
1  grade(s1,98).
2  grade(s2,45).
3  grade(s3,99).
```

The following rule defines the number of students who received an *A* on their test:

```
4  num_of(a,N) :-
5      findall(X, (grade(X,Y), Y>=90), L),
6      length(L,N).
```

Note that (G1,G2) denotes a conjunction of goals G1 and G2. Since *L* is a list and as such may contain duplicate entries, accidental duplication of records in the knowledge base could cause an incorrect answer. To avoid this we can replace *findall* by relation *set_of_all* defined as

```
set_of_all(X,G,L) :-
    findall(X,G,L1),
    rm_dupl(L1,L).
```

12.2.2 Parts Inventory Program

In this section we present a more advanced Prolog program that solves the *parts inventory problem*. Any business that makes something from parts that are in turn made from other parts is faced with the need to know how many of what part to keep in stock. The program in this section deals with a small number of bicycle parts, but it can be easily expanded to large, realistic examples while preserving the program structure. We simply need to add more facts to our knowledge base and tailor them to the business at hand. The following problem domain and program (with minor changes) came from William F. Clocksin and Christopher S. Mellish's book *Programming in Prolog: Using the ISO Standard* Clocksin and Mellish (2003), Fifth Edition, 2003, Ch. 3: Using Data Structures, pp. 64–66, and is used with kind permission of Springer Science+Business Media.

We are given a knowledge base that consists of a collection of basic bicycle parts together with the list of compound parts followed by their immediate components. We need to find the type and quantity of each basic part required to assemble more-complex ones. More precisely, we assume that our knowledge base contains a complete list of basic parts; e.g.,

```
1  basic_part(rim).
2  basic_part(nut).
3  basic_part(spoke).
```

```
4  basic_part(frame).
5  basic_part(brakes).
6  basic_part(tire).
```

By a lists of parts we mean a list of the form $[[P_1, K_1] \ldots [P_n, K_n]]$ where Ps are names of parts, if $i \neq j$ then $P_i \neq P_j$, and Ks are positive integers. $[P, K]$ is read as "K items of a part P." If all Ps of L are basic parts, we say that L is a list of basic parts. We also assume that the knowledge base contains a complete collection of compound parts together with information about the names and quantities of their immediate components; e.g,

```
7  components(bike,[[wheel,2],[frame,1],[steering,1]]).
8  components(wheel,[[spoke,4],[rim,1],[tire,1],[nut,5]]).
9  components(steering,[[brakes,2],[nut,10]]).
```

The first parameter of this relation is a compound part P, whereas the second is a list L of its immediate subparts (i.e., $[P_i, K]$ is in L iff P has exactly K immediate subparts of type P_i).

We are interested in defining a relation $parts\_required(N, P, L)$ that satisfies the following two conditions: For any positive integer N and a part P

1. there is a list L such that $parts\_required(N, P, L)$ is true;
2. if $parts\_required(N, P, L)$ is true then L is a list of basic parts required to assemble N parts of type P.

We start our design by defining $parts\_required(N, P, L)$ with the mode $parts\_required(+, +, -)$. The definition is given by two rules

```
10 parts_required(N,P,[[P,N]]) :-
11     basic_part(P).
12 parts_required(N,P,L) :-
13     components(P,C),
14     parts_for_list(C,L1),
15     times(N,L1,L).
```

where the relation $parts\_for\_list(C, L)$ satisfies the following conditions. For any list C of parts,

1. there is an L such that $parts\_for\_list(C, L)$ holds;
2. if $parts\_for\_list(C, L)$ holds, then L is a list of basic parts required to assemble parts from C, and relation $times(N, L_1, L_2)$ constructs list L_2 by replacing every element $[P, M]$ of L_1 by $[P, N * M]$.

To define $parts\_for\_list(C, L)$ with mode $parts\_for\_list(+, -)$ we need the following rules:

```
16  parts_for_list([ ],[ ]).
17  parts_for_list([[P,K]|T],L)  :-
18      parts_required(K,P,Lp),
19      parts_for_list(T,Lt),
20      combine(Lp,Lt,L).
```

Here $combine(L_1, L_2, L)$ is a new relation that appends two lists L_1 and L_2 of parts, transforms the result into a list of parts, and stores it in L.

To define relation $combine$, we first introduce an auxiliary relation $insert\_one(X, L_1, L_2)$, which inserts a list X of the form $[P, N]$ into a list L_1 of parts. The result L_2 should be a list of parts. For example,

```
insert_one([wheel,2],
              [[frame,1],[wheel,3]],
              [[frame,1],[wheel,5]]).
insert_one([wheel,2],
              [[frame,1]],
              [[wheel,2],[frame,1]]).
```

Here is the relation:

```
21  % mode insert_one(+,+,-)
22
23  insert_one(X, [], [X]).
24  insert_one([P,N1], [[P,N2] | T], [[P,N] | T]) :-
25      N is N1 + N2.
26  insert_one([P1, N1], [[P2,N2] | T1], [[P2,N2] | T ]) :-
27      diff(P1,P2),
28      insert_one([P1,N1], T1, T).
```

(You can see that arithmetic operators are defined in Prolog, as well as assignment (`is`).)

Now we can define relation $combine(L_1, L_2, L)$ such that

1. For every lists L_1 and L_2 of parts there is a list L such that $combine(L_1, L_2, L)$ holds.
2. If $combine(L_1, L_2, L)$ holds, then $[P, N]$ belongs to L iff the list of elements of L_1 and L_2 of the form $[P, K1], \ldots, [P, Km]$ is not empty and $N = K1 + \cdots + Km$; e.g.,

$$combine([[wheel, 2], [spoke, 5]], [[spoke, 1], [wheel, 3]],$$

$$[[spoke, 6], [wheel, 5]])$$

Note that the actual order of elements in the constructed list may differ.

```
29  % mode combine(+,+,-)
30
31  combine([],L,L).
32  combine([H | T], L1, L) :-
33      insert_one(H,L1,L2),
34      combine(T,L2,L).
```

To complete the assignment we define the relation $times(N, L_1, L_2)$ that satisfies the following two conditions:

1. For any positive number N and a list L_1 of parts, there is a list L_2 such that $times(N, L_1, L_2)$ holds.
2. If $times(N, L_1, L_2)$ holds, then $[P, K]$ is in L_2 iff $[P, K/N]$ is in L_1.

```
35  % mode times(+,+,-)
36
37  times(_,[],[]).
38  times(N,[[P,K]|T],[[P,M]|TN ]) :-
39      M is K*N,
40      times(N,T,TN).
```

Finally, we define $diff(X, Y)$:

```
41  eq(X,X).
42  diff(X,Y) :-
43      \+ eq(X,Y).
```

To run this program in Prolog, collect all the typewritten code into a file, say `parts.pl`. Launch Prolog from the directory that your code is in, consult the program, and ask it how many basic parts are required to assemble 10 bicycles or, say, 100 wheels. Here is a sample run:

```
?- [parts].
% parts compiled 0.00 sec, 7,504 bytes
true.

?- parts_required(10, bike, L).
L = [[spoke, 80], [rim, 20], [tire, 20],
     [frame, 10], [brakes, 20], [nut, 200]] .

?- parts_required(100, wheel, L).
L = [[spoke, 400], [rim, 100],
     [tire, 100], [nut, 500]] .

?- halt.
```

12.2.3 (*) Finding Derivatives of Polynomials

Here is another example of using Prolog to solve complex problems with elegance. In this section we write a program computing derivatives of polynomials – a typical and important example of *symbolic computation.* By polynomials we mean functions constructed from a variable x, integers, function symbols $+,-,*$, exponent $\char94$, and parentheses. Note that X^N is defined for a nonnegative integer N only. Among other things the program is aimed to illustrate the use of basic Prolog data structures – terms and lists. Those who use Sictus Prolog need to include a library module for list operations. For SWI Prolog this is not needed.

The derivative is computed using relation $derivative(F, DF)$ that, given a polynomial F, computes the canonical form DF of its derivative. For instance, both queries

```
derivative(3*x^2+4*x+1,DF).
derivative(4*x+3*x^2+1,DF).
```

are answered by

```
DF = 6*x+4
```

Queries

```
derivative(3*x^2-4*x+1,DF).
derivative((2*x+3)^2,DF).
```

are answered by

```
DF = 6*x-4
```

and

```
DF = 8*x+12
```

respectively.

```
1  %%%%%%%%%%%%%%%%%%%%%%%%%%%%%%%%%%%%%%%%%%%%%%%%%%%%%%
2  % COMPUTING DERIVATIVES of POLYNOMIALS
3  % For the purpose of this program polynomials are
4  % functions constructed from a variable x, integers,
5  % function symbols +, -, * and ^, and parentheses.
6  % Exponentiation X^N is defined for non-negative integer
7  % N. The derivative is only computed once. Multiple
8  % calls can lead to an infinite loop.
9
```

```
10  :-use_module(library(lists)). % not needed for SWI
11                                 % Prolog
12  %%%%%%%%%%%%%%%%%%%%%%%%%%%%%%%%%%%%%%%%%%%%%%%%%%%%%%%
13  % derivative(F,DF) computes a derivative DF of a
14  % polynomial F. The result is given in canonical form.
15  % type F, DF - polynomials.
16  % mode derivative(+,-)
17
18  derivative(F,DF) :-
19      der(F,G),
20      simplify(G,DF).
```

The derivative is computed in two steps. First *der* applies the rules of derivation to F to produce a polynomial G, which is then reduced to its canonical form DF by *simplify*.

```
21  %%%%%%%%%%%%%%%%%%%%%%%%%%%%%%%%%%%%%%%%%%%%%%%%%%%%%%%
22  % der(F,DF) computes a derivative DF of a polynomial F.
23  % type F, DF - polynomials.
24  % mode der(+,-).
25
26  der(N,0) :-
27      number(N).
28  der(x,1).
29  der(-x,-1).
30  der(F^0,0).
31  der(F^N, N*F^M*DF) :-
32      N>=1,
33      M is N-1,
34      der(F,DF).
35  der(E1*E2, E1*DE2 + E2*DE1) :-
36      der(E1,DE1),
37      der(E2,DE2).
38  der(E1+E2, DE1+DE2) :-
39      der(E1,DE1),
40      der(E2,DE2).
41  der(E1-E2,DE1-DE2) :-
42      der(E1,DE1),
43      der(E2,DE2).
44  der(-(E),DE) :-
45      der((-1)*E,DE).
```

One can now test the definition of *der*. Use your favorite Prolog system, consult the program, and ask the query der(x^2,D). Prolog will answer with D = 2*x^1*1. Clearly, the answer is correct, but to have a decent output it should be simplified and reduced to canonical form 2*x.

To simplify the resulting derivative we represent polynomials as lists of the form [...[Ci,Ni]...] where [Ci,Ni] corresponds to the term Ci*x^Ni. Polynomials written in this form are called **l-polynomials**. The derivative DF of F computed by der(F,DF) is translated into its equivalent l-polynomial, then written in canonical form, and, finally, transformed back into term form. A list L = [[C1,N1],...,[Ck,Nk]]) is called the **list-representation** of polynomial T = C1*x^N1 +...+ Ck*x^Nk. This change of representation greatly simplifies the reduction to canonical form.

Relation $simplify(P, SP)$

1. transforms polynomial P into equivalent l-polynomial SP;
2. combines like terms;
3. removes terms whose coefficients are 0;
4. sorts terms in decreasing order of exponents; and
5. converts the resulting l-polynomial back to canonical form.

For instance, query

```
simplify(3*x^2+x^2-2*x^2+0*x^3+x^4,SP).
```

is answered by

```
SP = x^4+2*x^2
```

The complete definition follows.

```
46  %%%%%%%%%%%%%%%%%%%%%%%%%%%%%%%%%%%%%%%%%%%%%%%%%%%%%%%%
47  % simplify(P,SP) iff SP is a canonical form of P
48  % type: P, SP - polynomials
49  % mode simplify(+,?)
50
51  simplify(P,SP) :-
52      transform(P,TP),
53      add_similar(TP,S),
54      remove_zero(S,S1),
55      poly_sort(S1,S2),
56      back_to_terms(S2,SP).
```

Next we describe each step in detail. Relation $transform(P, L)$ translates polynomial P into an equivalent 1-polynomial L. For instance, query

```
transform(3*x^2+4*x+1,L).
```

is answered by

```
L = [[3,2],[4,1],[1,0]]
```

Here is the definition:

```
57   %%%%%%%%%%%%%%%%%%%%%%%%%%%%%%%%%%%%%%%%%%%%%%%%%%%%%%%
58   % transform(T,[[C1,N1],...,[Ck,Nk]]) implies that
59   % T = C1*x^N1 +...+ Ck*x^Nk.
60   % type: T - polynomial, C - integer, N - nonnegative
     integer.
61   % mode: transform(+,?).
62
63   transform(C,[[C,0]]) :-
64       integer(C).
65   transform(x,[[1,1]]).
66   transform(-x,[[-1,1]]).
67   transform(A*B,L) :-
68       transform(A,L1),
69       transform(B,L2),
70       multiply(L1,L2,L).
71   transform(A^N,L) :-
72       transform(A,L1),
73       get_degree(L1,N,L).
74   transform(A+B,RT) :-
75       transform(A,RA),
76       transform(B,RB),
77       append(RA,RB,RT).
78   transform(A-B,RT) :-
79       transform(A,RA),
80       transform(-B,RB),
81       append(RA,RB,RT).
82   transform(-(A),R) :-
83       transform((-1)*A,R).
```

The definition uses two new relations, $multiply(L_1, L_2, L)$ and $get\_degree(L_1, N, L)$. The former simply multiplies two polynomials written in list form. For instance, a query

```
multiply([[1,2],[3,4]],[[2,3],[3,2]],Y).
```

is answered by

```
Y = [[2,5],[3,4],[6,7],[9,6]]
```

```
84  %%%%%%%%%%%%%%%%%%%%%%%%%%%%%%%%%%%%%%%%%%%%%%%%%%%%%%%%%%%
85  % multiply(L1,L2,L)  L is the product of L1 and L2
86  % type: L1,L2,L - 1-polynomials
87  % mode: multiply(+,+,-)
88
89  multiply_one(_,[],[]).
90  multiply_one([C1,N1],[[C2,N2]|R],[[C,N]|T]) :-
91      C is C1*C2,
92      N is N1+N2,
93      multiply_one([C1,N1],R,T).
94
95  multiply([],_,[]).
96  multiply([H1|T1],T2,T) :-
97      multiply_one(H1,T2,R1),
98      multiply(T1,T2,R2),
99      append(R1,R2,T).
```

The second relation, $get\_degree(L_1, N, L)$, used in *transform*, raises polynomial L_1 to the Nth degree. L is the nonsimplified result of this operation. Both polynomials are written in list form. For instance, query

```
get_degree([[3,2],[1,1]],2,L)
```

is answered by

```
L = [[9,4],[3,3],[3,3],[1,2]]
```

```
100  %%%%%%%%%%%%%%%%%%%%%%%%%%%%%%%%%%%%%%%%%%%%%%%%%%%%%%%%%%%
101  % get_degree(L1,N,L)  L is L1^N
102  % type: L1,L - 1-polynomials, N - nonnegative integer
103  % mode: get_degree(+,+,-)
104
105  get_degree(L1,0,[[1,0]]).
```

```
106  get_degree(L1,1,L1).
107  get_degree(L1,N,L)  :-
108      N > 1,
109      M is N-1,
110      get_degree(L1,M,L2),
111      multiply(L1,L2,L).
```

Returning to the definition of *simplify*, we define the second relation, $add\_similar(L_1, L_2)$, which simplifies l-polynomial L_1 by combining terms with like degrees. For instance, query

```
add_similar([[9,4],[3,3],[3,3],[1,2]],L)
```

is answered by

```
L = [[9,4],[6,3],[1,2]]
```

```
112  %%%%%%%%%%%%%%%%%%%%%%%%%%%%%%%%%%%%%%%%%%%%%%%%%%%%%%%%%%
113  % add_similar(L1,L2) implies that L2 is the result of
114  % adding up similar terms of L2.
115  % type: L1 and L2 are l-polynomials.
116  % mode: add_similar(+,?)
117
118  add_similar([],[]).
119  add_similar([[C1,N]|T],S) :-
120      append(A,[[C2,N]|B],T),
121      C is C1+C2,
122      append(A,[[C,N]|B],R),
123      add_similar(R,S).
124
125  add_similar([[C,N]|T],[[C,N]|ST]) :-
126      not_in(N,T),
127      add_similar(T,ST).
```

The relation $not\_in(N, L)$ holds if l-polynomial L does not contain a term with degree N. For instance, a query

```
not_in(2,[[1,2],[3,4]]).
```

is answered by *no*, whereas a query

```
not_in(1,[[1,2],[3,4]]).
```

returns *yes*.

```
128  %%%%%%%%%%%%%%%%%%%%%%%%%%%%%%%%%%%%%%%%%%%%%%%%%%%%%%%%%%%
129  % not_in(N,L) holds if an 1-polynomial L does not
130  % contain a term with degree N
131  % type: N - non-negative integer, L 1-polynomial
132  % mode: not_in(+,+)
133
134  not_in(_,[]).
135  not_in(_,[[]]).
136  not_in(N,[[_,M]|T]) :-
137       diff(N,M),
138       not_in(N,T).
```

The third relation of *simplify* is $remove\_zero(L_1, L_2)$. It holds if L_2 is obtained from L_1 by removing terms whose coefficients are 0. For instance, query

```
remove_zero([[3,4],[0,3],[0,2],[3,0]],X).
```

is answered by

```
X = [[3,4],[3,0]]
```

```
139  %%%%%%%%%%%%%%%%%%%%%%%%%%%%%%%%%%%%%%%%%%%%%%%%%%%%%%%%%%%
140  % remove_zero(L1,L2) iff list L2 is obtained from
141  % list L1 by removing terms of the form [0,N].
142  % type: L1,L2 1-polynomilas
143  % mode: remove_zero(+,?)
144
145  remove_zero([],[]).
146  remove_zero([[0,_]|T],T1) :-
147      remove_zero(T,T1).
148  remove_zero([[C,N]|T],[[C,N]|T1]) :-
149      diff(C,0),
150      remove_zero(T,T1).
```

The next step in our description of *simplify* is to sort terms in decreasing order of exponents. Sorting is needed for computing the canonical form of the derivative, and it is easier to do it while the derivative is still in list form. Here is an example. Query

```
poly_sort([[3,4],[5,1],[2,5]],X).
```

returns

```
X = [[2, 5], [3, 4], [5, 1]]
```

```
151  %%%%%%%%%%%%%%%%%%%%%%%%%%%%%%%%%%%%%%%%%%%%%%%%%%%%%
152  % poly_sort(L1,L2) sorts 1-polynomial L1 in decreasing
153  % order of exponents and stores the result in L2.
154  % type: L1,L2  1-polynomilas
155  % mode: poly_sort(+,-)
156
157  poly_sort([X|Xs],Ys) :-
158       poly_sort(Xs,Zs),
159       insert(X,Zs,Ys).
160  poly_sort([],[]).
161
162  insert(X,[],[X]).
163  insert(X,[Y|Ys],[Y|Zs]) :-
164       greater(Y,X),
165       insert(X,Ys,Zs).
166  insert(X,[Y|Ys],[X,Y|Ys]) :-
167       greatereq(X,Y).
168
169  greater([_,N1],[_,N2]) :-
170       N1 > N2.
171
172  greatereq([_,N1],[_,N2]) :-
173       N1 >= N2.
```

To complete the definition of *simplify* we define relation *back_to_terms*(L, T), which translates 1-polynomial L into its canonical equivalent, T. For instance, a query

```
back_to_terms([[3,2],[2,1],[1,0]],T).
```

is answered by

```
T = 3*x^2 + 2*x + 1
```

The definition of *back_to_terms* uses recursion on the length of 1-polynomial L. The base case is an 1-polynomial of length 1. Note, that instead of a simple rule

```
back_to_terms([[C,N]],C*x^N)
```

we have seven different rules. This happens because we are not merely translating back to terms, but are also doing some simplification along the way. For instance, instead of translating $[[1, 1]]$ as 1*x^1, we translate it simply as x. (We do not need to take care of the case where $C = 0$ because we have already removed these terms.) The last two rules of the definition take care of the inductive step. Relation *append* discussed earlier in this chapter is used to split the list L into list L_1 and a singleton $[[C, N]]$. If $C > 0$ then the translation of L is the sum of the translations of L_1 and $[[C, N]]$; otherwise, it is the difference of the translations of L_1 and $[[AC, N]]$ where AC is the absolute value of C.

```
174  %%%%%%%%%%%%%%%%%%%%%%%%%%%%%%%%%%%%%%%%%%%%%%%%%%%%%%%
175  % back_to_terms(L,T) computes a term-representation T
176  % of L. L is an l-polynomial sorted in decreasing order
177  % of exponents and not containing terms of the form [0,N].
178  % type: L l-polynomial, T polynomial.
179  % mode: back_to_terms(+,?)
180
181  back_to_terms([[1,1]],x).
182  back_to_terms([[-1,1]],-x]).
183  back_to_terms([[C,0]],C) :-
184        integer(C).
185  back_to_terms([[1,N]],x^N):-
186        diff(N,0),
187        diff(N,1).
188  back_to_terms([[-1,N]],-x^N):-
189        diff(N,0),
190        diff(N,1).
191  back_to_terms([[C,1]],C*x):-
192        diff(C,1),
193        diff(C,-1).
194  back_to_terms([[C,N]],C*x^N):-
195        diff(N,1),
196        diff(C,1),
197        diff(C,-1).
198  back_to_terms(L,F+T) :-
199        append(L1,[[C,N]],L),
200        diff(L1,[]),
201        C > 0,
```

```
202      back_to_terms(L1,F),
203      back_to_terms([[C,N]],T).
204 back_to_terms(L,F-T) :-
205      append(L1,[[C,N]],L),
206      diff(L1,[]),
207      C < 0,
208      abs(C,AC),
209      back_to_terms(L1,F),
210      back_to_terms([[AC,N]],T).
```

Finally we need

```
211 eq(X,X).
212 diff(X,Y) :-
213      \+ eq(X,Y).
214 abs(X,X) :-
215      integer(X),
216      X >= 0.
217 abs(X,Y) :-
218      integer(X),
219      X < 0,
220      Y is (-1)*X.
```

This completes our program. We hope that the examples of Prolog programs given in this chapter convince the reader that it is a valuable and interesting language in its own right. We encourage those interested in becoming proficient Prolog programmers to continue their study with several of the excellent textbooks currently available on the subject.

Summary

In this chapter we introduced important reasoning algorithms based on unification and resolution and demonstrated their use in interpreters for Prolog. The more general versions of resolution are used in automatic theorem proving and other important areas of logic-based reasoning.

The fact that resolution can be used to find elegant solutions to diverse computational problems is a consequence of the deep relationship between constructive mathematical proofs and algorithms. Recall that the proof is called **constructive** if it demonstrates existence of a mathematical object by exhibiting or providing a method for exhibiting such an object. As a result, an algorithm for building an object is often simply a part of a constructive proof of the object's existence (or can be automatically extracted from such a proof). That is exactly what is done by the Prolog interpreter, which seeks a constructive logical proof of the existence of an object X satisfying query $q(X)$. The proof uses the resolution and the rules of a program. The answer returned by the interpreter can be viewed as a conclusion reached by a logical reasoner about the truth or falsity of a statement given that reasoner's knowledge about the world. Similar relationships between constructive proofs and computation are used in a number of other systems (see, for instance, Mints and Tyugu (1988), Miglioli, Moscato, and Ornaghi (1988), Constable et al. (1986)).

References and Further Reading

Resolution for the full first-order logic was introduced in a seminal article by John Alan Robinson (1965). The SLD resolution first appeared in Kowalski and Kuehnm (1971). SLDNF resolution first appeared in Clark (1978). A somewhat more accurate version of the definition can be found in Apt and Doets (1994). There are a number of very good books on Prolog. A good practical introduction can be found in Clocksin and Mellish (2003). As a source for more advanced material see, for instance, Sterling and Shapiro (1994) and Covington, Nute, and Vellino (1997). Poole, Mackworth, and Goebel (1998) give a good introduction to artificial intelligence based on Prolog.

Exercises

1. If possible, unify the following pairs of atoms; otherwise, explain why they will not unify.

   (a) $p(X)$ and $r(Y)$.
   (b) $p(X, Y)$ and $p(a, Z)$.
   (c) $p(X, X)$ and $p(a, b)$.
   (d) $r(f(X), Y, g(Y))$ and $r(f(X), Z, g(X))$.
   (e) $ancestor(X, Y)$ and $ancestor(bill, father(bill))$.
   (f) $ancestor(X, father(X))$ and $ancestor(david, george)$.
   (g) $q(X)$ and $q(a)$.
   (h) $p(X, a, Y)$ and $p(Z, Z, b)$.
   (i) $p(f(X))$ and $p(g(a))$.
   (j) $p(X, X)$ and $p(f(Y), g(Z))$.
   (k) $p(f(X, g(X), g(g(Y))))$ and $p(f(g(X), V, g(Y)))$.

2. Trace the Prolog interpreter for query $p(Y)$ to the following program:

$$p(f(X)) \leftarrow q(X), r(X).$$
$$q(a).$$
$$q(b).$$
$$r(b).$$

3. Write definitions for the following list operations in Prolog. Do not use built-in predicates that are not mentioned in this chapter.
   (a) $reverse(L, R)$ where R is the list containing all elements of L in reverse order.
   (b) $last(X, L)$ where X is the last element of L.
   (c) $second(X, L)$ where X is the second element of L.
   (d) $remove(X, L, NoX)$ where NoX is the same as list L with all occurrences of element X removed.

4. We say that a list $[A_1, \ldots, A_n]$ where all As are different represents a set $\{A_1, \ldots, A_n\}$. When we talk about set operations we simply mean to treat the lists as representations of sets. Write definitions for the following predicates in Prolog. X, Y, and Z are lists. Do not use built-in predicates that are not mentioned in this chapter.
   (a) $union(X, Y, Z)$ where Z is a list representing the union of sets represented by X and Y.
   (b) $subset(X, Y)$ where X is a subset of Y.
   (c) $intersection(X, Y, Z)$ where Z is the intersection of X and Y.

Appendix A

ASP Solver Quick-Start

What follows is a very brief, operational introduction to two currently existing ASP solvers, `clingo` and DLV. Since the field is developing rapidly, we recommend that users of this information learn about the most current versions of these solvers. To find DLV, go to `http://www.dlvsystem.com`. To find `clingo`, go to `http://potassco.sourceforge.net/`. For quick access to the manuals, just search online for DLV `manual` or `clingo manual`.

To find all answer sets of a given program, type

```
clingo 0 program_name
```

or

```
dlv -n=0 program_name
```

The 0 tells the programs to return *all* answer sets. If you omit the parameter when calling `clingo`, the program will return only one answer set; DLV will return all answer sets. Changing the number will return the corresponding number of answer sets. Both systems use - and :- instead of $\neg$ and $\leftarrow$, respectively. Epistemic disjunction *or* is denoted by |.

Often we may want to limit what a solver will output when it prints answer sets because complete sets can be large and we may only be interested in a few predicates. When using `clingo`, it is useful to learn the #show commands. For example, if you had a program with predicate $mother(X, Y)$, and you included the following line in your program:

```
#show mother/2.
```

`clingo` would output only those atoms of the answer sets that are formed by predicate *mother*. Adding

```
#show -mother/2
```

will also yield all occurrences of negative literals formed by predicate *mother*.

When using DLV, a similar (but not identical) effect can be produced with command-line options:

```
dlv -filter=mother dlvfamily.lp
dlv -pfilter=mother dlvfamily.lp
```

The first will return all the literals formed by predicate *mother*; the second will only return atoms formed by this predicate.

There is also a useful program called `mkatoms`, which can be found at `http://www.mbal.tk/mkatoms/`. It formats the output of the solvers with one predicate per line. Simply pipe the output of the solver to it.

Here is a small example:

```
%% program basic_test.lp
p(a).
-q(a).
r(a) | -r(a).
```

Running this program with `clingo`

```
clingo 0 basic_test.lp | mkatoms
```

or with DLV

```
dlv basic_test.lp | mkatoms
```

will give two answer sets as follows:

```
p(a)
-q(a)
-r(a)
::endmodel
p(a)
-q(a)
r(a)
::endmodel
```

For programs with a comparatively small number of answer sets, DLV and `clingo` can be used to answer queries by simply computing the program's answer sets and using Definition 2.2.2 from Section 2.2.1. For instance, the answer to query $?p(a)$ to the above program should be $true$ because it is true in both answer sets, the answer to query $?q(a)$ should be $false$ because it is false in both answer sets, and the answer to query $?r(a)$ should be $unknown$ because it is true in one but not in the other.

Appendix B

Aspide

Here we describe a query-answering system implementing STUDENT. The system is incorporated into an integrated development environment for ASP called ASPIDE (Febbraro, Reale, and Ricca, 2011), which is designed for program development, computing answer sets, and running queries.

ASPIDE is not a solver in itself, but an interface. At the time of this writing, the query interface of ASPIDE could only be used with DLV (see Appendix A). However, ASPIDE is being actively developed and is designed to be extendable for use with other solvers. As usual, please see the documentation for updates.

To begin, download DLV from `http://www.dlvsystem.com`. ASPIDE can be found at `https://www.mat.unical.it/ricca/aspide/index.html` under the Download tab. Installation instructions are under the Documentation tab. Note that, when the ASPIDE Settings box shows up during the installation process, it should be sufficient to just set the DLV path and ignore the other settings, unless, of course, you want to use extensions of DLV such as DLVDB, DLT or a profiler. All paths can also be set later by choosing Preferences from the File menu.

The next window to pop up asks you to select a workspace in which ASPIDE will store your projects. Specify a path for the new directory or use the default. (ASPIDE will expect you to work with the files through its interface, so it is best, at least for now, not to modify the contents of this directory directly.)

To start working on a new project, select "New ▶ Project" from the File menu and give the project a name. The project name will appear on the left-hand side of your screen in the "Workspace Explorer" panel. To create a new file in an existing project, select "New ▶ File ▶ DLV File with Arithmetic Expressions" from the File menu.[1] ASPIDE will pop up

---

[1] There are some examples in the text that require this mode because DLV does not yet understand some notation by itself.

a window and ask you to select the project in which you want to create the file. Once this is done, you will see an editor and will be able to type in your program. If you are planning to work on an old file in an existing project, click on the arrow to the left of the project's name in the Workspace Explorer panel, causing the names of the project's files to appear below. To display a file in the editor, double-click the file name.

Once you have created and saved your file, you are ready to query your program or compute its answer sets. ASPIDE views all files in your project as comprising a single program. For instructions on querying or running a program contained in one or more selected file(s), see the section on configuring a run/query.

Running Queries

To run a query, select "Query" from the Execute menu (or click on the toolbar button that has a question mark). This will bring up a new window. Choose the checkbox labeled "Epistemic Mode." (The default query mode does not match the definition of query given in this book.) Your choice will be remembered for the duration of the ASPIDE session, but you will need to make this selection each time you restart the application.

Once this is done, type your query in the query input box. Make sure to end it with a question mark. To see the results, click the "Execute" button that appears next to the input box. The possible answers to a ground query are *true*, *false*, or *unknown*. If the query contains variables, the system will display the values of variables that make the query true and those that make the query false (it clearly labels which are true and which are false). ASPIDE does not display values of variables for which the answer to the query is *unknown*. (You may find it useful to select "Single Run" to display only the values for which a query is true.)

ASPIDE allows conjunctive queries where the conjuncts are separated by commas. For example, query

```
p,q?
```

will be true iff both p and q are true in all answer sets of the program.

The query input box also allows you to enter facts and rules followed by a query. For example, you can input

```
p.
q :- p.
q?
```

This is equivalent to asking query q to the original program expanded by the first two rules. This is useful if you want to add some information before you ask a query, but do not wish to make changes to your actual program.

Computing Answer Sets

To compute the answer sets of your program, select "Run" from the Execute menu (or click on the play button with your project's name on it in the toolbar). The default display will show you the output in table mode. On the left is a list of the predicates in your answer set; on the right are the parameters of the highlighted predicate (if they exist). To view an answer set represented as a collection of literals, select "Answer Set 1" shown above the predicates (or whichever answer set you wish to see).

Configuring a Run/Query

As we mentioned, by default ASPIDE treats all the files in a project as one program. Since you may be running many small programs, you will, most likely, wish to avoid creating too many projects and to have the ability to run only one file of the project at a time. To do this, select the file you wish to run/query in the Workspace Explorer, right-click,[2] and select "Run ▶ Run Directly" or "Run ▶ Query Directly" from the pop-up menu. Once this is done, "Run" and "Query" will remember your selection and only run the chosen file.

To run a program consisting of several files, select "Show Run Configuration" from the Execute Menu (or click on the "Show Run Configuration" button found on the toolbar between the "Query" button and the "Run" button). This action brings up a new window. Near the bottom you will see a large box with a list of files to be included in your configuration; if no files were previously selected, you will see a message saying that the default configuration consists of all files in your project. Pressing the green plus icon to the right of this box will allow you to add files to the list; clicking on the file name and pressing the red minus icon will remove the chosen file. The selected files will from then on be treated as one program by the "Run" and "Query" commands. Note that deselecting all files will result in the project being treated as a unit once again.

---

[2] For a one-button mouse, use Ctrl-Click.

Importing Projects and Files

If you wish to import files located outside of ASPIDE into an existing project, choose "Import DLV File" from the list in the gray panel on the main ASPIDE screen. (If you are currently working on a file, closing it will get you there.)[3] A pop-up allows you to select the project you want and browse for your file. ASPIDE makes a copy of the file and adds it to the list of files in the project.

You may also choose to create a new project consisting of an entire directory of files. In that case, choose "Import Project" and select the folder you wish to import. The name of the folder becomes the name of a new project.

There is a lot more you can do with ASPIDE and more than one way to do things, but we hope this introduction will allow you to run and query the examples and exercises given in this book.

---

[3] Note that if you have arithmetic operators in the parameters of your predicates, you will not be able to run the program that you import. Instead of using the import feature, copy and paste your original into a file created with the "Arithmetic Expressions" option.

Appendix C
Introduction to SPARC

In this appendix we give a brief introduction to SPARC (Balai, Gelfond, and Zhang, 2013), an extension of ASP that allows for the explicit representation of sorts and CR-rules (see Section 5.5). A more detailed description of the language and the corresponding software system can be found at `https://github.com/iensen/sparc/wiki`.

A SPARC program consists of three parts: *sort definitions*, *predicate declarations*, and *program rules*; the keywords `sorts`, `predicates`, and `rules` begin the corresponding sections. The first part explicitly defines sorts of objects of the program's domain, the second declares the program's predicates and the sorts of their parameters, and the third consists of a collection of standard ASP and cr-rules. For example, the family program from Section 4.1.1 can be rewritten in SPARC by

1. Explicitly specifying the sorts of the program.

```
sorts

#person = {john, sam, alice, bill, bob}.
#gender = {male, female}.
```

Sort names of SPARC are identifiers preceded by #.

2. Declaring program predicates and their parameters.

```
predicates

father(#person,#person).
mother(#person,#person).
gender_of(#person,#gender).
parent(#person,#person).
child(#person,#person).
brother(#person,#person).
```

3. Removing from the program rules 1–7, 18, and 32, which contain the information already present in the sort definition; and removing the sort information from the bodies of other rules:

```
rules

father(john,sam).
mother(alice,sam).
...
-father(X,Y):- father(Z,Y), X != Z.
-father(X,Y) :- not father(X,Y).
```

Note that the last rules are obtained by dropping sort information person(X) from

```
-father(X,Y) :- person(X),
                father(Z,Y),
                X != Z.
```

and person(X), person(Y) from

```
-father(X,Y) :- person(X), person(Y),
                not father(X,Y).
```

The SPARC solver uses the first two sections of the program to automatically extract and use the necessary sort information. This solves the issue with rule safety, shortens the rules, and allows implementation of checking for sort errors in the program.

As mentioned earlier the rule part of a SPARC program can contain cr-rules. For instance, the first CR-Prolog program from Section 5.5 can be written in SPARC as follows:

```
1  sorts
2  #s1 = {a}.
3
4  predicates
5  p(#s1).
6  q(#s1).
7
8  rules
9  p(a) :- not q(a).
10 -p(a).
11 q(a):+.
```

In addition to the explicit set notation for defining sorts, SPARC allows a number of other constructs that facilitate such definitions. For instance, to define a sort $\#s1$ consisting of numbers from 1 to 100, one can simply say

```
#s1 = 1..100.
```

New sorts can be obtained from old ones using set-theoretic operators. For instance, given sorts $\#undergraduate$ and $\#graduate$, sort $\#student$ can be defined as

```
#student = #undergraduate + #graduate
```

where $+$ stands for set-theoretic union. To define a sort $\#s2$ consisting of names b1, b2, . . . , b100, one can use the concatenation operator. The corresponding definition is

```
#s2 = [b][1..100]
```

or, if $\#s1$ is already defined,

```
#s2 = [b]#s1.
```

If f is an identifier and $\#s1$ and $\#s2$ are given, then the new sort

```
#s3 = f(#s1,#s2)
```

consists of records of the form $f(X, Y)$ where X is in $\#s1$ and Y is in $\#s2$. For instance, sort $\#default\_name$ used by the uncaring John program from Section 5.1.1 as a parameter of predicate ab can be defined in SPARC as

```
#default_name = d_cares(#person,#person).
```

An accurate and complete description of constructs used for defining sorts of SPARC can be found in the SPARC manual. The manual also contains information on downloading and running the SPARC solver and its query-answering system. You can find it at `https://github.com/iensen/sparc/wiki`. This page also contains a link to a collection of useful examples, many of which are SPARC versions of programs from this book.

Appendix D
Code

D.1 ASP Encoding of the Igniting the Burner Example

```
1  %% ------------------------------------------------------
2  %% ignite.lp
3  %% ------------------------------------------------------
4
5  section(s1).
6  section(s2).
7  section(s3).
8
9  valve(v1).
10 valve(v2).
11
12 connected_to_tank(s1).
13 connected(s1,v1,s2).
14 connected(s2,v2,s3).
15 connected_to_burner(s3).
16
17 fluent(inertial, burner_on).
18 fluent(inertial, opened(V)) :- valve(V).
19 fluent(defined, pressurized(S)) :- section(S).
20
21 action(open(V)) :- valve(V).
22 action(close(V)) :- valve(V).
23 action(ignite).
24
25 #const n = 4.
26 step(0..n).
27
28 %% ---------------------
```

```
29  %% AL System Description:
30  %% --------------------

31
32  %% pressurized(S) if connected_to_tank(S).
33  holds(pressurized(S),I) :- step(I),
34                             connected_to_tank(S).

35
36  %% pressurized(S2) if connected(S1,V,S2),
37  %%                     opened(V),
38  %%                     pressurized(S1).
39  holds(pressurized(S2), I) :- connected(S1,V,S2),
40                               holds(opened(V), I),
41                               holds(pressurized(S1), I).

42
43  %% -burner_on if connected_to_burner(S),
44  %%               -pressurized(S).
45  -holds(burner_on, I) :- connected_to_burner(S),
46                          -holds(pressurized(S),I).

47
48  %% open(V) causes opened(V).
49  holds(opened(V), I+1) :- occurs(open(V),I),
50                           I < n.

51
52  %% impossible open(V) if opened(V).
53  -occurs(open(V),I) :- holds(opened(V),I).

54
55  %% impossible open(V1) if connected(S1,V1,S2),
56  %%                        connected(S2,V2,S3),
57  %%                        opened(V2).
58  -occurs(open(V1),I) :- connected(S1,V1,S2),
59                         connected(S2,V2,S3),
60                         holds(opened(V2),I).

61
62  %% close(V) causes -opened(V).
63  -holds(opened(V), I+1) :- occurs(close(V), I),
64                            I < n.

65
66  %% impossible close(V) if -opened(V).
67  -occurs(close(V), I) :- -holds(opened(V), I).
```

```
68
69  %% ignite causes burner_on.
70  holds(burner_on, I+1) :- occurs(ignite, I),
71                            I < n.
72
73  %% impossible ignite if connected_to_burner(S),
74  %%                       -pressurized(S).
75  -occurs(ignite, I) :- connected_to_burner(S),
76                        -holds(pressurized(S), I).
77
78  %% CWA for Defined Fluents:
79  -holds(F,I) :- fluent(defined,F),
80                 step(I),
81                 not holds(F,I).
82
83  %% General Inertia Axiom
84  holds(F,I+1) :- fluent(inertial,F),
85                  holds(F,I),
86                  not -holds(F,I+1),
87                  I < n.
88  -holds(F,I+1) :- fluent(inertial,F),
89                   -holds(F,I),
90                   not holds(F,I+1),
91                   I < n.
92
93  %% CWA for Actions
94  -occurs(A,I) :- action(A), step(I),
95                  not occurs(A,I).
96
97  %% ----------------------
98  %% Simple Planning Module:
99  %% ----------------------
100 success :- goal(I),
101            I <= n.
102 :- not success.
103
104 1{occurs(A,I): action(A)}1 :- step(I),
105                               not goal(I),
106                               I < n.
```

```
107
108  %% ------------------
109  %% Initial Situation:
110  %% ------------------
111  -holds(burner_on, 0).
112  -holds(opened(v1),0).
113  holds(opened(v2),0).
114
115  %% -----
116  %% Goal:
117  %% -----
118  goal(I) :- holds(burner_on,I).
119
120  %% ------------------
121  %% Output formatting:
122  %% ------------------
123
124  #show occurs/2.
```

D.2 ASP Encoding of the Missionaries and Cannibals Example

```
1  %% ------------------------------------------------------
2  %% crossing.lp
3  %% ------------------------------------------------------
4
5  %% ----------
6  %% Signature:
7  %% ----------
8
9  %% Steps:
10  #const n = 11.
11  step(0..n).
12
13  location(bank1).
14  location(bank2).
15
16  %% Number of cannibals/missionaries:
17  num(0..3).
18
19  %% Number of Boats:
```

```
20  num_boats(0..1).
21
22  %% --------
23  %% Statics:
24  %% --------
25
26  %% opposite bank:
27  opposite(bank1,bank2).
28  opposite(bank2,bank1).
29
30  %% --------
31  %% Fluents:
32  %% --------
33
34  %% number of missionaries at location Loc is N:
35  fluent(inertial, m(Loc, N)) :- location(Loc), num(N).
36
37  %% number of cannibals at location Loc is N:
38  fluent(inertial, c(Loc, N)) :- location(Loc), num(N).
39
40  %% number of boats at location Loc is NB:
41  fluent(inertial, b(Loc, NB)) :- location(Loc), num(NB).
42
43  %% true if cannibals outnumber missionaries on the same
44  %% bank:
45  fluent(inertial, casualties).
46
47  %% --------
48  %% Actions:
49  %% --------
50
51  %% move NC (a given number of cannibals) and NM
52  %% (a given number of missionaries) to Dest
53  %% (a destination):
54  action(move(NC, NM, Dest)) :- num(NC), num(NM),
55                                    location(Dest).
56
57  %%-----------------------------------
58  %% Encoding of AL System Description:
```

```
59  %%------------------------------------

60

61  %% Moving objects increases the number of objects
62  %% at the destination by the amount moved.

63

64  holds(m(Dest, N+NM), I+1) :- holds(m(Dest,N),I),
65                               occurs(move(NC,NM,Dest),I),
66                               I < n.

67

68  holds(c(Dest, N+NC), I+1) :- holds(c(Dest,N),I),
69                               occurs(move(NC,NM,Dest),I),
70                               I < n.

71

72  holds(b(Dest, 1), I+1) :- occurs(move(NC, NM, Dest),I),
73                            I < n.

74

75  %% The number of missionaries/cannibals at the opposite
76  %% bank is 3 - number_on_this_bank. The number of boats
77  %% at the opposite bank is
78  %% 1-number_of_boats_on_this_bank.

79

80  holds(m(Source, 3-N),I) :- holds(m(Dest, N),I),
81                             opposite(Source,Dest).

82

83  holds(c(Source, 3-N),I) :- holds(c(Dest, N),I),
84                             opposite(Source,Dest).

85

86  holds(b(Source, 1-NB), I) :- holds(b(Dest,NB),I),
87                               opposite(Source,Dest).

88

89  %% There cannot be different numbers of the same type
90  %% of person at the same location.
91  -holds(m(Loc, N1), I) :- num(N1),
92                          holds(m(Loc, N2),I),
93                          N1 != N2.

94

95  -holds(c(Loc, N1), I) :- num(N1),
96                          holds(c(Loc, N2),I),
97                          N1 != N2.
```

```
98
99   %% A boat can't be in and not in a location
100  -holds(b(Loc, NB1), I) :- num(NB1),
101                           holds(b(Loc, NB2), I),
102                           NB1 != NB2.
103
104  %% A boat can't be in two places at once.
105  -holds(b(Loc1, N), I) :- location(Loc1),
106                          holds(b(Loc2, N),I),
107                          Loc1 != Loc2.
108
109  %% There will be casualties if cannibals outnumber
     %% missionaries:
110  holds(casualties,I) :- holds(m(Loc, NM),I),
111                         holds(c(Loc, NC),I),
112                         NM > 0, NM < NC.
113
114  %% It is impossible to move more than two people at the
115  %% same time; it is also impossible to move less than
     %% 1 person.
116  -occurs(move(NC,NM,Dest),I) :- num(NC), num(NM),
117                                 location(Dest), step(I),
118                                 (NC+NM) > 2.
119  -occurs(move(NC,NM,Dest),I) :- num(NC), num(NM),
120                                 location(Dest), step(I),
121                                 (NM+NC) < 1.
122
123  %% It is impossible to move objects without a boat at
     %% the source.
124  -occurs(move(NC,NM,Dest), I) :- num(NC), num(NM),
125                                  opposite(Source,Dest),
126                                  holds(b(Source,0),I).
127
128  %% It is impossible to move N objects from a source if
129  %% there aren't at least N objects at the source in the
     %% first place.
130  -occurs(move(NC,NM,Dest), I) :- num(NC), num(NM),
131                                  opposite(Source,Dest),
132                                  holds(m(Source,NMSource),I),
```

```
133                              NMSource < NM.
134  -occurs(move(NC,NM,Dest), I) :- num(NC), num(NM),
135                              opposite(Source,Dest),
136                              holds(c(Source,NCSource),I),
137                              NCSource < NC.
138
139  %%--------------
140  %% Inertia Axiom:
141  %%--------------
142
143  holds(F, I+1) :- fluent(inertial, F),
144                   holds(F,I),
145                   not -holds(F, I+1),
146                   I < n.
147
148  -holds(F, I+1) :- fluent(inertial, F),
149                    -holds(F,I),
150                    not holds(F, I+1),
151                    I < n.
152
153  %%----------------
154  %% CWA for Actions:
155  %%----------------
156
157  -occurs(A,I) :- action(A), step(I),
158                  not occurs(A,I).
159
160  %% -----------------
161  %% Initial Situation:
162  %% -----------------
163
164  holds(m(bank1,3), 0).
165  holds(c(bank1,3), 0).
166  holds(b(bank1,1), 0).
167  -holds(casualties,0).
168
169  %% -----
170  %% Goal:
171  %% -----
```

```
172
173 goal(I) :-
174    -holds(casualties,I),
175     holds(m(bank2,3),I),
176     holds(c(bank2,3),I).
177
178 %% ----------------
179 %% Planning Module:
180 %% ----------------
181
182 success :- goal(I),
183            I <= n.
184 :- not success.
185
186 1{occurs(A,I): action(A)}1 :- step(I),
187                              not goal(I),
188                              I < n.
189
190 #show occurs/2.
```

D.3 ASP Encoding of the Circuit Diagnostic Example

```
1  %% ------------------------------------------------------
2  %% circuit.lp
3  %% ------------------------------------------------------
4
5  %% ----------
6  %% Signature:
7  %% ----------
8
9  %% Components:
10 comp(r).   %% relay
11 comp(b).   %% bulb
12
13 %% Switches:
14 switch(s1).
15 switch(s2).
16
17 %% Fluents:
18
```

```
19  fluent(inertial, prot(b)).
20  fluent(inertial, closed(SW)) :- switch(SW).
21  fluent(inertial, ab(C)) :- comp(C).
22  fluent(defined, active(r)).
23  fluent(defined, on(b)).
24
25  %% Actions:
26
27  action(agent, close(s1)).
28  action(exogenous, break).
29  action(exogenous, surge).
30
31  action(X) :- action(agent, X).
32  action(X) :- action(exogenous,X).
33  #domain action(A).
34
35  %% Steps:
36
37  #const n = 1.
38  step(0..n).
39  #domain step(I).
40
41  %% -------------------
42  %% System Description:
43  %% -------------------
44
45  %% Causal laws:
46
47  %% close(s1) causes closed(s1)
48  holds(closed(s1),I+1) :- occurs(close(s1),I),
49                            I < n.
50
51  %% break causes ab(b)
52  holds(ab(b),I+1) :- occurs(break,I),
53                      I < n.
54
55  %% surge causes ab(r)
56  holds(ab(r),I+1) :- occurs(surge,I),
57                      I < n.
```

```
58
59 %% surge causes ab(b) if -prot(b)
60 holds(ab(b),I+1) :- occurs(surge,I),
61                     -holds(prot(b),I),
62                     I < n.
63
64
65 %% State constraints:
66
67 %% active(r) if closed(s1), -ab(r)
68 holds(active(r),I) :- holds(closed(s1),I),
69                       -holds(ab(r),I).
70
71 %% closed(s2) if active(r)
72 holds(closed(s2),I) :- holds(active(r),I).
73
74 %% on(b) if closed(s2), -ab(b)
75 holds(on(b),I) :- holds(closed(s2),I),
76                   -holds(ab(b),I).
77
78
79 %% Executability conditions:
80
81 %% impossible close(s1) if closed(s1)
82 -occurs(close(s1), I) :- holds(closed(s1),I).
83
84
85 %% CWA for Defined Fluents:
86
87 -holds(F,I) :- fluent(defined,F),
88               not holds(F,I).
89
90 %% General Inertia Axiom:
91
92 holds(F,I+1) :- fluent(inertial,F),
93                holds(F,I),
94                not -holds(F,I+1),
95                I < n.
96
```

```
97   -holds(F,I+1) :- fluent(inertial,F),
98                    -holds(F,I),
99                    not holds(F,I+1),
100                   I < n.
101
102  %% CWA for Actions:
103
104  -occurs(A,I) :- not occurs(A,I).
105
106  %% --------
107  %% History:
108  %% --------
109
110  obs(closed(s1),false,0).
111  obs(closed(s2),false,0).
112  obs(ab(b),false,0).
113  obs(ab(r),false,0).
114  obs(prot(b),true,0).
115
116  hpd(close(s1),0).
117
118  obs(on(b),false,1).
119
120  %% -------
121  %% Axioms:
122  %% -------
123
124  %% Full Awareness Axiom:
125  holds(F,0) | -holds(F,0) :- fluent(inertial, F).
126
127  %% Take what actually happened into account:
128  occurs(A,I) :- hpd(A,I).
129
130  %% Reality Check:
131  :- obs(F,true,I), -holds(F,I).
132  :- obs(F,false,I), holds(F,I).
133
134
135  %% ----------------------
```

```
136  %% Explanation Generation:
137  %% -----------------------
138
139  {occurs(A,K) : action(exogenous,A)} :- step(K),
140                                         K >= 0, K < n.
141
142
143  expl(A,I) :- action(exogenous,A),
144              occurs(A,I),
145              not hpd(A,I).
146
147  #show expl/2.
```

Bibliography

DLV Web Page. http://www.dlvsystem.com/dlvsystem/index.php/Home.

Smodels Web Page. http://www.tcs.hut.fi/Software/smodels/.

Abiteboul, Serge, Robert Hull, and Victor Vianu. *Foundations of Databases*. Addison Wesley, 1995.

Aker, Erdi, Ahmetcan Erdogan, Esra Erdem, and Volkan Patoglu. Causal Reasoning for Planning and Coordination of Multiple Housekeeping Robots. In *LPNMR*, pages 311–316, 2011.

Alferes, Jose Julio and Luís Moniz Pereira. *Reasoning with Logic Programming*. Springer, 1996.

Alviano, Mario, Wolfgang Faber, Gianluigi Greco, and Nicola Leone. Magic Sets for Disjunctive Datalog Programs. *Artificial Intelligence*, 187:156–192, 2012.

Anh, Han The, Carroline D. Kencana Ramli, and Carlos Viegas Damásio. An Implementation of Extended P-Log Using XASP. In *Proceedings of the 24th International Conference on Logic Programming*, ICLP '08, pages 739–743. Springer-Verlag, 2008.

Apt, Krzysztof R., Howard Blair, and Adrian Walker. Towards a Theory of Declarative Knowledge. In J. Minker, editor, *Foundations of Deductive Databases and Logic Programming*, pages 89–148, Morgan Kaufmann, 1988.

Apt, Krzysztof R. and Roland Bol. Logic Programming and Negation: A Survey. *Journal of Logic Programming*, 19:9–71, 1994.

Apt, Krzysztof R. and Kees Doets. A New Definition of SLDNF-Resolution. *Journal of Logic Programming*, 28:177–190, 1994.

Baader, Franz, Diego Calvanese, Deborah L. McGuinness, Daniele Nardi, and Peter F. Patel-Schneider, editors. *The Description Logic Handbook: Theory, Implementation, and Applications*. Cambridge University Press, 2003.

Balai, Evgenii, Michael Gelfond, and Yuanlin Zhang. Towards Answer Set Programming with Sorts. In *LPNMR*, 2013.

Balduccini, Marcello. USA-Smart: Improving the Quality of Plans in Answer Set Planning. In *PADL'04*, Lecture Notes in Artificial Intelligence (LNCS), Jun 2004.

Balduccini, Marcello. CR-MODELS: An Inference Engine for CR-Prolog. In C. Baral, G. Brewka, and J. Schlipf, editors, *Proceedings of the 9th International Conference on Logic Programming and Non-Monotonic Reasoning (LPNMR'07)*, volume 3662 of *Lecture Notes in Artificial Intelligence*, pages 18–30. Springer, 2007.

Balduccini, Marcello. CR-Prolog as a Specification Language for Constraint Satisfaction Problems. In *LPNMR*, pages 402–408, 2009.

Balduccini, Marcello. Learning and Using Domain-Specific Heuristics in ASP Solvers. *AI Communications*, 24(2):147–164, 2011.

Balduccini, Marcello. An Answer Set Solver for Non-Herbrand Programs: Progress Report. In *ICLP (Technical Communications)*, pages 49–60, 2012.

Balduccini, Marcello and Michael Gelfond. Diagnostic Reasoning with A-Prolog. *Journal of Theory and Practice of Logic Programming (TPLP)*, 3(4–5):425–461, Jul 2003.

Balduccini, Marcello and Michael Gelfond. The AAA Architecture: An Overview. In *AAAI Spring Symposium 2008 on Architectures for Intelligent Theory-Based Agents (AITA08)*, 2008.

Balduccini, Marcello, Michael Gelfond, and Monica Nogueira. A-Prolog as a Tool for Declarative Programming. In *Proceedings of the 12th International Conference on Software Engineering and Knowledge Engineering (SEKE'2000)*, pages 63–72, 2000.

Balduccini, Marcello, Michael Gelfond, and Monica Nogueira. Answer Set Based Design of Knowledge Systems. *Annals of Mathematics and Artificial Intelligence*, 47: 183–219, 2006.

Balduccini, Marcello and Sara Girotto. Formalizing Psychological Knowledge in Answer Set Programming. In *Twelfth International Conference on the Principles of Knowledge Representation and Reasoning (KR2010)*, May 2010.

Baral, Chitta. *Knowledge Representation, Reasoning, and Declarative Problem Solving*. Cambridge University Press, Jan 2003.

Baral, Chitta and Juraj Dzifcak. Solving Puzzles Described in English by Automated Translation to Answer Set Programming and Learning How to Do that Translation. In *Thirteenth International Conference on the Principles of Knowledge Representation and Reasoning (KR2012)*, 2012.

Baral, Chitta and Matt Hunsaker. Using the Probabilistic Logic Programming Language P-log for Causal and Counterfactual Reasoning and Non-Naïve Conditioning. In *Proceedings of IJCAI-2007*, pages 243–249.

Baral, Chitta and Michael Gelfond. Logic Programming and Knowledge Representation. *Journal of Logic Programming*, 19(20):73–148, 1994.

Baral, Chitta and Michael Gelfond. Reasoning Agents in Dynamic Domains. In *Workshop on Logic-Based Artificial Intelligence*. Kluwer Academic Publishers, 2000.

Baral, Chitta and Michael Gelfond, and J. Nelson Rushton. Probabilistic Reasoning with Answer Sets. *TPLP*, 9(1):57–144, 2009.

Baral, Chitta and Jorge Lobo. Defeasible Specifications in Action Theories. In *Proceedings of IJCAI-97*, pages 1441–1446, 1997.

Baral, Chitta, Sheila A. McIlraith, and Tran Cao Son. Formulating Diagnostic Problem Solving Using an Action Language with Narratives and Sensing. In *Proceedings of the 2000 KR Conference*, pages 311–322, 2000.

Bidoit, Nicole and Christine Froidevaux. Minimalism Subsumes Default Logic and Circumscription in Stratified Logic Programming. In *Proceedings of the Logic in Computer Science Conference*, pages 89–97, 1987.

Bidoit, Nicole and Christine Froidevaux. Negation by Default and Unstratifiable Logic Programs. *Theoretical Computer Science*, 79(1):86–112, 1991.

Blackburn, Patrick and Johan Bos. *Representation and Inference for Natural Language: A First Course in Computational Semantics*. CSLI Publications, 2005.

Boenn, Georg, Martin Brain, Marina De Vos, and John Fitch. Automatic Music Composition Using Answer Set Programming. *TPLP*, 11(2–3):397–427, 2011.

Boole, George. *An Investigation of the Laws of Thought: On Which Are Founded the Mathematical Theories of Logic and Probabilities. George Boole's Collected Logical Works*. Walton and Maberly, 1854.

Brewka, Gerhard and Thomas Eiter. Preferred Answer Sets for Extended Logic Programs. *Artificial Intelligence*, 109:297–356, 1998.

Brewka, Gerhard, Ilkka Niemela, and Miroslaw Truszczynski. Answer Set Optimization. In *Proceedings of IJCAI-03*, pages 867–872. Morgan Kaufmann, 2003.

Brewka, Gerhard, Ilkka Niemela, and Miroslaw Truszczynski. Preferences and Nonmonotonic Reasoning. *AI Magazine*, 29(4):69–78, 2008.

Calimeri, Francesco, Tina Dell'Armi, Thomas Eiter, Wolfgang Faber, Georg Gottlob, Giovanbattista Ianni, Giuseppe Ielpa, Christoph Koch, Nicola Leone, Simona Perri, Gerard Pfeifer, and Axel Polleres. The DLV System. In Sergio Flesca and Giovanbattista Ianni, editors, *Proceedings of the 8th European Conference on Artificial Intelligence (JELIA 2002)*, Sep 2002.

Chen, Weidong, Terrance Swift, and David S. Warren. Efficient Top-Down Computation of Queries under the Well-Founded Semantics. *Journal of Logic Programming*, 24 (3):161–201, 1995.

Chintabathina, Sandeep, Michael Gelfond, and Richard Watson. Modeling Hybrid Domains Using Process Description Language. In *Answer Set Programming: Advances in Theory and Implementation*, volume 142 of *CEUR Workshop Proceedings*, pages 303–317. CEUR-WS.org, 2005.

Clark, Keith. Negation as Failure. In H. Gallaire and J. Minker, editors, *Logic and Data Bases*, pages 293–322. Plenum Press, 1978.

Clocksin, William F. and Christopher S. Mellish. *Programming in Prolog: Using the ISO Standard (5th ed.)*. Springer, 2003.

Cohen, Jacques. A View of the Origins and Development of Prolog. *Communications of the ACM*, 31(1):26–36, Jan 1988.

Colmerauer, Alain and Philippe Roussel. The Birth of Prolog. In Thomas J. Bergin, Jr. and Richard G. Gibson, Jr., editors, *History of Programming Languages II*, pages 331–367. ACM, 1996.

Constable, Robert L., Stuart F. Allen, Mark Bromley, W. Rance Cleaveland, J. F. Cremer, R. W. Harper, Douglas J. Howe, Todd B. Knoblock, N. P. Mendler, Prakash Panangaden, Scott F. Smith, and James T. Sasaki. *Implementing Mathematics with the Nuprl Proof Development System*, PRL Project, Cornell University, 1986.

Covington, Michael A., Donald Nute, and Andre Vellino. *Prolog Programming in Depth*. Prentice-Hall, 1997.

Dantsin, Evgeny, Thomas Eiter, Georg Gottlob, and Andrei Voronkov. Complexity and Expressive Power of Logic Programming. *ACM Computing Surveys*, 33(3):374–425, Sep 2001.

Davis, Martin George Logemann, and Donald W. Loveland. A Machine Program for Theorem-Proving. *Communications of the ACM*, 5(7):394–397, 1962.

Davis, Martin and Hilary Putnam. A Computing Procedure for Quantification Theory. *Communications of the ACM*, 7:201–215, 1960.

de Kleer, Johan, Alan K. Mackworth, and Raymond Reiter. Characterizing Diagnoses and Systems. *Artificial Intelligence*, 56(2–3):197–222, 1992.

Delgrande, James P., Torsten Schaub, and Hans Tompits. A Framework for Compiling Preferences in Logic Programs. *Journal of Theory and Practice of Logic Programming (TPLP)*, 3(2):129–187, 2003.

Delgrande, James P., Torsten Schaub, Hans Tompits, and Kewen Wang. A Classification and Survey of Preference Handling Approaches in Nonmonotonic Reasoning. *Computational Intelligence*, 20:308–334, 2004.

Dijkstra, Edsger W. Under the Spell of Leibniz's Dream. *Information Processing Letters*, 77(2–4):53–61, 2001.

Dimopoulos, Yannis, Jana Koehler, and Bernhard Nebel. Encoding Planning Problems in Nonmonotonic Logic Programs. In *Proceedings of the 4th European Conference on Planning*, volume 1348 of *Lecture Notes in Artificial Intelligence (LNCS)*, pages 169–181, 1997.

Dix, Jürgen. Classifying Semantics of Logic Programs (Extended Abstract). In *LPNMR*, pages 166–180, 1991.

Doherty, Patrick, Joakim Gustafsson, Lars Karlsson, and Jonas Kvarnström. TAL: Temporal Action Logics Language Specification and Tutorial. *Electronic Transactions on Artificial Intelligence*, 2:273–306, 1998.

Doherty, Patrick, John McCarthy, and Mary-Anne Williams, editors. *Logic Programs with Consistency-Restoring Rules*, AAAI 2003 Spring Symposium Series, Mar 2003.

Domingos, Pedro and Daniel Lowd. Markov Logic: An Interface Layer for Artificial Intelligence. Morgan & Claypool, 2009.

Erdem, Esra and Vladimir Lifschitz. Tight Logic Programs. *Theory and Practice of Logic Programming*, 3:499–518, 2003.

Fages, François. Consistency of Clark's Completion and Existence of Stable Models. *Journal of Methods of Logic in Computer Science*, 1(1):51–60, 1994.

Febbraro, Onofrio, Kristian Reale, and Francesco Ricca. ASPIDE: Integrated Development Environment for Answer Set Programming. In *Logic Programming and Nonmonotonic Reasoning – 11th International Conference, LPNMR 2011, Vancouver, Canada, May 16–19, 2011. Proceedings*, volume 6645, pages 317–330, 2011.

Ferraris, Paolo, Joohyung Lee, and Vladimir Lifschitz. A New Perspective on Stable Models. In *IJCAI*, pages 372–379, 2007.

Ferraris, Paolo, Joohyung Lee, and Vladimir Lifschitz. Stable Models and Circumscription. *Artificial Intelligence*, 175:236–263, 2011.

Fikes, Richard and Nils J. Nilsson. STRIPS: A New Approach to the Application of Theorem Proving to Problem Solving. Technical Note 43R, AI Center, SRI International, 1971.

Fitting, Melvin. A Kripke-Kleene Semantics for Logic Programs. *Journal of Logic Programming*, 2(4):295–312, 1985.

Fitzpatrick, Richard. *Euclid's Elements*. University of Texas at Austin, Institute for Fusion Studies Department of Physics, 2007.

Frege, Gottlob. Begriffsschrift, a Formal Language, Modeled upon that of Arithmetic, for Pure Thought. In J. van Heijenoort, editor, *From Frege to Gödel: A Source Book in Mathematical Logic*, pages 1–82. Harward University Press, 2002 (1879).

Gebser, Martin, Roland Kaminski, Benjamin Kaufmann, Max Ostrowski, Torsten Schaub, and Sven Thiele. Engineering an Incremental ASP Solver. In *ICLP*, pages 190–205, 2008.

Gebser, Martin, Roland Kaminski, Benjamin Kaufmann, and Torsten Schaub. *Answer Set Solving in Practice*, volume 6 of *Synthesis Lectures on Artificial Intelligence and Machine Learning*. Morgan & Claypool, 2012.

Gebser, Martin, Ronald Kaminski, Benjamin Kaufmann, Max Ostrowski, Torsten Schaub, and Sven Thiele. A User's Guide to gringo, clasp, clingo, and iclingo. http://potassco.sourceforge.

Gebser, Martin, Benjamin Kaufmann, Ramon Otero, Javier Romero, Torsten Schaub, and P. Wanko. Domain-Specific Heuristics in Answer Set Programming. In *Proceedings of the Twenty-Seventh Conference on Artificial Intelligence*, AAAI'2013. AAAI Press, 2013.

Gebser, Martin, Torsten Schaub, and Sven Thiele. GrinGo: A New Grounder for Answer Set Programming. In *LPNMR*, pages 266–271, 2007.

Geffner, Hector and Blai Bonet. Synthesis Lectures on Artificial Intelligence and Machine Learning. Morgan & Claypool, Jun 2013, Vol. 7, No. 2, pages 1–141.

Gelder, Allen Van, Kenneth A. Ross, and John S. Schlipf. The Well-Founded Semantics for General Logic Programs. *Journal of ACM*, 38(3):620–650, 1991.

Gelfond, Michael. On Stratified Autoepistemic Theories. In *Proceedings of Sixth National Conference on Artificial Intelligence*, pages 207–212, 1987.

Gelfond, Michael. Representing Knowledge in A-Prolog. In A. C. Kakas and F. Sadri, editors, *Computational Logic: Logic Programming and Beyond*, pages 413–451. Springer, 2002.

Gelfond, Michael and Daniela Inclezan. Yet Another Modular Action Language. In *Proceedings of the Second International Workshop on Software Engineering for Answer Set Programming10*, pages 64–78, 2009.

Gelfond, Michael and Daniela Inclezan. Some Properties of System Descriptions of ALd. *Journal of Applied Non-Classical Logics*, 23(1/2):105–120, 2013.

Gelfond, Michael and Vladimir Lifschitz. The Stable Model Semantics for Logic Programming. In *Proceedings of ICLP-88*, pages 1070–1080, 1988.

Gelfond, Michael and Vladimir Lifschitz. Classical Negation in Logic Programs and Disjunctive Databases. *New Generation Computing*, 9(3/4):365–386, 1991.

Gelfond, Michael and Vladimir Lifschitz. Representing Action and Change by Logic Programs. *Journal of Logic Programming*, 17(2/3&4):301–321, 1993.

Gelfond, Michael and Vladimir Lifschitz. Action Languages. *Electronic Transactions on AI*, 3, 1998.

Gelfond, Michael and Vladimir Lifschitz. The Common Core of Action Languages B and C. In *Working Notes of the International Workshop on Nonmonotonic Reasoning (NMR)*. 2012.

Gelfond, Michael, Vladimir Lifschitz, and Arkady Rabinov. What Are the Limitations of the Situation Calculus? In R. S. Boyer, editor, *Automated Reasoning: Essays in Honor of Woody Bledsoe*, pages 167–180. Springer, 1991.

Gelfond, Michael and Nelson Rushton. Causal and Probabilistic Reasoning in P-log. In R. Dechter, H. Geffner, and J. Halpern, editors, *A Tribute to Judea Pearl*, pages 337–359. College Publications, 2010.

Gelfond, Michael, Nelson Rushton, and Weijun Zhu. Combining Logical and Probabilistic Reasoning. In *AAAI Spring 2006 Symposium*, 2006.

Gelfond, Michael and Tran Cao Son. Reasoning with Prioritized Defaults. In *Third International Workshop, LPKR'97*, volume 1471 of *Lecture Notes in Artificial Intelligence (LNCS)*, pages 164–224, Oct 1997.

Ghallab, Malik, Dana Nau, and Paolo Traverso. *Automated Planning: Theory and Practice*. Morgan Kaufmann, 2004.

Ginsberg, Matthew L. and David E. Smith. Reasoning about Action I: A Possible Worlds Approach. *Artificial Intelligence*, 35(2):165–195, 1988.

Giunchiglia, Enrico, Joohyung Lee, Vladimir Lifschitz, Norman McCain, and Hudson Turner. Nonmonotonic Causal Theories. *Artificial Intelligence*, 153:105–140, 2004.

Giunchiglia, Enrico, Yulia Lierler, and Marco Maratea. Answer Set Programming Based on Propositional Satisfiability. *Journal of Automated Reasoning*, 36:345–377, 2006.

Giunchiglia, Enrico and Vladimir Lifschitz. An Action Language Based on Causal Explanation: Preliminary Report. In *AAAI/IAAI*, pages 623–630, 1998.

Godel, Kurt. *On Formally Undecidable Propositions of Principia Mathematica and Related Systems*. Dover Publications (1992), 1931.

Green, Cordell. Application of Theorem Proving to Problem Solving. In *Proceedings of the 1st International Joint Conference on Artificial Intelligence*, IJCAI'69, pages 219–239, San Francisco. Morgan Kaufmann Publishers, 1969.

Green, Cordell. The Application of Theorem-Proving to Question-Answering Systems. Unpublished Doctoral Dissertation, Stanford University, 1969.

Hamscher, Walter, Luca Console, and Johan de Kleer, editors. *Readings in Model-Based Diagnosis*. Morgan Kaufmann Publishers, 1992.

Hayes, Patrick J. and John McCarthy. Some Philosophical Problems from the Standpoint of Artificial Intelligence. In B. Meltzer and D. Michie, editors, *Machine Intelligence 4*, pages 463–502. Edinburgh University Press, 1969.

Hilbert, David. *Foundations of Geometry*. Open Court, 1980 (1899).

Hilborn, Ray and Marc Mangel. *The Ecological Detective*. Princeton University Press, 1997.

Hoos, Holger H. and Thomas Stützle. Local Search Algorithms for SAT: An Empirical Evaluation. *Journal of Automated Reasoning*, 24:421–481, 2000.

Inclezan, Daniela. An Application of ASP to the Field of Second Language Acquisition. In *LPNMR*, 2013.

Janhunen, Tomi, Ilkka Niemela, and Mark Sevalnev. Computing Stable Models via Reductions to Difference Logic. In *LPNMR*, pages 142–154, 2009.

Jaynes, Edwin T. *Probability Theory: The Logic of Science*. Cambridge University Press, 2003.

Kakas, Antonis C. and Rob Miller. Reasoning about Actions, Narratives and Ramification. *Electronic Transactions on Artificial Intelligence*, 1:39–72, 1997.

Kakas, Antonis C., Rob Miller, and Francesca Toni. E-RES: Reasoning about Actions, Events and Observations. In *LPNMR*, pages 254–266, 2001.

Kautz, Henry A. and Bart Selman. Planning as Satisfiability. In *ECAI*, pages 359–363, 1992.

Koller, Daphne and Nir Friedman. *Probabilistic Graphical Models: Principles and Techniques*. MIT Press, 2009.

Kowalski, Robert A. The Early Years of Logic Programming. *Communications of the ACM*, 31(1):38–43, January 1988.

Kowalski, Robert A. *Logic for Problem Solving*. North-Holland, 1979.

Kowalski, Robert. Database Updates in the Event Calculus. *Journal of Logic Programming*, 12(1):121–146, 1992.

Kowalski, Robert. Using Meta-Logic to Reconcile Reactive with Rational Agents. In *Meta-Logics and Logic Programming*, pages 227–242. MIT Press, 1995.

Kowalski, Robert and Donald Kuehnm. Linear Resolution with Selection Function. *Artificial Intelligence*, 2(3,4):227–260, 1971.

Kowalski, Robert A. and Marek Sergot. A Logic-Based Calculus of Events. *New Generation Computing*, 4(4):319–340, 1986.

Leibniz, Gottfried. *Leibniz Selection*. Charles Scribner's Sons, 1951.

Leone, Nicola, Gerald Pfeifer, Wolfgang Faber, Thomas Eiter, George Gottlob, Stefania Perri, and Francesco Scarcello. The DLV System for Knowledge Representation and Reasoning. *ACM Transactions on Computational Logic*, 7:499–562, 2006.

Leone, Nicola, Pasquale Rullo, and Francesco Scarcello. Disjunctive Stable Models: Unfounded Sets, Fixpoint Semantics and Computation. *Information and Computation*, 135:69–112, 1997.

Lierler, Yuliya and Marco Marateo. CMODELS Web Page. http://www.dlvsystem.com/dlvsystem/index.php/.

Lifschitz, Vladimir. Computing Circumscription. In *Proceedings of the International Joint Conference on Artificial Intelligence*, IJCAI'85, pages 121–127. Morgan Kaufmann Publishers, 1985.

Lifschitz, Vladimir. Answer Set Programming and Plan Generation. *Artificial Intelligence*, 138:39–54, 2002.

Lifschitz, Vladimir, Leora Morgenstern, and David Plaisted. Knowledge Representation and Classical Logic. In Frank van Harmelen, Vladimir Lifschitz, and Bruce Porter, editors, *Handbook of Knowledge Representation*, pages 3–88. Elsevier, 2008.

Lifschitz, Vladimir and Alexander A. Razborov. Why Are There So Many Loop Formulas? *ACM Transactions of Computational Logic*, 7(2):261–268, 2006.

Lin, Fangzhen. Embracing Causality in Specifying the Indirect Effects of Actions. In C. Mellish, editor, *Proceedings of IJCAI-95*, pages 1985–1993. Morgan Kaufmann, 1995.

Lin, Fangzhen and Raymond Reiter. State Constraints Revisited. *Journal of Logic and Computation*, 4(5):655–678, 1994.

Lin, Fangzhen and Yuting Zhao. ASSAT: Computing Answer Sets of a Logic Program by SAT Solvers. *Artificial Intelligence*, 157(1–2):115–137, 2004.

Liu, Guohua, Tomi Janhunen, and Ilkka Niemela. Answer Set Programming via Mixed Integer Programming. In *KR*, 2012.

Lloyd, John W. *Foundations of Logic Programming*, 2nd edition. Springer Verlag, 1987.

Manna, Marco, Ermelinda Oro, Massimo Ruffolo, Mario Alviano, and Nicola Leone. The HₐLεX System for Semantic Information Extraction. *T. Large-Scale Data- and Knowledge-Centered Systems*, 5:91–125, 2012.

Marek, Viktor W. *Introduction to Mathematics of Satisfiability*. Chapman & Hall/CRC Studies in Informatics Series. CRC Press, 2009.

Marek, Viktor W., and V. S. Subrahmanian. The Relationship between Logic Program Semantics and Nonmonotonic Reasoning. In *ICLP*, pages 600–617, 1989.

Marek, Victor W. and Miroslaw Truszczynski. *Nonmonotonic Logics: Context Dependent Reasoning*. Springer-Verlag, 1993.

Marek, Victor W. and Miroslaw Truszczynski. Stable Models and an Alternative Logic Programming Paradigm. In K. R. Apt et al., editors, *The Logic Programming Paradigm: A 25-Year Perspective*, pages 375–398. Springer-Verlag, 1999.

McCarthy, John. Programs with Common Sense. In M. Minsky, editor, *Semantic Information Processing*, pages 403–418. MIT Press, 1959.

McCarthy, John. Circumscription – A Form of Non-Monotonic Reasoning. *Artificial Intelligence*, 13(1–2):27–39, 1980.

McCarthy, John. Situations, Actions, and Causal Laws. Technical Report Memo 2, Stanford Artificial Intelligence Project, Stanford University, 1983.

McCarthy, John. *Formalizing Common Sense, Papers by John McCarthy*, edited by V. Lifschitz. Ablex, 1990.

McCarthy, John. Elaboration Tolerance. http://www-formal.stanford.edu/jmc/elaboration/, 1998.

McDermott, Drew V. and Jon Doyle. Non-Monotonic Logic I. *Artificial Intelligence*, 13 (1–2):41–72, 1980.

McDermott, Drew, Malik Ghallab, A. Howe, C. Knoblock, A. Ram, M. Veloso, D. Weld, and D. Wilkins. PDDL – The Planning Domain Definition Language. Tech. Rep. CVC TR-98-003/DCS TR-1165, Yale Center for Computational Vision and Control, 1998.

Mellarkod, Veena S., Michael Gelfond, and Yuanlin Zhang. Integrating Answer Set Programming and Constraint Logic Programming. *Annals of Math and Artificial Intelligence*, 53(1–4):251–287, 2008.

Miglioli, Pierangelo, Ugo Moscato, and Mario Ornaghi. PAP: A Logic Programming System Based on a Constructive Logic. In *Foundations of Logic and Functional Programming*, volume 306 of *Lecture Notes in Computer Science*, pages 141–156, 1988.

Minker, Jack. On Indefinite Data Bases and the Closed World Assumption. In *Proceedings of CADE-82*, pages 292–308, 1982.

Minker, Jack and Dietmar Seipal. Disjunctive Logic Programming: A Survey and Assesment. In *Computational Logic: Logic Programming and Beyond*, 2002, pages 472–511. Lecture Notes in Artificial Intelligence, Springer.

Mints, Gregory and Enn Tyugu. The Programming System PRIZ. *Journal of Symbolic Computation*, 5(3):359–375, June 1988.

Moore, Robert C. Semantical Considerations on Nonmonotonic Logic. In *Proceedings of the 8th International Joint Conference on Artificial Intelligence*, pages 272–279. Morgan Kaufmann, Aug 1983.

Mueller, Erik T. *Commonsense Reasoning*. Morgan Kaufmann, 2006.

Nerode, Anil and Richard A. Shore. *Logic for Applications*. Graduate Texts in Computer Science. Springer-Verlag GmbH, 1997.

Niemela, Ilkka. Logic Programs with Stable Model Semantics as a Constraint Programming Paradigm. *Annals of Mathematics and Artificial Intelligence*, 25(3–4): 241–273, 1999.

Niemela, Ilkka and Patrik Simons. Smodels – An Implementation of the Stable Model and Well-Founded Semantics for Normal Logic Programs. In *Proceedings of the 4th International Conference on Logic Programming and Non-Monotonic Reasoning (LPNMR'97)*, volume 1265 of *Lecture Notes in Artificial Intelligence (LNCS)*, pages 420–429, 1997.

Niemela, Ilkka, Patrik Simons, and Timo Soininen. Extending and Implementing the Stable Model Semantics. *Artificial Intelligence*, 138(1–2):181–234, Jun 2002.

Nillson, Nils. Shakey the Robot. Technical Report 323, AI Center, SRI International, 1984.

Nilsson, Nils J. Probabilistic Logic. *Artificial Intelligence*, 28(1):71–87, 1986.

Nogueira, Monica, Marcello Balduccini, Michael Gelfond, Richard Watson, and Matthew Barry. An A-Prolog Decision Support System for the Space Shuttle. In Alessandro Provetti and Tran Cao Son, editors, *Answer Set Programming: Towards Efficient and Scalable Knowledge Representation and Reasoning*, AAAI 2001 Spring Symposium Series, Mar 2001.

Ostrowski, Max and Torsten Schaub. ASP Modulo CSP: The Clingcon System. *TPLP*, 12(4-5):485–503, 2012.

Pearce, David. A New Logical Characterisation of Stable Models and Answer Sets. In *In Proceedings of NMELP 96, LNCS 1216*, pages 57–70. Springer, 1997.

Pearce, David. Equilibrium Logic. *Annals of Math and Artificial Intelligence*, 47(1–2): 3–41, 2006.

Pearl, Judea. *Heuristics: Intelligent Search Strategies for Computer Problem Solving*. Addison-Wesley Longman Publishing, 1984.

Pearl, Judea. *Probabilistic Reasoning in Intelligent Systems: Networks of Plausible Inference*. Morgan Kaufmann, 1988.

Pearl, Judea. *Causality: Models, Reasoning, and Inference*. Cambridge University Press, 2000.

Pednault, Edwin P. D. ADL and the State-Transition Model of Action. *Journal of Logic and Computation*, 4(5):467–512, 1994.

Pereira, Luís Moniz and Carroline Kencana Ramli. Modelling Decision Making with Probabilistic Causation. *Intelligent Decision Technologies*, 4(2):133–148, 2010.

Pinto, Javier. Occurrences and Narratives as Constraints in the Branching Structure of the Situation Calculus. *Journal of Logic and Computation*, 8(6):777–808, 1998.

Pinto, Javier and Raymond Reiter. Reasoning about Time in the Situation Calculus. *Annals of Mathematics and Artificial Intelligence*, 14(2–4):251–268, 1995.

Poole, David. Representing Diagnosis Knowledge. *Annals of Mathematics and Artificial Intelligence*, 11:33–50, 1994.

Poole, David. The Independent Choice Logic and Beyond. In L. De Raedt, editor, *Probabilistic Inductive Logic Programming*, pages 222–243. Springer, 2008.

Poole, David and Alan K. Mackworth. *Artificial Intelligence – Foundations of Computational Agents*. Cambridge University Press, 2010.

Poole, David, Alan Mackworth, and Randy Goebel. *Computational Inteligence: A Logical Approach*. Oxford University Press, 1998.

Przymusinska, Halina and Teodor Przymusinski. Weakly Stratified Logic Programs. *Fundamenta Informaticae*, XIII:51–65, 1990.

Przymusinski, Teodor C. On the Declarative and Procedural Semantics of Logic Programs. *Journal of Automated Reasoning*, 5:167–205, 1995.

Przymusinski, Teodor. On the Declarative Semantics of Deductive Databases and Logic Programs. In Jack Minker, editor, *Foundations of Deductive Databases and Logic Programming*, pages 193–216. Morgan Kaufmann, 1988.

Rao, Georgeff. Modeling Rational Agents within a BDI-Architecture. In *Proceedings of the 2nd International Conference on Principles of Knowledge Representation and Reasoning*, pages 473–484. Morgan Kaufmann Publishers, 1991.

Reiter, Raymond. On Closed World Data Bases. In *Logic and Data Bases*, pages 119–140. Plenum Press, 1978.

Reiter, Raymond. A Logic for Default Reasoning. *Artificial Intelligence*, 13(1–2):81–132, 1980.

Reiter, Raymond. A Theory of Diagnosis from First Principles. *Artificial Intelligence*, 32:57–95, 1987.

Reiter, Raymond. *Knowledge in Action – Logical Foundations for Specifying and Implementing Dynamical Systems*. MIT Press, Sep 2001.

Ricca, Francesco, Giovanni Grasso, Mario Alviano, Marco Manna, Vincenzino Lio, Salvatore Iiritano, and Nicola Leone. Team-Building with Answer Set Programming in the Gioia-Tauro Seaport. *TPLP*, 12(3):361–381, 2012.

Robinson, John Alan. A Machine-Oriented Logic Based on the Resolution Principle. *Journal of the ACM*, 12(1):23–41, January 1965.

Ross, Kenneth. A Procedural Semantics for Well Founded Negation in Logic Programs. *Journal of Logic Programming*, 13(1):1–22, 1992.

Sakama, Chiaki and Katsumi Inoue. Prioritized Logic Programming and Its Application to Commonsense Reasoning. *Artificial Intelligence*, 123:185–222, 2000.

Sandewall, Erik. *Features and Fluents (Vol. 1): The Representation of Knowledge about Dynamical Systems*. Oxford University Press, 1994.

Sato, Taisuke and Yoshitaka Kameya. PRISM: A Language for Symbolic-Statistical Modeling. In *IJCAI*, pages 1330–1339, 1997.

Shanahan, Murray. A Circumscriptive Calculus of Events. *Artificial Intelligence*, 77:249–284, 1995.

Shanahan, Murray. *Solving the Frame Problem: A Mathematical Investigation of the Commonsense Law of Inertia*. MIT Press, 1997.

Simons, Patrik. *Extending and Implementing the Stable Model Semantics*. Dissertation, Helsinki University of Technology, 2000.

Soininen, Timo and Ilkka Niemela. Developing a Declarative Rule Language for Applications in Product Configuration. In *Proceedings of the First International Workshop on Practical Aspects of Declarative Languages*, May 1999.

Son, Tran Cao, Chitta Baral, Nam Tran, and Sheila A. McIlraith. Domain-Dependent Knowledge in Answer Set Planning. *ACM Transactions on Computational Logic*, 7(4):613–657, 2006.

Sowa, John F. *Knowledge Representation: Logical, Philosophical and Computational Foundations*. Brooks/Cole Publishing, 2000.

Sterling, Leon and Ehud Shapiro. *The Art of Prolog (2nd ed.): Advanced Programming Techniques*. MIT Press, 1994.

Subrahmanian, V. S. and Carlo Zaniolo. Relating Stable Models and AI Planning Domains. In *Proceedings of ICLP-95*, pages 233–247. 1995.

Syrjanen, Tommi. Implementation of Logical Grounding for Logic Programs with Stable Model Semantics. Technical Report 18, Digital Systems Laboratory, Helsinki University of Technology, 1998.

Tarski, Alfred. *Introduction to Logic and the Methodology of Deductive Sciences*. Dover Publication, 1995 (1941).

Thielscher, Michael. A Theory of Dynamic Diagnosis. *Linkoping Electronic Articles in Computer and Information Science*, 2(11), 1997.

Thielscher, Michael. *Action Programming Languages*. Synthesis Lectures on Artificial Intelligence and Machine Learning. Morgan & Claypool Publishers, 2008.

Touretzky, David S. *The Mathematics of Inheritance Systems*. Research Notes in Artificial Intelligence. Morgan Kaufmann, 1986.

Tran, Vien, Khoi Nguyen, Tran Cao Son, Enrico Pontelli. A Conformant Planner Based on Approximation: CpA(H). *ACM Transaction on Intelligent Systems and Technology*, 4(2), 2013.

Taylor, Bonnie and Michael Gelfond. Representing Null Values in Logic Programming. In Anil Nerode and Yuri Matiyasevich, editors, *LFCS*, volume 813 of *Lecture Notes in Computer Science*. Springer, 1994.

Truszczynski, Miroslaw, Victor W. Marek, and Raphael A. Finkel. Generating Cellular Puzzles with Logic Programs. In *IC-AI*, pages 403–407, 2006.

Tu, Phan Huy, Tran Cao Son, Michael Gelfond, and A. Ricardo Morales. Approximation of Action Theories and Its Application to Conformant Planning. *Artificial Intelligence*, 175(1):79–119, 2011.

Turner, Hudson. Representing Actions in Logic Programs and Default Theories: A Situation Calculus Approach. *Journal of Logic Programming*, 31(1–3):245–298, Jun 1997.

Ullman, Jeffrey D. *Principles of Database and Knowledge-Base Systems*. Computer Science Press, 1988.

Vennekens, Joost, Marc Denecker, and Maurice Bruynooghe. CP-Logic: A Language of Causal Probabilistic Events and Its Relation to Logic Programming. *TPLP*, 9 (3):245–308, 2009.

Whitehead, Alfred N. and Bertrand Russell. *Principia Mathematica, 3 vols*. Cambridge University Press, 1910, 1912, 1913.

Wooldridge, Michael. *Reasoning about Rational Agents*. MIT Press, 2000.

Zaniolo, Carlo. Design and Implementaion of a Logic Based Language for Data Intensive Applications. In R. Kowalski and K. Bowen, editors, *Logic Programming: Proceedings of the Fifth International Conference and Symposium*, pages 1666–1687, 1988.

Zhu, Weijun. A New Algorithm for P-log Inference Engine. In *Workshop on Answer Set Programming and Other Computing Paradigms (ASPOCP) 2010*, 2010.

Zhu, Weijun. *PLOG: Its Algorithms and Applications*. PhD thesis, Texas Tech University, College of Engineering, Department of Computer Science, 2012.

Index